HAMLYN LECTURE SERIES

KAHN-FREUND'S

LABOUR AND THE LAW

AUSTRALIA AND NEW ZEALAND
The Law Book Company Ltd.
Sydney: Melbourne: Perth

CANADA AND U.S.A.
The Carswell Company Ltd.
Agincourt, Ontario

INDIA
N. M. Tripathi Private Ltd.
Bombay
and
Eastern Law House Private Ltd.
Calcutta *and* Delhi
M.P.P. House
Bangalore

ISRAEL
Steimatzky's Agency Ltd.
Jerusalem: Tel Aviv: Haifa

MALAYSIA: SINGAPORE: BRUNEI
Malayan Law Journal (Pte.) Ltd.
Singapore

PAKISTAN
Pakistan Law House
Karachi

Kahn-Freund's

LABOUR
AND THE LAW

by

Paul Davies, M.A., LL.M

Fellow of Balliol College, Oxford;
Lecturer in Law at the
University of Oxford

Mark Freedland, LL.B., M.A., D. Phil.,

of Gray's Inn, Barrister;
Fellow of St. John's College, Oxford;
University Lecturer in Labour Law
at the University of Oxford

THIRD EDITION

LONDON
STEVENS & SONS
1983

First Edition 1972
Second Edition 1977
Third Edition 1983

Published by
Stevens & Sons Ltd. of
11 New Fetter Lane, London
Computerset by Promenade Graphics Ltd., Cheltenham
Printed in Scotland

British Library Cataloguing in Publication Data
Kahn-Freund, *Sir* Otto
　　Sir Otto Kahn-Freund's Labour and the law.—
　　3rd ed.—(The Hamlyn lectures)
　　1. Labour law and legislation—Great Britain
　　I. Title　　II. Davies, Paul　　III. Freedland,
　　Mark　　IV. Kahn-Freund, *Sir* Otto. Labour
　　and the law　　V. Series
　　344.104'1　　KD 3040

　　Hb　ISBN 0–420–46220–1
　　Pb　ISBN 0–420–46230–9

PREFACE

Since the publishers of this book have been kind enough to allow its editors the space for an Introduction in which to explain their objectives and substantive methods in editing the text, there is need only for one or two preliminary matters in this preface.

The most important of these are acknowledgments. The first of these, which is implicit in the whole project of a third edition, is to Otto Kahn-Freund himself. Our work as editors is intended as a tribute to his enormous contribution to our subject, and as an acknowledgment of the inspiration we derived from his teaching and friendship. Lady Kahn-Freund and Sylvia Kahn-Freund have given this project their kind support and approval and have taken a most helpful interest in it, the latter also contributing the Index. We are also grateful to the Hamlyn Trustees for their approval of the project. The publishers have been more than patient with our efforts to keep up to date with successive legislation and proposals for legislation. Despite most helpful advice and comment from various colleagues—particularly Professors Lord Wedderburn and Javillier and Miss Elizabeth Fox—the responsibility for errors and omissions is ours alone.

In a few passages, as will be explained in the Introduction, we have indicated differences between our own views and those of the original author; those passages are enclosed in square brackets. For the rest, it is our privilege to be able to re-state the original in what we hope is an appropriately up-dated form. We have sought to take account of developments up to September 1, 1983.

Balliol College Oxford and
St. John's College Oxford
St. Giles' Day, 1983.

Paul Davies
Mark Freedland

CONTENTS

TABLE OF CASES

TABLE OF STATUTES

TABLE OF STATUTORY INSTRUMENTS

LABOUR AND THE LAW—THIRD EDITION

THE task of preparing in 1983 a new edition of *Labour and the Law* to follow the second edition of 1977 is indeed a difficult one. There are a number of reasons for this. The most important is that we are conscious of being, at best, craftsmen working in the studio of the Master, perhaps safe to be entrusted with the fine detail but incapable of adequately reproducing the inspiration for the whole broad canvas. Moreover, if *Labour and the Law* is to be compared with a painting, it must be with one of those great tableaux of the past in which the face of the painter keeps appearing in the background among the crowd. For this is an intensely personal work; it is both consciously and unconsciously an elaborate statement of Kahn-Freund's particular outlook upon British labour law. There is no one who, by virtue of his own contribution to our understanding of the subject, had or has a better claim to make a personal statement in relation to it and to advance that statement as authoritative; but the extent to which he did so in *Labour and the Law* poses peculiar problems for us in editing his work, and perhaps indicates the unwisdom of our attempting to do so.

The text that follows this introduction represents our efforts to deal with these difficulties, while maintaining *Labour and the Law* as a living text rather than an annotated classic, which would be the other alternative. We have at one or two points in the course of the text indicated specific differences between our views and Kahn-Freund's. But there is a further sense in which we feel it necessary now to supplement the text, and that will require a few pages of introduction by us here. There have been, in the six years since the second edition was written, momentous developments for labour law, developments both legal, social and concerned with governmental policy. It is in many ways a different world from that of 1977. There have been a number of qualitative changes in the approach of government to the employment relationship, and these suggest to us the need for some re-examination of the framework of Labour Law if that subject, as an academic discipline, is to maintain its credentials as offering an explanatory framework of the legal regime within which the employment relationship operates.

Labour and the Law is the definitive description of a framework of labour law organised around the concept of collective bargaining. The central purpose of labour law is seen as that of maintaining an equilibrium between employers and workers by ensuring the effective operation of a voluntary system of collective bargaining. Beyond that, labour law is seen as concerned with protecting the social rights of workers, but even that is in a sense subsidiary to the main aim. This pre-occupation with collective bargaining with which *Labour and the Law* is imbued is important in two ways, one less immediately obvious than the other. First and more obviously it represents a most significant statement of values in relation to labour law. This is not a novel remark of ours; Kahn-Freund is recognised as the exponent of collective laissez-faire, and if one at any stage lost sight of his special identification with it, that was merely an indication of the extent to which it had become part of a widely shared orthodoxy about labour law—an orthodoxy which to quite a considerable extent from 1945 onwards at least until the 1960s transcended political divisions.

Secondly, and less obviously, *Labour and the Law* typifies the way in which, for Kahn-Freund (and in consequence for a generation of labour lawyers), the emphasis on collective bargaining operated not only as a statement of values but also as a guide to the proper confines of the subject of labour law. In *Labour and the Law*, the topics for discussion are evaluated in terms of their relationship to the collective bargaining system, and receive greater or lesser attention according to their degree of relevance to that system. Our concern in this Introduction is to suggest the need for some degree of re-examination of this second and less obvious way in which, in *Labour and the Law*, the whole subject of labour law is approached via collective bargaining. We think it requires some scrutiny as an explanatory framework, whatever its validity as a social ideal.

It is worth noting in passing that Kahn-Freund himself in his last published work in this area expressed serious doubts on the latter score—that is, as to the continuing validity of collective laissez-faire as a social ideal. This was in *Labour Relations: Heritage and Adjustment*, published in 1979 from a set of lectures given to the British Academy in 1978. In these lectures he stressed the dangers inherent in the British tradition of direct trade union democracy, and in the linked tradition of union control of access to jobs. He continues by indicating doubts about the capacity of the existing collective bargaining system to respond to the great social demands which had come to be made of it, and concludes, "That which, on previous occasions, I have called 'collective laissez-faire' may be in need of adjustment more than any other part of the British heritage" (at p.88). One may admire the willingness this demonstrates to re-examine even his own contribution to the received orthodoxies of labour law; but it is worth noting that in *Heritage and Adjustment* even this fundamental questioning of accepted values is not seen as suggesting any reformulation of the conceptual framework of labour law. It is of no small importance that Kahn-Freund regarded these lectures as being about labour relations rather than about labour law. It was as if he had come to regard the social problems under discussion as being outside the framework of labour law because they could not be contained within the structure of collective laissez-faire.

We are far from suggesting that there is any easy way out of the crisis of values which Kahn-Freund confronted in *Heritage and Adjustment*. But we do suggest that there is some scope for a re-casting of the conceptual framework of labour law—indeed, some necessity therefor—if developments of recent years are to be adequately explained. Since the time of the second edition of *Labour and the Law* and the time of *Heritage and Adjustment*, there has been in power an administration which has rejected the political commitment to collective laissez-faire far more fundamentally than any other post-war government. This is evident from some of the measures contained in the Employment Acts of 1980 and 1982 and from extra-statutory measures such as the abolition of the Fair Wages Resolution. One thinks in particular of the abolition of the statutory procedure for obtaining trade union recognition, of the abolition of Schedule XI of the Employment Protection Act 1975 and of the statutory prohibition upon the imposition of trade union recognition requirements in commercial contracts. From the perspective of *Labour and the Law*, these measures represent a simple dismantling of the structures of labour law. From the perspective of the government taking these measures, they no doubt represent a positive approach towards labour law. This apparent paradox is largely the result of a conflict of values and is not, as such, resoluble by means of any single formula. But in so far as it poses a problem about the conceptual structure of labour law, there may be something more that can be said about it.

Our suggestion is that the developments of the last five years to which we have referred should be viewed not in isolation from the events of earlier years, but as pointing out the necessity for an appreciation of a continuing governmental perspective upon labour law which is not primarily based on collective laissez-faire. The point is that successive governments have throughout the post-war years been centrally concerned with the control of inflation. In particular they have until very recently been concerned to reconcile that goal with that of maintaining a high level of employment. Moreover, it has been perceived by governments throughout the period that there is a degree of tension between these two goals, a potentiality for conflict of which the collective bargaining system could prove the very vehicle and expression. This was already made clear as a prognosis in the White Paper, *Employment Policy*[1] of 1944 in which the government's responsibility for maintaining "a high and stable level of employment" in post-war Britain was asserted. It has been seen as a major problem by all subsequent governments of differing political outlooks, although they have, of course, varied in the priority they have accorded to the problem and in the ways they have sought to resolve the conflict. In particular, one may contrast attempts to resolve the conflict while remaining within the terms of the problem as thus stated with attempts to resolve the conflict by transcending it—as in their very different ways certain versions of the industrial democracy thesis and certain of the monetarist and free market policies of the present government seek to do.

The point we wish to make in this Introduction is that to take this particular problem—in short the problem of inflation resulting from collective bargaining—as the focus for analysis and to say by implication that it was the most important problem perceived by governments in the post-war period, is to some extent to re-write the way in which *Labour and the Law* looks at this period and the way in which labour lawyers generally have looked at their subject. For example, from the accepted perspective, it is traditional to see the establishment of the Donovan Commission[2] as the major expression of government concern with labour relations problems in its period and therefore to identify the major labour relations issue for labour lawyers at that time and beyond as being the problems of the levels and type of industrial conflict, particularly unofficial and unconstitutional strikes. But the eventual implementation of the Donovan prescription of formalising establishment-level bargaining machinery, even if it has reduced the scale of the problem of unofficial and unconstitutional strikes, did little if anything to alter the fact of union bargaining power at a time of high employment. That is why successive governments, including the Labour government in power when the Donovan

---

[1] Cmd. 6527.
[2] Royal Commission on Trade Unions and Employers' Associations, Chairman: Lord Donovan, established in 1965, reported in 1968 (Cmnd. 3623).

Commission reported, were never able to view the Donovan prescription as a sufficient response to the problems as they viewed them, for all the lip-service that was paid to the Donovan Report. For although the Donovan Commission was far from unaware of or unconcerned about the problem of inflation, they were committed to a frame of reference in which inflation was a marginal problem, and the majority at least of the Commission were concerned to find solutions to labour relations problems within the voluntarist framework, so far as the collective bargaining system was concerned. From a governmental standpoint, on the other hand, the inflation problem was the more significant one and that is why Donovan was of limited impact from their point of view.

To apply this theme systematically to the developments of the post-war period would be a major undertaking and would be inappropriate as an Introduction to *Labour and the Law*. Suffice it here to indicate some ways in which we think the analysis contained in *Labour and the Law* might be supplemented by the kind of analysis we have suggested. First of all, let it be noted that if we are talking about decisions by governments to exercise greater control by law over the collective bargaining process because of the latter's inflationary consequences, then we are dealing with a revolutionary change in the nature of labour law. For as Kahn-Freund himself showed, the hall-mark of the collective bargaining system was its autonomous, self-regulatory nature and the hall-mark of labour law was its abstentionist stance in relation thereto. So there was little scope here for the sort of adaptation that Renner[3] describes, whereby existing legal rules and institutions could be tacitly fashioned to serve new purposes. Those who formulated the aims and directions of labour law early in the post-war period both at a govenmental and an academic level (and there was initially, at least, quite a high measure of accord between them) tended to conceive of it as having mainly *social* functions, above all those of redressing the inequality of power as between individual employee and employer and providing machinery for resolving the inevitable conflicts of interest between employers and trade unions. To attempt to harness this system to the economic function of controlling the inflationary consequences of collective bargaining would necessarily be to effect revolutionary changes in it.

In what precise ways, then, has our labour law been influenced

---

[3] *Institutions of Private Law and their Social Functions* (1949) (Introduction by O. Kahn-Freund) pp. 24 *et seq*.

by the need to control inflation, ideally while preserving a high level of employment? We suggest that many of the developments in labour law in the last twenty or more years can usefully be seen as forming part of a number of strategies whose aim has been to meet that need. There have been four main types of strategy, with a complex inter-relationship: (1) incomes policy; (2) social contract; (3) legal restrictions; (4) control by the market. Again it must be stressed that we are not in this Introduction seeking to develop an alternative history of labour law in the last twenty years in terms of these strategies, but are simply seeking to indicate ways in which the perception of these strategies might supplement the existing analysis. Let us consider that relatively limited issue in relation to each of the four suggested strategies.

(1) *Incomes policy.* The most obvious expression of government's perceived need to reconcile its employment and inflation goals has been, of course, the development of incomes policy. The first of these post-war policies can be identified as early as 1948, its outlines being contained in the White Paper, *Statement on Personal Incomes Costs and Prices* (Cmd. 7321). Since then few years have passed when an incomes policy of one sort or another has not been in force. These policies have varied greatly in their shape and institutional structure: they have variously been statutory or voluntary; agreed, imposed or acquiesced in; general or confined to the public sector only; enforced by independent agencies, agencies under government control or by no agencies. No policy has lasted more than two to three years; in that time each has gone through a reversal phase; each has differed from its predecessor and its successor. So they are difficult to systematise. But a few general points are worth making.

The machineries established for the operation of incomes policies as such have not tended to have a great impact upon the contours of that which is traditionally accepted as labour law even when they have taken a predominantly statutory form. For example even the incomes policy of 1966, which was the most dependent upon statutory support, sought to deal with the problem in a self-contained way in the Prices and Incomes Act 1966, minimising the impact upon the traditional categories of labour law. So it has been tempting for labour lawyers to regard incomes policies as offering at best a very marginal source of labour law both because of their primary non-statutory nature and because they have to some extent been consciously isolated from traditional labour law.

But the substance is very different from the form. Incomes policies have in fact gone to the heart of labour law by encroaching very directly upon the autonomy of collective bargaining and the whole voluntarist stance in relation to collective bargaining. In the late 1960s it was thought there might be an effective voluntarist response to this sort of governmental pressure by the evolution of productivity bargaining. But that never really met the sort of demands upon the collective bargaining system that successive governments felt impelled to make. One result was that incomes policies challenged the traditional role of the Ministry of Labour—later the Department of Employment—as the provider of voluntary conciliation and arbitration in industrial disputes. The tension between that traditionally impartial approach to industrial disputes and governmental commitment to particular views as to the level at which settlements should be achieved was ultimately irresoluble and led indirectly to the hiving-off in 1975 of the conciliation and arbitration functions from the Department of Employment to ACAS. This was of the first importance to labour law traditionally so called.

But although incomes policies had in these senses a heavy impact upon labour relations and labour law, their outstanding single feature has been their ultimate failure to provide a permanent solution to the dilemma between low inflation and high employment. No permanent machinery has been established; no incomes policy seems to have achieved more than temporary success; most have ended in *débâcle*. Hence governments have searched for alternative ways of resolving the problem and have adopted further strategies, to some extent a development out of incomes policy, in an attempt to do so. These strategies have had other and perhaps even more fundamental effects upon the shape of labour law.

(2) *Social contract.* One such strategy to develop out of incomes policy is that whereby it is sought to achieve the effect of income restraint by agreement essentially between the govenment and the trade unions. The main example has been the Social Contract of 1975–77, but it was a strategy also attempted in 1972 when the Conservative government engaged in (abortive) negotiations with the unions in which terms were sought for the suspension of the operation of the Industrial Relations Act. Such a strategy may have an impact upon labour law traditionally so called if the passing of labour legislation is part of the *quid pro quo* for acceptance by the unions of wage restraint. That this was the main function of the Employment Protection Act 1975 may serve to explain its rather incoherent nature, because within the traditional stance of British labour law the Trade Union and Labour Relations Acts 1974–76 had given most of what could be provided.

The Employment Protection Act 1975 in attempting to provide "modern employment rights" came up against a fundamental conceptual problem of our labour law and this perhaps explains the flawed nature of the recognition procedure and the ambiguity about the purposes of Schedule 11.

Moreover, the Social Contract of 1975 was more than simply an agreed form of incomes policy. It had the potentiality, and to some extent the actuality, of enlarging the scope of labour law at a more fundamental level, because of its aim of involving the union movement, through the T.U.C., in a much wider range of government social and economic policies than just incomes on the one hand and labour legislation in a traditional sense on the other. Social contract philosophy involved acceptance of the fact of union power in a high employment economy but it coupled acceptance with an attempt to redirect it away from simple wage-bargaining and into a wider range of social, political and economic objectives. One can see industrial democracy of the kind advocated by the Bullock Committee Report[4] as an attempt to repeat the process at the level of the employing enterprise. The Social Contract was short-lived and the Bullock initiative was stillborn. Had they or either of them become permanent parts of the landscape, they would have tended towards the development of new levels of bargaining—between T.U.C. and government and between enterprises and unions—in addition to the traditional national industry-level and establishment level bargaining. The T.U.C. and government level bargaining would have involved a greater commitment by the T.U.C. to the method of political action as against the method of industrial action, with consequent changes in relations between the T.U.C. and its affiliated unions. To the extent that these developments were even put on the map of labour law as potentialities in the Social Contract period, this represents a change in the discourse of labour law which is indirectly attributable to the central concern of governments with the control of wage inflation.

(3) *Legal restriction.*[5] The strategy of legal restriction consists in the use of the law to reduce the freedom of trade unions and groups of workers to give full expression to their bargaining

---

[4] Report of the Committee of Inquiry on Industrial Democracy (Chairman: Lord Bullock), Cmnd. 6706, 1977.

[5] We acknowledge our debt for this particular phrase and, more generally and importantly, for stimulation of our ideas to J. Clark and Lord Wedderburn, "Modern Labour Law—Problems, Functions and Policies" in Wedderburn, Lewis and Clark (eds.) *Labour Law and Industrial Relations: Building on Kahn-Freund* (1983).

strength by reducing their legal freedom to engage in industrial action. The impact of such a strategy upon labour law traditionally so-called is obvious enough, but it is worth stressing its interconnection with the control of wage inflation. This may arise in at least two main forms. First, the need for such a strategy may be suggested where government has failed to secure agreement for its policies either from the T.U.C. as a whole or from the particular unions involved and has decided to "stand firm." Often this has occurred, inevitably, in public sector pay claims where government as employer or as paymaster to the nationalised industries has effectively determined pay policy. In such circumstances the problem of the General Strike about the distinction between economic and political disputes[6] has tended to re-emerge, as have issues about secondary action, emergency procedures and the protection of uninvolved parties (which may be identified with the protection of the public interest). In this way there may arise a demand for a strategy of legal restriction which will in reality be concerned with effectuating governmental anti-inflation policies though it will not tend to be perceived in those terms.

On the other hand, a strategy of legal restriction may be adopted as the result of a more fundamental perception that it offers of kind of pre-emptive alternative to an incomes policy. The point of governmental control is seen as being shifted so that it operates no longer, as under incomes policy, at the level of the collectively agreed settlement, but at the prior level of the ability of unions to apply the sort of pressure that is likely to result in a high level of settlement. This sort of thinking was to be found in the White Paper *In Place of Strife* (Cmnd. 3888, 1969) and to quite an extent shaped the Industrial Relations Act 1971 and, in a rather different way, the Employment Acts 1980–82. The difference perhaps consists in the fact that an advantage which could be claimed for the strategy in the earlier period was that, if successful, it would be compatible with the maintenance of the collective bargaining system and high levels of employment and even with a public policy in favour of collective bargaining. By 1980, the government would have little interest in making such a claim because they were turning increasingly to the fourth strategy to which we will now refer.

(4) *Control by the market.* Under this strategy, the commitment to high levels of employment is abandoned and the public policy of support for collective bargaining is reversed. The result is likely to be a reduction in the bargaining strength of trade unions but this

---

[6] See below p. 317.

time by a direct attack upon the economic conditions that have given rise to that strength rather than by an attempt to use the law to control the forms of expression of that strength, as under the third strategy. In this strategy labour law traditionally so called is likely to play a less central role than under the third strategy, though, of course, given the history of support in public policy for collective bargaining since 1917/18, an element of dismantling of existing structures is likely to be aimed at through legislation. This strategy underlies the thinking of the present government as expressed in the Employment Acts of 1980 and 1982.

Moreover it is a strategy which also dictates a particular approach to measures for job creation and employment subsidy. Under this strategy, such measures will either be reduced to a minimum as being counter-productive to the struggle against worse inflation; or such measures will be framed in such a way as to cut across the contours of collective bargaining in an attempt to limit their inflationary consequences or even to use them in a counter-inflationary sense, as where the Young Workers Scheme[7] seeks to promote the employment of young people at rates of pay significantly lower than those achieved by collective bargaining. Such developments serve to emphasise the centrality to labour law of job creation and employment subsidy measures which have, like incomes policies, tended to be regarded as very marginal by labour lawyers both because their sources fall outside the normal statutory and case-law purview of labour lawyers and because they have tended to be perceived as existing in the purely economic sphere rather than in that primarily social sphere with which labour lawyers have tended to be concerned.

In conclusion, then, what claims, if any, can be made for this analysis according to anti-wage-inflation strategies? Again, we wish to stress that we advance it here as no more than a major foot-note to *Labour and the Law* which it is necessary to add by reason of events subsequent to the second edition of this work. But it may perhaps be claimed as a justification for such a foot-note that it helps to bring incomes policies more fully into the discourse of labour law; that it indicates the existence of a particular kind of functional continuity between the different strategies described without in any way suggesting an equivalence between them; and that it strengthens the case at certain points for a widening of the parameters of labour law. On the one hand we feel that it would be artificial and slightly incongruous to attempt to intrude that analysis into the text of *Labour and the Law*. On

---

[7] See Freedland (1982) 11 I.L.J. 41.

the other hand we feel that it is with the continuing development of this kind of analysis that Kahn-Freund was concerned when he wrote both the first two editions of *Labour and the Law*, and that he would have approved of the aim of keeping the book up to date at a conceptual as well as at a descriptive level, even if he might have disagreed with the manner of our trying to do so. If the readers of this edition are left with any sense of conviction at all as to how the author himself might have re-written his book in 1983, our aim will have been to that extent achieved.

CHAPTER 1

INTRODUCTION

SOME REFLECTIONS ON LAW AND POWER

I

THIS book has its origins in a series of Hamlyn Lectures given by Otto Kahn-Freund (its original sole author) in 1972. As a Hamlyn lecturer, Kahn-Freund was entrusted with the task of trying to elucidate one branch of the law of the United Kingdom and of comparing it with the corresponding institutions and principles of other nations. This book seeks to do that and also, where appropriate, to place due emphasis on whatever assistance the legislature and the courts have been able to give to the development of labour relations in this country, especially by a policy of self-restraint which at certain times has distinguished the law in this country far more than that of other nations. However, anyone who surveys the history and structure of labour law must become aware of the inherent tension between the social demands of the employment relationship and the spirit and possibilities of the common law. The evolution of an orderly and (compared with many other countries) even today reasonably well-functioning system of labour relations was one of the great achievements of British civilisation. This system of collective bargaining rests on a balance of the collective forces of management and organised labour. To maintain it has on the whole been the policy of the legislature during the last hundred years or so. The welfare of the nation has depended on its continuity and growing strength. This is a sentiment shared, it is to be hoped, by all political parties represented in Parliament. However, the common law knows nothing of a balance of collective forces. It is (and this is its strength and its weakness) inspired by the belief in the equality (real or fictitious) of individuals; it operates between individuals and not otherwise. Perhaps one of the most important characteristics of civil litigation is that the public interest is not represented in the civil courts. It is this, and not only the personal background of the judiciary, which explains the inescapable fact that the contribution which the courts have made to the orderly development of collective labour relations has been slight indeed. More than that, on a number of vitally important occasions Parliament has had to intervene to redress the balance which had been upset by court decisions capable of exercising the most injurious influence on the relations between capital and labour. Thus this book is not primarily concerned with the common law.

If it is important to an understanding of labour law to accept the limitations of the common law, it is equally important to realise the limitations of the law as a whole in this area, as elsewhere. The law governing labour relations is one of the centrally important branches of the law–the legal basis on which the very large majority of people earn their living. No-one should be qualified as a lawyer–professionally or academically–who has not mastered its principles. But the law can make only a modest contribution to the standard of living of the population. On some matters it is crucial. Safety at work is an obvious example, though even here we must see its limitations. But the level of wages, nominal or real, and the level of employment, which are the vital issues, can only marginally be influenced by legal rules and institutions, and this truism holds good for a communist as well as for a capitalist society. Minimum wage legislation should not be decried as it can do and has done a great deal here and abroad to help those on the bottom rungs of the social ladder. Nor should one disparage legislative provisions for guarantee payments protecting workers against a sudden fall in income due to market fluctuations or unforseen occurrences. But these are marginal influences on social welfare, and in times of recession it is quickly apparent how very marginal they are. This same social welfare depends in the first place upon the productivity of labour, which in turn is to a very large extent the result of technical developments. It depends in the second place on the forces of the labour market, on which the law has only a slight influence. It depends thirdly on the degree of effective organisation of the workers in trade unions to which the law can again make only a modest contribution. What the lawyer can do and what the legislator can do remains important, but far more important is the work of the engineer and the scientist, and the creative organiser in industry. Law is a secondary force in human affairs, and especially in labour relations.

The origins of this book in the Hamlyn Lectures also affect its scope and its method of approach. This is not a systematic text-book on labour law, and many important matters such as the organisation of the labour market and the problems of training and apprenticeship are not discussed. It is a book about collective labour relations and the law rather than about individual employment law. The topics that have been selected as being central are the sources of the rules governing labour relations, various factual and legal aspects of collective bargaining and agreements, and some of the legal norms which apply to the trade unions themselves, as well as to disputes between them and their members and the representatives of management. Inevitably the labour legislation of 1971, 1974, 1975, 1976, 1980 and 1982 must play a central part in this discussion of labour law; but we shall not discuss these statutes in precise detail except where it is strictly necessary to do so. Instead, the book will concentrate on the principles underlying labour legislation, and will do so in the light of the history and structure of labour relations and labour law in this country. There is no lack of legal literature on the new legislation and on labour law in general. The purpose of the Hamlyn Lectures which were the starting point of what follows was to see things in perspective, and that is what this book endeavours to do.

II

Law is a technique for the regulation of social power. This is true of labour law, as it is of other aspects of any legal system. Power–the capacity effectively to direct the behaviour of others–is unevenly distributed in all societies. There can be no society without a subordination of some of its members to others, without command and obedience, without rule makers and decision makers. The power to make policy, to make rules and to make decisions, and to ensure that these are obeyed, is a social power. It rests on many foundations, on wealth, on personal prestige, on tradition, sometimes on physical force, often on sheer inertia. It is sometimes supported and sometimes restrained, and sometimes even created by the law, but the law is not the principal source of social power.

Labour law is chiefly concerned with this elementary phenomenon of social power. And—this is important—it is concerned with social power irrespective of the share which the law itself has had in establishing it. This is a point the importance of which cannot be sufficiently stressed. We are speaking about command and obedience, rule making, decision making, and subordination. As a social phenomenon the power to command and the subjection to that power are the same no matter whether the power is exercised by a person clothed with a "public" function, such as an officer of the Crown or of a local authority, or by a "private" person, an employer, a trade union official, a landlord regulating the conduct of his tenants. The subordination to power and the nature of obedience do not differ as between purely "social" or "private" and "legal" or "public" relations. It is a profound error to establish a contrast between "society" and the "state" and to see one in terms of co-ordination, the other in terms of subordination. As regards labour relations that error is fatal. It is engendered by a view of society as an agglomeration of individuals who are co-ordinated as equals; by a myopic neglect or deliberate refusal to face the main characteristic of all societies, and not least of industrial societies, which is the unequal distribution of power. The law does and to some extent must conceal the realities of subordination behind the conceptual screen of contracts considered as concluded between equals. This may partly account for the propensity of lawyers to turn a blind eye to the realities of the distribution of power in society.

The principal purpose of labour law, then, is to regulate, to support and to restrain the power of management and the power of organised labour. These are abstractions. In their original meanings the words "management" and "labour" denoted (as they still do) not persons, but activities; the activities of planning and regulating production and distribution and co-ordinating capital and labour on the one hand, the activity of producing and distributing on the other. But even if, by a now common twist of language, "management" and "labour" are used to denote not activities but the people who exercise them, they remain abstractions. "Management" may be a private employer, a company, a firm. It may be an association of employers, or an association of associations, such as the Confederation of British Industry. It may be a public corporation such as the National Coal Board, British Railways or an Area Health Authority. It may be a local authority or it may be that largest of all "managers" which in most countries is called the State or the Government and which in this country appears in the symbolic disguise of the "Crown." In a concrete situation, however, this word "management" may be used to designate a foreman at the assembly line, a production manager, a factory manager, or a board of directors or head of a department. The word is always used to identify the individual or corporate body who in a given situation wields that power to define policy, to make rules, and above all decisions, through whose exercise management manifests itself to those who are its subordinates. To manage means to command.

"Labour," too, is an abstraction. To the Confederation of British Industy "labour" presumably denotes in the first place the Trades Union Congress, to a foreman it may principally denote a shop steward, to every employer it denotes the men and women subject to his managerial power, and also the union or unions with whom he or the association of which he is a member negotiates.

This ambiguity of the terms "management" and "labour" if applied to persons rather than to activities is important: it means that by "labour relations," the relations between "management" and "labour" we understand all sorts of relationships, individual and collective, and that hence the orbit of what we are accustomed to call labour law comprehends matters of industrial safety as well as of industrial disputes, of collective agreements as well as of job security, in short anything that can arise between managers and those subject to managerial power.

Nor is it possible neatly to separate these two categories of persons.[1] One of the most significant features of our contemporary economic and social development is the rapidly growing overlap of "management" and "labour." A production manager or the head of one of a chain of stores is "management" if seen from below and "labour" if seen from above. A steadily increasing number of men and women are employed to exercise managerial, and even entrepreneurial functions. It is an inevitable consequence of the growth of the units of enterprise, and of that separation of management and of policy making from ownership which results from the technical development of industrial societies, and it matters little in this context whether we consider the private or the public sector of the economy. It is however also a phenomenon which, as we shall have to point out on a subsequent occasion, has very important repercussions in the structure of labour relations and of labour law.

To gauge the distribution of managerial power and to identify its location is not always an easy task. The Royal Commission on Trade Unions and Employers' Associations (the Donovan Commission) spent a great deal of time and energy on this quest,[2] and especially on the problem of how power was shared between boards of directors and the lower echelons, whether "line" or "personnel" management, where and by whom rules affecting workers were in fact made, and where and by whom they were

---

[1] See—as regards publicly owned industries—Bell, "The Development of Industrial Relations in Nationalised Industries in Post-War Britain" (1975) 13 Brit. J. of Ind.Rel. 1 at 12; see also Weir, "Radical Managerialism:Middle Manager's Perceptions of Collective Bargaining" (1976) 14 Brit.J. of Ind.Rel. 324.

[2] Royal Commission on Trade Unions and Employers' Associations 1965–1968 Report (Cmnd. 3623) (in future quoted as "Donovan Report"), Pt. III, esp. paras. 83 *et seq.* See also V. G. Munns, *Employers' Associations,* Royal Commission Research Paper No. 7, esp. paras. 146 *et seq.;* H. A. Clegg, *The Changing System of Industrial Relations in Great Britain* (1979), esp. Chaps. 3 and 4.

applied, that is, who wielded the power of discipline. The Donovan Commission was also much concerned to find how the rule making powers were distributed between employers and their associations, again—as we shall see—a problem which is of fundamental importance for the law and its development.

To trace the distribution of managerial power is a difficult task in any given society, no less difficult where the means of production are publicly owned than where they are privately owned. To find who has power on the side of labour is equally, if not more, difficult.[3] Here, however, we can establish as clear and hardly controverted one elementary proposition which will explain a great deal of what we have to say. The individual employee or worker—we use these words indiscriminately[4]—has normally no social power, because it is only in the most exceptional cases that, as an individual, he has any bargaining power at all. Such exceptional cases exist of course—one can think of a high powered managerial employee with unique experience, a top rank scientist, or even a highly skilled craftsman whom the employer cannot easily replace, in short, of those whom Alan Fox calls "occupants of high discretion roles."[5] For our purposes these cases are atypical and therefore irrelevant in the present context.Typically, the worker as an individual has to accept the conditions which the employer offers. On the the labour side, power is collective power. The individual employer represents an accumulation of material and human resources, socially speaking the enterprise is itself in this sense a "collective power." If a collection of workers (whether it bears the name of a trade union or some other name) negotiate with an employer, this is thus a negotiation between collective entities, both of which are, or may at least be, bearers of power.

---

[3] Donovan Report, paras. 46 *et seq.,* 96 *et seq.,* see also W. E. J. McCarthy, *The Role of Shop Stewards in British Industrial Relations,* Royal Commission Research Paper No. 1, esp. Chaps. D and E; McCarthy and Parker, *Shop Stewards and Workshop Relations, ibid.* No. 10, *passim*; Clegg, *loc.cit.* Chap.2.

[4] Here and throughout we use the words "employee" and "worker" indiscriminately to designate all those working under contracts of employment, irrespective of the nature of their work and irrespective of their place in the hierarchy of the enterprise or public service concerned. As used here, the two words are synonymous and have the same meaning as "servant" at common law. There are many (divergent) statutory definitions of "workman." For a statutory definition of "employee" and of "worker," see Trade Union and Labour Relations Act 1974, s. 30 (1); Employment Protection Act 1975, s.126 (1)—the latter term denotes a status, *i.e.* a person who works or normally works or seeks to work under a contract of employment, a contract for personal services, or in employment under or for the purposes of a government department.

[5] Alan Fox, *Beyond Contract: Work, Power and Trust Relations* (1974), pp. 57 *et seq.,* esp. p. 61.

But the relation between an employer and an isolated employee or worker is typically a relation between a bearer of power and one who is not a bearer of power. In its inception it is an act of submission, in its operation it is a condition of subordination, however much the submission and the subordination may be concealed by that indispensable figment of the legal mind known as the "contract of employment." The main object of labour law has always been, and we venture to say will always be, to be a countervailing force to counteract the inequality of bargaining power which is inherent and must be inherent in the employment relationship. Most of what we call protective legislation—legislation on the employment of women, children and young persons, on safety in mines, factories, and offices, on payment of wages in cash, on guarantee payments, on race or sex discrimination, on unfair dismissal, and indeed most labour legislation altogether— must be seen in this context. It is an attempt to infuse law into a relation of command and subordination.

We have said that all this is necessarily inherent in the employment relationship. Capital resources cannot be utilised by anybody (whether the body be private or public) without exercising a command power over human beings. This is, or ought to be, a common-place. In any event one has not heard of any legal system which has sought to replace the relation of subordination by a relation of co-ordination. Except in a one man undertaking, economic purposes cannot be achieved without a hierarchical order within the economic unit. There can be no employment relationship without a power to command and a duty to obey, that is without this element of subordination in which lawyers rightly see the hallmark of the "contract of employment." However, the power to command and the duty to obey can be regulated. An element of co-ordination can be infused into the employment relationship. Co-ordination and subordination are matters of degree, but however strong the element of co-ordination, a residuum of command power will and must remain. Thus, the "when" and the "where" of the work must on principle be decided by management, but the law may restrict the managerial power as to the time of work by prohibiting work at night or on Sundays, and as to the place by seeking to prevent overcrowding and other insalubrious conditions. More than that: the law may create a mechanism for the enforcement of such rules and it may protect the worker who relies on its operation. By doing so the law limits the range of the worker's duty of obedience and enlarges the range of his freedom. This, without any doubt, was the original and for many decades the primary function of labour law. But the most elementary knowledge of the history of labour relations in this country and abroad yields the insight that, standing by itself, the law is not very effective in these matters. For centuries Parliament tried, first in a growing number of trades and then generally, to prevent unfair competition, to protect the workers, above all, to protect the monetary economy by prohibiting the payment of wages in kind and also to suppress managerial devices such as the "tommy shop" designed to restrain whatever consumer's choice society allowed the worker to exercise.[6] But although the duty to pay wages in current coin of the realm was imposed by the Truck Act of 1831 on the employers of manual workers[7] and the "tommy shop" most sternly prohibited,[8] we have the clearest evidence that these and other prohibited practices such as the deduction of fines continued far into the second half of the nineteenth century,[9] and that Parliament improved the situation but did not wholly solve the problem when in 1887 it introduced a system of inspection to enforce this legislation.[10] Where labour is weak—and its strength or weakness depends largely on factors outside the control of the law—Acts of Parliament, however well intentioned and well designed, can do something, but cannot do much to modify the power relation between labour and management. The law has important functions in labour relations but they are secondary if compared with the impact of the labour market (supply and demand) and, which is relevant here, with the spontaneous creation of a social power on the workers' side to balance that of management. Even the most efficient inspectors can do but little if the workers dare not complain to them about infringements of the legislation they are seeking to enforce. The Truck Acts and other protective legislation began to be effectively enforced when membership in trade unions gave the workers the strength to insist on the maintenance of the legal standards, and modern legislation acknowledges this fact. It enables recognised[11] trade unions to

---

[6] Beginning with a statute applying to woollen cloth making, passed in 1464. All these statutes are enumerated in the statute of 1831 (1 & 2 Will. 4, c.36) by which they were repealed. See Report of the Committee on the Truck Acts (Karmel Report) 1961, para. 4.

[7] *i.e.* those employed in the trades specified in the original s. 19 of the Truck Act 1831, which was subsequently replaced by s. 2 of the Truck Amendment Act 1887.

[8] Truck Act 1831, s. 2.

[9] See the *Transactions and Results of the National Association of Coal etc. Miners of Great Britain*, London (1863), quoted, Webb, *Industrial Democracy* (1926 ed.), p.317, n.2.

[10] Truck Amendment Act 1887 (Bradlaugh's Act), s.13 (2). See Karmel Report, para.8.

[11] See below, Chap. 4.

appoint, from amongst the employees of an undertaking, "safety representatives" who must co-operate with the employer so as to ensure health and safety at work, to check the effectiveness of the relevant measures, and, if necessary, insist on the appointment of a permanent safety committee.[12] The law does, of course, provide its own sanctions, administrative, penal, and civil, and their impact should not be underestimated, but in labour relations legal norms cannot often be effective unless they are backed by social sanctions as well, that is by the countervailing power of trade unions and of the organised workers asserted through consultation and negotiation with the employer and ultimately, if this fails, through withholding their labour. The law seeks to restrain the command power of management. How far it succeeds in doing so depends on the extent to which the workers are organised. The law also seeks to restrain the power of the unions. How far it can do so depends on the attitude of the employers.

We have said that it is difficult to locate the seat of power on the side of labour. Countervailing labour power is not synonymous with trade union power, but even if it were, the problem would be exceedingly complex. Who has the rule making power and the decision-making power inside the trade union movement and inside a given union? The problem is strictly analogous to the corresponding problem on the management side. Here, on the union side, we also have a relation of subordination, of command and obedience, and necessarily so. How far then, is the subordination of the individual union member to the union's rule and decision-making power mitigated by his share in the making of these rules and of these decisions? How much reality is there in the democratic right of members to participate in these processes? And—a different but a connected question—where are the decisions made: at the centre, in the regions, in the branches? Or outside these local branches, on the shop floor, by shop stewards or by the "direct democracy" of the "work group," with the assistance of or perhaps in defiance of the shop steward?[13] A trade

---

[12] Health and Safety at Work Act 1974, s. 2 (4), (6) and (7). s. 2 (5) was repealed by the Employment Protection Act 1975, s. 116 and Sched. 15, so as to give to recognised unions the exclusive power of appointing safety representatives and to remove the possibility of their election by the workforce. See on the earlier developlments, R. Howells and D. Lewis, "Worker Participation in Safety" (1974) 3 I.L.J. 87.

[13] See the evidence collected by Clegg, *loc cit.,* pp.41 *et seq.,* and in Boraston, Clegg and Rimmer, *Workplace and Union* (Warwick Studies in Industrial Relations, 1975) a series of case studies on the relation between full time union officers, branch officers, and workplace organisation.

union shares with a company or a government department or a county council the quality of being a collective unit and whether the law treats it as a corporate person in the technical sense is irrelevant in this context. By saying that a collective entity exercises social power you have said very little until you have also said who (that is which individuals) have that power inside the collective unit. We should not speak about the power of "the State" or "the Crown," but of that of civil servants, or Ministers, or Members of Parliament. For the same reason an analysis of the impact the law has on labour relations is only a fragment unless it takes into account the internal structure of the trade unions and of the trade union movement as a whole, the relations between the unions and the TUC, between unions and their officers and branches, above all between unions and their members. Here too, the law may have the role of a force countervailing the subordination of the individual to the bearer of a social power. The need for protecting the worker against unfair dismissal by the employer should be seen in conjunction with the need for protecting him against arbitrary expulsion by the union.[14]

As a power countervailing management the trade unions are much more effective than the law has ever been or can ever be. This is not only true in this country, it also applies where the law has played a larger part in the development of labour relations than in Britain; in Continental countries such as France or Germany, in Australia and New Zealand, and in the United States and Canada.

Everywhere the effectiveness of the law depends on the unions far more than the unions depend on the effectiveness of the law. The effectiveness of the unions, however, depends to some extent on forces which neither they nor the law can control. If one looks at unemployment statistics and at the statistics of union membership, one can, at least at certain times, see a correlation. Very often, as employment falls, so does union membership.[15] Nothing contributed to the strength of the trade union movement as much as the maintenance over a number of years of a fairly high level of employment, contributed, that is, to its strength in relation to

---

[14] This was the view taken by the Donovan Commission (Cmnd. 3623, Chaps. 9 and 11)

[15] See "Trade Unionism"—the Evidence of the Trades Union Congress to the Donovan Commission, para. 364: "The most important factor determining the level of trade union membership is the level of the economy"; and G. S. Bain, "The Labour Force" in *British Social Trends Since 1900*, A. H. Hasley *et al.*, editors (London: Macmillan, 1972); G. S. Bain and F. Elsheikh, *Union Growth and the Business Cycle* (1976).

management. A high level of employment strengthens the unions externally, but it may (it does not always) weaken them internally. Under conditions of high employment the locus of rule- and decision-making power shifted on the labour side in many industries (the motor car industry is the textbook example in this country) from the union administrations to spontaneous, amorphous and often ephemeral work groups on the shop floor; sometimes, but only sometimes, led by shop stewards who represent the union on the spot.[16] On the labour side as on the management side we have witnessed a decentralisation of power; a movement of power from the centre to the periphery. This transformation of the power structure of labour relations became at certain times one of the decisive factors in the development of the law. It resulted from the development of the labour market which reduced the effectiveness of central wage fixing and the authority of the union over its members. The wage drift and the wildcat strike were Siamese twins. These may have been ephemeral phenomena, but union activity through shop stewards at plant—sometimes at enterprise—level is likely to remain one of the central features of labour relations in this country, and the law now recognises this by protecting workers against dismissal or other disciplinary measures by reason of such activity, and by guaranteeing that they have the necessary facilities and free time.[17]

The characteristic feature of the employment relation is thus that the individual worker is subordinated to the power of management but that power of management is co-ordinated with that of organised labour. The regulation of labour results from the combination of these processes of subordination and of co-ordination, of the rules made unilaterally by the employer in conjunction with those agreed between him or his association and the union through collective bargaining, including bargaining at plant level. In some foreign countries, especially on the European Continent, the law has created a statutory representation of the workers in the plant or enterprise, and a third regulatory factor thus appears in the shape of the rule- and decision-making power of this "works council" or body of "delegates" or "internal committee" which may sometimes act unilaterally, but more

---

[16] This was one of the important findings of the Donovan Report: (Cmnd. 3623) Chap 3, especially paras. 96 *et seq.*, with the conclusion that (para. 107) "there is no question that this is largely due to the choice of management." For recent developments see W. Brown (ed.), *The Changing Contours of British Industrial Relations* (1981), Chaps. 2 and 4.

[17] See Chap. 7.

normally bilaterally with management. Nothing of this kind exists in this country and some may regret this,[18] but, of course, here, and also in other countries,[19] many of the functions of such statutory bodies are fulfilled by shop stewards, *i.e.* union representatives elected by union members at the workshop and confirmed by the union through their credentials. For us the dominating feature of labour relations must be the adjustment of the managerial rule- and decision-making power and of collective bargaining. This is the reality of things, in the language of the law that reality is concealed. There the unilateral rule- and decision-making power of management is presented as based on a "contract,"[20] on the free will of the employer and the employee. The central problem how to adjust managerial power and the co-ordinated power of labour and management appears to the legal mind as a problem of the relation between the collective agreement and the contract of employment, made between the individual worker with his employer. In fact the worker does not participate in the making of the rules which govern his work, any more than the citizen, as a citizen, participates in the making of the laws he has to obey. Nor does "democracy" mean that those who have to obey rules have an active share in making them, and this is true of political as well as of "industrial" democracy. In both spheres—the political and the industrial—democracy means that those who obey the rules have a right (and a moral duty) to select those who represent them in making the rules. In this country where, as we have just said, there are no statutory works councils or the like, the unions and the unions alone fulfil in relation to the worker, as a worker, the democratic function which Parliament fulfils in relation to the citizen as a citizen. The citizen has the legal right and the moral duty to vote. The worker has the legal right and the moral duty to be a member of the relevant union. He may

---

[18] See the symposium *La représentation des travailleurs sur le plan de l'entreprise dans le droit des pays membres de la* C.E.C.A., Luxembourg 1959. More up to date: "Workers' Participation and Collective Bargaining in Europe" C.I.R. Study No. 4, HMSO 1974; "Employee Participation and Union Structure" Bulletin of the Eur. Comm., Suppl. 8/75 (the Commissions's "Green Paper"); Batstone & Davies, "Industrial Democracy, European Experience" HMSO 1976; Blanpain, "The Influence of Labour on Management Decision Making" (1975) 3 I.L.J., p. 5; Sorge, "The Evolution of Industrial Democracy in the Countries of the European Community" (1976) 14 Brit. J. of Ind. Rel., p. 274.

[19] *e.g.* in France: *sections syndicales and délégués syndicaux,* since the statute of December 27, 1968 (now *Code du Travail,* 1974, Art. L 412–10 *et seq.*) recognised by law, alongside the *délégués du personnel (ibid.* Art. L 420 *et seq.*) who are elected by the entire workforce, irrespective of organisation.

[20] Or on a similar relation during its temporary interruption, Employment Protection (Consolidation) Act 1978, Sched. 13,paras. 9 and 10.

have the legal freedom not to be a member of a union, just as the citizen is free not to vote. But he has no more a moral right to abstain from being a union member than a citizen has to abstain from voting. The equation of the "freedom not to associate" with the "freedom to associate" is a fallacy. We shall come back to this in a subsequent chapter.

Nothing is more misleading than the ambiguity of the word "freedom" in labour relations. By restraining the power of management over the individual worker the law limits the range of the worker's duty to obey rules made by management. Protective legislation thus enlarges the worker's freedom, his freedom from the employer's power to command, or, if you like, his freedom to give priority to his own and his family's interests over those of his employer. Yet paradoxically, such liberating legislation must appear to the lawyer as a restraint on freedom, on the "freedom of contract" which in this context is the term the law uses for the subjection of the worker to the power of management, or as "statutory restrictions," the name given in older textbooks to legislation passed for the protection of the workers. This paradox cannot be condemned. It is necessary for the law to see relations of subordination in terms of co-ordination, that is, an act of submission in the mask of a 'contract,' because this is the fiction through which it exorcises the incubus of "compulsory labour." One should not underestimate the real significance of verbal magic. During the Second World War when the law permitted "direction of labour"[21] and removed most of the parties' freedom to make and to terminate contracts of employment by requiring for both acts the permission of the representative of the Ministy of Labour in all industries "essential" to the war effort,[22] this fiction of the "contract," of the "free" intention of the parties was maintained, and of an employee directed to a job or of an employer forced against his intention to keep on a worker it could have been said, as the Romans said in a different context, *"quamquam coactus voluit."* And even today the employer's freedom to choose his workers and the worker's freedom to choose his employer is seriously curtailed in dock employment and has to be in the interest of the "decasualisation" of labour.[23]

---

[21] Defence Regulation 58A, sparingly used in practice. See Ministry of Labour and National Service, Report for the years 1939–46, Cmd. 7225, pp. 40 *et seq.*

[22] Under the Essential Work Orders.

[23] See the Dock Workers Employment Scheme 1967 in Sched. 2 to the Dock Workers (Regulation of Employment) (Amendment) Order 1967 (S.I. 1967 No. 1252), in due course to be replaced by a new Scheme under Dock Work Regulation Act 1976, ss. 4 and 5; see also Sched. 3.

Nevertheless, even here the law sees the relationship as one based on a freely concluded contract, and thus upholds the tradition that the law abhors compulsory labour.[24] This is a necessary approach to the problem of freedom, but it is the use of words as symbols expressing a policy, an aspiration, a tradition, and not as symbols denoting a reality. The danger begins if "freedom of contract" is taken for a social fact rather than a verbal symbol. As a social fact that which the law calls "freedom of contract" may in many spheres of life (not only in labour relations) be not more than the freedom to restrict or to give up one's freedom. Conversely, to restrain a person's freedom of contract may be necessary to protect his freedom, that is, to protect him against oppression which he may otherwise be constrained to impose upon himself through an act of his legally free and socially unfree will. To mistake the conceptual apparatus of the law for the image of society may produce a distorted view of the employment relation. This in turn may lead to the uncritical and undiscriminating application to it of rules developed for relations of real co-ordination (where the parties are "at arm's length") such as most commercial contracts, and this has in fact happened in the history of British labour law. The most conspicuous example was the imputation to the worker of an "intention" to "assume" certain risks of injury, especially those caused by the negligence of fellow workers, the notorious doctrine of "common employment," now abolished by statute.[25] It is not the only example.[26] The courts have often had to face difficult problems arising from the limitations of the managerial rule- and decision-making power such as the problem of what personal risks a worker could be required to undertake,[27] and how far the employer could go in

---

[24] The celebrated principle of Equity not specifically to enforce a contract of employment: *Lumley* v. *Wagner* (1852) 1 De G. M. & G. 604 shows how easily this can be done indirectly through injunctions. For the principle itself, Treitel, *The Law of Contract* (5th ed.), pp. 758 *et seq.* It is now codified in s. 16 of the Trade Union and Labour Relations Act 1974, which may have an effect on indirect enforcement through injunction. It is not affected by the decision of the Court of Appeal in *Hill* v. *Parsons* [1972] Ch. 305 which dealt with a situation described by Lord Denning M.R. as an "exception" (see Freedland, *The Contract of Employment* (1976) pp. 277–278, 298–299). Nor is it affected by the power to order reinstatement or re-engagement under s.69 of the Employment Protection (Consolidation) Act 1978.

[25] Abolished as far as personal injuries are concerned:Law Reform (Personal Injuiries) Act 1948, s.1.

[26] Perhaps the best example of this dream world of "implied intentions" is *Lister* v. *Romford Ice and Storage Co. Ltd.* [1957] A.C. 555.

[27] *e.g. Bouzourou* v. *Ottoman Bank* [1930] A.C. 277; *Ottoman Bank* v. *Chakarian*, ibid. 277; *Palace Shipping Co.* v. *Caine* [1907] A.C. 386; *Robson* v. *Sykes* [1936] 2 All E.R. 612.

determining the time and the place of work and the work itself.[28] In making decisions in such cases the courts were tracing the outer limits of the "managerial prerogative," but what was quite frequently a dilemma between respect for the needs of management and respect for the freedom and for the dignity of the individual appeared in the deceptive disguise of "interpreting" a non-existent "intention of the parties." We can, however, see in recent legislation on equal pay that the unilateral rule making power of management, the power to make, and to communicate to the workers, a "pay structure," is beginning to be openly recognised.[29]

Protective legislation which cannot be "contracted out" of limits the parties' legal freedom of contract. No worker coming within the scope of a maximum hours law can validly promise to work more than the maximum set by statute. To put it differently: though he gives this promise he remains free not to keep it. This illustrates the ambiguity of the word "free" in this context. The enlargement of the worker's freedom, however, is of little factual importance. It means no more than that the law will not assist the employer to enforce the promise. He can still enforce it through such social pressures as are at his disposal, or rather he could do so if the purely negative sanction of the voidness of the promise had not been under-pinned by positive sanctions such as inspection and penalties, and even these, as we have said, are often ineffective as long as the workers are not effectively organised.

III

In concluding these introductory observations, we must make one further fundamental point. Any approach to the relations between management and labour is fruitless unless the divergency of their

---

[28] Under the redundancy payments legislation many occasions are arising on which the scope of the managerial power over type and place of work has to be defined by the court. See Grunfeld, *The Law of Redundancy*, (2nd ed., 1980) *passim*. The cases on the employers' power to send the worker to a place in a different part of the country are of special importance: they concern the control of the employer over the whole of the worker's life. The decisions in *O'Brien* v. *Associated Fire Alarms Ltd.* [1968] 1 W.L.R. 1916 (C.A.) and in *Mumford* v. *Boulton & Paul (Steel Constructions) Ltd.* [1971] I.T.R. 76 should be contrasted with *Stevenson* v. *Teeside Bridge and Engineering Ltd.* [1971] 1 All E.R. 296. Such cases are numerous. See, *e.g. Sutcliffe* v. *Hawker Siddeley* [1973] I.C.R 560 (N.I.R.C.); *Maher* v. *Fram Gerrard* [1974] I.C.R. 31 (N.I.R.C.); *U.K. Atomic Energy Authority* v. *Claydon* [1974] I.C.R. 128 (N.I.R.C.); *Rowbotham* v. *Lee* [1975] I.C.R. 109; *Jones* v. *Associated Tunnelling Co. Ltd.* [1981] I.R.L.R. 477.

[29] Equal Pay Act 1970, s.3.

interests is plainly recognised and articulated.[30] This is true of any type of society one can think of and certainly of a communist as much as of a capitalist society. There must always be someone who seeks to increase the rate of consumption and some who seek to increase the rate of investment. The distribution of the social product between consumption and investment can only be determined by a constant and unending dialogue of powers, no matter whether this takes place at the bargaining table, in Parliament, or in the recesses (more or less dark) of government offices. The dialogue may result in all sorts of things: in an ill assorted huge pile of agreements, hardly comprehensible to anyone unfamiliar with the arcana of a trade or industry, in the fragments of a statutory incomes policy, in guidelines formulated in a "social contract"[31] or in a tidy national plan. One cannot think of any person who in our century has done more to substitute a legally organised dialogue for ordeal by battle than the late Mr. Justice Higgins, the principal Founding Father of the Australian system of arbitration and conciliation. It was he who said[32] that "the war between the profit-maker and the wage-earner is always with us," *i.e.* the war between those who argue for more investment (and who to a limited, sometimes a very limited, extent represent the welfare of future generations at the expense of the present) and those who argue for a maintained or improved standard of living now. This is what labour law is very largely about. This is also what a good deal of politics is about; who can read the pages of any history of the Soviet Union since 1917 without realising how true this is even in a communist country?

There is, however, one interest which management and labour have in common: it is that the inevitable and necessary conflicts should be regulated from time to time by reasonably predictable procedures, procedures which do not exclude the ultimate resort to any of those sanctions through which each contending part must—in case of need—assert its power. Such procedures may—and this is an important point—prevent any change in existing

---

[30] Alan Fox, *Industrial Sociology and Industrial Relations* (1966) (Royal Commission Research Paper No. 3). The author distinguishes between a "pluralistic" and a "unitary" frame of reference. Subsequently he submitted the pluralist conception to a stringent criticism: *Beyond Contract: Work, Power and Trust Relations* (1974), Chap. 6, pp. 248 *et seq.* This in turn was subject to a—largely convincing—counter-critique by Clegg, "Pluralism in Industrial Relations" (1975) 13 Brit. J. of Ind. Rel., 309.

[31] *i.e.* a political compact—not, of course a "contract" in the legal sense. See p. 68 below.

[32] H. B. Higgins, *A New Province for Law and Order* (1922) p. 1; "war" meaning conflict of interest, not industrial stoppage.

conditions (the status quo) until they have been exhausted.[33] It is however sheer utopia to postulate a common interest in the substance of labour relations. To dig up the roots of this utopia of a "pre-established harmony" of management and labour would be a fascinating task for a sociologist: he would probably discover laissez-faire doctrines as well as a very crude type of Marxism and most certainly those (more or less bogus) ideological constructions which were used by Mussolini to bolster up the *"stato corporativo,"* and he would also observe how the utopia can degenerate into the sham romanticism of the feudalistic trappings used by Hitler for his labour laws. Much more important: this belief that there are not really two sides of industry may induce unenlightened employers to hinder their workers in exercising their freedom of organisation, to refuse negotiations with genuine trade unions and to set up sham organisations controlled by management. It may also be invoked by enlightened employers inclined to adopt an attitude of paternalistic benevolence. It may however also (whether consciously or not) have a powerful influence on the minds of trade union leaders anxious to blur the line between labour and managment, attaching exaggerated hopes to "participation" and elevating "co-determination" almost to the level of a religious belief, though far less of this can be observed here than in some foreign countries. Whatever the source of this "unitary" approach to labour relations, and whatever the use to which it is put in practice, it should be firmly rejected. The conflict between capital and labour is inherent in an industrial society and therefore in the labour relationship. Conflicts of interest are inevitable in all societies. There are rules for their adjustment, there can be no rules for their elimination. To that extent there is a certain parallel between labour relations and international relations. There must be rules designed to promote negotiation, to promote agreement, and to promote its observance, and there must be rules designed to regulate the use of such social pressure as must be available to both sides as weapons in the conflict. It will be our principal concern in the following chapters to discuss some of those rules, but before we do so, we shall have to say something about the sources of labour regulation in general.

---

[33] See on this in detail Anderman, "The 'Status Quo' issue in industrial disputes procedures: some implications for labour law" (1975) 4 I.L.J. 131.

CHAPTER 2

SOURCES OF REGULATION

1. THE ROLE OF THE COMMON LAW

IN the formulation of the rules which regulate the relations between employers and workers the common law has played a minor role. The courts have had a share, but only a small share, in their evolution. For this there are a number of reasons:

(*a*) The rules and principles in which we are interested are designed to govern the normal typical behaviour of the parties (hours of work, length of overtime, rates of wages, etc.); case law can only deal with pathological situations. The rules which are needed in labour relations must work *ex ante*. They must direct people what to do or not do, before and not after they have acted. Case law operates *ex post;* it does establish rules, but not before something has gone wrong. The normal function of a court is to lock the stable door after the first horse has bolted so as to keep the other horses in; normally it is only a statute that can protect the first horse. The courts have played (and continue to play) a most important role in interpreting statutes. The Truck Acts were a good example in the past,[1] the redundancy payments legislation is a very good prominent example at the present moment[2] and so are the provisions on unfair dismissal.[3] The courts also made contributions to the regulation of the employment relation through applying the common law; but if one looks at the cases one finds that they are mainly about the unforeseen and about the exceptional: whether the employer must pay wages if the worker is sick,[4] or if the employer cannot provide work owing to

---

[1] Esp. such leading cases as *Hewlett* v. *Allen* [1894] A.C. 383; *Williams* v. *North's Navigation Collieries* [1906] A.C. 136; *Pratt* v. *Cook* [1940] A.C. 437; *Williams* v. *Butlers Ltd.* [1975] I.C.R. 208.

[2] For an excellent analysis, see Grunfeld, *The Law of Redundancy* (2nd ed., 1980).

[3] Employment Protection (Consolidation) Act 1978, Pt. V, as amended by Employment Act 1980, ss. 6–10.

[4] See, *e.g. Marrison* v. *Bell* [1939] 2 K.B. 187 (C.A.); *Petrie* v. *MacFisheries* [1940] 1 K.B. 258; *O'Grady* v. *Saper* [1940] 2. K.B. 469; *Orman* v. *Saville Sportswear Ltd.* [1960] 1 W.L.R. 1055, *Mears* v. *Safecar Security Ltd.* [1982] I.C.R. 626; *Howman & Son* v. *Blyth* [1983] I.C.R. 416. See Hepple and O'Higgins,

commercial[5] or technical[6] circumstances, whether the worker is under an obligation to undergo unforeseen physical risks,[7] whether there are cases in which, to protect his reputation or skill, the worker can claim to do particular jobs[8] and also, of course, how and when the employer can use discipline such as dismissal[9] or suspension.[10] The one aspect of the employment relation which has been predominantly shaped by the courts is the employer's liability for accidents suffered by the worker at his work.

If one compares the formative influence of the courts on commercial relationships (sale of goods, carriage of goods and passengers, insurance, etc.) with the role they have played in the employment relationship, the contrast is staggering. Even where statutes have been passed to codify the law governing certain kinds of commercial contracts, they have largely been a summary of the prodigious previous case law on the subject.[11] The obligations of the seller to deliver goods of the agreed quantity and quality at the agreed time and place can be developed out of rulings made in situations where the court found that he delivered too little or not in accordance with sample or description or too late or at the wrong place. What is meant by a seaworthy ship you can define very effectively by deciding a long line of cases in which the ship was in fact unseaworthy. But the price the buyer has to pay, the freight the shipowner can claim, the quantity of goods the seller has to deliver or the time or voyage or number of lay days for which the ship is at the charterer's disposal are settled by the contract. Businessmen do not generally expect the law to direct their normal behaviour. What they want to know from the court is what they can claim and what they must expect to pay if things

---

Employment Law (4th ed, 1981) paras. 339–341; Freedland,*The Contract of Employment* (1976) pp. 108 *et seq.*; certain statutory entitlements to sick pay from the employer are now conferred by the Social Security and Housing Benefits Act 1982 Pt. I—see below, p. 33, n. 23.

[5] *e.g. Devonald* v. *Rosser and Sons* [1906] 2 K.B. 728 (C.A.).

[6] *Browning* v. *Crumlin Valley Collieries Ltd.* [1926] 1 K.B. 522 (C.A.).

[7] See Chap. 1, n. 27 above.

[8] See, *e.g. Clayton* v. *Oliver* [1930] A.C. 209; *Collier* v. *Sunday Referee Publishing Co. Ltd.* [1940] 2 K.B. 647.

[9] See, *e.g. Churchward* v. *Chambers* (1860) 2 F. & F. 229; *Jupiter General Insurance* v. *Shroff* [1937] 2 All E.R. 67; *Laws* v. *London Chronicle Ltd.* [1959] 1 W.L.R. 698(C.A.)

[10] *e.g. Hanley* v. *Pease and Partners Ltd.* [1915] 1 K.B. 698; *Warburton* v. *Taff Vale Ry.* (1902) 18 T.L.R. 420; *Wallwork* v. *Fielding* [1922] 2 K.B. 66; *Marshall* v. *English Electric Co. Ltd.* [1945] 1 All E.R. 655; *Bird* v. *British Celanese Ltd.* [1945] K.B. 336.

[11] *e.g.* the Sale of Goods Act 1893 (now 1979); the Marine Insurance Act 1906.

have gone contrary to expectations. Employers and workers however must expect the law to play a part in regulating their mutual obligations and rights. The difference between the role played by the law in individual commercial and in individual industrial relations reflects the difference in the expectations society attaches to the law in different spheres of life. It reflects the difference between a sphere of life in which the parties to contracts make their agreements articulate and a sphere of life in which the so-called contract is usally no more than a blank to be filled from outside. "From outside" means that the law must do a great deal of what the contract does in commercial relations: to regulate the day-to-day normal duties of the parties. It can be done by statute or by collective agreements, not by the courts. Demurrage charges have a vague affinity with overtime rates. Look at the difference in the source of regulation. This difference may have been partially obscured by legislation controlling the terms on which contracts may be made particularly with regard to exemption clauses; the most important of these is the Unfair Contract Terms Act 1977. Such legislation is primarily concerned with the protection of the consumer of goods and services, in the sense of the private citizen consumer as distinct from the commercial consumer. Although such legislation has some impact on contracts between commercial contractors, it is still true to say that commercial contracting is in most areas far less closely regulated by statute than are contracts, and the terms of contracts, by and on which the employment relationship is constituted.

(b) The law is expected to have a share in the regulation of normal behaviour in relations between employers and employed. Examples abound. Think of safety and health, of hours of work, of minimum wages and guarantees against loss through abnormal events, of periods of notice and redundancy payments and remedies for unfair dismissal, and an untold number of other things. But statutes are not the primary factor in filling the blank of the empty "contract of employment." The primary factor is of course the collective agreement. Its pivotal formative influence on the mutual obligations of employers and workers has also greatly reduced the influence of the courts. More than once matters orignally left to case law were subsequently regulated by collective bargaining—more clearly and probably more effectively. Take for example the problem whether the employer must pay the worker if he cannot do the work owing to causes for which neither he nor the employer is responsible, an enormously important matter in practice—weather, power cuts, a transport strike, stoppage in the supply of raw materials, tools, or accessories. There is, *e.g.* in

Germany, on this matter a very large body of intricate case law,[12] here there are hardly any cases at all,[13] and this is not due to the amounts involved being small, they are not, and—quite apart from legal aid—this is just the sort of issue a union might have taken up through a test case. Hardly any cases, and a statute which covers no more than a fraction of the problem.[14] Why? Is not the, or at least a, reason that, since and partly as a result of the Second World War[15] this Gordian knot—it may involve the "partial performance of an entire contract"[16]—has been cut by the "guaranteed week"[17] provisions of numerous collective agreements?

This is also true, but not nearly to the same extent, of the questions whether the worker can claim his pay when he is sick and, if yes, whether the employer can deduct the sickness benefit

---

[12] For a first introduction into the complexities of the German case law, see Hueck-Nipperdey, *Grundriss des Arbeitsrechts.* (4th ed., 1968) pp. 76 *et seq.* For a very good analysis of the situation in the orignal six EEC countries, Yamaguchi, *La Théorie de la Suspension du Contrat de Travail* (Paris, 1963), *passim.* See also Camerlynck, "Rapport de Synthèse," para. 118 in C.E.C.A., *Le Contrat de Travail dans le Droit des Pays Membres de la C.E.C.A.* (Luxembourg 1965), pp. 98 *et seq.*

[13] See Hepple and O'Higgins, *loc. cit.,* para 359. The only relevant cases appear to be *Browning* v. *Crumlin,* above, n. 6, and *Minnevitch* v. *Café de Paris* [1936] 1 All E.R. 884. How many unreported county court cases there are is anybody's guess. Some mention of the issue is to be found in *Dakri (A.) & Co. Ltd.* v. *Tiffen* [1981] I.C.R. 256 at p. 260.

[14] Employment Protection (Consolidation) Act 1978, ss. 12–18.

[15] The guaranteed week provisions in collective agreements as well as in statutory minimum wage orders (in which they were made possible by the Wages Councils Act 1945) had their origin in the Essential Work Orders; the worker was unable to quit and had to be guaranteed a minimum income at the work place to which he was tied, despite interruptions of work by air raids and other events.

[16] See Glanville Williams, "Partial Performance of an Entire Contract" (1941) 57 L.Q.R 373 at p. 490.

[17] Example of a "Guaranteed Week" Agreement: "All hourly rated manual workers who have been continuously employed by a federated firm for not less than four weeks shall be guaranteed employment for four days in each normal week. In the event of work not being available for the whole or part of the four days, employees covered by the guarantee will be assured earnings equivalent to their consolidated time rate of 34 hours." (This is subect to elaborate conditions.) (Agreement between the Engineering Employers' Federation and the Confederation of Shipbuilding and Engineering Unions of February 15, 1957, *Handbook of National Agreements* (1964 ed)., p. 65.) Agreements such as this, by being in corporated in the contracts of employment, continue to operate alongside the statutory provisions on "guarantee payments" (Employment Protection (Consolidation) Act 1978, ss 12 *et seq.,* esp. s. 16). The vitality of collective bargaining on this matter is demonstrated by the number of exemption orders made under s. 18 of the Act. See Davies and Freedland, *Labour Law: Text and Materials* (1979), pp 203–208.

the worker gets under the Social Security Act.[18] There is a considerable body of case law here, but it is ambiguous.[19] In some foreign countries this has been settled by statue,[20] not in this country. There is however a growing practice of handling this matter through sick pay schemes (which, however, are not necessarily jointly agreed) and a Committee[21] appointed by the National Joint Advisory Council of the (then) Ministry of Labour report in 1964 that 57 per cent. of all employees were covered by a scheme, largely but by no means exclusively for non-manual workers. Such schemes are organised either by individual firms or on an industry-wide basis and the Committee found that "schemes negotiated at industry level appear to be spreading."[22] Recently statute has intervened in this area, not, however, with the primary intention of settling the question of the employee's entitlement to sick pay from his employer (though it may have the effect in practice of persuading employers and trade unions to devote greater attention to that issue), but in order to relieve the social security system of an administrative burden. During the first eight weeks of sickness in any year most employees no longer have an entitlement to sickness benefit from the social security system. Instead, they have an entitlement to sick pay from the employer of very approximately the same amount, and the employer recoups the amount paid by him in discharge of his statutory obligation from the social security system.[23]

Or, to take still another example, the exceedingly thorny question of what a piece rate worker can claim if the employer does not give him any work. The Court of Appeal dealt with this as far back as 1906.[24] and made a "Praetorian" ruling on the basis of a calculation of average earnings over a previous period. This however seems to have been completely superseded by the now almost universal practice of providing a minimum ("fall back") guarantee for piece rate workers, on the basis of the corresponding

---

[18] Social Security Act 1975, ss. 14 *et seq*.

[19] See the cases in n.4, above and Freedland, *loc. cit.*, pp. 108.

[20] See the publication of the European Coal and Steel Community, mentioned in n. 12, above. Such legislation exists, *e.g.* in Belgium, Italy, the Netherlands and Western Germany.

[21] Ministry of Labour, *Sick Pay Schemes,* Report of a Committee of the N.J.A.C. on Occupational Sick Pay Schemes, 1964.

[22] Para. 133, "Most of the workers without any cover are manual employees in private industry."

[23] See Income During Initial Sickness: A New Strategy (Cmnd. 7864, 1980), noted in (1980) 9 I.L.J. 193, which led eventually to the Social Security and Housing Benefit Act 1982. See Richard Lewis, (1982) 11 I.L.J. 245.

[24] *Devonald* v. *Rosser and Sons* [1906] 2 K.B. 728.

time rates, often with an added percentage(*e.g.* "time and a quarter"). In 1906 the Court of Appeal raised with its ruling at least as many unsolved problems of calculation as it settled, but the courts do not seem to have been troubled with their solution. The reason is plain. The great success of collective bargaining had reduced the need for the intervention of the courts.

This may partly explain the surprising fact that, until very recently, this has been one of the few European countries without a system of inexpensive, easily accessible, labour tribunals for the handling of individual disputes. This is now in the course of being changed. Industrial tribunals,[25] consisting of a lawyer chairman, an employer and an employee, exercise exclusive jurisdiction in matters arising between employer and employee under recent statutes.[26] It may—one hopes soon—extend to all disputes arising from contracts of employment, except those on damages for personal injuries, and this jurisdiction will be concurrent with that of the ordinary courts.[27] At the same time it is worth sounding a note of warning. The entrustment of a wide range of issues arising out of the employment relationship to industrial tribunals and to the courts on appeal from them does inevitably tend to judicialise the employment relationship, however informally and empirically those tribunals conduct their business. Even the most enlightened of lawyers may at times overlook the social costs of too broad an extension of their sphere of operation.[27a]

(*c*) Lastly, as we have seen, rules governing labour relations are an attempt to mitigate the disequilibrium inherent in the employ-

---

[25] Created originally under the Industrial Training Act 1964. The best survey of the situation on the Continent is Aaron (ed.), *Labor Courts and Grievance Settlement in Western Europe* (Univ. of Calif. Press, 1971); and esp. for France also: McPherson and Meyers, *The French Labor Courts: Judgment by Peers* (Univ. of Illinois, 1966)—a model of procedural fact investigation—and B.W. Napier, "The French Labour Courts—An Institution in Transition" (1979) 42 M.L.R. 270. For Britain see Wedderburn and Davies, *Employment Grievances and Disputes Procedures in Britian* (Univ. of California Press, 1969). This should be read with Chap. X of the Donovan Report.

[26] See Davies and Freedland, *op. cit.* Chap. 10.

[27] Under the Employment Protection (Consolidation) Act 1978, s. 131, this may be done by delegated legislation. The Employment Appeal Tribunal has appellate jurisdiction in all cases decided by the Tribunals, but usually only on points of law. A further appeal lies—with leave—to the Court of Appeal or the Court of Session.

[27a] The theme which is hinted at here was extensively developed by Hugh Collins in a most significant two-part article about the unfair dismissal legislation ("Capitalist Discipline and Corporatist Law" (1982) 11 I.L.J. 78, 170) in which he characterises that legislation as essentially corporatist in its ambition to judicialise the termination of the employment relationship.

ment relation. The common law, however, ignores any disequilibrium of power which results from normal social relations, as distinct from abnormal personal conditions (infancy, mental disorder). It ignores the realities of social constraint and of economic power: it did so even at a time when the employer was and the worker was not in a position to invoke the aid of the criminal law, to say nothing of the threat of the workhouse; the worker's obligation to obey the lawful commands given by management and the employer's obligation to remunerate the worker are contractual obligations freely incurred among equals. *Pacta sunt servanda.* Contractual promises, however informal, must be kept. This can be mitigated by statute, and this of course has happened frequently and still continues to happen: it is the essence of the legislation on maximum hours and on minimum wages, on the restriction of juvenile employment and on many other things. Contractual promises can however also be declared void by the courts without the support of a statute. This happens when a court holds that a contractual promise is against "public policy" such as a contract to bribe an official or to trade with the enemy, or, in a different sphere, not to get married. In the light of the history of labour relations one might have thought that the courts would have had many opportunities of declaring as being against public policy contracts of employment of an extortionate character, "sweating contracts" such as led to the passing of the Trade Boards Act of 1909. No case is known in which a court invalidated a contract of employment by reason of gross exploitation, but neither is a case in which a court was given an opportunity of doing so. Exploited workers are not plaintiffs in courts of law—until the days of legal aid they had no access to the courts—nor are they defendants—they are not worth powder and shot. The remedies through which their obligations were enforced were not those of the law of contract; if it was done through law at all it was, until well into the second half of the nineteenth century, done through the poor law or the criminal law.

There is, as far as one can see, only one aspect of the employment relationship which did induce the courts to lift the veil of equality and to allow the fact of subordination to impinge upon the validity of contractual promises. The courts have declared to be illegal and void promises given by employees not to compete with the employer or to restrict their competition, in so far as such promises related to the period after the termination of their employment. They thus protected against 'restraint of trade' the supply in the labour market, except in so far as the employer, by imposing the promise, was protecting his own trade or technical secrets. Here of course the critical situation arises after the employment relation has come to an end, and the employee can afford to rely on the invalidity of his undertaking. Moreover, whilst unquestionably protecting the employee, the courts here also protected the consumer, and possibly the employer's competitors. The House of Lords formulated the relevant principles mainly in three leading decisions between 1894 and 1916[28] but they have been frequently applied since then. The important point is that these principles differ quite radically from those applied in other "restraint of trade" situations, *e.g.* where a man sells his business and promises the purchaser not to compete with him in a certain area. Here the courts will uphold promises which they would have struck down if given by an employee to his employer (with reference to the time after the end of the relationship). One reason is that the public has a greater interest in preventing employees from depriving themselves of their freedom to compete than in preventing (presumably elderly) vendors of businesses from doing so. Another reason however is that vendor and purchaser are, but employer and employee are not, " at arm's length."[29] "There is obviously more freedom of contract between buyer and seller than between master and servant or between an employer and a person seeking employment."[30]

This does show that the courts can pay attention to the reality of subordination which lurks behing the facade of contractual equality, but they do not normally do so, and this is another reason why the vast bulk of labour regulation had to be provided by legislation and by collective agreements. Moreover, even if the courts had been willing to pierce the veil of equality it would have made little difference in that large majority of cases in which the fact of subordination itself would have prevented the employee from relying on the law. We repeat that the main characteristic of the "restraint of trade" situation is the comparative freedom which the (former) employee has to invoke the law: where the former employer enjoys something like a monopoly in the relevant market, even this may be problematic.

These remarks about the role played by the courts refer to the individual relation between employers and employees. The far

---

[28] *Nordenfeldt* v. *Maxim Nordenfeldt Co. Ltd.* [1894] A.C. 535; *Mason* v. *Provident Clothing Co.* [1913] A.C. 724; *Morris* v. *Saxelby* [1916] 1 A.C. 688.

[29] *Fitch* v. *Dewes* [1920] 2 Ch. 159 (C.A.) at p. 188 (Younger L.J.)

[30] *Per* Lord Macnaghten in the *Nordenfeldt case, supra*, at p. 566. It is interesting to contrast the approach of the modern Court of Appeal where the employee is in a strong bargaining position: *Littlewoods Organisation* v. *Harris* [1977] 1 W.L.R. 1472.

greater impact which they have had on trade union law and on the law of labour disputes we shall discuss below.[31]

2. REGULATORY LEGISLATION

Statutes such as those on working hours, on safety, on payment of wages in cash without deductions, etc., are early examples of what one can call regulatory legislation. By this we mean legislation directly laying down rules of employment. Such legislation is used quite obviously to restrict the power of managment, and to do so quite irrespective of whether or not and to what extent the workers are organised. Nevertheless, we can see that, especially in this country, the policy of the law has always been not to regulate the employment relation by statute where this could effectively be done through collective bargaining. The result is that, until fairly recently, such regulatory legislation (whether on wages or on hours, or on safety, health and welfare) was deliberately directed towards subjects which do not lend themselves well to collective bargaining (safety at work is an example) or which, owing to weakness of organisation or for other reasons, were not in fact dealt with in collective agreements. Perhaps the growth (both in size and scope) and the general significance of collective bargaining in the country restricted the growth and reduced the significance of such regulatory legislation: a comparison with the development of the law in some foreign countries, *e.g.* in France, suggests that this was the case.

But one should not exaggerate this. Quite clearly we have seen in our days and we continue to see a revival and a very considerable increase of regulatory legislation. This does not refer even in the first place to the expansion of safety, health and welfare legislation into new areas such as agriculture[32] and office work.[33] Nor does it refer to the growth of social security law. What matters far more in the present context is that legislation has been extended so as to cover the loss of wages as a result of interruption of work—or, to be more precise, of certain selected causes of interruption of work, because we still do not have a general

---

[31] See Chaps. 7 and 8.

[32] Agriculture (Safety, Health and Welfare Provisions) Act 1956.

[33] Office, Shop and Railway Premises Act 1963. This statute and the one mentioned in the previous note, belongs, together with the Factories Act 1961, the Mines and Quarries Act 1954, and many others, to those which are being progressively replaced by a system of regulations and approved codes of practice under the Health and Safety at Work, etc., Act 1974, as amended by Employment Protection Act 1975, Sched. 15.

provision embracing all such causes due to neither party's fault. But the law now to some extent seeks to protect employees against loss of wages through market fluctuations, cessation of the supply of raw materials, weather conditions and other abnormal occurrences. It does so by providing for a statutory "guarantee payment,"[34] and this means that regulatory legislation has entered a field hitherto entirely left to collective bargaining. Further: a woman who loses wages by absence from work owing to pregnancy or confinement is in certain limits entitled to maternity pay.[35] Here—at long last—our law has created a right well known in foreign countries, and extended its protective intervention to an area hitherto neglected by collective agreements as well as by the law itself. This development can be well understood if one considers the weakness in the past of trade union organisation and of collective bargaining in industries and trades where female work prevails. This is changing rapidly, and so is the composition of the workforce.[35a] The history of the rights of the working woman is of special interest to anyone who sees the law primarily as the product of changing social conditions

The most noteworthy—and in practice by far the most important—extension of regulatory legislation, however, is concerned with the duties it imposes upon the employer at the moment when the employment is terminated. We have now a system of statutory minimum terms of notice[36] (to be given by both sides, but only on a minor scale by the employee) and of redundancy payments.[37] We have elaborate legislation against unfair dismissal[38] under which an employee may be entitled to be reinstated (*i.e.* have his old contract restored), to be re-engaged under a new contract, or be compensated, and we have the right of a woman after absence owing to pregnancy or confinement to return to her job.[39] Thus

---

[34] Employment Protection (Consolidation) Act 1978, ss. 12 *et. seq.* To a large degree, however, the aim of these provisions seems to have been, not the protection of individual employees, as the re-allocation of the burden of support from the social security stystem to the employer. See Davies and Freedland, *op. cit.,* pp. 289–292 and see also the same process at work in relation to sick pay (above).

[35] Pt. III, as amended by the Employment Act 1980, ss. 11–13.

[35a] The labour force in Great Britain is estimated to have increased by over 2 million between 1961 and 1981 entirely due to the increasing participation of married women: see *Social Trends* (the annual governmental analysis of social statistics) Vol. 13 (1982) at p. 51.

[36] Employment Protection (Consolidation) Act 1978, Pt. IV.

[37] *Ibid.* Pt. VI.

[38] *Ibid.* Pt V as amended by Employment Act 1980, ss. 6–10.

[39] *Ibid.* ss. 45–48, as amended by Employment Act 1980, ss. 11–12.

regulatory legislation has laid some essential foundations for a law of job security, re-inforced by a worker's right to a written statement of the reasons for his dismissal.[40]

Still—and this is a point of importance for the technique of rule making in this country—some of these provisions, especially those on redundancy payments[41] and on unfair dismissals,[42] are destined to yield to any regulation through collective agreement which complies with certain minimum standards and is approved by the Secretary for Employment. Especially the law of unfair dismissals was originally intended to be only subsidiary (a "long stop"), and autonomous regulation was hoped to predominate in practice. This did not happen, but as a pattern of legislation this remains important. Since all these minimum standards are enacted for the benefit of the workers, it is—quite apart from collective agreements—of course always open to an employer to grant more generous rights or benefits.[43]

The most far reaching regulation of employment conditions by law is the compulsory determination of the wages and other conditions of employment themselves. This has been done by what is still generally called "minimum wage legislation" because it originated in the Trade Boards Act of 1909[44] and in the Corn Production Act 1917[45] which applied to wages only. But subsequently it was extended, first to paid holidays, and now, under the Wages Councils Act of 1979 and the Agricultural Wages Acts for England and Wales and for Scotland of 1948 and 1949, as amended

---

[40] *Ibid.* s. 53.

[41] *Ibid.* s. 96.

[42] *Ibid.* ss. 65–66. The same pattern of legislation can be found in Social Security Act 1975, s. 158 and Sched. 19. The method of permitting statutory standards to be contracted out of by collective agreement, but not by individual contract, is well known abroad: see, *e.g.* the German Decree on Working Hours of 1938, s. 7. See also Factories Act 1961, s. 117. The Employment Protection Act 1975 provides a similar possibility in respect of arrangements for consultation and notification in the event of redundancy (s. 107)and the 1978 Act contains such provisions in respect of guarantee payments (s.18). In fact only these last have been extensively used in practice. For discussion as to why this might be, see Davies and Freedland, *op. cit.,* pp. 203–208.

[43] *Ibid.* s. 49(3): A shorter notice is treated as detrimental to the employee even if it is the one he has to give. Rights under the 1978 Act cannot generally be varied by contract of employment either way (s. 140). It must be considered that the employer can claim repayments ("rebates") out of public funds for redundancy and maternity payments.

[44] For its pre-history and history see Bayliss, *British Wages Councils* (1962).

[45] This Act and the Agricultural Wages Act 1940 were the principal stepping stones to the modern system of national wage fixing in agriculture.

in 1975,[46] to all conditions of employment. Here Parliament has created a floor of wages and other conditions for workers who find it difficult to establish and to enforce bilaterally agreed collective levels, either because their organisation is weak or because—as in agriculture—the labour force is scattered in small enterprise units. Such wages and other conditions are only minimal: it is open to the employer to pay higher wages or grant better conditions, and this happens in practice. We shall have to come back to this matter in other contexts.[47]

In the course of the years there have been changes in the nature of the standards created by regulatory labour legislation, and also in the sanctions through which they are enforced.

In the first place there is a general tendency to pass from the "thou shalt not" to the "thou shalt." Legislation, *e.g.* on maximum hours, on the employment of women on certain types of work or at certain times, on the employment of children or young persons, is prohibitive, or, if you like, negative: it is forbidden to employ certain persons for more than a stated number of hours, or on certain processes, or at certain times or places, or at all.[48] Contrast more modern legislation, such as that on minimum wages and conditions, on periods of notice, on guarantee or maternity or redundancy pauments, or on re-instatement after unfair dismissal or of a woman after pregnancy or confinement. All this imposes positive obligations to make certain payments or to re-instate. To some extent regulatory legislation which in bygone days merely restrained the exercise of managerial power, now guides its exercise into channels defined by social or industrial public policy.

Safety legislation has of course always been "positive." It has, since its inception, said, and it contines to say to the employer "thou shalt," for example, ensure that dangerous machinery is securely fenced[49] or that ladders do not slip.[50] But more recently the law has proceeded further. Under the Health and Safety at Work etc. Act of 1974 there is now a general "duty of every employer to ensure, as far as reasonably practicable, the health, safety and welfare of all his employees."[51] Over and above all

---

[46] Employment Protection Act 1975, Scheds. 9, 10.

[47] See esp. Chap. 6.

[48] *e.g.* Factories Act 1961, ss. 69 (as amended by S.I. 1974 No. 1941), 74, 86 *et seq.;* Children and Young Persons Act 1933, s. 18, as amended by the Children Act 1972.

[49] Factories Act 1961, s. 14, as amended by S.I. 1974 No. 1941.

[50] *Ibid.* s. 28(5).

[51] s. 2(1). The extent, in the sense of the rigorousness, of this obligation was considered, and rather restrictively defined, in *West Bromwich Building Society Ltd.* v. *Townsend* [1983] I.C.R. 257.

special standards of safety (some of which are of a highly technical nature) this general statutory duty involves an obligation to take certain kinds of affirmative action, the nature of which is expressly defined. Thus, the employer is by statute responsible for the provision and maintenance not only of reasonably safe plant, *i.e.* material equipment, but also of a reasonably safe system of work,*i.e.* organisation, selection, supervision of his personnel, and, linked with this, there is a duty to inform, to instruct and to train employees so far as this is necessary and reasonably practicable to ensure health and safety at work. At the same time the law spells out the duty of every employee while at work to take reasonable care for the health and safety of himself and others and to co-operate with the employer in the maintenance of the standards he has to observe.

It is here, above all in this particular problem of standards of safety at work, that the courts have paved the way for legislation: the standards now formulated by statute are similar to, though not strictly identical with, those which the courts have for many years read into or out of the employer's "duty of care" implied in the principles of the common law of negligence. In that sense the standards of the common law and those of public policy crystallised in statutes are converging. There is this difference, however, that the sanction attached to the statutory standards is, generally speaking, penal, whilst the courts have developed their own standards mainly in connection with the employer's (*i.e.* in practice generally the insurer's) civil liability to indemnify the employee or his dependants. Safety legislation has never in the past in so many words imposed civil liabilities, but for almost a century the courts have held that a "breach of statutory duty" involves civil liability at common law,[52] and as regards duties imposed by regulations made under the Act of 1974, but not as regards those contained in the Act itself, this is now affirmed by statute.[53] The general obligations imposed by the statute are enforced in the criminal courts, but the civil courts are not prevented from holding, and are likely to hold, that, on established principles, a violation of these obligations gives rise to a civil action, not indeed under the statute, but by virtue of the rules of the judge-made common law.

Obligations imposed by such "protective" legislation—no matter whether it refers to hours of work, to safety, health and

---

[52] The leading case is *Groves* v. *Lord Wimborne* [1898] 2 Q.B. 402 (C.A.).
[53] Health and Safety at Work etc. Act 1974, s. 47.

welfare, or even to certain aspects of wage payments[54]—are generally imposed by the law, not, as you would expect, on the employer as an employer, that is as the party to the contract of employment, but as the occupier of the premises. They are in the social sense managerial obligations, and as we have said, restrictions on the rule- and decision-making powers of management. Management involves the control of material as well as of human resources. The law says that it is as a controller of material and not of human resources that the employer must observe *e.g.* provisions on safety and on hours of work. A sociologist might say that the command power of management is here concealed behind the screen of the power exercised through the occupation of "premises." From the lawyer's point of view what matters are the practical consequences of this approach to managerial obligations. If, for example, a worker is injured in an accident due to his employer's failure to have dangerous machinery properly fenced he (or, if the accident is fatal, his widow or next-of-kin) can claim compensation from the employer. But normally they will not claim for a breach of the contract of employment,[55] but for the breach of a general "statutory" duty imposed by the law upon the "occupier" of the premises for the benefit of all those who have entered them lawfully.[56] In the civil courts protective legislation of this type is enforced through the law of tort and not generally through the law of contract. Whatever the ideological root of these arrangements, in practice they are sensible and beneficial. To rely on such legislation a person injured in an accident does not have to show that there is any contract between him and the occupier at all. Thus, if owing to a breach of statutory duty incumbent on the occupier a man is injured who is or was employed by a contractor doing some building or repair work in, say, a factory, he can recover damages from the factory owner ("occupier") which in practice means from his insurance company.[57] An independent contractor such as a window cleaner can rely on these safety

---

[54] Factories Act 1961, ss. 135, 136, s. 136 is now replaced by s. 9 of the 1974 Act.

[55] Never in a fatal case when the claim is based on the Fatal Accidents Act 1976, and not normally in a non-fatal case although in such a case it is legally possible: *Matthes* v. *Kuwait Bechtel Corporation* [1959] 2 Q.B. 57 (C.A.).

[56] See *e.g. Smith* v. *Cammell Laird* [1940] A.C. 242 (shipyard). Whether in a given case a particular person can recover damages will often depend on the wording of the particular Regulations: see, *e.g. Wingrove* v. *Prestige* [1954] 1 All E.R. 576 (C.A.).

[57] Employers' Liability (Compulsory Insurance) Act 1969.

provisions,[58] and so can, in certain circumstances at least, workers employed by a "labour only" subcontractor[59]—a matter of great and growing importance especially in the building industry.[60] This very characteristic feature of British labour legislation, however, has recently undergone a change which is of more technical than material significance. The Health and Safety at Work etc. Act 1974 imposes obligations on the employer in relation to his employees[61] and also to others who many be affected by the way he conducts his undertaking.[62] It imposes[63] separate obligations on those in control of non-domestic premises towards those who, without being employed by them, use the premises made available to them as a place of work or as a place where they may use plant or substances provided for their use there. These provisions signify a change in, and a rationalisation of, legislative method. They remove what had been an anomaly of legislation peculiar to this country, without sacrificing the practical advantages to which it gave rise.

We find thus that in so far as protective legislation of what we may describe as the "older" type—though the particular statute or regulation in question may be of very recent vintage—has a creative rather than a prohibitive function, it operates through the law of tort. The "thou shalt" is (apart from the criminal law, of course) enforced through delictual, not through contractual, actions. In legislation of more recent origin however a different technique is applied. There the law moulds the contract itself. This is true of minimum wage laws and also, *e.g.* of the Equal Pay Act of 1970[64] and of the minimum notice provisions.[65] The parties to

---

[58] The principle was laid down by the Court of Appeal in *Lavender* v. *Diamints Ltd.* [1949] 1 K.B. 585, and affirmed by the House of Lords in *Wigley* v. *British Vinegars Ltd.* [1964] A.C. 307, where however the action was dismissed on other grounds.

[59] *Donaghey* v. *Boulton & Paul Ltd.* [1968] A.C. 1. Much depends on the facts. See *Mulready* v. *Bell* [1953] 2 Q.B. 117 (C.A.). Some of the reasoning in this case was disapproved of by the House of Lords in the *Donaghey* case. For a constructive approach in the Court of Appeal, see *Ferguson* v. *John Dawson & Partners (Contractors) Ltd.* [1976] 1 W.L.R. 1213.

[60] Report of the Committee of Inquiry under Professor E. H. Phelps Brown into Certain Matters concerning Labour in Building and Civil Engineering, Cmnd. 3714 (1968), esp. Chaps. VI and VII.

[61] s.2

[62] s.3.

[63] s.4.

[64] s.1(1) and (2); see Sched. 1, Pt. II of the Sex Discrimination Act 1975.

[65] Employment Protection (Consolidation) Act 1978, s. 49(3) and (4)

the contract of employent are, by a statutory fiction, deemed to make the contract on the basis of the statutory terms: "the only effect of the statute on that contract is to insert, against, it may be, the overt agreement of the parties, the proper rate of wages,"[66] or, we may add, the proper other conditions. The terms of the statute can be contracted out of only for the benefit of the worker, and if the parties purport to agree on terms less favourable to him or her (a wage lower or a term of notice shorter than the minimum) or on terms less favourable than those applied to a member of the other sex doing the same or equivalent work, they are nevertheless deemed to have contracted for the minimum or for equal treatment, and the worker's claim for the difference is accordingly (by fiction) a contractual claim. The general fiction of a "contractual" intent of the worker to which we have referred earlier is here countered by a special fiction that the content of the statute was contractually intended by the employer, if you like a "contervailing fiction." This is in many countries (and indirectly to some extent, as we shall see, in this country) a way of enforcing the minimum codes of wages and other terms of employment laid down in collective agreements or awards. Here too the obligation to pay no less than a stated minimum takes effect as part of the contract.[67] Thus if the employer has exacted from the worker a promise to work at a wage lower than the collectively agreed or imposed minimum, that promise is displaced by the collective norm, just as in the case of minimum wage legislation it is displaced by the statutory norm. Not all legislation on wages operates through this device of the "contractual sanction." Sometimes, *e.g.* when applying the rules of the Truck Acts which forbid deductions from wages,[68] the courts consider claims for the difference as "statutory" and not as "contractual"—a technical difference which may be very important when it comes to deciding at what time such a claim is barred owing to lapse of time.[69] This is, rather surprisingly, also adopted for the regulation of guarantee payments[70] and other matters.[71] But, generally speaking, one can

---

[66] Lord Wright M.R. in *Gutsell* v. *Reeves* [1936] 1 K.B. 272 at p. 283.
[67] Employment Protection Act 1975, Sched. 11, paras 11, 12 and 16 (now repealed). See below, Chap. 6.
[68] Truck Act 1831, s. 3; Truck Act 18986, ss. 1–3.
[69] *Pratt* v. *Cook, Son & Co. (St. Paul's) Ltd.* [1940] A.C. 437.
[70] 1978 Act, ss. 12 *et seq.*, s. 16.
[71] *e.g.* "protective awards" (1975 Act, ss. 101 *et seq.*). Also maternity pay (1978, s. 37), but this is understandable because here the employer is entitled to a rebate out of a public fund which he cannot claim for money owed under a contract. For the time being this technique has the advantage of clarifying the jurisdiction of the Industrial Tribunals.

say that the idea of moulding the contract through legislation is a technique of growing importance, here and abroad. It shows the awareness of the legislature that the contract of employment is, as we have said, generally no more than a tool of legal thought, and that the substance of the mutual obligations of employer and employee is settled either unilaterally by the employer or bilaterally by collective bargaining or by the law itself.

In its early stages regulatory legislation was mainly concerned with the protection of those sections of the working population which were or were deemed to be in exceptional need of it, and with the conditions under which their work was performed. It dealt with the employment and the working hours of women, children and young persons, with safety at work, and also with the method of wage payments and the calculation of wages; the latter being a protection of employers against a very insidious type of undercutting.

Much of this earlier legislation shows a very interesting feature, characteristic of the way in which law often develops in this country. It frequently originates in statutes applicable to a particular sector of the economy, and in the course of time the principles embodied in such statutes are gradually generalised. This was, for example, the case with legislation on hours of work which at first applied to the textile industry exclusively before it was extended to other industries, until much later it became law for factories in general.[72] Still later similar legislation was passed for the retail trade.[73] All this extended over more than three quarters of a century. A similar development can be observed in the legislation on the method of wage payments, except that here the process begins much earlier and is today not yet concluded. Prohibitions of truck in particular trades go back as far as the late Middle Ages. As the industrial revolution proceeded the number of such statutes increased rapidly in the course of the eighteenth century.[74] Finally this legislation was consolidated in the Truck Act of 1831. That statute was no longer restricted to particular trades or industries, but it defined its personal scope of application through an enumeration of various categories of workers,[75] and it was not until 1887[76] that this clumsy enumeration was replaced by

---

[72] Hutchins and Harrison, *A History of Factory Legislation,* esp. Chaps. VII and VIII.

[73] The legislation consolidated in the Shops Act 1950 goes back to 1912.

[74] See n. 6 in Chap. 1.

[75] s. 19 (repealed in 1887).

[76] Truck Amendment Act 1887, s. 2; the definition of a "workman" in s. 2, now amended by the Statute Law (Repeals) Act 1973, was originally contained in the Employers and Workmen Act 1875 which was repealed by the Act of 1973.

a global reference to "manual workers." The final step of extending this protective legislation to non-manual workers has often been recommended[77] but never been taken.[77a] And lastly, to give a third example of gradual expansion, we can consider the special and important legislation designed to enable piece rate workers to check the correctness of the assessment of their work and thus of the calculation of their wages. The provision for the appointment by the workers of checkweighmen applied at first in the mining industries[78] and was extended to a large number of other branches of the economy by a statute of 1919.[79] The provision making it incumbent on the employer to give to piece rate workers written particulars of the work expected and of the rate of remuneration promised for each unit of work applied at first only to a few sectors of the economy, whilst today the "particulars clause" in the Factories Act[80] is of very wide application, and, like the checkweighing statute of 1919, capable of being extended to further industries by delegated legislation.

One would be tempted to call this a "trial and error" method of legislation, if one was satisfied that there had been a deliberate policy behind this progress from the particular to the general. But there is, as far as is known, no evidence that there was more in it than the hazard of pressures and counterpressures. A different picture is presented by that second "layer" of labour legislation which had its starting point in the first Trade Boards Act of 1909. This is the point at which the law begins to take an interest in the quantum, the rates of wages, as distinct from the method of payment (though through the prohibition of deductions the Truck Acts, as interpreted since a fundamental decision of the House of Lords of 1906,[81] had had an indirect effect on the size of the wage packet). Ever since its inception in the Act of 1909 British minimum wage law (as distinct, *e.g.* from French[82] and American

---

[77] Home Office Committee on the Truck Acts 1908; Karmel Report, para. 47.

[77a] A consultative document issued by the Department of Employment in March 1983 recommends that protection against deduction from wages should be extended to all employees but only as part of a process which would involve repeal of the Truck Acts and thus a reduction in the degree of protection afforded to employees with regard to deductions from wages.

[78] Coal Mines Regulation Act 1887, ss. 13 and 14.

[79] Checkweighing in Various Industries Act 1919.

[80] Factories Act 1961, s. 135, as amended by S.I. 1975 No. 1012, and s. 135A; see Hutchins and Harrison, *loc. cit.* p. 220. This was first introduced in the long-since repealed Factories and Workshops Act 1891, s. 24.

[81] *Williams* v. *North's Navigation Collieries* [1906] A.C. 136.

[82] On the *Salaire minimum interprofessionnel de croissance (Code du Travail* 1974 Art. L 141–1 *et seq.*, see Camerlynck et Lyon–Caen, *Droit du Travail* (10th ed., 1980), paras. 288 *et seq.* pp. 366 *et seq.*

legislation)[83] has had the characteristic of being selective. Minimum remuneration is not fixed for the whole of the economy, but for carefully chosen categories of workers. It is one of the examples of the ad hoc nature of so much of British labour legislation. Minimum remuneration is fixed only for workers in need of a statutory "floor" of wages and this was subsequently extended, first to holidays and holiday remuneration[84] and then to all other terms and conditions of employment.[85] Criteria for selecting these workers have changed as one minimum wage statute followed another, and this has enabled this legislation to be adjusted to changing social conditions. The Trade Boards Act of 1909 was passed against tremendous opposition: it was considered as a revolutionary step, an interference by the legislature with the sacred law of demand and supply. Hence Parliament proceeded cautiously: the minimum wage principle at first applied only to four selected industries in which "sweating" was notorious, but the Act envisaged the extension of its scope through delegated legislation.[86] But the conditions under which this was permitted were so restrictive and the procedures which had to be observed were so complex that very little use could be made of these provisions.[87] The second Trade Boards Act passed in 1918 as a result of one of the recommendations of the Whitley Committee set up in 1916 to consider post-war social policy,[88] and subsequently the Wages Councils Acts of 1945[89] and 1959[90] very much enlarged the power to extend the scope of this legislation. This was a conscious policy of experiment and gradual expansion. But even under the present Act of 1979[91] a most elaborate procedure, now centring on an investigation by the Advisory, Conciliation and Arbitration Service,[92] must be observed before the Secretary of

---

[83] Fair Labour Standards Act 1938 (as amended) s. 6, which covers every employee engaged in or producing goods for interstate or foreign commerce, but not (s. 3(*e*)) agriculture, *i.e.* the one industry designated in this country by statute as being in need of minimum wage determination.

[84] Wages Councils Act 1956

[85] Wages Councils Act 1959, s. 11.

[86] The "Provisional Orders" procedure.

[87] See Bayliss, *loc. cit.,* pp. 11–12.

[88] Second Report of the Committee on Relations between Employers and Employed, Cd. 9002 (1918).

[89] Especially by enabling the Secretary of State to create minimum wage machinery in view of an anticipation that adequate bargaining machinery will cease to exist in future.

[90] ss. 1 and 2.

[91] s.3

[92] For the Advisory, Conciliation and Arbitration Service, see below, Chap. 5.

State for Employment can set up a wages council for a new category of workers, and interested persons have the right to be heard at various stages of the proceedings, not to mention the role played by both Houses of Parliament[93] in checking the exercise of the power of the executive to organise the fixing of minimum remuneration for a branch of the economy. However, a very considerable use has been made of this procedure since the Second World War. In the post-war period minimum wage legislation (that is the Wages Councils Act and the two Agricultural Wages Acts) covered nearly four million workers, between one-fifth and one-sixth of the labour force, practically the whole of the retail trade, much of the catering industry, and of course agriculture, apart from many others.[94] To a large extent minimum wage law has become a measure to protect white collar workers.[94a] We shall say more about this below.

We can today speak about a third layer of protective legislation. This consists of the various statutes consolidated in 1978,[95] intended to guarantee to the worker an enlarged measure of security against abrupt or unfair dismissal, and payments on redundancy. These statutes, to which we have already referred, show a further stage in the development of the personal scope of such legislation: none is restricted to particular branches of the economy. With certain exceptions they apply to all those employed by private or public employers, no matter whether their work is "manual" or "non-manual."

This point is of importance. Today we consider it as almost a matter of course that protective legislation should cover white collar as well as manual workers. This was not always so. Take the question of hours of work of women and young persons. One can say that the legislation of 1833[96] was the beginning, in any meaningful sense, of the restriction of hours of work for children and young persons in industry, and the same can be said of the

---

[93] Wages Councils Act 1979, s. 29.

[94] Written Evidence of the Ministry of Labour to the Donovan Commission, Fifth Memorandum, para. 6 (p.115); Donovan Report, paras. 226–227.The system reached its peak in 1947 with 69 councils and boards; at the end of 1979, as a result of amalgamation and abolition, the number stood at 36: ACAS, *Industrial Relations Handbook* (1980), p. 33 and see below, Chap. 6.

[94a] A valuable survey of the recent and current operation of the Wages Councils system is to be found in Craig, Rubery, Tarling and Wilkinson, *Labour Market Structure, Industrial Organisation and Low Pay*, (Cambridge, 1982), Chap. 2.

[95] Employment Protection (Consolidation) Act 1978, Pts. IV to VI.

[96] Factory Act 1833. See for an analysis of its historical significance S. E. Finer, *The Life and Times of Sir Edwin Chadwick*, Chap. II.

Factory Act of 1844[97] as regards the employment and working hours of women. The first step to arrive at similar protective regulations for shop assistants was not taken until 1886.[98] The Factories Act of 1961 is a milestone on a road which the law began to travel far more than a century ago but the Shops Act of 1950 has an ancestry which does not go back much further than the First World War. Similarly with health, welfare and safety. For industry we see the beginnings of relevant legislation in the 1860s and 1870s[99] but it is only since 1963 that we have had a code of health, welfare and safety for offices and shops[1] The minimum wage law, as we have pointed out, was originally enacted to prevent sweating of manual workers in a number of trades. Today its most important field of application is in the white collar field,[2] especially in the retail trade. All this reflects one of the most significant social developments of our time. With the rapid growth of the distributive sector of the economy and, perhaps even more important, with the even more rapid technical development of industry, a steadily increasing proportion of the working population has become engaged on non-manual work, whether clerical or technical. In 1911, 18.7 per cent. of the employed population were non-manual workers, but in 1971 this figure had risen to 42.7 per cent.[3] In the United States where this process had been more rapid and gone much further, only 34.6 per cent. of the industrial working population were said to be manual workers by the mid-1970s.[4] Until far into the nineteenth century the typical clerical worker did not consider himself as part of the working class, and it is not surprising that, compared with the unions of manual workers, the now quickly growing trade unions of clerical and technical employees were late comers. The expansion of the personal scope of regulatory legislation reflects the growing insight that the relation of subordination between employer and worker is the same whether the worker is employed on the assembly line or in the office. What we have said applies to all non-manual workers

---

[97] See on this and on the older history of factory law in general the useful survey in Mansfield Cooper and Wood, *Outlines of Industrial Law*, 4th ed., Chap. VII, esp. pp. 175 *et seq.*; and 5th ed., pp 220 *et seq.*

[98] For the Shop Hours Regulation Act 1886, see Mansfield Cooper and Wood, *loc. cit.* (6th ed.), p. 321.

[99] Hutchins and Harrison, *loc. cit.,* Chap. 10.

[1] See above, n. 33, p. 37.

[2] See above, n. 94, p. 48.

[3] See Bain and Price (1976) 14 Brit. J. of Ind. Rel. 339 at p. 345.

[4] The relevant statistics published by the Federal Bureau of Labour Statistics are conveniently printed in the "The News," 1976 *World Almanac,* p. 89. This does not include service workers or farm workers.

including foremen and others who exercise supervisory or even managerial functions. We have already referred to the ambivalent situation of these managerial or entrepreneurial employees. This has given rise and still gives rise to serious problems of freedom of organisation, of trade union recognition, and—especially in this country—of inter-union relations. What matters at the moment is the character of regulatory legislation. Here we can see a real change in the scope of the law, an expansion over the last half century or so in a new direction. This extension to white collar workers is a good example of the response of the law to a fundamental social change. It is no more than an absurd atavistic freak that, as we have seen, the main body of our Truck Laws applies to manual workers only. It is a further significant fact that white-collar workers have formed an important, perhaps even a dominant, section of the workers who bring claims to industrial tribunals under the various new statutory employment rights. This applies particularly to the law of unfair dismissal. In this way, the importance of the white collar sector in employment[5] law has tended to be, as it were, geometrically increased in recent years.

Lastly, we can see how the method of enforcing regulatory legislation is changing. Take as an example the employer's duty to inform the worker in writing of the work he is expected to do, of the remuneration to which he is entitled, and of the calculation of the wages he is getting. Under the older legislation, *e.g.* under the particulars clause in the Factories Act[6] to which we have already referred and which applies to piece workers, the only remedy to enforce compliance is a prosecution before the magistrates and fine.[7] And so it was with the employer's duty to give to his employees written particulars of their terms of employment under the original Contracts of Employment Act of 1963.[8] But in 1964[9] things changed with the establishment of the new industrial tribunals.[10] Thus in 1965[11] the clumsy penal sanction of the employer's duty to give particulars under the 1963 Act was

---

[5] It is important to note that the white-collar sector includes most of the retail and distributive workers. That is a sector of the economy in which unionisation is relatively low. This tends to reinforce the link between lack of unionism and recourse to industrial tribunals. Thus it stresses the nature of statutory employment rights as a substitute in practice for collective bargaining rather than as an adjunct to it.

[6] s. 135, see above, n. 80.

[7] *Ibid.* s. 155.

[8] ss. 4, 5.

[9] Industrial Training Act 1964.

[10] Above, n. 25, p. 34.

[11] Redundancy Payments Act 1965, s. 38, introducing a new s. 4A into the 1963 Act, now Employment Protection (Consolidation) Act 1978, s. 11.

replaced by empowering the tribunal, on a reference of a dispute to its jurisdiction, to determine particulars itself and these are then "deemed to have been given by the employer to the employee."[12] Now, in addition to being entitled in advance to be informed in writing about their wages and other terms, employees also have a right to an itemised pay statement, showing the gross amount of the wage or salary, the deductions, and the net amount.[13] Here, too, any dispute can be referred to an industrial tribunal, and as an ultimate sanction, this can order the employer to pay to the employee the amount of any deduction not properly specified.[14] We can expect that these methods of shaping the mutual rights of employers and employees through the direct action of these expert tribunals will increasingly replace the circuitous and ineffective enforcement of social standards through criminal proceedings.

3. THE BORDERLINE BETWEEN LEGISLATION AND COLLECTIVE BARGAINING

The rules of employment are thus, in the main, either an emanation of the managerial power of the employer or they are a complex amalgam of legislation and of collective agreements. The share which these sources of rules have in the whole varies from place to place and, a matter of special importance in this country at present, it also varies from time to time. Its analysis is a fascinating task for legal, economic and social historians and for students of comparative labour relations and labour law. To generalise is always dangerous, but in this matter it is hazardous because the cultural, economic, geographic, historical and political factors which determine the borderline of legislation and collective bargaining are legion and their significance and mutual relation sometimes change very rapidly. Take the problem of job security, and the connected problem of redundancy payments. Britain is the classical country of collective bargaining, and for reasons rooted in the political history and the social structure of the two countries regulatory legislation has played a greater role in France than here. Yet, it is now fair to say that redundancy payments which are based on a statute in this country[15] developed in France largely

---

[12] *Ibid.* s. 11(5) and (6). The exact extent of the powers thus conferred upon tribunals is in some doubt: *Construction Industry Training Board* v. *Leighton* [1978] I.R.L.R. 60, *cf.* WPM *Retail Ltd.* v. *Lang* [1978] I.R.L.R. 243 (E.A.T.), *Mears* v. *Safecar Security Ltd.* [1982] I.C.R. 626 (C.A.).

[13] *Ibid.* ss. 8–10 (generalising and modifying provisions made for a special situation in the Payment of Wages Act 1960).

[14] s. 11(8). The complex details are ommitted here.

[15] Employment Protection (Consolidation) Act 1978, Pt. VI.

through collective bargaining,[16] though eventually they were regulated by statute.[17] Job security on the other hand is dealt with by the most elaborate body of legislation in Germany[18] (which has no scheme of redundancy payments) and is now centrally important as a subject of legislation (far more than of collective bargaining) in this country.[19] In the United States on the other hand job security is more fully developed than anywhere else for that minority of workers who are the beneficiaries of the collective bargaining system.[20] We are not suggesting that this bewildering picture could not be sorted out in terms of cause and effect, but the sorting out would require a thorough-going investigation taking in matters as different as the effect of the federal constitutional system of the United States on the evolution of labour law, the political histories and allegiances of the trade unions in Britian and in France, the structures of the various collective bargaining systems, the political history of the countries concerned in relation to their social and economic histories, and the volume and pace of their industrialisation.

Having said this, we shall now risk the broad generalisation that regulatory legislation is apt to prevail over collective bargaining where and when the political pressure power of the workers exceeds their industrial pressure power and, with great caution, this proposition can be reversed. It is sometimes (but not always) the case that, as the unions get industrially stronger, the significance of collective bargaining grows and that of legislation diminishes whilst, as their political influence increases, so does the volume and significance of regulatory legislation.[20a] Developments

---

[16] See for a detailed discussion of this impressive development Despax, *Conventions Collectives*, para. 153, pp. 246 *et seq.*, in Camerlynck (ed.), *Traité de Droit Du Travail*, Vol. 7. See also Camerlynck et Lyon-Caen, *Droit du Travail, loc. cit.* paras. 183 *et seq.*, pp. 229 *et seq.*

[17] *Code du Travail,* 1974, Art. L 122–9 *et seq.*; Art. R 122–1.

[18] Kündigungsschutzgesetz of August 10, 1951, amended in 1969, and reissued in its amended form on August 25, 1969. The fundamental principles of this statute go back to the law on Works Councils of 1920.

[19] Employment Protection (Consolidation) Act 1978, Pt. V, as amended by Employment Act 1980, ss. 6–10.

[20] The literature is immense. R. W. Fleming, *The Labor Arbitration Process* (Univ. of Illinois Press 1967), is a very good introduction. For a detailed survey of legal problems, Summers and Wellington, *Labor Law*, pp. 666 *et seq.*

[20a] [Kahn-Freund makes a dichotomy between industrial pressure power and political pressure power. May not the 1970s in Britain be seen in retrospect as a period in which the two were partly conflated, so that perhaps for the first time the development of legislation was crucially influenced by what was fairly directly industrial pressure power? When the Labour government was in power, the linking factor was surely the Social Contract.]

in France may be said to illustrate this.[21] In Italy we have seen how growing trade union strength can produce a generalisation of principles hitherto developed by collective bargaining and their transformation into law.[22] Developments in this country since 1963, but especially since 1974, have shown how quickly the scene of rule making can shift, and legislation can come to the forefront. This development illustrates the point that the boundary between legislation and collective bargaining may largely result from the facts of political and economic history. As has been pointed out on previous occasions,[23] one of the cardinal facts of British social and political history is that the industrial revolution preceded the extension of Parliamentary franchise to the working class. Through the early formation of trade unions a collective counter-vailing power of labour developed in many industries long before the unions had achieved that political pressure power which results from the voting strength of their members. It is impossible to prove the point, but it is more than tempting to think that here we have a clue to the difference between the British trade unions and their opposite numbers on the Continent of Europe as regards attitudes towards regulatory legislation.[24] The unions in this country were traditionally disinclined to put their trust in legislation to be applied by courts of law. It appears that a pattern of thought and of action had developed during the formative periods of the British trade union movement, and this was totally different from the attitude of the unions in countries in which the unions themselves were to some extent the creatures of political parties. In our own time a far-reaching transformation of attitudes was, it seems, engendered by the growing political influence of the unions. We are not for a moment suggesting that the whole complex problem can be solved with this glib formula. No doubt things such as the political split in the unions of some Continental

---

[21] See Despax, *loc. cit.* (n. 16, p. 52), Introduction.

[22] Italian law No. 604 of July 15, 1966; *Lex,* July–December 1966, p.1335; this transformed and generalised the content of collective agreements, previously concluded between the top organisations. *"Norme sui licenziamenti individuali"*—a statute on job security. In Sweden the provisions of the Employment Protection Act 1974, on dismissals and lay-offs have taken the place of those of the Basic Agreement of 1938. See F. Schmidt, *Law and Industrial Relations in Sweden* (1977), p.27.

[23] O. Kahn-Freund, *Labour Law: Old Traditions and New Developments* (Toronto, 1968).

[24] See the illuminating article by Allan Flanders (published posthumously), "The Tradition of Voluntarism" (1974) 12 Brit J. of Ind. Rel., 352. See also Wedderburn of Charlton, "Industrial Relations and the Courts" (1980) 9 I.L.J. 65, esp. pp. 83–86.

countries (France, Italy, Belgium, in a different way the Netherlands[25]) play their role, and so does—we have already hinted at this—the fact that in federal countries (the United States is the principal but not the only example) the unions may operate over the whole territory, but regulatory legislation is largely outside the federal power. The re-interpretation by the Supreme Court of the Interstate Commerce Clause of the Federal Constitution in and since 1936[26] has been a most powerful factor promoting the growth of regulatory legislation in the United States.

Regulatory legislation—we have already indicated this—played in the past a much greater role in the great countries of Continental Western Europe than here, and France is perhaps the best example to illustrate the contrast.[27] Take the problem of working hours. With the exception of some industries confronting peculiar problems (of which the coal mining industry is the most important[28]) the working hours of adult men have never been regulated in this country by statute. They are of course regulated by collective agreements. One cannot think of any other major country not to have passed legislation in this matter. In France not only working hours but even rates of overtime pay are laid down in statutes.[29] So are holidays with pay,[30] which, as a general principle, have always been left to collective bargaining here.[31] An elaborate body of complex legislation exists in France by which a national minimum wage is established which varies with the cost of living.[32] All these matters continue to be dealt with by law in this country only in relation to workers who are rightly or perhpas sometimes wrongly assumed not to have the collective power to achieve these things through union action. We are of course referring to those within the range of the minimum wage laws we

---

[25] For a brief survey, see O. Kahn-Freund "Labour Law and Social Security" in Stein and Nicolson (ed.), *American Enterprise in the Common Market. A Legal Profile* (Ann Arbor, 1960), Vol. I, Chap. VI, at pp. 381 *et seq.*

[26] *N.L.R.B.* v. *Jones & Laughlin Steel Corpn.,* 301 U.S. 1 (1937).

[27] But collective bargaining today plays a much more important, and complex, role in the development of general norms in France than previously: Despax, *op. cit. Mise à Jour 1974*, pp. 1–11.

[28] Coal Mines Regulation Act 1908 (as amended).

[29] *Code du Travail*, 1974, Art. L 212–1 *et seq.*; Camerlynck et Lyon-Caen, *loc. cit.* paras. 233 *et seq., * pp. 302 *et seq.*

[30] *Code du Travail*, 1974, Art. L 223–1 *et seq.*; Camerlynck et Lyon-Caen, *loc. cit.* paras. 248 *et seq., * pp. 321 *et seq.*

[31] The Holidays with Pay Act 1938 in no way detracts from the validity of this statement.

[32] *Code du Travail*, 1974, Art. L 141–1 *et seq.*

have mentioned, which cover, as we have said, between 16 and 20 per cent. of the total labour force.[33]

This disparity of the ranges of legislation and of collective bargaining has repercussions at the international level. The first Convention ever to have been passed by the International Labour Organisation was the celebrated Washington Convention of 1919 which sought to give effect to the principle of the 48-hour-week.[34] Most of the major industrial countries have ratified this Convention. The United Kingdom never did. The reason no doubt was that, to implement its obligations in the event of a ratification of the Washington Convention, the Government of the United Kingdom would have had to ask Parliament to legislate on a matter which is traditionally left to collective bargaining in this country. This was in 1919, but since then the extent to which a State member of the ILO can live up to its international obligations under a ratified Convention otherwise than by legislation and especially through a collective bargaining practice has become a matter of much discussion.[35] The International Labour Office has taken the view that on principle it is for each member to determine the measures to be taken to make the norms of a Convention effective in its territory,[36] but its late Director-General regarded it as "undesirable" to erect into "an axiom of policy" the principle that Conventions can be implemented otherwise than by legislation.[37] What matters in our context is that, against this background, an increasing number of Conventions provide in a variety of ways for the supplementing of legislation by collective agreements, and even specify "that there is no obligation to legislate where satisfactory compliance is secured by collective agreements."[38] A similar provision applicable to some of its provisions can be found in the European Social Charter.[39] We have mentioned all this to show how the co-existence of these alternative sources of standards has had its influence on international law making.

---

[33] See above, n. 94, p. 48.

[34] Convention No.1 Limiting the Hours of Work in Industrial Undertakings to Eight in The Day and Forty-eight in the Week, in force since June 13, 1931.

[35] Valticos, *Droit International Du Travail* (1970), para. 615, pp. 544 *et seq.* (Camerlynck (ed.) *Traité de Droit du Travail*), Vol. 8; Jenks, *The Application of International Labour Conventions by means of Collective Agreements* (Festgabe für A. N. Makarov, 1958), pp. 197 *et seq.*; Preface to *International Labour Code* (I.L.O. 1952). Vol. I, pp. LXXVI *et seq.*

[36] *See International Labour Code* Vol. I, p. 277, n. 464, and p. 863, n. 352.

[37] Jenks, *loc. cit.* p. 199.

[38] *Ibid.* p. 202.

[39] Art. 33.

Conversely, however, international standards have powerfully contributed to the growth of regulatory legislation in this country. A considerable body of labour legislation resulted from the ratification by the United Kindom of ILO Conventions,[40] or from the acceptance of ILO Recommendations.[41] Moreover, the fact that certain aspects of regulation were more highly developed among other members of the European Economic Community stimulated legislation here: an example is the protection of pregnant women against dismissal,[42] the right to maternity pay,[43] and a woman's right to return to her job after absence due to pregnancy or confinement.[44] Another example is the power of an industrial tribunal to order the reinstatement or re-engagement of a worker who has been unfairly dismissed.[45] A Directive of the Council of EEC[46] is the basis of the provisions which make it incumbent on an employer to consult a recognised union before dismissing an employee by reason of redundancy and to notify the Deparment of Employment at stated intervals before reducing its workforce on that ground,[47] while another Directive[48] has been implemented by statutory regulations[49] giving workers some protection (however incomplete) of their interests in the event of a transfer of the ownership of the undertaking in which they are employed. It is a third Directive[50] which has by its interpretative effect upon Article 119 of the Treaty of Rome placed the United

---

[40] *e.g.* Employment of Women, Young Persons and Children Act 1920; Hours of Employment (Conventions) Act 1936; Merchant Shipping (International Labour Conventions) Act 1925, See Johnston. "The Influence of International Labour Standards on Legislation and Practice in the United Kingdom" (1968) 79 Int. Lab. Rev. 465 *et seq.*

[41] Thus, the Termination of Employment Recommendation, 1963 (Recommendation No. 119) has had a considerable influence on legislation on unfair dismissal. See generally- *The Impact of International Labour Conventions and Recommendations* (I.L.O., 1976), with further references. In 1982 Recommendation No. 119 was replaced by a new Convention and a new Recommendation, which the U.K. Government has yet to decide whether it will ratify. See Napier, (1983) 12 I.L.J. 17.

[42] Employment Protection (Consolidation) Act 1978, s. 60.

[43] *Ibid. ss* 33–44, as amended by Employment Act 1980, s. 11.

[44] *Ibid.* ss. 33, 45–48, as amended by Employment Act 1980, ss. 11–12.

[45] *Ibid.* ss. 69 *et seq.*

[46] No. 75/129. See Freedland. (1976) 5 I.L.J. 24 *et seq.*

[47] Employment Protection Act 1975, ss. 99–107. See below, Chap. 4.

[48] No. 77/187.

[49] The Transfer of Undertakings (Protection of Employment) Regulations 1981 (S.I. 1981 No. 1794); see Davies and Freedland, *Transfer of Employment*, (1982).

[50] No. 75/117.

Kingdom under an obligation to expand the scope of the equal pay legislation to give fuller effect to the principle of equal pay for work of equal value.[51] The influence on the Equal Pay Act 1970 of the relevant ILO Convention of 1951[52] and the European Social Charter[53] are obvious, whilst the Sex Discrimination Act 1975 owes far more to American than to international or European models. In sum: if in the past reluctance to legislate has been an obstacle to the acceptance of international standards, we have seen more recently how international and foreign standards have in their turn helped to promote a more positive attitude to regulatory labour legislation in this country.[54]

These international influences are among the many and variegated factors which, as we have said, affect the policies determining how regulation is distributed between legislation and collective agreements. This is the historical way of looking at the problem. One can also look at it pragmatically, that is one can ask what can be achieved by either method. If one does, one is struck by the not unusual dilemma of quantity versus quality. The coverage of a statute is all embracing, but very frequently the effect of collective agreements is limited to workers in the better organised industries. In this country some 60 or 65 per cent. of all those in employment are directly or indirectly covered by collective agreements,[55] but this is an exceptionally large percentage; even in the United States the corresponding figure is between 30 and 35 per cent.[56] On the other hand that which can be achieved for the workers through legislation is very frequently far below that which they can get through collective bargaining. The contrast becomes evident if one compares the statutory minimum wages

---

[51] An obligation asserted by the European Court of Justice in Case 61/81 *EEC Commission* v. *U.K.* [1982] I.C.R. 578.

[52] Convention concerning Equal Remuneration for Men and Women for Work of Equal Value (No. 100) of 1951, in force since May 1953. The United Kingdom has now ratified the Convention.

[53] Art. 4(3) which the United Kingdom has not ratified.

[54] Indeed, in some cases, as with the minimum wage legislation, it seems likely that ratification by the U.K. of the relevant international agreement, in the case of Wages Councils ILO Convention No. 26 of 1928, is what temporarily protects the domestic legislation from repeal or drastic reform.

[55] See Donovan Report, para.38

[56] This estimate is based on figures in the *Directory of National and International Unions in the U.S. 1973*, pp. 87–88, published by the U.S. Department of Labour. The collective agreement coverage in 1972 was about 26 million, out of an estimated employed labour force of about 82 million. We owe these figures to the helpfulness of Prof. Clyde W. Summers of the University of Pennsylvania Law School.

laid down in this country under the Wages Councils Act, or (in a very different way) in the United States in the Fair Labor Standards Act, with what workers in this country or in America get under collective agreements. Legislation can rarely do more than establish a "floor." It is however a floor on which all can stand, all those who work and whose political vote may influence legislation even if they are too poorly organised to lift themselves to a higher level. It is —and this is for example now becoming a decisive matter in France[57]—above all a groundfloor for an edifice of collective bargaining. Legislation and collective bargaining are not necessarily alternative, indeed they may frequently be supplementary sources of regulation. It may however also happen—and the Donovan Commission thought that this was sometimes the case with minimum wage legislation[58]—that the existence of statutory regulation, far from promoting collective bargaining, actually proves to be a hindrance to its development or progress. It was on this ground that the Employment Protection Act[59] changed the law so as to facilitate the transformation of statutory into voluntary regulation: a wages council can now be converted into a statutory joint industrial council consisting only of representatives of the two sides without independent members, a transition from the creation of statutory standards to collective bargaining.

Legislation is generally more rigid than collective bargaining, and obviously much less responsive to economic change. Collective agreements are concluded for a year, sometimes for two or three, sometimes (and in this country normally) without a time limit. If management has, at times of prosperity and a high level of demand, consented to high standards of labour conditions, it may find itself unable to maintain them (especially in labour intensive industries) when demand slackens and prices fall. In this situation the flexibility of collective bargaining allows an adjustment of the agreed standards to changed conditions, whilst it may (if only for lack of Parliamentary time) be out of the question to amend a statute. This cuts both ways, because organised labour can afford at times of recession to make temporary concessions in collective bargaining, being conscious of the fact that, when the demand for labour increases, it will be able to press for a return to the high standard. And, of course, the fact that the collectively agreed

---

[57] See above, n. 21, p. 53.
[58] Report, paras. 260 *et seq.*
[59] ss. 90–94, and Sched. 8. See now Wages Councils Act 1979, Pt. II. These powers have not yet in fact been utilised.

standards are more flexible makes it easier for the unions to obtain improvements in this form than through legislation. The rigidity of the legislative process may perhaps be one of the reasons why everywhere the legislative standards are comparatively low. One may also be tempted to think that, from this point of view, the British system of fixing minimum wages and other conditions through tripartite wages councils and Agricultural Wages Boards for separate categories of workers is superior to the system of a national minimum wage adopted in the United States where a new statute is needed in each case to adjust the standard to changed conditions. It is probably superior even to the French system under which the national minimum wage varies automatically (in a most complicated way) with the cost of living.

The rigidity of legislation compared with the flexibility of collective bargaining has given rise to an international problem the traces of which are still visible in the Treaty of Rome. The borderline between the two types of regulation is, for purely historical and political reasons, drawn differently in economically comparable countries. In a competitive market this gives an advantage to countries in which the range of collective bargaining is wide and the range of legislation narrow, or, in the language of the Treaty of Rome,[60] it may "distort" competition. This was the difficulty facing the French Government at the time when the EEC was in the course of being established. France insisted on a special Protocol[61] attached to the Treaty of Rome (and forming an integral part of it)[62] the purpose of which was, during a transitional period, to protect the French economy against the disadvantages it was thought it might suffer in the common market as a result of the rigidity of its legislation on overtime and overtime rates, compared, *e.g.* with the flexibility of the collectively agreed standards in force in the German Federal Republic. For the same reason it was in the French interest that by the Treaty itself, member States undertook to "endeavour to maintain the existing equivalence of paid holiday schemes."[63] Whether problems of this nature will play a role in the enlarged Community may depend on the market situation during the next few years: such problems are of course much more important in a buyer's than in a seller's market.[64]

---

[60] Art. 3(*f*).
[61] Protocol concerning certain Provisions affecting France, Pt. II.
[62] Art. 239
[63] Art. 120.
[64] Today the reverse problem of legislation "distorting competition" by subsidising employment is perhaps more common. See Freedland (1980) 9 I.L.J. 254 for a discussion of EEC influence on the form of U.K. employment support schemes.

Up to now we have spoken about regulatory labour legislation,
about the law as an instrument for creating standards to be
observed by employers and workers individually and for creating
individual rights and obligations. This, however, is not, on the
whole, the type of legislation which in this country is likely to give
rise to big political controversies. These controversies turn around
the use of state power, but not—generally—its use for the direct
intervention between individual workers and employers, *e.g.* for
the purpose of restraining the managerial power as against the
individual worker or the range of the individual's subjection to
managerial power. Political battles are however—and have been
for a long time—fought about the power relation between
management and labour as collective forces, the use of the law for
the purpose of strengthening or of curbing the power of
managment against the unions or of the unions against management. The legislation here envisaged seeks to promote collective
bargaining, to ensure the observance of collective agreements, to
define and to delineate the freedom of organisation and the
freedom to strike, and the right to promote union interests at the
level of the plant or enterprise, for instance, by means of the
closed shop. It may also deal with the participation of union or
workers' representatives in the making of managerial decisions.
Above all, it seeks to establish certain standards of behaviour
between employers and unions or their representatives (*e.g.* shop
stewards) in their mutual dealings. This was what the Industrial
Relations Act 1971 was about and what the Trade Union and
Labour Relations Acts 1974–76, and, to some extent, the
Employment Protection Act 1975, and the Employment Acts 1980
and 1982 are about. The legislation here involved does not settle
wages, hours or other conditions of employment, but it makes
rules for their settlement, chiefly by the collective parties
themselves, and for the enforcement of the terms they have
settled. It establishes "rules of the game," Queensberry Rules so
to speak. We call such legislation "auxiliary" in contrast to
"regulatory" legislation, though sometimes its effect may be to
restrain rather than to advance collective bargaining.[65]

---

[65] Roy Lewis, "The Historical Development of Labour Law" (1976) 14 Brit. J. of
Ind. Rel. 1, concludes a very able survey of the history of British auxiliary
legislation with the observation (p.15) "that the one indubitably fundamental
and irreversible trend is the ever-increasing extent of the legal regulation of the
British system of industrial relations." This is entirely correct as regards
regulatory legislation, but not as regards auxiliary legislation, and may therefore
be somewhat misleading in the context in which it appears.

Rules for promoting the improvement of labour relations can of course be made by statute, and are constantly made that way. Statutes, however, have to be—or in any event are in this country—expressed in a style which most people cannot understand. They operate or seek to operate with sharply delineated concepts and they are entirely deficient in those subtle shades of expression which to the sensitive and sensible human being convey much more than the inhuman circumlocution of legal definitions. Owing to the style which—for better or for worse—has come to be used in the drafting of statutes and statutory instruments, these documents have a very slender chance of exercising any educative or opinion-forming influence on those whose conduct they seek to regulate. If it is desirable to seek to influence human behaviour through rules, it is better not to apply the traditional methods of legislation. Thus, in order to guide users of the road, to produce, *e.g.* reasonably decent relations between pedestrians and motorists, the law has resorted to the device of the Highway Code[66] which does not give rise to legal rights and duties, but whether or not a road user has complied with it may be evidence for establishing a liability or a defence. Under the Industrial Relations Act 1971,[67] the Secretary of State published a similar Code of Practice for industrial relations which was, under the Act, approved by both Houses of Parliament and has been in operation, except so far as superseded by subsequent more specialised codes, since the end of February 1972. The task of making new Codes of Practice was, by the Employment Protection Act 1975,[68] entrusted to the Advisory, Conciliation and Arbitration Service, about which we shall say more in a subsequent chapter. The Code made under the 1971 Act and continued in force by the 1974 Act deals with the mutual dealings of management and union representatives in their day-to-day practice. It is couched in terms of benevolent advice or admonition as to how to shoulder the responsibilities the two sides of industry have towards one another, and how to translate them into rules of good behaviour of, say, shop stewards, foremen and managers in their mutual dealings. It also advises management on manpower policies, above all it seeks to improve the channels of communication and of consultation, and it has a great deal to say about collective bargaining, about employee representation at the place of work and about grievance disputes. It also dealt with disciplin-

---

[66] Road Traffic Act 1972, s. 37.
[67] ss. 2–4; see S.I. 1972 No. 179.
[68] s. 6.

ary procedures, but the relevant portions of the Code of Practice of 1972 have been replaced by Code of Practice No. 1 of the A.C.A.S., in force as from June 20, 1977 under the title "Disciplinary Practice and Procedure in Employment." A.C.A.S. Code No. 2—in force as from August 22, 1977—is about "Disclosure of Information to Trade Unions for Collective Bargaining Purposes," and replaces the corresponding provisions of the 1972 Code. The A.C.A.S. has also published a third code of Practice, on "Time Off for Trade Unions Duties and Activities."—in force from April 1, 1978. To the subject matter of Code of Practice No. 2 and of Code No. 3 we shall return in later chapters.[69]

The idea of having such codes is essentially sound. Whether the Code made under the 1971 Act has fulfilled its mission in guiding the behaviour of management and union representatives, is a difficult question to answer. This is in a sense a new approach towards creating standards of industrial relations. The first chairman of A.C.A.S. has stated the view that the code on disciplinary procedures "undoubtedly has had a big influence on industrial relations practice," notably by encouraging the introduction of "practices on discipline and dismissals which have helped good industrial relations." On the other hand, he thought that the code on time off had had a lesser effect because circumstances vary so much from firm to firm, and the code on disclosure of information had had an impact on a number of large firms but its impact on smaller firms had been "very limited indeed."[70]

With the passage of the Employment Act 1980, however, the practice of issuing codes of practice achieved a much more controversial status. By that Act,[71] the Secretary of State for Employment had conferred upon him a power parallel to that of A.C.A.S. to issue codes of practice, and he exercised that power in 1980 to issue codes on picketing and on closed shop agreements and arrangments (the latter being re-issued in 1983 after the Employment Act 1982 had made further changes in the law). It was largely because these are controversial topics, where the degree of consensus between management and unions is low, that a power to issue codes was conferred upon the Secretary of State. The Service, which is governed by a Council intended to be

---

[69] See on all this A.C.A.S. Annual Report 1976, Part I, pp. 40–41.
[70] House of Commons, Employment Committee, Minutes of Evidence, October 13, 1980, para. 336.
[71] s.3.

representative of both sides on industry, must be consulted by the Secretary of State when preparing a code, but the Service declined to make any comments on the first two Codes issued by the Secretary of State.[72]

Also because of the controversial nature of the first two topics chosen for codes of practice issued by the Secretary of State, it has not proved possible for the codes to confine themselves to benevolent advice or admonition. Two examples may be given. First, in disputed areas the parties naturally have a legitimate interest in knowing the legal status of rules which it is suggested in an official document that they should abide by. Like A.C.A.S. codes, the rules of the Secretary of State's codes do not automatically give rise to liability for failure to abide by them, but industrial tribunals (and, which is new, the courts) must take into account provisions of the codes in determining any matter to which the rules of the code are relevant.[73] But some of the more striking provisions of the codes cannot be easily related to questions of liability. Thus, the Code of Practice on Picketing says that pickets should take great care to ensure that their activities do not hinder the provision of essential supplies and services.[74] But the Code makes no attempt to link this admonition to the legal rules governing picketing which, as we shall see,[75] are today very strict, both as regards criminal and as regards civil liability, but do not seem to turn on the essential nature or otherwise of the goods or services being provided by those who are being picketed.

Second, in some cases where a provision of the codes is relevant to the exercise by a tribunal of its discretion, the codes appear to wish to pre-empt the exercise of that discretion by the tribunal. Thus the Code of Practice on Picketing provides that "disciplinary action should not be taken or threatened by a union against a member on the ground that he has crossed a picket line which it had not authorised or which was not a member's place of work."[76] Similarly, the Code of Practice on Closed Shop Agreements and Arrangements says that "disciplinary action should not be taken or threatened by a union against a member on the grounds of refusal to take part in industrial action called for by the union," *inter alia*,

---

[72] Employment Committee, *op. cit.,* para. 325. "The reason why the Council of A.C.A.S. took this view was that they wished to maintain their impartiality . . ."
[73] s.3(8).
[74] Code of Practice on Picketing (1980), paras. 37–38.
[75] See below, Chap. 8.
[76] Para. 36.

where the action was in breach of a procedure agreement; or where the action had not been affirmed in a secret ballot.[77] In both cases the provisions might be relevant to the question of whether a union had unreasonably expelled a person from membership of the union in a closed shop situation[78]; in both cases the provision of the code is put in an unqualified manner; in none of the cases would the member's compliance with the union's instructions necessarily have involved the member in an unlawful act. Will an industrial tribunal feel free to override the "advice" of the codes and, if not, will the codes not have succeeded in making legislation without going through the scrutiny of the full Parliamentary process? That these questions can be seriously raised perhaps demonstrates the difficulties inherent in the technique of using codes of practice where there is no genuine "best practice" embodied in the industrial relations activities of employers and unions to which all can be encouraged to aspire.

In the following chapters we turn from regulatory legislation to a discussion of auxiliary law. To understand the legal framework of collective bargaining, however, we must introduce into the discussion an element which so far has been absent. This is the function of the law to protect expectations in labour relations, expectations of management and expectations of labour. With this we shall deal in the next chapter.

---

[77] Para. 61.
[78] Employment Act 1980, s.4. See below, Chap. 7.

CHAPTER 3

PURPOSES AND METHODS OF
COLLECTIVE BARGAINING

WE now turn to what has been called "auxiliary legislation," that is, those branches of labour law which are designed to promote collective bargaining as well as the making and the observance of collective agreements. Before doing so, however, we must, to make the law comprehensible, say something about the purposes and about the methods of collective bargaining. These are the remarks of lawyers who must disclaim any ability or intention to establish a new theory of collective bargaining—the modest aim is to introduce the following discussion on the law.[1]

1. PURPOSES OF COLLECTIVE BARGAINING

We must remind ourselves that one of the purposes of all rules, legal or otherwise, is to protect such expectations as society approves, and which one generally calls "legitimate expectations." The fundamental principle *pacta sunt servanda,* that contractual promises must be kept, is a very clear illustration. So is the legal protection of property and so is legislation providing for health and educational services accessible to the entire population. The critical situations are those in which legitimate expectations clash. This is apt to happen where social powers support conflicting expectations, and it is at these neuralgic points that the rules of conduct become most acutely necessary. We have said before that one of the primary purposes of law is the regulation of social power. The regulation of social power may involve an adjustment of conflicting expectations and it may, although it need not, be for the law to provide the rules designed to adjust conflicting expectations and to provide the sanctions for the enforcement of such rules. Whenever you are faced with a conflict between

---

[1] The literature on the theory of collective bargaining is immense, especially in America. For a critical survey of contemporary theories, see Flanders, "Collective Bargaining: A Theoretical Analysis" (1968) 6 Brit. J. of Ind. Rel. 1; Flanders, *Industrial Relations, What is wrong with the System?* (1965); also McCarthy and Ellis, *Management by Agreement* (1973); Clegg, "Pluralism in Industrial Relations" (1975) 13 Brit. J. of Ind. Rel. 309; Hyman, "Pluralism, Procedural Consensus and Collective Bargaining" (1978) 16 Brit. J. of Ind. Rel. 16.

expectations of social powers, there arises the problem of the frontiers of the law. The long history of monopoly versus competition in markets for commodities and services, the even more acute problem of race relations in mixed societies, and the long saga of the struggle between religious conformity and toleration, are all cases in point. So is the problem of labour relations.

It follows from what we have said before that the legitimate expectations of labour and of management belong to those which are inevitably in conflict. Management can legitimately expect that labour will be available at a price which permits a reasonable margin for investment, and labour can equally legitimately expect that the level of real wages will not only be maintained but steadily increased. Management can claim a legitimate interest in obtaining for each job the most qualified worker available; labour can claim a legitimate interest in obtaining a job for each worker who is unemployed. Management can and must always expect that the arrangements of society (through law or otherwise) ensure that labour is as mobile as possible in the geographical as well as in the occupational sense; labour must always insist that workers enjoy a reasonable measure of job security so as to be able to plan their own and their families' lives. Managment expects to plan the production and distribution of goods or supply of services on a basis of calculated costs and calculated risks, and requires society to guarantee the feasibility of such planning by protecting it against interruption of these processes; labour well realises that without the power to stop work collectively it is impotent, and expects to be able to interrupt the economic process if this is necessary in order to exercise the necessary pressure. Management's interest in planning production and in being protected against its interruption is the exact equivalent to the worker's interest in plannning his and his family's life and in being protected against an interruption in his mode of existence, either through a fall of his real income or through the loss of his job. All this is palpably obvious, except for a person blinded by class hatred either way. The point is that even this almost inexcusably platitudinous confrontation of expectations and interests which labour law is designed to protect shows how much they are in conflict. It also shows that they can be temporarily adjusted through "give and take."[1a]

[1a] [This sentence perfectly encapsulates Kahn-Freund's pluralist position *vis-à-vis* the collective labour relationship. It is to be acknowledged that many would regard it, and its claim to be a corollary of what is said earlier in the paragraph, as controversial.]

But what about the expectations of the public, of the consumer? One of his principal expectations is that there will be an uninterrupted flow of goods and services, and it is at this point that the law may have to play an important role in reducing the number and the magnitude of industrial stoppages. The question whether and how far the law can be effective in doing so we shall examine in the last chapter. But the equally important expectation of the consumer that the goods and the services will be available at stable prices raises a far more difficult issue. It is at this point that we can very clearly see the frontiers of the law.

It is entirely beyond our possibilities and outside our terms of reference to discuss the means which are available to a government for formulating and carrying into effect a wages policy in particular and an incomes policy in general. That it can be done seems to be clear—the history of the wage policy of the Netherlands[2] seems to show that it can even be done over a considerable period. It can however only be done on the condition that the two sides of industry are prepared actively to apply it, and that the organisations on both sides have sufficient authority to carry that policy into effect in relation to the individual units of management and the individual work groups. Legal restraints— the application of legal sanctions—can sometimes work over a short period, and we have had recent examples of these, but they cannot by themselves achieve anything. The Prices and Incomes Acts imposed such restraints,[3] but the reality behind the governmental incomes policy was the Statement of Intent which emanated from the two sides of industry.[4] Wage restraints can

[2] Based originally on the Extraordinary Decree on Labour Relations of October 5, 1945, but completely changed in 1963. See Levenbach, "Collective Bargaining in the Netherlands" (1953) 16 M.L.R. 453; Pen, "The Strange Adventure of Dutch Wage Policy" (1963) 1 Brit. J. of Ind. Rel. 318. Prof. Pen's article demonstrates that the system rested on consent, and that the continuity of the co-operation of both sides (organised in the Foundation of Labour) was the condition of such success as it had. The system broke down in the sixties, in spite of the 1963 reforms, and was formally abolished by the Wages Act 1970. Under that Act, the government has only limited powers to impose temporary wage-freezes, which powers may be supplemented by ad hoc legislation. See "The Netherlands" in *International Encyclopaedia for Labour Law and Industrial Relations*, Vol. 6, pp 62–64.

[3] Prices and Incomes Acts 1966, 1967 and 1968. An analysis of these now obsolete provisions is to be found in Kahn-Freund, *Labour Law: Old Traditions and New Developments*, pp. 15 *et seq.*

[4] Joint Statement of Intent on Productivity, Prices and Incomes of December 16, 1964. See, for a survey of the history of incomes policy in this country, Clegg, *The Changing System of Industrial Relations in Great Britian* (1979), Chap. 9, and also H. A. Turner, "Collective Bargaining and the Eclipse of Incomes Policy, Retrospect, Prospect and Possibilities" (1970) 8 Brit. J. of Ind. Rel. 197.

only be imposed by organised labour and management on themselves, and can only be imposed by their agreement. The law can at best play the role of a "midwife." It can be an instrument in creating the climate of opinion in which the organisations can be persuaded to adopt a policy of restraint and in which they can in turn persuade their own members to act on it. To do this, one of the best means may be to appeal to people's reason rather than to their emotions, and unquestionably the law can contribute to this by setting up a body such as the former National Board for Prices and Incomes,[5] whose Reports made a unique contribution to the understanding of the facts of industrial relations. What is impossible is that any government (outside a totalitarian dictatorship) can, by threat of legal sanctions, impose upon the two sides of industry an incomes policy which either of them rejects. Between 1975 and 1979 the necessary agreement between government, management, and labour was given the name of a "social contract." There is, however, nothing new in the underlying idea. It is a truism that, in a democracy, there can be no incomes policy without an understanding of this nature, whatever its name. What matters is the collective understanding—how far it is given the form of "law" is comparatively unimportant. Thus, the early period of the "social contract" was a relatively successful one, judging by the criterion of how far increases in earnings coincided with the targets set by the policy (even though the targets often implied a fall in the standard of living). The crucial element in this success was the agreement between the TUC and the Government on the need for and the shape of the incomes policy,[6] and legislation was confined to an essentially subordinate role, *e.g.* in relieving from contractual liability employers who limited their wage increases in order to comply with the norms of the policy.[7] When the political agreement between Government and trade union movement evaporated in the late 'seventies, so did the policy's effectiveness, even when the Government made attempts to bolster the policy by seeking to use its power as a purchaser of goods and services against government contractors who exceeded the policy's norms.[8]

---

[5] Originally set up as a permanent Royal Commission under a Royal Warrant of April 8, 1965, and put on a statutory basis by the Prices and Incomes Act 1966, now abolished.

[6] See, *e.g. The Attack on Inflation*, Cmnd. 6151, 1975, paras. 1–11.

[7] Remuneration, Grants and Charges Act 1975, s.1.

[8] *Holliday Hall & Co. Ltd.* v. *Chapple, The Times*, February 4 and 7, 1978. The constitutional propriety of the government's use of its powers in this way was not ultimately decided.

We are concerned with the relation between management and organised labour, and, for an understanding of the role the law plays or does not play in that relation, the notion of countervailing power is indispensable. The conflicting expectations of labour and of management can be temporarily reconciled through collective bargaining: power stands against power. Through being countervailing forces, management and organised labour are able to create by autonomous action a body of rules, and thus to relieve the law of one of its tasks. More than that, the two sides of industry have at their disposal sanctions to enforce these rules against the other side and against the employers and workers on their own side. It is the conflict of interests which makes their agreements a valid instrument of "social engineering." But where is the power countervailing the combined forces of labour and management? No sanctions the law has at its disposal can effectively compel them to impose a restraint on wages if they are determined not to impose it. The only social technique available is persuasion, which technique may be taken to include the creation by Government of economic conditions such that employers cannot pay and workers will not ask for large increases in wages. This is borne out by experience in a number of countries. It has—we shall see it—important consequences in the law governing collective agreements.[9]

In the light of what we have said it is not difficult to summarise the purposes of collective bargaining: by bargaining collectively with organised labour, management seeks to give effect to its legitimate expectation that the planning of production, distribution, etc., should not be frustrated through interruptions of work. By bargaining collectively with management, organised labour seeks to give effect to its legitimate expectations that wages and other conditions of work should be such as to guarantee a stable and adequate form of existence and as to be compatible with the physical integrity and moral dignity of the individual, and also that jobs should be reasonably secure. This definition is not intended to be exhaustive. It is intended to indicate (and this is important for the law) that the principal interest of management in collective bargaining has always been the maintenance of industrial peace over a given area and period, and that the principal interest of labour has always been the creation and the maintenance of certain standards over a given area and period, standards of distribution of work, of rewards, and of stability of employment. The relative significance of these various objectives varies from

---

[9] See below, Chap. 6.

country to country. Thus the market regulating function of collective bargaining, its decisive role in job distribution, is far greater in this country than in the countries of the European Continent; this may reflect the strength of the guild tradition in the British labour movement, a tradition which has had its influence in other countries, including the United States.

2. METHODS OF COLLECTIVE BARGAINING

It is when we come to methods of collective bargaining that national differences become really prominent. We are going to touch upon three aspects of this fascinating subject: the difference between institutional or dynamic and contractual or static bargaining, the significance of "custom and practice," and the level of bargaining.

(a) Dynamic versus static bargaining

One can distinguish two types of bargaining procedures. They are distinguishable as types, but there are many overlaps and hybrid forms. One is sometimes referred to as the institutional or dynamic, the other as the contractual or static method.[10] The use of the term "contractual" in the present context is not intended to prejudge the issue we shall discuss later on, whether a collective agreement is or is not a legally enforceable contract. "Contractual" is here simply intended to mean that the parties, that is, the employer or employers or employers' association and the union or unions, come together, negotiate, arrive at an agreement, and then disperse, to renew their negotiations as the need arises either because the time of the expiry of the agreement approaches or, if there is no time limit, either side desires a change. By contrast the "institutional" or "dynamic" method consists in the creation of a permanent bilateral body, known as a joint industrial council, a conciliation board, or a joint committee, on which both sides are represented by an equal number of members, sometimes (in a minority of cases) with an independent chairman presiding.[11] To

---

[10] "Intergroup Conflicts and their Settlement" (1954) 5 Brit. J. of Sociology, 193, esp. pp 202 *et seq*, reprinted in Kahn-Freund, *Selected Writings* (1978), p. 41; Spyropoulos, *Le Droit des Conventions Collectives de Travail dans les pays de la C.E.C.A.* (1959), pp 26 *et seq.*

[11] A "statutory joint industrial council" (see above Chap. 2) has no independent members (and thereby differs from a wages council) (Wages Councils Act 1979, Part II). If the two sides cannot agree, ACAS may be requested to try to settle the matter and thus to fulfil the functions of the independent members of a wages council (s.11). The orders of a statutory industrial council are legally enforceable (ss. 14–15).

this body the parties give a constitution and a code of procedure, but they leave it to the body thus created by unamimous resolutions to settle the wages and other substantive conditions of the industry. This "dynamic" method is widespread in this country,[12] more so than in any other comparable country with the important exception of Belgium, which is in many ways the country most similar to Britain in these matters.[13] This distinction between the two methods of collective bargaining is very important in the context of this book because it is (to say the least of it) exceedingly difficult to apply to collective bargaining of the "institutional" variety the categories of the law of contract; the traditional prevalence of this method in some of the most important branches of the British economy goes some way towards explaining why collective agreements are not considered as legal contracts in this county.[14] Moreover, since this "dynamic" or "institutional" method consists in the passing of resolutions by a joint body which is always free to modify its own decisions, provided it does so unanimously, it encourages "open ended" agreements and discourages the fixing of time limits. More important: the body which lays down the conditions is often also the body which interprets its own resolutions. Over a large area of British industrial relations the rule-making and the decision-making processes, the, as it were, "legislative" and "judicial" functions are as indistinguishable as they were in the constitution

---

[12] Ministry of Labour, *Industrial Relations Handbook* (1961), Chaps. III–V; Sharp, *Industrial Conciliation and Arbitration in Great Britain* (1950), Chaps. II–VIII. For an analysis of five of the most important industries, see Marsh and McCarthy, *Disputes Procedures in Britain,* Royal Commission Research Paper No. 2, Pt. (2). In Pt. 1, Mr. Marsh analyses "The Preference for Procedural over Substantive Rules" in paras. 67–74.

[13] On the Belgian system of *commissions paritaires*, see Horion, *Nouveau Précis de Droit Social Belge* (2nd ed., 1969) paras. 232–247, pp. 140 *et seq.* The late Prof. Paul Horion, a leading authority in Belgian labour law, surmised (see *loc. cit.* 1st ed. 1965, para. 167, p. 133) that the autonomous growth of collective bargaining and the abstention of the legislature may have been due to the English example. This observation is omitted from the second ed. of the book. For up-to-date information about the *commissions paritaires*, see *International Encyclopedia for Labour Law and Industrial Relations*, Vol. 2, "Belgium", paras. 306–16 and 340–41.

[14] See below, Chap. 6. Nor were they in Belgium before the law of December 5, 1968 on collective agreements and bilateral commissions, (Art. 19 of which gave them binding force (see however Art. 4)). Horion, *loc. cit.,* para. 184, p. 143, points out that this was by reason of the parties' lack of contractual capacity. Horion, however, considered the lack on contractual intention as a possible additional reason.

of medieval England.[15] Within these processes of institutional bargaining every dispute about existing "rights" can be turned into a dispute about "interests" by the simple device of solving it through a new and possibly retrospective resolution. This may help us to understand why there is so little room in British industrial practice and labour law for that distinction between "conflicts of right" and "conflicts of interest" which is elementary and basic in the labour law systems of many comparable countries.[16] The countries which draw this sharp distinction between the making of rules and their application include the United States,[17] and The Commonwealth of Australia, where the courts have held[18] that it is—within the framework of the federal compulsory arbitration system—guaranteed by the Federal Constitution which insists on the separation of powers. This shows that the separation of conflicts of rights and conflicts of interests is of course perfectly compatible with the common law, that is, with casuistic legal thinking, whilst the Belgian example shows that the dynamic or institutional method of bargaining can exist in a country with systematic legal thinking. The structure of industrial relations has nothing to do with the structure of the law. Australia, the United States, and Great Britain have similar legal traditions and different systems of collective bargaining. The same is true of Belgium and France.

Nevertheless, there is an extraordinary similarity between the spirit of the common law and the spirit of industrial relations in Britain. The common law is permeated by a deep distrust, by an almost obsessional fear of "tidiness." So is much in the British system of industrial relations. Both sides have a traditional desire for solving problems "ad hoc," as they arise. So does the common law. Is not this what we mean by "case law"? Traditionally it has been the tendency of the common law to avoid the commitment inherent in the acceptance of general norm-codifying legislation. It has never had much confidence in the solution of unpredictable problems through the syllogistic application of a major premise; it

---

[15] McIlwain, *The High Court of Parliament, passim.*

[16] *This distinction is recognised in every comparable country except this country. For France, see Code du Travail* (1974), Art. L 525–4, al. 2 and 3. See Benjamin Aaron (ed.) *Labour Courts and Grievance Settlement in Western Europe* (1971).

[17] It appears, *e.g.* in the Railway Labor Act 1926, where different statutory procedures have been laid down for these two different types of dispute.

[18] The decision of the High Court in *R.* v. *Kirby, ex p. Boilermakers' Society of Australia* (1956) 92 C.L.R. 254 was affirmed by the Privy Council, *Att.-Gen.* v. *R., ex p. Boilermakers' Society of Australia* [1957] A.C. 288. It led to a reconstruction of the system of compulsory arbitration: Counciliation and Arbitration Act 1956.

has always preferred to rely on the ability of the decision-maker to deal with new situations in the light of what are called "their own facts." However much scholars have elucidated the principle of precedent,[19] no one has ever succeeded in lifting the dark veil which surrounds the relation between law finding and law making in the common law. And just as in the common law the judge is rule maker and decision maker all at once, so in the dynamic system of collective bargaining the parties ignore the difference between interpreting a new rule and making a new one. The common law develops not through deductive syllogisms but through analogical reasoning from previous fact situations,[20] and similarly new collective rules are made out of existing conflicts by asking "how have we dealt with similar situations in the past?" But, as in the common law, the fluidity of the substantive norm is in this method of collective bargaining balanced by the firmness of the code of procedure. The expectation of the parties to know in advance what the decision will be may often remain unprotected, but they can at least rely on the strict observance of rules as to how it will be made. In so far as the predictability of the decision is safeguarded, this is done less through logical processes of reasoning from the general to the particular than through a regulated method of bilateral, that is, dialectical, argument. For decades British statutes[21] spoke of terms and conditions of employment established by machinery of negotiation or arbitration, where elsewhere legislation speaks of collective agreements or awards, and this practice still prevails.[22] It is the "machinery" which counts, the procedure, the "remedy," not its product, the agreement, the "code," or the "right."

This similarity is not coincidental. The common law (and we must of course include equity) is "lawyers' law" in the sense that it is law made by lawyers for lawyers, a set of rules to guide the lawyer as to when he may and how he should proceed, how he should argue, how he should produce evidence, how he should

---

[19] Cross, *Precedent in English Law* (3rd. ed., 1977) (Clarendon Law Series), see pp. 26 *et seq.* about the great mystery of the "declaratory theory" of the common law.

[20] Levi, *An Introduction to Legal Reasoning* (University of Chicago Press, 1949). Dean Levi argued that the basic pattern of all legal reasoning was "reasoning by example."

[21] Conciliation Act 1896; Industrial Courts Act 1919; S.R. & O. 1940 No. 1305; S.I. 1951 No. 1376; Wages Councils Act 1959; Terms and Conditions of Employment Act 1959, s. 8, etc.; all these, except Pt. II of the Industrial Courts Act, have been repealed.

[22] See Employment Protection Act 1975, ss 3 (2), 4 (1) (c), 98, Sched. 11 (the latter two provisions are now repealed).

draft documents—a body of craft rules developed by and in the lawyers' guilds for their members, and handed down from master to apprentice. It is not in its origin or in its structure (as many other legal systems are) in the first place a systematic body of norms to be applied by judges and other servants of the State, but a set of remedies to be used by advocates. Fortunately these characteristics of the common law have been progressively eroded in a century and a half of law reform, but they are still present. They explain the procedural character of the common law, just as the guild spirit and tradition explain many of the characteristics of British industrial relations. These characteristics are not necessarily praiseworthy. One wonders whether we do not need a Jeremy Bentham in the world of industrial relations.

[The distinction which Kahn-Freund draws in the above passage bewtween dynamic and static models of bargaining is of the utmost importance because of the difficulties dynamic bargaining places in the way of any simple distinction between conflicts of right and of interest and because of the encouragement dynamic bargaining gives to ad hoc decision making. It may be wondered, however, whether it is correct to identify dynamic methods of bargaining exclusively with institutional forms of bargaining machinery (defining institutional forms as permanent bilateral bodies with equal representation of both sides). As Kahn-Freund himself seemed to recognise, the outstanding example of dynamic bargaining is probably provided by "unreformed" bargaining by shop stewards at plant and work-group level, and yet bargaining machinery at this level is often anything but institutionalised.[23] Contrariwise, there seems no reason in principle why a joint, standing body should not adopt a "contractual" model of bargaining, *i.e.* of periodic meetings to settle all outstanding issues between the parties; and some evidence does exist that standing bodies at national level, especially in the public service sector, do operate in this way.[24] Since institutional forms of bargaining machinery are identified predominantly with multi-employer bargaining, usually at national level, and since, at least in manufacturing industry, multi-employer bargaining is now much less significant than single-employer bargaining at establishment or enterprise level,[25] the crucial question has become how far single-employer bargaining accords with a dynamic rather than static model.]

---

[23] See the second edition of this book at pp. 66–67; and see below, pp. 85–86.
[24] Clegg, *op. cit.*, pp. 104–123.
[25] See W. Brown (ed.), *The Changing Contours of British Industrial Relations* (1981), Chap. 1.

(b) Custom and practice

The parallel does not end here. Like the common law, British collective bargaining is a "mystery" in both the connected meanings of that word. It is a secret and a craft, the French *métier*. The rules are largely esoteric. It is still controversial among the historians[26] whether a direct link can be established between the remnants of the medieval guilds (of which the Inns of Court are of course a surviving example) and the infant trade unions of the eighteenth century. From our point of view it does not matter very much. As we have already said, the guild spirit is present. The world of industrial relations has its own language and its own etiquette. Most important, the etiquette, whilst well understood and rigidly observed, remains largely inarticulate, and most certainly and deliberately uncodified. It is known as "custom and practice,"[27] sometimes as "trade practices." Such is their importance that, to make a more rational use of the labour force possible in the interest of national survival, statutes had to be passed under the impact of both World Wars[28] to promise the unions the subsequent restoration of these practices, so as to induce them to relax apprenticeship rules, waive manning scales and demarcation lines, agree to the admission of women to certain jobs, etc., in short to agree to what is known as "dilution of labour." In 1940 Ernest Bevin tried to bring some order into this chaos by making provision for the codification of trade practices, and, when he was Minister of Labour, he created a statutory mechanism for this purpose.[29] One remembers that this great trade union leader had his background in the transport industry.[30] Perhaps he did not fully appreciate the resistance of craft unions and other craft organisations to the idea of a codification of customs or etiquettes. In any event, this attempt to make industrial relations less esoteric ended

---

[26] Sidney and Beatrice Webb, *History of Trade Unionism* (1926 ed.), pp. 12 *et seq.*, denied that there was such link. Brentano, *Die Arbeitergilden der Gegenwart* (1871–72), was at one time understood or, as the Webbs point out, probably misunderstood, as affirming it.

[27] See Clegg, *loc. cit.* pp. 24–31. The *Final Report of the Committee of Inquiry under the Rt. Hon. Lord Devlin into certain matters concerning the Port Transport Industry*, Cmnd. 2734 (1965), is a textbook on custom, ritual and etiquette. See also, for a persuasive sociological analysis, W. Brown, *Piecework Bargaining* (1973), esp. Chap. 4. The author shows striking similarities between the principle of precedent in the law and the growth of custom and practice in industry.

[28] Restoration of Pre-War Practices Act 1919; Restoration of Pre-war Trade Practices Acts 1942 and 1950.

[29] Conditions of Employment and National Arbitration Order, S.R. & O. 1940 No. 1305, Art. 6.

[30] Allan Bullock, *The Life and Times of Ernest Bevin*, Vol. I (1960).

in complete failure, and the relevant provisions, long since revoked,[31] remained a dead letter.

Not as if "custom and practice" mattered only for the craft unions of skilled workers. Far from it. The purpose of many of them is to protect the workers against unemployment, and what some call "restrictive practices," others call "protective rules."[32]

This is not the only explanation why they exist or continue to exist. Another is tradition, the law of inertia.[33] One thinks of manning scales, of demarcation lines, of the artificial creation of overtime, and of course especially of apprenticeship rules which sometimes remind one of the apprenticeship legislation of Elizabeth I.[34] Such restrictive practices or "arrangements" are sometimes simply tacitly accepted by management, and sometimes expressly agreed[35] upon. They are not the only examples of "custom and practice." Many of the rules which govern the daily working lives of the workers are of this character: not only "who does what," but also "when" and "where" he does it. The "tea break" and "washing-up time" are only examples which happened to hit the headlines.

As we have said, these customs and practices are extremely well understood by those concerned, by the "insiders," and often they are inseparably intertwined with rules that happen to find their way into formulated collective agreements, even where they themselves have not been so formulated. Of course, any formal agreements have to be read in the light of these uncodified practices, and they are so read by employers and workers who know their own industry. But they are not necessarily so read by lawyers,[36] and to separate formal collective agreements from the traditional custom and practice which are their environment may be a Procrustean operation. It is almost as if a foreign lawyer tried to understand an English statute without seeing its common law background. Since 1960[37] many collective agreements have been

---

[31] Industrial Disputes (Amendment and Regulation) Order (S.I. 1958 No. 1796).

[32] *Restrictive Labour Practices,* Royal Commission Research Paper No. 4 (Pt. 2), written by the secretariat, esp. paras. 14 *et seq.,* and Lupton, *On the Shop Floor,* 1963, as quoted in para. 37 of the Appendix to the above-mentioned paper.

[33] See *ibid.* paras. 17 *et seq.,* 25.

[34] Statute of Apprentices 1562.

[35] Para. 3 of the paper quoted in n. 26.

[36] The peace clause in *Rookes* v. *Barnard* [1964] A.C. 1129 was treated as legally binding, the closed shop understanding was not. This was, however, largely due to an admission made by the defendants before Sachs J.

[37] Flanders, *The Fawley Productivity Agreement* (1964); National Board for Prices and Incomes, *Productivity Agreements,* Report No. 36, Cmnd. 3311 (1967);*Productivity Bargaining,* Royal Commission Research Paper No. 4 (Pt. 1), written by the Secretariat.

directed towards the raising of productivity through the abandonment of customs restricting output, or restricting the optimal use
of the labour force by management. How can one begin to
understand such agreements in isolation from their customary
background? This is only one particularly striking example. Trade
union rules are another, as the House of Lords decided in 1972,[38]
when it held that a union rule book cannot be interpreted as
lawyers interpret commercial contracts or statutes. The rule book
does not codify the union's constitution, but only a fragment, so
that, *e.g.* (as was held in the case) the constitutional authority of a
shop steward may, whatever the rule book says, have to be
"reasonably implied from custom and practice."[39] The difference
between the interpretation of commercial contracts and of union
rule books arises from the nature of labour relations, and the
House of Lords would have had to draw the same distinction if,
instead of a rule book, it had to interpret a collective agreement.
Like the rule book, the formulated agreement may be no more
than the tip of the iceberg visible to the outsider, just as the Law of
Property Acts or the Companies Acts are not only incomprehensible but may be misleading to anyone unfamiliar with the case law
to which they sometimes create exceptions without stating the
rule.

The common law, far more than the legal systems of other
comparable countries, has, as befits its guild origin and spirit, its
own esoteric language, and it has, as a mere glance at the Annual
Statements of the Senate of the Inns of Court and the Bar clearly
shows, a well understood, complex, uncodified set of rituals and
etiquettes. To understand or to teach the English law of procedure
without taking account of these is a hopeless quest. They include
the pre-entry closed shop,[40] demarcation rules and manning
scales. Like industrial apprenticeship rules and even manning
scales and demarcation lines, one of their purposes is to maintain
standards of performance, and of course, professional ethics and
they also have the effect of spreading job opportunities and
warding off unemployment. Perhaps the parallel does not end
even here. At the back of all formulated rules of the common law
there is the rule of what is called "reason," an amalgam of ethical
convictions, traditions, and prejudices which, in its relation to

---

[38] *Heatons Transport (St. Helens) Ltd.* v. *T.G.W.U.* [1972] I.C.R. 308. See
Hepple, "Union Responsibility for Shop Stewards" (1972) 1 I.L.J. 197.

[39] Lord Wilberforce, *loc. cit.* at p. 394.

[40] See, on the closed shop in the organisation of the English legal profession
Harman J. in *Huntley* v. *Thornton* [1957] 1 All E.R. 234 at pp. 2391–240A.

positive rules of law, may be compared to that part played in industry by trade practices in relation to collective agreements.

Where collective bargaining is of the "institutional" type, those called upon to adjust the formulated resolutions or decisions to new or newly revealed situations can always do so in the light of the custom and practice which they know. This may be one of the reasons why so few of these councils, boards and committees have an impartial chairman from outside. But custom and practice also play their role in industries which do not have a permanent negotiating machinery. The engineering industry is an example. Unlike, *e.g.* the building industry, it has no such machinery. Yet "custom and practice" is perhaps nowhere more important than in some sections of the engineering industry.[41]

One may wonder whether this approach to industrial relations as a "mystery" does not partly explain the desire to keep outsiders and above all to keep the lawyers out. It is certainly not the only explanation; a great deal of that has to be found not in the characteristics of British industrial relations but in the characteristics of the law. Nor can this tendency or policy always be approved, but at least it ought to be understood. There is a fear, more or less articulate, that the interpretation of an agreement as if it were a body of clear and precise terms, self-contained and to be understood in the light of the categories of contract interpretation, would distort its spirit. In this respect the resistance to the intrusion of the law can be compared to the traditional resistance of many members of the legal profession to the intrusion of legislation into their lawyers' law. Do we not sometimes hear or read about the "interference" of statutes with the "law," just as in the world of industrial relations we hear references to the "interference" of the law itself?

This proud autonomy, this spirit of independence and of self-government, is deeply rooted in English history. You may say that it is a surviving pre-capitalist element in modern society. The British system of collective bargaining is as impressive an achievement as the common law. There were times when it was superior to the corresponding arrangements of other countries. But in a competitive world craft rules and etiquettes, custom and practice can turn from a blessing into a curse. Like so much in the common law, the existing system of collective bargaining may have had its day. To say the least, many of its aspects, and not least the

---

[41] Marsh, *Industrial Relations in Engineering* (Oxford 1965), p.93. In a sense the whole of Mr. Marsh's book is an explanation of the complex reasons for this phenomenon. See also Brown (1973), *op. cit., passim.*

restrictions on the optimal use of labour, are in desperate need of urgent and radical reform. This reform must come from inside. To think that it can be achieved through the creation of a "legal framework" was as realistic as the idea that the common law could, by a stroke of the legislative pen, be transformed into a codified system. A utopian belief in the omnipotence of the law can do no good, and much harm.[42]

(c) The level of bargaining

To understand the relation between collective bargaining and the law, and the reasons why this is different in this country from what it is in many foreign countries, one must, lastly, consider the level of bargaining, that is: who are the parties to collective agreements, and what is their territorial scope of application?

One of the outstanding features of the collective bargaining system of Britain (which it shares with those of other countries of Western Europe, but not that of the United States) is that frequently the agreement aimed at is collective on both sides: the bargaining partner on the side of the management is very often an employers' association; this is a dominant feature of British collective bargaining, not only in the private but also in the public sector of the economy. Local authorities also bargain through associations. Despite the great and growing importance of bargaining by individual employers, a large proportion of the labour force is still governed by agreements made by an employers' association with one or more trade unions.[43] This may cover the whole of an industry on a national level ("industry wide bargaining") or on a regional, district or local basis. We are beginning to hear a great deal about multinational or supra-national bargaining (with associations or with multinational employers) but this is as yet only a pious aspiration. All bargaining by employers' associations always refers to a territorial unit, very often the various territorial levels are interlocked; some matters are regulated on a national, others on a regional basis, or, in defined limits, regional agreements may supplement those made on a nation-wide basis.

---

[42] These arguments are developed at greater length in Kahn-Freund, *Labour Relations: Heritage and Adjustment* (1979), esp. Chap. 2.

[43] For a survey of the role of employers' associations in wage and other collective bargaining, see the evidence of the CBI to the Donovan Commission, para. 49, paras. 106 *et seq.*, paras. 126 *et seq.*, and the tabulated survey in Appendix 2. See also V. G. Munns, *The Functions and Organisation of Employers' Associations in Selected Industries*, Royal Commission Research Paper no. 7, paras. 148 *et seq.*

More important even: where agreements are made by employers' associations, it is almost inevitable that they should be supplemented by further agreements or understandings between individual employers and unions. These may apply to the whole of an enterprise or, a different matter, a factory or plant (the difference is so important because of the central importance of multi-plant enterprise in this country). As we shall have to point out, they may operate at an even lower level. This has to be understood in the light of the traditional function of local, regional, and national bargaining. This is very largely to provide a minimum for all, that is, for all those employed by the employers and in the localities covered by the agreement. Industry-wide or regional or local agreements generally codify minima, not standards. This is a vital matter.[44]

It would, however, be a mistake to believe that in this country individual employers bargain only in order to supplement agreements made by their associations. They may also negotiate with unions to the exclusion of employers' associations. This may be due to a variety of reasons. One may be the dominating position of an employer in an industry, whether in the public sector, such as that of the National Coal Board, or in the private sector, such as that of Imperial Chemical Industries. Another reason may be that the employer disapproves of employers' associations, which may account for the fact that some large British subsidiaries of American corporations (Ford, Vauxhall) are not members of employers' associations.

The prevailing system in the United States is bargaining by individual employers either for all or some of their plants or for a particular plant. As time proceeds it is becoming clearer that this American system has great advantages, or, better perhaps, that it would be for the benefit of labour relations in this country if a large dose of this American method was injected into it, without destroying territorial bargaining in so far as it is more appropriate.[45] Plant bargaining is apt to be richer in content than territorial bargaining, that is, it can be extended to topics which cannot otherwise be included in the bilateral rule-making process. Pensions schemes are an example.[46] Another example, though this

---

[44] The debate to which this point has given rise over the proper interpretation of the now-rescinded Fair Wages Resolution and now-repealed Sched. 11 of the Employment Protection Act 1975 is discussed below in Chap. 6.

[45] This was one of the most fundamental conclusions of the Donovan Commission. See Cmnd. 3623, paras 162 *et seq.*

[46] They are a "mandatory" bargaining subject in the U.S.; *Inland Steel Co.* v.*N.L.R.B.*, 170 F. (2d) 247 (1948). See Summers and Wellington, *Labor Law*, p. 645.

is not uncontroversial, is productivity bargaining.[47] In Continental countries, such as Germany, and (not quite to the same extent) France and Belgium the statutory works council or staff delegates make agreements with the employer which supplement the collective agreements made by the unions with the employers' association.[48] No such plant agreements with statutory status exist here, nor does anyone seem to want them.[49] All the more important that the British system of industrial relations should be adjusted to that need for systematic and orderly regulation "on the spot" which the Americans enjoy through their collective plant agreements, and, *e.g.* the Germans through the statutory agreements between management and the works council. More important than all this: wages agreed at plant or enterprise level are likely not to be minima but standards, and thus a far surer foundation for cost calculation than territorial minima supplemented by "fragmented" and informal understandings arrived at on the shop floor. We shall have to come back to this. A development in this direction might also reduce the number of wildcat strikes which sometimes result from the deficiencies of the present methods of bargaining at plant and lower levels. Nevertheless, enterprise or plant bargaining can never supersede territorial bargaining in industries comprising many small entrepreneurial units, and even in large-scale enterprise there are likely to be matters which lend themselves most easily and conveniently to territorial bargaining, such as the length of the working week or of the annual holiday. By the same token a multi-plant enterprise such as Imperial Chemical Industries or British Leyland, Woolworths or Marks and Spencers, the National Coal Board or British Railways, may find that some matters must be regulated by

---

[47] See Answers 1139 *et seq.* in the Oral Evidence of the Engineering Employers' Federation to the Donovan Commissions, November 23, 1965, Minutes No. 6.

[48] In Germany this is of central importance: Works Constitution Law *(Betriebsverfassungs-Gesetz),* 1972. s. 77. For a survey of the situation in the original six Member States of the Euopean Communities, see Vol III of the Labour Law Publications of the High Authority of the ECSC: *La Représentation des Travailleurs sur le Plan de l'Entreprise dans le Droit des Pays Membres de la C.E.C.A.* (1959), partly overtaken by new developments, for which see the references n. 18, p. 23 above.

[49] See the rejection by the TUC of works councils of the German pattern: *Industrial Democracy, A Statement of Policy* (1974), para 93. For a more favourable view see I. L. Roberts, "The Works Constitution Act in West Germany, Implications for the United Kingdom" (1973) 11 Brit. J. of Ind. Rel. 338. See *Report of the Committee of Inquiry on Industrial Democracy* (Bullock Report), Cmnd. 6706, 1977, Chaps. 6 and 10; but see also the Minority Report.

agreements covering the whole of the undertaking, and others at the level of the plant.[50]

Two or more employers may of course enter into a collective agreement jointly without forming an association, and two or more employers' associations may do so without forming a super-federation. Nor is there anything to prevent one or more employers from being thus associated with one or more employers' associations. The result is that, on the management side, the collective agreement is, in the words of the Trade Union and Labour Relations Act,[51] "made by or on behalf of . . . one or more employers or employers' associations."An employers' association may either have individual members or be a federation of constituent or affiliated organisations—the CBI could, if it chose, be party to a collective agreement,[52] but it may also have individual members as well as affiliated associations.[53]

On the workers' side, however, we get a very different picture. As we said in the first chapter, the individual worker, as distinct from the individual employer, does not enter into the process of adjusting social power which is the essence of collective bargaining. He can never make a collective agreement, nor can any number of workers who do not form an association. On the workers' side, therefore, as the Act says,[54] the agreement is always made "by or on behalf[55] of one or more trade unions." Two or more trade unions may thus bargain jointly, a most common and most important feature of British industrial relations, and a necessary method for overcoming the consequences of multiunionism. Moreover, a federation of unions is itself a trade union,[56] and the purposes of joint collective bargaining may thus be fulfilled either by forming a permanent federation, such as the Confedera-

---

[50] Bell, "The Development of Industrial Relations in Nationalised Industries in Great Britain" (1975) 13 Brit. J. of Ind. Rel. 1.

[51] s. 30.

[52] s. 28(2).

[53] s. 30.

[54] s. 30.

[55] In some continental countries, *e.g.* in Scandinavia, in Belgium, in Italy, and to a minor extent in Germany, "interindustrial"agreements, concluded by the top organisations (the equivalents of the TUC and CBI) continue to be decisively important, *e.g.* the famous Swedish "Basic Agreement" between the Swedish Employers' Confederation and the Confederation of Swedish Trade Unions of December 20, 1938, and repeatedly amended. See Folke Schmidt, *Law and Industrial Relations in Sweden* (1977), pp. 26 *et seq.*, and, on the utilisation of this system for a wages policy. A. Victorin, (1975) 19 *Scandinavian Studies in Law* 293. No such agreements exist as yet in this country, but, through the "on behalf" formula they could be accommodated in the statutory definition.

[56] Trade Union and Labour Relations Act 1975, s. 28(1).

tion of Shipbuilding and Engineering Unions or, formerly, the Printing and Kindred Trades Federation or by co-operating ad hoc. The TUC is itself a "trade union" and, like the CBI, could therefore be a collective bargaining party.

There must thus be at least one association on the workers', and there may be an association on the employers', side. This gives rise to a legal problem over which in some Continental countries buckets of printers' ink have been spilt in the course of many years.[57] Does an organisation when entering into a collective agreement act as principal (*i.e.* on its own account) or as agent for its members, or both? To answer the question one must remember than an employer can, but a worker cannot, be a party to an agreement. From this, it seems to follow that a trade union, when bargaining collectively, acts always and exclusively as a principal, and that this is a matter of law. On the hand, it is a question of fact whether in a given case an employers' association intends to act in one or the other capacity or in both, though, especially in the case of a large organisation with many (presumably small) firms as members, the intention is likely to be for the association to act as principal.[58] There are good reasons why the "agency" theory cannot be right if applied to the workers' side. If you consider the union as an agent, you involve yourself in a tangle of problems of the law of agency[59]: think only of those members who joined the union after the making of the agreement, or of those who on a ballot voted against it, to say nothing of nice little problems concerning members under 18 years of age. Much more important: the obligations a union undertakes and the rights it acquires are collective by nature, they cannot be performed or claimed by an individual. This is true of the creation of joint committees etc. and of the observance of stipulated procedures, and of all terms on the distribution of jobs, on demarcation, on the closed shop, in short, of everything that has to do with the conditions for the making of contracts of employment rather than the terms of concluded contracts.[60] And for the reasons we have sufficiently emphasised,

---

[57] For a survey of this literature see Jacobi, *Grundlehren des Arbeitsrechts*, (1927), p. 179. For France, See Despax, *Conventions Collectives*, p. 29 (Camerlynck (ed.), *Traité de Droit du Travail*, Vol. 7).

[58] *Cf. N.U.G.S.A.T.* v. *Albury Bros. Ltd.* [1979] I.C.R. 84 (C.A.) This also obviates the difficulty which otherwise might arise when a newly formed company joins an employers' association which has concluded a collective agreement. A company cannot ratify a contract made on its behalf before it was incorporated: *Kelner* v. *Baxter* (1867) L.R. 2 C.P. 174.

[59] See Donovan Report, para. 477.

[60] See the problem which arose in *R.* v. *National Arbitration Tribunal, ex p. Crowther* [1948] 1 K.B. 424.

this is the only legal analysis reconcilable with social reality,[61] the reality of the collective agreement as a treaty between social powers. An organisation of organisations, such as the Confederation of Shipbuilding and Engineering Unions or, in the past, the Printing and Kindred Trades Federation may, and constantly does, bargain collectively as an agent for its affiliated organisations. The Trade Union and Labour Relations Act takes account of this in the definition to which we have referred,[62] but this has of course nothing to do with the problem we are here considering. Even before the 1974 Act it was clear[63] that an organisation of workers acted as principal and not as agent for its members, and this, as we shall see, has consequences both as regards the effect of the agreement on the contracts of employment, and in connection with the law governing trade disputes and industrial sanctions. Apart from special statutory provisions such as exist, *e.g.* in Sweden,[64] the agreement itself imposes no obligation on union members,[65] and an unconstitutional strike is not a breach by the workers of the agreement if it is a strike organised or financed by the union. It may of course be a breach by the union. Nor, an equally important point, can an individual member of the union derive any rights from the agreement as such, as distinguished from his contract of employment the content of which has been determined by the collective agreement. The idea, mooted at one time in some Continental countries[66] and also in the United States,[67] that a collective agreement could operate as a third party beneficiary contract and that individual union members could,

---

[61] See Flanders, "Collective Bargaining—A Theoretical Analysis" (1968) 6 Brit. J. of Ind. Rel. 1 at 24–25.

[62] "On behalf of " in s. 30.

[63] It was clear even before the (now repealed) Industrial Relations Act 1971, which itself clarified the matter (s. 166), and it remained clear after its repeal. See however, an *obiter dictum* of Lord Denning M.R. in *Chappell* v. *Times Newspapers Ltd.* [1975] I.C.R. 145 at p. 172.

[64] Act on the Joint Regulation of Working Life, 1976, s. 26. See F. Schmidt, *loc.cit.,* pp. 234 *et seq.*

[65] For a discussion of s. 18(4) and (5) of the 1974 Act see below, Chap. 6.

[66] Jacobi, *loc. cit.,* p. 243, nn. 45–46; Raynaud, *Le Contract Collectif de Travail,* 1901, pp. 277 *et seq.*

[67] Smith, Merrifield and St. Antoine, *Labor Relations Law* (4th ed.), p. 822; Gregory, *Labor and the Law* (2nd ed., 1961), p. 447, discussing the position at common law. However, the courts have interpreted s. 301 of the Labor-Management Relations Act 1947 as permitting the individual employee to sue his employer for breach of the collective agreement for discharging him without just cause if the union in breach of its duty of fair representation has not properly processed the employee's grievance: *Hines* v. *Anchor Motor Freight* 424 U.S. 554 (1975).

either against an employer or against an employers' association, claim rights in the capacity of third parties for whose benefit the agreement has been made, seems to have fallen into limbo, and rightly so. In England the question does not arise because the law does not, in principle, allow anyone to derive rights from a contract to which he is not a party, and in Scotland, where the law is different, no one seems as yet to have thought of this ingenious idea. No wonder, considering that only in the most exceptional circumstances can a collective agreement be regarded as a contract in the legal sense at all.[68]

The real crux of the problem of the bargaining "level" however lies in the emergence of the ad hoc "work group"[69] as a collective bargaining party on the workers' side. Traditionally one sees the trade union represented by its central, regional or local officers as the bargaining party, and one assumes that there is a neat distinction between the matters handled at these various levels. This is the classical picture of collective bargaining painted by Sidney and Beatrice Webb.[70] Frequently the reality of our own time still corresponds to this model, but on other occasions it does not. Bargaining about wages may—and in many industries does—occur at several levels simultaneously. One of these levels is often the plant, and on the workers' side it may be conducted not by the constitutional representatives of the union, but by an informal "autonomous" work group[71] holding out (and sometimes striking) for wage increases above those agreed by the union.[72] We have already referred to this shifting of power from the centre to the periphery,[73] to this, in Allan Flanders' words[74] "fragmenta-tion" of collective bargaining. The Donovan Commission[75] identified it as the principal evil of industrial relations in this country at the time of its Report in 1968, but there is evidence that its significance has decreased since then.[76] Moreover, the com-

---

[68] Trade Union and Labour Relations Act 1974, s. 18(1) to (3). See below, Chap. 6.
[69] Clegg, *loc. cit.*, Chap. 2.
[70] *Industrial Democracy*, Pt. 2, Chap. 2.
[71] See Flanders, *Collective Bargaining: Prescription for Change* (1967), p. 29.(This book is the revised version of the evidence the late Allan Flanders gave to the Donovan Commission.)
[72] Evidence of the CBI to the Donovan Commision, paras. 60 *et seq.*; Evidence of the Engineering Employers' Federation, paras. 19 *et seq.*; Donovan Report, Chap. VII.
[73] See above, Chap. 1.
[74] *Loc. cit.*, p. 28.
[75] Chap. 3, see esp. paras. 143 *et seq.*
[76] Wilders and Parker, "Changes in Workplace Industrial Relations 1966–1972" (1975) 13 Brit. J. of Ind. Rel. 22 and W. Brown (ed.) *The Changing Contours of British Industrial Relations* (1981) Chap. 3.

bined efforts of employers and unions, and the work, formerly, of the Commission on Industrial Relations,[77] and now of the Advisory, Conciliation and Arbitration Service[78] may succeed in rationalising shopfloor bargaining. This type of bargaining is, however, likely to remain a feature of our industrial relations.[79] Very often it is a continuous process, just like the collective bargaining process at a higher level which is of the "institutional" or "dynamic" type.[80] Shopfloor bargaining, like "institutional" bargaining, thus illustrates the great difference between collective bargaining and contract making in the clear and traditional legal sense. Even that form of agreement which outwardly resembles a contract may not create anything final, but may be no more than a momentary stop in an unending process.

We are stating this as a fact. It is, perhaps, a deplorable fact, and it may be said that it signifies a deterioration of collective bargaining. To a certain degree it has unquestionably frustrated one of the original purposes of collective bargaining, which is to enable management to calculate its costs on a reasonably predictable basis. But it is one thing to deplore something, and another to ignore it. Those who at one time thought that collective agreements could be made into legally binding contracts by the *ipse dixit* of the legislature were, as events have shown,[81] insufficiently aware of the social facts to which we have referred.

Of the many peculiar characteristics of British collective bargaining we have emphasised three: the institutional or dynamic method, the influence of custom and practice, and the complex structure of the bargaining levels. All this bears a close relation to the connection or lack of connection between industrial relations and the law, and, as we have pointed out more than once, helps to explain why hitherto the law had so little to do with this world of labour relations

Nevertheless, it would be utterly wrong to think that the law had no share in the shaping of collective labour relations in this country until its shortlived intervention in a new role under the Act of 1971. On the contrary: whilst before 1971 it did little to induce the parties to bargain collectively, it made a great and successful effort

---

[77] Industrial Relations Act 1971, ss. 120–123. Now abolished.
[78] Employment Protection Act 1975, ss. 1 *et seq.*, esp. s. 4. See below. The ACAS was first established by Royal Warrant in Sept. 1974 (see Benedictus (1976) 5 I.L.J. 12).
[79] See Boraston, Clegg and Rimmer, *Workplace and Union*, above n. 13, p. 20.
[80] See above, n. 10.
[81] See below, Chap. 6.

to help parties willing to bargain in coming to terms, and, in an indirect way, it also encouraged the observance of concluded agreements.

It is to these three aspects of labour law that we shall now have to turn: the law as a factor in promoting the bargaining process, as a factor in promoting the concluding of agreements, and as a factor in promoting their application and observance.

These matters we shall discuss in the following three chapters.

CHAPTER 4

COLLECTIVE BARGAINING AND THE LAW: PROMOTING NEGOTIATION

1. GENERAL BACKGROUND

COLLECTIVE bargaining presupposes that both unions and employers and their associations are willing to bargain collectively. Willingness to bargain is of course quite different from willingness to agree, and legislation designed to promote negotiation quite different from legislation designed to promote agreement. The willingness of an employer or of an employers' association to bargain with a particular union is know as the "recognition" of that union.[1] One of the most fundamental issues in labour law is whether the law seeks to induce or to compel employers to recognise unions, and, if so, under what conditions. It is a complex issue, because the problem is not the recognition of unions in the abstract, but that of a particular union or unions and it may thus involve questions of a choice between competing unions. Nor is it a problem of collective bargaining in the abstract, but of bargaining on particular matters, and it may thus involve questions of selecting the topics on which employers are under an obligation to negotiate. These difficult matters may be involved, but they need not be. Where an employer refuses to have anything to do with unions altogether, and there still are such employers, the problem of recognition appears untrammelled by any inter-union issues or by the demarcation of negotiable and non-negotiable issues.

The contrast between the development of the law of this country and some other countries, especially of the United States and Canada, but also of Sweden, is most striking. It is here that we can most clearly see the results of the early industrial revolution. In many branches of the British economy the trade unions secured

---

[1] In the Employment Protection Act 1975, "recognition" in relation to a trade union means its recognition by an employer, or two or more associated employers, to any extent for the purpose of collective bargaining (s. 126(1)). This excludes recognition by employers' associations ("associated employers"— see s. 126(1) and 1974 Act, s. 30(5)—are not an employers' association). This reflects the structure of the (now repealed) recognition procedure under the 1975 Act. See below.

their recognition by the employers at a very early stage,[2] far back in the nineteenth century. At first this was true only in certain very important industries, and in many of these until well into the last quarter of the nineteenth century mainly of the skilled workers. After the great struggles during the quarter of a century preceding the outbreak of the First World War—struggles vividly reflected in the case law of that period—collective bargaining spread to the unskilled workers and, very important, to the service industries, especially to transport, including the railways (which was the most controversial matter of all,[3] witness the *Taff Vale*[4] and *Osborne*[5] cases). The law however had no share in the advancement of collective bargaining. During the period from the repeal of the Combination Acts in 1824,[6] that is, from the moment unions ceased to be illegal, until the lifting of the threat of prosecutions for criminal conspiracy in 1875,[7] the criminal courts made it difficult for the unions to use the strike weapon to establish their recognition. During the second formative period of trade unions, that is, after the decisive Dock Strike of 1889,[8] and until the statute of 1906,[9] similar action was repeatedly taken by the civil courts. At both periods the role of the law in promoting collective bargaining was negative rather than positive. At the time of the outbreak of the Second World War trade unions, at least of manual workers, had secured their recognition over wide areas of the economy, more so than in many other comparable countries, but the law had not made it incumbent on any employer to bargain with a union, nor on any union to bargain with an employer. Nor does it seem that either employers or unions desired the law to intervene in this direction. After the Second World War the nationalisation statutes which were then enacted imposed on the public corporations in charge of publicly owned industries an obligation to seek consultations with unions appearing to the corporation in question to be appropriate ones with a view to the

---

[2] Sidney and Beatrice Webb, *Industrial Democracy*, Pt. 2, Chaps. 2 and 3; Clegg, Fox and Thompson, *A History of British Trade Unions since 1889*, Chap. 1.

[3] Only after the railway strike of 1911 did the Amalgamated Society of Railway Servants (subsequently National Union of Railwaymen) obtain recognition from the railway companies. Sidney and Beatrice Webb, *History of Trade Unionism*, (Revised ed., 1926), pp. 528–530.

[4] *Taff Vale Ry.* v. *Amalgamated Society of Railway Servants* [1901] A.C. 426.

[5] *Amalgamated Society of Railway Servants* v. *Osborne* [1910] A.C. 87.

[6] Combination Laws Repeal Act 1824.

[7] Conspiracy and Protection of Property Act 1875,s.3.

[8] Clegg, Fox and Thompson, *loc. cit.*, pp. 55 *et seq.* Perhaps the myth or historic "image" of that dramatic event is even more important than its actual effect.

[9] Trade Disputes Act 1906. See further below, Chap. 8.

conclusion of agreements on negotiating procedures and various related matters.[10] This obligation seems to have been more of political than of legal significance.[11] The reason is that none of the public corporations is likely to refuse bargaining altogether, and the only relevant context of a statutory obligation would have been that of an inter-union dispute. The statutes, however, are (perhaps wisely) framed so as to give to the corporations a wide range of discretion in selecting the union with which they wish to negotiate,[12] and as long as they exercise this discretion, one cannot see how a court could intervene through an order of mandamus.[13]

Here the contrast to the development in the United States is most instructive. The National Labor Relations Act of 1935, one of the great achievements of the President Franklin Roosevelt's First Term, conferred on employees the legal right "to bargain collectively through representatives of their own choosing"[14] and imposed a corresponding legally enforceable obligation on employers, the violation of which was and remains today an "unfair labor practice."[15] The National Labor Relations Board, which is an administrative authority, can order an employer to bargain with a union, but it cannot order him to make an agreement. In other words, the enforcement of this obligation to bargain does not in any sense of the word involve compulsory arbitration.[16] Yet, it is enforcement in the strict legal sense. If the employer does not comply with an order of the Board, the Board can take steps to obtain an enforcement order from the appropriate federal court,[17]

---

[10] Sir Norman Chester, *The Nationalization of British Industry 1945–1951* (1975) pp. 782–796.

[11] K. W. Wedderburn, *The Worker and the Law* (2nd. ed., 1971) p. 165.

[12] *i.e.* which in their opinion are "representative" or "appropriate."

[13] *Gallagher* v. *Post Office* [1970] 3 All E.R. 712; *R.* v. *Post Office ex p. A.S.T.M.S.* [1981] I.C.R. 76 (C.A.). In the latter case it was emphasised that the Post Office did not have a discretion to consult such appropriate unions as it thought fit, but was under a duty to consult all unions which it considered appropriate, and it must give fair and reasonable consideration to the question of whether a particular union was appropriate. However, the Court of Appeal upheld the Post Office's determination that A.S.T.M.S. in the circumstances was not an appropriate union, even though it had a high degree of support amongst the employees in question. *Cf.* the Court of Appeal's decision in *UKAPE* v. *ACAS* [1979] I.C.R. 303, discussed below at p. 101.

[14] s. 7. This was preceded by a similar provision in the Railway Labor Act 1926, as amended in 1936, and by a similar provision on the National Industry Recovery Act 1933, which was, however, declared unconstitutional by the Supreme Court in *Schechter Poultry Corpn.* v. *U.S.*, 295 U.S. 495 (1935).

[15] s.8 (*a*)(5).

[16] On compulsory arbitration, see Chap. 5.

[17] s. 10.

and non-compliance with that order is contempt of court. A corresponding obligation to bargain with employers was imposed upon the unions by the Taft-Hartley Act of 1947.[18] The person against whom an order of the Board is directed can himself take the initiative in challenging its validity in the appropriate federal court.[19]

When this legislation was passed in America, struggles between rival unions were frequent, and these struggles were aggravated by the growth of industrial alongside craft unions (which was partly the result of the Act itself) and by the split, in 1938, of the trade union movement as a whole into two rival groups, the American Federation of Labor (the existing organisation) and the new Congress of Industrial Organisations.[20] Hence, quite inevitably, the legal right to recognition by the employer had to be linked with a highly sophisticated and complex procedure designed to determine with what union the employer would have to bargain.[21] If necessary, this procedure culminates in an election in the plant, ordered and organised by the National Labor Relations Board.[22] But more than that, to eliminate all further trouble, the American legislature took a step by which it introduced into the law a principle of fundamental importance, and, as far as one can see, quite unknown to any European system including our own[23]: once a union is designated as the "statutory bargaining representative," it represents not only its own members, but all workers in the "statutory bargaining unit," which is normally the plant, but can also be a "craft," or, whatever this mysterious word may mean, a "class" of workers. This concept of the "statutory bargaining representative"[24] was pregnant with consequences of the greatest legal and political significance, as was inevitable in a multiracial society. The union was placed under a statutory duty to give "equal protection," *i.e.* representation, to all workers in the unit, irrespective of membership, irrespective of race, creed or anything else.[25]

Legislation of a similar though not identical character has been

---

[18] s.8 (*b*)(3).
[19] s.10 (*f.*).
[20] Smith, Merrifield & St. Antoine, *op. cit.*, pp. 42 *et seq.*
[21] s.9.
[22] s.9 (*c*).
[23] See, however, section 4 below, on Pt. IV of the Employment Protection Act 1975.
[24] Summers and Wellington, *op. cit.*, p. 512.
[25] *Steele* v. *Louisville and Nashville R.R. Co.*, 323 U.S. 192 (1944); Lechmann, "The Union Duty of Fair Representation" (1971) 30 Fed. B.J. 280, 291.

enacted in Canada, both at the federal level, and, with important variations, in all the Provinces.[26]

In the United States collective bargaining got a very considerable stimulus from this legislation. Under it the scope and content of collective bargaining is in practice largely determined by the National Labor Relations Board and by the courts: in determining whether the employer has complied with his duty to bargain, they must inevitably decide about what he has to negotiate.[27] In spite of all this, however, even today collective bargaining covers a comparatively modest portion of the labour force. In Europe, including this country, legislation of this type was unknown until fairly recently. A general statutory recognition procedure was not introduced in this country until 1971. It was repealed with the legislation that created it in 1974, but reintroduced in a modified form in 1975. In 1980, the second set of statutory provisions was repealed and has not been replaced. We shall discuss below[28] what lessons can be learned from this short-lived and often controversial experiment of providing direct support for the extension of collective bargaining. However, almost at the same moment that the British government was repealing the statutory recognition procedure for the second time, the French government, as part of the *"lois Auroux,"* so named after the then Minister of Labour in the socialist government under President Mittérand, was introducing a duty to bargain into French labour law. We have already had cause to remark upon the relatively recent and weak development of collective bargaining in France (and hence, it was suggested, the much stronger growth of regulatory legislation in that country as compared with Britain).[29] The law of November 13, 1982[30] aims boldly to alter this state of affairs through the mechanism of a duty to bargain. Unlike the United States and British legislation, whose aim is or was almost entirely the encouragement of bargaining at establishment or enterprise level, the new French legislation aims to encourage both single-employer bargaining and bargaining at industry level.[31] Although the main emphasis of the legislation can perhaps be said to be upon bargaining at enterprise level, since at industry

---

[26] Carrothers, *Collective Bargaining Law in Canada,* (1965) Chaps. 6–17. The Federal Industrial Relations and Disputes Investigation Act 1948 was, in varying forms, imitated in all the Provinces. See Carrothers, pp. 60 *et seq.*

[27] See Wellington, *Labor and the Legal Process* (1968), p. 75.

[28] pp. 95 *et seq.*

[29] Above, p. 52.

[30] Amending Title III of Book 1 of the *Code du Travail.*

[31] See new Arts. L.132–12 and L.132–27 to L.132–29.

level the duty to bargain is confined to trade unions and employers' associations which are already parties to a collective agreement for the industry,[32] nevertheless fears have been expressed by some commentators that it will be too great a task for the law to develop simultaneously bargaining at two levels, especially at a time when economic circumstances have forced the French government to resort to quite restrictive forms of incomes policy.[33] In interesting contrast to the British legislation, which eschewed penal sanctions in this area,[34] the French legislation imposes upon the employer who fails to comply with the new duty a criminal penalty. However, whilst laying down a procedure the employer must follow, the new French legislation does not explicitly require the employer to bargain "in good faith," the requirement which has been the centrepiece of the enormous judicial exegesis of the statutory obligation to bargain in the United States.[35] Whilst it is clear that the duty to bargain is not *"une obligation de résultat,"* the French judges will have to answer questions, such as whether the duty implies that the employer must adopt reasonable bargaining methods or make reasonable compromises in responding to the unions' demands, with little help from the legislative text. It will be interesting to see if, whether consciously or not, there is any cross-fertilisation from the United States experience to the very different circumstances of French industrial relations.

There is one prominent exception to the statement that statutory recognition procedures in Europe are of recent origin. This is the Swedish Act on the Joint Regulation of Working Life of 1976[36] which takes the place of a statute of 1936 respecting the right of association and the right of collective bargaining.[37] This gives to the trade unions and also to employers and their organisations a "right to negotiation" and imposes a corresponding obligation on the other side. A violation of this obligation

---

[32] See new Art. L.132–12. That it was thought necessary to place such a statutory obligation upon parties to an existing bargaining arrangement is itself a comment upon the state of desuetude into which some areas of French collective bargaining had fallen.

[33] See the stimulating article by R. Soubie, "L'obligation de négocier et sa sanction" *Droit Social*, January 1983, and generally the contents of the articles published in that issue of *Droit Social* under the heading, "Les Reformes—IV."

[34] See below, pp. 114 *et seq.*

[35] See Robert A. Gorman, *Labor Law* (1976), Chap. 20.

[36] ss. 10 *et seq.*, printed in English translation in Folke Schmidt, *Law and Industrial Relations in Sweden* (1977), pp. 235 *et seq.*

[37] Printed in Folke Schmidt, *The Law of Labour Relations in Sweden,* (1962) pp. 251 *et seq.*

entails a liability to pay heavy damages.[38] The structure of the Swedish trade unions made it unnecessary to establish an elaborate procedure for the settlement of inter-union disputes, but there is a provision[39] which gives a limited protection to minority unions. The unions' right to negotiate is re-inforced by a far-reaching right to information, including the inspection of the employer's books and accounts and other relevant documents.[40]

Our interest in this Swedish legislation is especially aroused by the reasons for which it was enacted. These were linked with the transformation of the labour force to which allusion was made in the first chapter. It appears that by the early 1930s manual workers had largely secured from the employers the recognition of the unions as their bargaining representatives. However, as in this country, the growing body of non-manual workers, and especially of clerical workers in private industry and trade, met with frequent and stiff resistance on the employers' part when seeking to organise unions, to join unions, and to initiate collective bargaining. The Swedish statute of 1936 was passed in order to protect the freedom of organisation and the negotiating rights of these workers.

This corresponds very much to the state of affairs which was revealed in this country by the research organised by the Donovan Commission.[41] It was largely, but not exclusively, with an eye to the need for developing collective bargaining among the white collar workers that the Donovan Commission recommended that the law should impose on employers an obligation to recognise unions.[42] This was however not, as in America, to be given effect through legal compulsion, but through voluntary settlement proceedings before the appropriate body,[43] and, in the event of

---

[38] Folke Schmidt, _Law and Industrial Relations in Sweden_ (1977) p. 102.

[39] s.13 of the 1976 Act.

[40] _Ibid._ s. 19.

[41] See G. S. Bain, _Trade Union Growth and Recognition,_ Royal Commision Research Paper No. 6; and also Bain, _The Growth of White Collar Unionism_(1970); Bain and Price, "Union Growth and Employment Trends in the United Kingdom, 1964–1970" (1972) 10 Brit. J. of Ind. Rel. 366; "Union Growth Revisited: 1948–1974 in Perspective" (1976) 14 Brit. J. Ind. Rel. 339. The latter article shows how rapidly things are changing: as of 1974, 36 per cent. of all union members were white collar workers, and 35.2 per cent. of all white collar workers were union members. By 1978, it has been estimated, 48 per cent. of white-collar workers employed in manufacturing industry in establishments of at least 50 employees were union members: W. Brown (ed.), _The Changing Contours of British Industrial Relations_ (1981) p. 51.

[42] Cmnd. 3623, paras. 220 _et seq._

[43] Then the Commission on Industrial Relations, now the Advisory, Conciliation and Arbitration Service (ACAS). See below.

the employer rejecting its recommendation or evading negotiations with the union, through the binding unilateral determination of wages and other conditions by what was then the Industrial Court[44] and is now the Central Arbitration Committee.[45] Whilst American legislation says to the employer: "if you do not make a genuine attempt to come to terms with the union, we shall punish you for contempt until you do," the Donovan proposals and the laws which carried them into effect said: "very well, you do not want to negotiate, we cannot force you, but, if you persist in this, you will have to pay and otherwise treat your workers in accordance with terms in the shaping of which you had no part." This however was expected to happen only in the most exceptional situations.

To some extent the (now repealed)[46] provisions of the Industrial Relations Act 1971[47] were based on these recommendations. However, in at least three vital respects they adopted a diametrically different policy. In the first place the 1971 Act followed the American pattern in linking the recognition procedure with the settlement of inter-union conflicts and thus made the entire recognition problem appear as merely incidental to the solution of inter-union disputes, and to the reduction of their injurious effect on the industry. Secondly, the Act reserved the power of enforcing recognition to those trade unions which were "registered," and, as things developed in practice, the refusal of all major unions attached to the TUC to be registered turned the mechanism of the Act principally—but by no means entirely[48]—into an instrument for the use of an insignificant minority of unions, often, but not always, "staff associations," sometimes created under managerial influence. The provisions of the statute, intended to promote

---

[44] Created by the Industrial Courts Act 1919, in 1971 renamed Industrial Arbitration Board, now abolished and replaced by the Central Arbitration Committee. See below. The former Industrial Court (which was an arbitration board) must not of course be mixed up with the National Industrial Relations Court, created by the Industrial Relations Act 1971, and abolished by the Trade Union and Labour Relations Act 1974. For brevity this was often referred to as the "Industrial Court," but it had nothing to do with the arbitration board of that name which since 1971 and until its demise was called the Industrial Arbitration Board.

[45] Employment Protection Act 1975, s. 10 and Sched. 1. See below.

[46] Trade Union and Labour Relations Act 1974, s.1.

[47] ss. 44–55, ss. 121–122.

[48] See Weekes, Mellish, Dickens and Lloyd, *Industrial Relations and the Limits of Law. The Industrial Effects of the Industrial Relations Act 1971* (Oxford 1975), Chap. 5, esp. pp. 131 *et seq.* The main exception was the National Union of Bank Employees. See, *e.g. N.U.B.E.* v. *Barclays Bank Ltd.* [1973] I.C.R. 167; *N.U.B.E.* v. *Anglia Building Society* [1973] I.C.R. 197.

collective bargaining, had occasionally a disruptive effect in encouraging small registered minority unions as against the recognised but unregistered majority union and thus provoked or exacerbated, instead of settling or assuaging, interunion conflicts, as happened in the already celebrated or notorious dispute in the Post Office.[49] Thirdly, a key positon was given to the (now abolished) National Industrial Relations Court, and to the extent to which this was done the ultimate control of recognition and its enforcement acquired the characteristics of a judicial process. One of the centrally important aspects of this was the prohibition of all strikes and other industrial action for the purposes of obtaining recognition, as long as proceedings before the Court were "pending,"[50] or after it had either made an order or (for two years) after it had received a report from the Commission on Industrial Relations.[51]

2. TRADE UNION RECOGNITION UNDER THE EMPLOYMENT PROTECTION ACT

In all these, and in some other, directions, the relevant provisions of the Employment Protection Act 1975 signified a complete break with the policy of 1971 and largely a return to, and in some respects a development beyond, the Donovan Recommendations. A "recognition issue" was now defined[52] as an issue arising from a request by a trade union to be recognised by an employer (or two or more associated employers)[53] for purposes of collective bargaining, and the subtitle of the relevant group of provisions is no longer "recognition of sole bargaining agent," but "trade union

---

[49] *i.e.* the dispute between the recognised, but unregistered Union of Post Office Workers (about 2000,000 members, including about 40,000 telephonists) and the registered, but unrecognised Telecommunication Staff Association (about 10,000 members) about the latter's right to display notices, etc. on post office premises, a dispute which ended with the TSA's victory in the Court of Appeal (*Post Office* v. *Crouch* [1973] I.C.R. 366) and the House of Lords (*Post Office* v. *Union of Post Office Workers* [1974] I.C.R. 378). One's instinctive desire to sympathise (to paraphrase Lord Denning M.R.) with "David" against "Goliath" should be overcome by one's insight into the urgent need for stable labour relations. Further litigation culminated in the decision of the House of Lords in *UPW* v. *TSA* [1974] I.C.R. 658.

[50] As defined in s. 54 of the Act, a fair sample of its immense legal complexity.

[51] s.55.

[52] Employment Protection Act 1975, s. 11(3). The corresponding formulation in s. 45(1) of the 1971 Act referred to the determination of the bargaining unit and of the sole bargaining agent.

[53] *i.e.* parent, subsidiary or sister companies: Employment Protection Act 1975, s. 126(1) in conjunction with Trade Union and Labour Relations Act 1974, s. 30(5). Note that there is no reference to employers' associations. See below.

recognition."[54] The promotion and the extension of collective bargaining were thus treated as the dominant policies of the law. These policies might involve the need for answering three questions: Should the employer be induced to bargain at all? If so, about what? And if so, with whom? The last is the "inter-union" question, and it thus appears as only one of three. Moreover, the difference between registered and unregistered unions had disappeared: under the provisions of the 1974 Act[55] discussed in a subsequent chapter, a union may be "listed," but listing, although a pre-requisite to a certificate of independence,[56] no longer carried the connotation of state control of the union's rule-book. Lastly, not only the courts, but also the Department of Employment had ceased to participate in the recognition procedure which had been entrusted to the ACAS.[57]

An even more obviously striking aspect of the 1975 Act's provisions was the extent to which they were used. As we have seen, the corresponding provisions of the 1971 Act could be activated only, so far as unions were concerned, by registered trade unions. The 1975 Act procedure, on the other hand, was open to all "independent"[58] trade unions, and, whereas only 64 applications were made for recognition under the 1971 Act.[59] ACAS under the 1975 Act handled, 1,610 recognition issues between February 1, 1976 and August 15, 1980. In 69 per cent. of the cases the Service achieved a conciliated settlement during the course of its investigations into the issue, and in about half of these cases the employer granted some form of recognition. In 15 per cent of cases no agreement was reached and the service issued a report. In two thirds of reports recognition was recommended but less than half of such reports were accepted by the employers concerned.[60] Yet, in spite of this apparently high rate of success, especially in achieving conciliated settlements, on June 29, 1979

---

[54] Compare the heading preceding s. 44 of the 1971 Act with that preceding s. 11 of the 1975 Act.

[55] s.8, as amended by Employment Protection Act 1975, Sched. 16. Pt.III and by the Trade Union and Labour Relations (Amendment) Act 1976, s. 1 (c).

[56] The Certification Officer under s.8 of the 1975 Act has the power and the duty conclusively to decide whether a union is independent or not. This applies only to "listed" unions.

[57] *i.e.* the Advisory, Conciliation and Arbitration Service.

[58] The notion of independence is discussed *infra* at pp. 213 and 283.

[59] See Weekes, *op. cit.,* p. 302. In a further 34 cases, applications were made which objected to existing bargaining arrangements.

[60] ACAS, *Annual Report 1980,* p. 31. Chap. 8 of the Report contains a detailed consideration of the ACAS experience under the statutory recognition procedure.

the chairman of ACAS wrote to the Secretary of State for Employment stating the view of its governing council to be that "it cannot satsifactorily operate the statutory recognition procedures as they stand"[61] and that the Service's effectiveness in its other areas of responsibility was being undermined by its obligations under the recognition procedure. The response of the incoming Conservative government was not to reform the statutory procedure, but to repeal the relevant provisions of the 1975 Act, so that British labour law reverted once again to its pre-1971 posture of containing no general[62] procedure by which employers could be legally compelled to recognise and bargain with appropriate trade unions. The sudden demise, after a period of experimentation of less than a decade, of the stautory recognition procedure seems attributable to three causes: the extent of the control which the courts, initially at least, seemed to wish to exercise over the service's functioning; the difficulties which the Service's tripartite Council had in developing criteria to decide recognition issues; and the diminished commitment of the new Conservative Government ment to the traditional policies of encouraging the growth of collective bargaining. We shall look at each cause in turn.

(a) ACAS and the courts

The recognition procedure contained in the 1975 Act was premised upon a policy of excluding the courts. In contrast to the 1971 Act's procedure, references of recognition issues were to be made by independent trade unions directly to ACAS[63] (and not via a court) and, if the result of the Service's investigation were a recommendation in favour of recognition, that recommendation would be operative of its own force[64] and would not need the approval of any court, still less approval in a court-ordered ballot. Enforcement of the recommendation was by means of binding unilateral arbitration by the Central Arbitration Committee on a claim for improved terms and conditions of employment,[65] which, as we have seen, was also the enforcement procedure under the 1971 Act, but under the 1975 Act the Committee had to determine also the prior question of whether the recommendation was being

---

[61] The chairman's letter is reproduced as Appendix C to the *Annual Report 1979*.

[62] The provisions in the public sector, discussed above, remain in force. The separate provisions for Northern Ireland based on the 1975 Act but contained in the Industrial Relations (Northern Ireland) Order 1976, arts. 7–8, also remain in force.

[63] Employment Protection Act 1975, s. 11(1).

[64] s.15(1).

[65] s.15(2)(*b*) and (6).

complied with,[66] a task entrusted under the 1971 Act to the National Industrial Relations Court.[67] No provision was made for an appeal from the Service's recommendation.

However, merely to give the courts no formal role in the recognition procedure could not be effective to exclude them from their common law jurisdiction of ensuring that public authorities act within the law. No attempt was made expressly to exclude the common law supervisory jurisdiction of the ordinary courts, and it is doubtful whether such an attempt, if it had been made, would have proved completely effective. Nevertheless, the 1975 Act was drafted so as to give the Service a very broad discretion, thus apparently reducing the scope for argument that the Service had exceeded its powers or acted improperly in some other way. The 1975 Act, as we have noted, no longer contained concepts such as "bargaining unit" or "sole bargaining agent" and their associated statutory definitions.[68] Instead, if the Service failed to settle the issue by conciliation during the course of its investigations into it—and such conciliated settlements were expected and indeed proved to be the main way of resolving these matters—then the Service's duty was stated in neutral terms as being to "prepare a written report setting out its findings, any advice in connection with those findings and any recommendation for recognition and the reasons for it" or, where no recommendation was made, the reasons for not making one.[69] The Act was virtually bereft of criteria which would compel the Service to make or not to make a recommendation for recognition in any particular set of circumstances or which would, if it did make a recommendation, determine the content of the recommendation.[70]

The approach embodied in the Act might thus be thought to be that policy on recognition issues should be developed by ACAS, under the guidance of its tripartite Council. It was not, however, until extensive litigation had been pursued in the courts that this perception was reaffirmed by the House of Lords in early 1980, but by this time the die was cast, for the then Government had determined upon the repeal of the procedure. Indeed, the first case to come before their lordships went against the Service.

---

[66] s.16(2)(*a*).
[67] Industrial Relations Act 1971, ss. 101(1) and 105(5).
[68] s.44 (*a*) and (*c*).
[69] Employment Protection Act 1975, s. 12 (4).
[70] s. 12(5) of the Act required the Service to specifiy the employer, unions and workers covered by the reommendation, the level at which recognition was to be granted, and the subjects of bargaining, but it did not specify how these matters were to be determined.

Although the Service was generally left very free by the Act in the conduct of its investigations into recognition issues, it was provided that "the Service shall ascertain the opinions of workers to whom the issue relates by any means it thinks fit."[71] In the case of *Grunwick Processing Laboratories Ltd.* v. *ACAS*[72] the employer in question had refused to provide the Service—he was under no legal obligation to do so—with the names and addresses of the majority of the workforce, so that the Service had been able to obtain the opinions only of the union members amongst the workforce, who were in fact on strike at the time in pursuit of their claim for recognition and who were, not surprisingly, overwhelmingly in favour of recognition being granted. On the basis of the opinions expressed by this part of the workforce, the Service recommended in favour of recognition, which recommendation was held by the House of Lords to be *ultra vires* the Service. The provision quoted above placed upon ACAS a mandatory (rather than a directory) duty to obtain the opinions of the workforce as a whole, and the duty was not to be qualified by the implication of words such as "so far as reasonably practicable." The courts' expressed policy of protecting the interests of the workforce as a whole was, it might be thought, only doubtfully implemented by allowing the employer to hinder the Service's investigations in this way, and the decision seems to have contributed to a growing reluctance by employers to cooperate fully with the Service's investigations.[73] By the end of 1979 the Service estimated that in over one quarter of the cases then being handled full cooperation was not forthcoming and in some 11 cases, including Grunwick itself, the Service had ultimately to conclude that it could not ascertain the opinions of the workforce as a whole and that it was therefore in no position to make a recommendation one way or another.[74] Thus, although the House of Lords had been careful to point out in the judgements that ACAS need not obtain the opinion of every single worker and that the provision quoted above gave the Service a wide discretion as to the means by which it obtained the employees' opinions (a questionnaire being one only of the available methods), nevertheless the decision did coincide with a growing dissatisfaction on the part of employers with the recognition procedure and encouraged them to withhold the voluntary cooperation with ACAS investigations on which the procedure was premised.

---

[71] s. 14(1).
[72] [1978] I.C.R. 231 (H.L.).
[73] ACAS, *Annual Report 1979*, p. 27.
[74] ACAS, *Annual Report 1980*, p. 77.

Although the *Grunwick* decision was an important one for the Service, it was concerned with the procedure for investigation of recognition issues and not with the heart of the recognition question, *viz.* the criteria on which recognition was to be granted or refused, in relation to which the Act had taken such pains to make the Service the sole judge. This, however, was the question at the centre of the litigation arising out of a claim for recognition at W. H. Allen Ltd.[75] The issue was referred by UKAPE, a non-TUC union, on behalf of some 150 professional engineers amongst whom UKAPE had a high level of support. The employer had granted a very minimal form of recognition[76] in respect of those workers to a TUC union, which was also a member of the Confederation of Shipbuilding and Engineering Unions (CSEU), the recognised bargaining partner of the Engineering Employers' Federation (EEF) at national level in this industry, and of which UKAPE, again, was not a member. Although UKAPE would normally have been regarded by the Service as having a strong claim to recognition by the employer on account of the level of employee support, the Service, supported by the employer and EEF as well as by the TUC union, recommended against recognition, essentially on the grounds that it was undesirable further to fragment representation arrangments in the engineering industry by granting recognition, at least in these particular circumstances, to a non-CSEU union.

The report of ACAS was declared void by May J. and the Court of Appeal. Lord Denning M.R. took the view that the provision in the Act that "the Service shall be charged with the general duty of promoting the improvement of industrial relations and in particular of encouraging the extension of collective bargaining,"[77] required the Service to place the extension of collective bargaining as a goal above that of improving industrial relations. This might be thought not to be an obvious reading of the words, and by applying this duty, which is contained in the first section of the Act and governs the whole of the Service's activities and not just its role in the now-repealed recognition procedure, the Master of the Rolls came close to suggesting that the only proper matter to which the Service could give consideration was the wishes of the employees. The majority of the court concurred in the result on

---

[75] *UKAPE* v. *ACAS* [1979] I.C.R. 303 (C.A.); [1980] I.C.R. 201 (H.L.)

[76] This was described as "non-procedural" recognition, which did not give the union the right to raise collective issues and probably did not amount to "recognition" at all as far as the statutory definition of the term was concerned. See s. 11(2)—now s. 126(1)—of the 1975 Act.

[77] s.1(2).

the basis that the Service had not made sufficient findings to justify its conclusions, but both lines of reasoning were rejected by the House of Lords. Giving the leading speech Lord Scarman concluded that "it is plain that it is Parliament's intention that recognition issues are for ACAS and the Central Arbitration Committee. It is their discretion, their judgment, which is to determine such issues."[78] The scope of judicial review was correspondingly to be restricted. A month later the House of Lords handed down its decision in the case of *EMA* v. *ACAS*,[79] which confirmed the Service's discretion not to proceed with its investigation into a complicated recognition dispute, involving a variety of inter-union rivalries, whilst it attempted to utilise voluntary conciliation machinery, notably the Bridlington procedures of the TUC, to resolve at least some of the competing claims. The two decisions of the House of Lords did much to restore the Service's control over both the procedure and the substance of the legislative provisions on recognition, but, as we have seen, both decisions came too late.

(b) ACAS Council and recognition

The corollary to the legislative view (eventually accepted also by the courts) that the development of policy on recognition matters was not to be in the hands of the courts was that such policy should be developed by the Service itself and, in particular, by the governing council of ACAS. This may have seemed in 1975 an unproblematic proposition. After all, the Commission on Industrial Relations, in many ways the predecessor to ACAS, had made considerable progress in developing criteria for the identification of appropriate unions in such cases and some, though rather less, progress on criteria for the identification of appropriate groups of workers to be represented.[80] In one crucial respect, however, the CIR differed from ACAS. The Commission consisted entirely of persons appointed as independent experts in industrial relations (though they came from a variety of backgrounds), whilst it was seen as vital in securing the support of employers and trade unions for ACAS after the traumas of the Industrial Relations Act that the Council of the Service should be predominantly a representative body. Thus, three of the ten members are nominated in effect by the CBI and three by the TUC.[81] Three members only are

---

[78] [1980] I.C.R. at p. 210.
[79] [1980] I.C.R. 215 (H.L.).
[80] CIR, *Trade Union Recognition: CIR Experience* (1974).
[81] Sched. 1, para. 2.

independents with no representative function, and the final member is the full-time chairman. The tripartite constitution of ACAS is seen as a way of giving reality to the formal legal position, as enshrined in the Act, of the Service as an independent body corporate, not "subject to directions of any kind from any Minister,"[82] though, of course, the Government does control the size of the Service's budget.

However, the tripartite nature of the Council made it difficult for the Council to develop criteria for recognition cases, for in contrast to the other work which ACAS has been given, which we shall examine in the next chapter and where there is a high degree of consensus between employers and employees, recognition is not an uncontroversial matter.[83] Trade unions probably tend to the view that any group of members who wish to bargain with their employer ought to be entitled to do so, provided that the union which represents them would not thereby be trespassing on another union's sphere of influence. This view makes little concession to queries about whether those members form a coherent group for bargaining purposes or what proportion of the group the union members represent. Employers, on the other hand, tend to stress the need to have employees in coherent groups for the purposes of bargaining and to wish the major factor in the assessment of coherence to be the organisational structure and needs of the employer. Once a coherent group has been defined, recognition should be granted or refused simply by determining whether a majority of the group want it. This approach might result in making the achievement of recognition a very difficult task for trade unions in certain circumstances, *e.g.* to take a common problem, where in a multi-plant company the employer insists on a bargaining unit for a particular grade of worker that is company-wide.

The practice of ACAS, building on that of the CIR, was somewhat in between the two views. The Service paid attention to the need to have coherent bargaining groups, but regarded union organisation as being as important as employer structure in determining them. The Service was also concerned about the level of employee support within the group for recognition, but was never committed to a simple majority test. The question was whether there was sufficient support within the group to establish viable collective negotiations with the employer; in some cases less

---

[82] Sched. 1, para. 11(1).
[83] H. A. Clegg, *The Changing System of Industrial Relations in Great Britain* (1979), pp. 415–419.

than a majority might be enough.[84] Given the differences of
opinion between employers and trade unions, this middle course
became increasingly difficult to sustain, especially as employers'
attitudes began to harden generally against the Labour Government's legislation of 1974–1976. In his letter to the Secretary of
State of June 29, 1979 the Chairman of ACAS stated bluntly: "nor
has it been possible for the Council to agree on any such criteria
for recognition which would be generally applicable,"[85] and a
projected code of practice on recognition was never produced.
Indeed, the Chairman expressed the fear that lack of consensus
over recognition matters was hampering the Service in its other
areas of activity, where consensus ought to be readily achievable.
This line of thought even led the Council, through its Chairman, to
criticise the failure of the draftsmen of the Act to include criteria
for recognition in the statute.[86] This point sits rather oddly in a
letter which also complained of the degree to which it then
appeared the courts had fettered ACAS's discretion. Any set of
statutory criteria that would have effectively relieved the Council
of the need to resolve its internal divisions would both have
removed the Service's flexibility in particular cases and have
provided an open invitation to judicial scrutiny on the grounds that
the Service had not properly implemented its statutory mandate.

(c) Government policy and collective bargaining

Whether the conflict between the need for flexibility and
discretion and the tripartite composition of the ACAS Council
could have been resolved can only be guessed at, for the
Conservative Government, elected in 1979, decided not to reform
but to repeal the recognition procedure of the 1975 Act. One
question that is raised is whether this decision represents a
fundamental change in the attitude of government towards the
encouragement of collective bargaining. It has been public policy
in Britain, at least since the Whitley Committee Reports of the
First World War and perhaps even earlier, to encourage the
spread of collective bargaining. That policy has been more or less
strongly expressed at different times, but it has remained. On the
other hand the implementation of that public policy was not seen
to require legislation until the Industrial Relations Act 1971, so
that repeal of the recognition provisions does not necessarily

---

[84] On the early approach of ACAS to recognition issues see ACAS, *Annual Report
    1976,* Chap. 9, and Dickens, "ACAS and the Union Recognition Procedure"
    (1978) 9 I.L.J. 160.
[85] *Op. cit.* at p. 111.
[86] *Ibid.*

represent an abandonment of the public policy. Moreover, the recognition procedure of the 1975 Act can be seen as the greatest departure from the traditional "non-interventionist" stance of British labour law towards positive encouragement of collective bargaining that the legislation of 1974–1976 contained,[87] and therefore, perhaps, to some extent as aberrant. Further, the need for such a legal procedure, closely identified by the Donovan Commission with the spread of white-collar employment, may be questioned. Since the Donovan Commission reported, British trade unions have in fact made great strides in the recruitment of such workers, even in the private sector of the economy,[88] and yet it is not clear how great a contribution to this growth the various procedures for encouraging recognition have made. Thus, the 1975 Act procedure, in spite of its high rate of use, resulted in recognition only in respect of some 65,000 workers (an average of some 130 workers in each case where the Service achieved some form of recognition from the employer) and ACAS has concluded that "recognition stemming directly from section 11 references . . . had no more than a marginal impact except in one or two sectors of industry."[89] On the other hand, throughout the period of operation of the procedure the Service handled a greater number of recognition issues under its voluntary conciliation powers, which have not been altered by the 1980 Act and which are discussed below,[90] and recognition was achieved by these means in respect of some 77,500 workers.[91] Even greater strides were made by unions through voluntary efforts that did not even require ACAS conciliation. What is unclear is how far the presence of statutory procedure in the background was essential to the success of these voluntary efforts.

The above arguments might suggest that repeal of the statutory recognition procedure is not necessarily inconsistent with a public policy favourable to recognition. On the other hand, there is evidence that this public policy has indeed undergone a sea change. Traditional public policy has usually been formulated in terms of a choice between collective bargaining and individual

---

[87] "The attempt to reconstruct in 1974 a non-interventionist structure of collective labour law may be inconsistent with too many interventions by statute at the *collective* level . . . ": Lord Wedderburn of Charlton, "The New Structure of Labour Law in Britain." (1978) 13 *Israel Law Review* 455.

[88] Some figures are given in Bain and Price, "Union Growth Revisited: 1948–1971 in Perspective" (1976) 14 Brit. J. of Ind. Rel. 339. The authors do attach significance to the climate of public policy favouring recognition.

[89] ACAS, *Annual Report 1980*, pp. 99–100.

[90] Chap. 5.

[91] *Op. cit.* p. 65.

bargaining (or, more likely, unilateral imposition of terms by the employer) from the point of view of which is the more equitable and efficient method of resolving conflicts of interest. This viewpoint is well expressed in the following passage from the First General Report of the C.I.R:

> "Employees naturally have a collective interest in such matters as pay and conditions. In our view, the task of managment is most effectively and acceptably performed by recognising that interest, allowing for its organisation and expression and seeking to reconcile the interests of the employees with other aspects of management responsibility. We do not believe that where pay and conditions are determined solely by the management this means that there is no conflict of interest; it merely means that the method of resolving the conflict is by unilateral management decision. Such a system may produce good pay and conditions and be accepted without overt protest, but we think that more is to be gained in terms of efficiency and satisfaction when the employees concerned are actively associated with management in joint consideration of these matters."[92]

A more recent concern with collective bargaining is expressed in terms of its economic effects, notably its impact upon the external labour market (in terms of inflation in particular) and upon the labour market within firms (mainly in terms of working practices). It would not be surprising if a Government committed to a more market-oriented analysis of economic problems (as that elected in 1979 was) should accord the public policy itself, and not just certain manifestations of it, a low priority. And we shall see in later chapters that it was not only recognition procedure that was repealed in 1980 but also the much more long-standing legal policy of underpinning the results of national and district collective bargaining by bringing underpaid employees into line with the minimum levels settled by collective agreement, whilst subsequently the Fair Wages Resolution has been rescinded, wages councils subjected to criticism from government ministers, and requirements of union recognition in commercial contracts made unlawful.

3. DISCLOSURE OF INFORMATION

In the Employment Protection Act 1975 the provisions containing the statutory recognition procedure, which has now

---

[92] Cmnd. 4417, 1970, para. 31.

been repealed, appeared in Part I of the Act which is entitled, "Machinery for Promoting the Improvement of Industrial Relations." In addition to the recognition procedure the Act contained, and continues to contain, the provisions establishing ACAS and setting out its "voluntary" functions[93] and provisions for the disclosure of information by employers for the purposes of collective bargaining. Thus, perhaps rather oddly, the legislative policy of promoting collective bargaining by requiring the disclosure of information where bargaining arrangments already exist is continued, whereas the policy of using the law to promote collective bargaining by encouraging the establishment of bargaining arrangements has been severely curtailed.[94]

(a) The two aspects of "disclosure" in labour relations

If the law imposes on employers a duty to disclose to the workers' side financial and other information concerning the past record, present state, and future prospects of the enterprise, it may pursue two different (though allied) objectives. It may be the policy of the law to enable the unions to negotiate, without being, by lack of factual knowledge—as the 1975 Act says[95]—"to a material extent impeded in carrying on . . . collective bargaining." The obligation to disclose is thus subservient to the promotion of collective bargaining, and this is its only function and purpose under the present law. It provides for disclosure to recognised unions of information by the employer relating to his undertaking.

An employer's legal duty to keep the workers informed about the state of the enterprise may however also have (but does not have under the present British law) the object of strengthening the interest of the individual worker in the prospects of the undertaking, and perhaps of enabling him thereby also to gauge his own prospects within it, to assess the degree of job security and the chances of improving the position he enjoys. The 1971 Act (which also provided for disclosure of information to trade unions, albeit "registered" unions only[96]) had a provision[97] by which larger employers had to supply each of their employees with an annual

---

[93] These are discussed below in Chap. 5.

[94] The various provisions applying to specific areas of the public sector continue unaffected by the repeal of the general recognition procedure. See above p. 89.

[95] s. 17(1) (a), the duty to disclose information to recognised trade unions imposed upon companies by the Industry Act 1975, Part IV (repealed by the Industry Act 1980) was not directly linked with collective bargaining, but served the need "for consultation between Government, employers and workers on the outlook for a particular sector of manufacturing industry" (s. 28(1)).

[96] Industrial Relations Act 1971, s. 56.

[97] *Ibid.* s. 57.

statement relating to the past financial year. This provision has been dropped in the 1975 Act.[98] Under the present law workers are entitled to information exclusively for bargaining purposes, *i.e.* in their capacity as union representatives. This may express the deliberate policy—visible throughout the present law—not to encourage collective activities or relations within the plant or enterprise other than those between the union or unions (and their representatives) and the employer. The disclosure of information to the workforce of an enterprise irrespective of union membership is regarded as undesirable within the framework of such a policy, as undesirable as, *e.g.* the election of a works council of the French or German pattern which the TUC rejects[99] or even the election by the workers (in addition to appointment by the union) of safety representatives at plant level which was envisaged by the Health and Safety at Work, etc., Act 1974,[1] in a provision repealed by the Act of 1975.[2] It could be argued that the provision in the 1971 Act about the annual statement did not make much sense in the absence of a statutory works council or similar body to whom the statement could be made, as is the case under the German Works Constitution Law of 1972.[3] The German works councils deal with individual grievances, but they also enter for certain purposes into agreements with the employer.[4] Their right to obtain information must be seen in both contexts. In this country—as, *e.g.* in the United States—the trade unions are the

---

[98] Many employers do in fact make certain information available to their employees individually, but that is now regarded as a matter for the companies and their employees to decide for themselves. The present Government does not propose to implement the recommendation of the Bullock Committee that companies provide copies of their statutory annual report and accounts to employees on the grounds that these "will not . . . in many cases be the most appropriate means of presenting information to employees" *Company Accounting and Disclosure* (Cmnd. 7654, 1979), p.8.

[99] *Industrial Democracy,* a Statement of Policy by the Trades Union Congress, 1975, para. 93.

[1] *Ibid.* s. 57.

[2] Employment Protection Act 1975, s. 116; Sched. 15, para. 2. S. 2(4) of the Health and Safety at Work Act 1974, which refers to the appointment of safety representatives by a recognised union, remains in force.

[3] ss. 106 *et seq.* A comparison of the matters to be disclosed to the German works council (or its "economic committee") according to s. 106(3) and those which should be disclosed to negotiators in the opinion of the TUC (*Industrial Democracy, supra,* para. 77) shows that the unions in this country demand far more specific information about the economic performance and prospects of the enterprise than is vouchsafed to the German statute which (see below) is in other respects superior to our present law.

[4] *Ibid.* s. 85 and s. 77.

only collective representation the workers have, the only counter-vailing power on their side. The law has implemented the policy of the TUC to reject statutory plant or enterprise representation. Consequently only unions or—this is vital—union representatives at enterprise and especially at plant level are under the 1975 Act entitled to information. These representatives may of course be full time officials, but they may also be shop stewards negotiating at plant level or shop stewards' committees negotiating at enterprise level. The ACAS Code[5] recommends that the trade unions should keep the employer informed of the names of the relevant representatives, and that, whenever possible, two or more recognised unions should co-ordinate their requests.

Where a statutory workers' council system is in place, it is also easy for the employer to know whom he must consult. In the U.K. where the law turns upon the recognition of an independent trade union, it may not always be clear whether relations between employer and union have developed to the point of falling within the statutory definition of recognition as being "recognition of the union by an employer, to any extent, for the purpose of collective bargaining."[6] The Court of Appeal has held that membership by an employer of an employers' federation which bargains with the union is not by itself recognition of the union by the employer member of the federation.[7] This decision reflects the policy of the Donovan Commission, embodied in the current legislation, that, where the law is used to support and encourage collective bargaining, it should be bargaining at plant, company or group (see the reference to "associated employers")[8] level that benefits, rather than multi-employer bargaining at district or national level within an industry. The Court of Appeal also held in this case that the preliminary direct contacts between union and employer did not on the facts tip the scales in favour of recognition, apparently because they did not demonstrate that the employer had accepted the union for the purposes of joint regulation of the employees'

---

[5] ACAS Code No. 2, paras. 17, 18.
[6] Employment Protection Act 1975, s. 126(1).
[7] *N.U.G.S.A.T.* v. *Albury Bros.* [1979] I.C.R. 1076.
[8] Employers are associated "if one is a company of which the other (directly or indirectly) has control, or if both are companies of which a third person (directly or indirectly) has control": Trade Union and Labour Relations Act 1974, s. 30(5). This definition of associated employers, dependent as it is upon the presence of a limited company, is wholly inadequte for, indeed often inapplicable to, the public service sector of the economy: *Merton L.B.C.* v. *Gardiner* [1981] I.C.R. 186 (C.A.).

terms and conditions of employment, but only for discussion on these matters.[9]

All this does not however fully explain why the employer's duty to give information to workers individually and irrespective of collective bargaining negotiations has now completely disappeared. As said above, a provision of this type may serve the individual interest of the worker, quite outside any collective nexus. The TUC itself, in formulating its policy in 1974,[10] whilst laying the main emphasis on disclosure for negotiating purposes, also took the view that individual workers should, as of right, be entitled to all information circulated to shareholders, and, in addition, to information about terms and conditions of employment, job specifications and employment prospects, and that they have the statutory right to see their personal files and to have them explained. Hence the TUC then favoured a statutory regulation embracing both objectives of disclosure as formulated above, but the Act of 1975 adopted only one of the two aspects of this policy.

(b) Recognition and disclosure

Disclosure for the purpose of facilitating collective bargaining is no more than one aspect of recognition. Negotiation does not deserve its name if one of the negotiating partners is kept in the dark about matters within the exclusive knowledge of the other which are relevant to an agreement. The financial record and prospects of the enterprise are obviously relevant to wage negotiations, but intended changes in production methods may— to take only one further example—be equally significant for bargaining about possible redundancies and their consequences. In the United States an employer who does not provide the necessary information to the union is considered as having refused to bargain in good faith and thus as having committed an "unfair labor practice."[11] In this country it is very doubtful whether the courts would have allowed the ACAS and the CAC to give so wide an interpretation to the statutory term "recognition." It was therefore necessary specially to provide that a trade union may by a request in writing make it legally incumbent on an employer to

---

[9] See also *R.* v. *CAC ex p. B.T.P. Tioxide Ltd.* [1982] I.C.R. 843 on the status of individual grievance representation under the statutory definition of collective bargaining.

[10] *Industrial Democracy*, above, para. 72.

[11] This has been established law since shortly after the passing of the National Labor Relations Act. The *locus classicus* is the opinion of Mr. Justice Black, (delivering the opinion of the United States Supreme Court) in *National Labor Relations Board* v. *Truitt Manufacturing Co.*, 351 U.S. 149 (1956). See further Gorman, *loc. cit.*, pp. 409–415.

disclose to its representatives such relevant information closely linked with the duty to negotiate. To be able to make this request, the union must not only be "independent,"[12] but it must be recognised by the employer. More than that: the employer's duty to disclose is circumscribed by the scope of the recognition. That is: he does not have to disclose anything that does not refer to the workers or to the matters with reference to whom or to which the union is recognised. If the union has been recognised only with respect to workers on the production line, it cannot ask for information on intended technical changes which affect the maintenance workers only, and if it has not succeeded in extending the scope of bargaining to pensions schemes, it cannot request the employer to inform it about their funding. On the other hand, it does not follow that a union may not ask successfully for information which relates to workers in respect of whom the union is not recognised, provided that the information is relevant to bargaining about other workers in respect of whom the union is recognised. Where the two sets of workers are represented by different unions, such claims may be controversial in industrial relations terms, and the CAC, whilst upholding the principle, has proceeded cautiously when awarding disclosure in such circumstances.[13]

(c) What must be disclosed

Nothing need be disclosed that does not refer to the undertaking involved or to that of an "associated employer," *i.e.* of a parent, subsidiary or sister company.[14] Nor is the union entitled to any information unless its absence would impede collective bargaining "to a material extent." But further than this the law cannot go in specifying what can be demanded. All it can do for further specification is to refer to "good industrial practice" and to leave it to the ACAS through its flexible Codes to fill in the blank.[15] Nor is the 1975 Act more specific in defining what need not be disclosed.[16] The employer may withhold any facts if their disclosure would be incompatible with national security or with a statutory prohibition, or a breach of the confidence or privacy of third persons, or if he has obtained them for the purpose of legal

---

[12] Employment Protection Act 1975, s. 17(1), (3).
[13] *Daily Telegraph Ltd. and Institute of Journalists,* Awards Nos. 78/353 and 78/353A.
[14] *Ibid.* s. 17(1), s. 126(1); Trade Union and Labour Relations Act 1974, s. 30(5).
[15] Employment Protection Act 1975, s. 17(4). See ACAS Code No. 2, para. 11 where some examples are given.
[16] *Ibid.* s. 18(1).

proceedings, but also anything whose disclosure "would cause substantial injury to the employer's undertaking for reasons other than its effect on collective bargaining."[17] What is "substantial injury?" It is certainly a little less far-reaching than "serious prejudice to the interest of the undertaking," the corresponding formula used in the 1971 Act.[18] Clearly it covers (as it should) marketing information which may be used by commercial competitors or unpatented technical information. Could one perhaps say that it covers such information as, according to the principles of the common law, an employer may protect by an agreement with an employee on his activities after the termination of his employment?[19] Would one not destroy the utility of the employer's duty to disclose if one gave to these words a much wider meaning?

(d) How disclosure is to be made

If the union so requests, it must be in writing, but this is perhaps a minor point.[20] The major point is whether the union can ask for documentary material to support it. Here the law is more anxious to protect the employer from trouble and expense than to enable the union to verify his statements. He need not produce any documents, he need not even allow the union to inspect documents, let alone copy or make extracts from them, except if he has prepared the document for the purpose of conveying or confirming information to the union. No question therefore of any right of the workers' side to see a company's accounts, or to ask an accountant to do so on their behalf.[21] This is very different in countries in which works councils have such rights of information.[22] Nothing, perhaps, can show more clearly than this

---

[17] s. 18(1) (*e*)—Contrast the German Works Constitution Law 1972, s. 106(2): "unless the technical or commercial secrets of the enterprise are put in jeopardy."

[18] Industrial Relations Act 1971, s. 158(1) (*e*).

[19] *i.e.* trade secrets and technical unpatented information: *Mason* v. *Provident Clothing etc. Co.* [1913] A.C. 688. The ACAS Code, paras. 14 and 15, goes a little further.

[20] Employment Protection Act 1975, s. 17(5) (or, if previously made orally, confirmed in writing).

[21] s. 18(2) (*a*).

[22] *e.g.* German Works Constitution Law, 1972, s. 106(2) ("production of the necessary documentation"). Similarly in France, where the workers' representatives have the right to see the accounts and to use the services of an accountant. These rights have recently been much extended by the law of October 28, 1982, amending the *Code du Travail*. See especially new Art. L.434–5, creating in large enterprises a *Commission économique* within the *Comité d'entreprise*, and new Art. L.435–6, concerning the use of experts. For an analysis see G. Couturier, "L'accès du comité d'entreprise à l'information économique et financière" *Droit Social*, January, 1983, p. 26. For Sweden, see above, p. 94.

provision how far all the discussions on "participation" are still removed from the reality of things. That the employer cannot be asked to provide information if to compile or assemble it would involve him in a disproportionate amount of work or expense is only reasonable, but to assess the value the information would have to the union against the trouble and cost it would cause to the employer may be a delicate task in a given case.[23]

(e) Enforcement of the duty to disclose

Enforcement of the duty to disclose is by way of a complaint to the Central Arbitration Committee and a claim to be arbitrated upon by the Committee that terms and conditions of employment be improved. The CAC can trace its ancestry to the "Industrial Court" created, as we shall see,[24] by the Industrial Courts Act 1919, as a result of one of the recommendations of the Whitley Committee set up by Lloyd George during the First World War to prepare the ground for the post-war reorganisation of labour relations. It was conceived of as primarily an organ for agreed arbitration, and as such we must look at it more closely in a subsequent chapter. It continued under the 1971 Act, though under the new name Industrial Arbitration Board.[25] Now the CAC has taken the place of that Board.[26] Like the Board, it is tripartite; it sits with an impartial chairman and one representative of either side of industry, but not of the industry before the Committee.[27] More important: it is independent, not subject to any governmental directions,[28] and its members have, within the terms of their appointments, security of tenure.[29] Although ACAS is consulted by the Secretary of State before he appoints the chairman and deputy chairman, and although ACAS nominates the other members and pays their remuneration as well as that of the chairman, the Commitee is as independent from the Service as it is from the Department of Employment and other branches of Government.

The Donovan Commission recommended that the sanction against an employer who rejected a recommendation for recognition should be binding unilateral determination of wages and other conditions of employment.[30] This was the sanction utilised in the

---

[23] Employment Protection Act 1975, s. 18(2).
[24] Below, Chap. 5.
[25] Industrial Relations Act 1971, s.124.
[26] Employment Protection Act 1975, s. 10.
[27] Sched. 1, para. 14.
[28] Para. 27.
[29] Para. 15(1).
[30] Cmnd. 3621, para. 273.

1971 Act in respect of both the duty to recognise and the duty to disclose information,[31] and this policy was perpetuated by the 1975 Act[32] and it continues in respect of disclosure of information even after the 1980 Act, although, as we have seen, the recognition procedure has now fallen away. Thus, in respect of both recognition and disclosure the 1975 Act provided an essentially indirect sanction. Unlike American federal law the Act did not provide for an enforcement of the obligation to bargain by mandatory court injunctions.[33] If the employer refused to recognise the union, he might lose his right to set terms and conditions of employment to the Central Arbitration Committee, but he could not, ultimately, be compelled to enter into joint regulation of them with the union. Because of the experience of the Committee and its predecessors with voluntary arbitration they were seen as the natural forum for the enforcement of the new sanction of compulsory unilateral arbitration.

However, in one respect the 1975 Act went beyond the 1971 Act. Under the latter the Industrial Arbitration Board had been seen as the appropriate body to determine the claim for improved terms and conditions of employment, but the question of whether the duty to recognise or to disclose had been broken was for the National Industrial Relations Court.[34] With the abolition of that Court in 1974, the CAC had transferred to it in addition the question of whether the duties had been broken.[35] So there came to be conferred upon the Committee tasks of statutory construction and application very similar to those imposed, say, upon the Employment Appeal Tribunal in relation to matters such as consultation over redundancies.[36] On the matter of recognition the Committee had thus to determine whether the employer "was not then taking such action by way of or with a view to carrying on negotiations as might reasonably be expected to be taken by an employer ready and willing to carry on such negotiations as are envisaged by the recommendation."[37] This was the British

---

[31] Industrial Relations Act 1971, ss. 102(2) (*c*) and 105(5) (*a*).

[32] Employment Protection Act 1975, ss. 16 and 21.

[33] It is interesting to note that under the 1971 Act the N.I.R.C. could order the employer to fulfil his duty to disclose, which order would have been backed by the sanctions of contempt of court: s. 102(2) (*b*). However, this procedure was never tested because the disclosure provisions of the 1971 Act were never brought into force.

[34] Industrial Relations Act 1971, s. 101.

[35] Employment Protection Act 1975, ss. 16(1), 19 and 20.

[36] See below.

[37] s. 15(2).

circumlocution equivalent to the American requirement of "bargaining in good faith." Only after the CAC had upheld the union's complaint that the employer was not so acting could it go on to the next stage of adjudicating upon the claim for improved terms and conditions of employment for those workers in respect of whom the employer had failed to recognise the union.[38] In fact, the interpretation of this provision gave rise to little difficulty in practice, though it had much potential for problems, because in the great majority of the 29 complaints which came before the Committee before the procedure was repealed the employer freely admitted that he was not complying the with the Service's recommendation, often because he did not accept its legitimacy.[39]

With regard to the duty to disclose also the Committee has to determine a complaint that the duty is not being complied with as well as a claim for improved terms and conditions of employment. However, the CAC plays a much more central role in the enforcement of the duty to disclose information than in the recognition procedure: a union desiring recognition must apply to the ACAS,[40] but a union desiring to complain that the employer failed to give the information to which it is entitled must go direct to the CAC.[41] The Service comes into all this only if the CAC refers the complaint to it for conciliation.[42] If this is not done or if conciliation fails, the further proceedings are entirely in the hands of the CAC. The difference in the structure of the two types of procedure is easy to understand; the law did not lay down (as other legal systems do) that an employer is under a general duty to recognise unions; not even the Code of Industrial Relations Practice recommends union recognition.[43] Hence the duty to recognise a union was not created by the statute itself, but by the recommendation made by the ACAS when dealing with a recognition issue. The role of the ACAS was not to declare whether an existing duty has been fulfilled or violated, but to establish that duty. This is what we call a "constitutive" act requiring an administrative apparatus such as the ACAS has at its disposal, and the CAC has not. The duty to disclose, on the other hand, is established by the statute itself. Hence the union's

---

[38] s. 16(6).
[39] CAC, *Annual Report 1980* para. 3.6–3.7.
[40] Employment Protection Act 1975, s.11(1).
[41] s.19(1).
[42] s.19(3).
[43] It merely gives advice on how employers should handle recognition claims. See paras. 82–86.

"request" is made to the employer, not, as in the case of recognition, to the ACAS, and hence the task of the authorities involved is not to create a duty but to declare whether or not an existing duty has been fulfilled, a "judicial" and not an "administrative" task to which the CAC is better adapted than the ACAS.

A further consequence of this, however, must be that the procedure before the CAC is somewhat more complicated in disclosure than in recognition proceedings where all the spade work was done by the ACAS by the time the case reached the CAC. The disclosure procedure before the CAC develops in three stages: the first[44] is the hearing of the complaint ending with a declaration as to what information should have been furnished by the employer (and when) and giving him a further period to do so. The second[45] begins (after the end of this period) with a "further complaint" by the union that the employer has not complied with the duty to disclose, and, after a further hearing, ends with a further declaration by the CAC that, and how far, the complaint is well founded. The third stage[46] (which may coincide with the second) is opened by a claim made by the union that the terms and conditions of the workers concerned should be settled by an award made by the CAC. When made, this award has the same effect as an award made by the CAC had in recognition proceedings: its terms are compulsorily implied in the contracts of employment and cannot, to the employee's detriment, be validly abrogated by an individual contract. In other words: the law says to the employer; "if you do not provide the union with the information it needs to bargain with you about wages and other conditions, then an impartial authority may, at the union's request, unilaterally fix those wages and conditions." But the law does not say how an obligation to disclose is enforced, if the information involved did not refer to wages, hours, etc., *i.e.* conditions capable of being incorporated in a contract of employment, but, *e.g.* to problems of procedure for the settlement of disputes or facilities for union activities which concern the relation between the union itself and the employer and not those between the employer and any individual employee. The distinction between these two different kinds of relationship is, as we shall see, quite fundamental.

The question may be raised as to how successful the sanction of unilateral arbitration is likely to be. At the time of writing only a handful of disclosure cases have reached the stage of adjudication

---

[44] Employment Protection Act 1975, s. 19(4)–(6).
[45] s.20.
[46] s.21.

upon a claim,[47] but somewhat more substantial evidence is available from the recognition procedure.[48] An early question raised was whether the Committee might award, if this was claimed, that the employer should recognise the trade union, an obligation which would, like all awards on claims, become a compulsorily implied term in the contracts of employment of the employees covered by the award. After some hesitation the Committee rejected this approach, not so much because such terms could not be formulated in appropriate language as because it was conceived of as inconsistent with the notion of an "indirect" sanction which the legislation was seen to contain.[49] Thus, the sanction upon the employer was to be his loss to the Committee of the freedom to set substantive terms and conditions. Even here the Committee trod cautiously and in fixing these terms the Committee refused to penalise the employer for his failure to grant recognition by making, say, awards of substantial increases in pay, fearing the distortions in pay structures generally that might result. Instead, the Committee saw itself as providing a substitute for the bargaining that should have taken place had the recommendation been complied with, though it was perhaps prepared to take a fairly sanguine view of the results of that bargaining in achieving the employees' goals.[50] The approach the Committee adopted was doubtless the one most consistent with its tasks under its other jurisdictions and the one most conducive to the avoidance of anomalous pay structures, but, as ACAS has pointed out, "there is little evidence that, once involved in the complaints procedures,

---

[47] The use of the disclosure provisions amounted to some 133 complaints under s. 19 over the period 1977 to 1980, so that this procedure is being used much less intensively than the recognition procedure was used. See H. Gospel and P. Willman, "Disclosure of Information: the CAC Approach." (1981) 10 I.L.J. 10.

[48] See the analysis by B. Doyle, "A Substitute for Collective Bargaining?—The Central Arbitration Committee's Approach to Section 16 of the Employment Protection Act 1975" (1980) 9 I.L.J. 154.

[49] CAC, *Annual Report 1980*, para. 38; *Road Transport Services (Hackney) Ltd. and Transport and General Workers' Union*, Award No. 78/677. After some hesitation the Committee did, however, in some cases insert into its award a procedure for representation on individual grievances: *Uniroyal Ltd. and Association of Scientific, Technical and Managerial Staffs*, Award No. 79/27. *Cf. Commodore Business Machines (U.K.) Ltd. and Electrical, Electronic, Telecommunication and Plumbing Union*, Award No. 78/339.

[50] *John Wyeth and Brother Ltd. and Association of Scientific, Technical and Managerial Staffs*, Award No. 78/808. The Committee referred to its award as a "substitute for the hard bargain which recognition, had it been granted, would have provided."

employers were persuaded by the nature of the remedies. . . . to change their position."[51] It remains to be seen whether the sanction will be any the more effective in relation to the duty to disclose.

4. CONSULTATION ON REDUNDANCIES

When referring to international influences on our labour legislation reference was made to the provisions of the Employment Protection Act imposing on employers an obligation to consult unions before dismissing any one of their employees as redundant.[52] In a sense this too belongs to the group of rules and institutions designed to promote collective bargaining. The Act does not say so, but merely imposes on the employer a duty to consider, and reply to, representations made by union representatives in the course of the consultations, and, if he rejects them, to say why.[53] This is a kind of collective bargaining, and it is for this reason that we mention it here.

It would be quite wrong to think that these provisions deal only with "mass dismissals." The employer must consult the appropriate union at the earliest opportunity if he wishes to make a single employee redundant—but, if he intends to dismiss a large number he is obliged to begin the consultations at least a certain period before the first dismissal is to take effect, and what that time is depends on how many employees are to be dismissed within one establishment (it is the "establishment" which counts, not the undertaking which may comprise many establishments) and on how soon they are to be dismissed—sometimes the period is 90 days and sometimes 30 days before the first dismissal takes effect.[54]

Like the duty to disclose, this duty to consult is linked with union recognition: what we have just loosely called the "appropriate" union is the one which the employer has recognised for the purposes of collective bargaining with respect to the class ("description") of employees to which any one to be dismissed

---

[51] ACAS, *Annual Report 1980*, p.91.
[52] ss. 99 *et seq.* (Pt. IV), based on EEC Council Directive No. 75/129. See Freedland (1976) 5 I.L.J. 24 *et seq.*
[53] s. 99(1) and (7).
[54] s. 99(3): 90 days if 100 or more are to be dismissed within 90 days or less, 30 days if 10 or more are to be dismissed within 60 days or less. The original period for redundancies of 10 or more was 60 days, but in 1979 the Government by statutory instrument reduced it to 30 days because the longer period was thought to be a "damaging burden" upon employers, especially small employers.

belongs.[55] And the representative to be consulted is a union official or any other person authorised to carry on collective bargaining—this may be a full time officer or, in a given situation, it may be a shop steward or a convener of shop stewards. Like so much in labour legislation, the procedure here formulated is not more than what any enlightened employer would do in any event. This is especially true of the particulars he has to disclose in order to make sense of the consultation.[56] These must be given in writing and include matters such as the reasons why redundancy dismissals are necessary, the number and description of those to be dismissed and of those employed at the establishment and belonging to the same description as those to be dismissed, the proposed method of selection (which may be important in connection with claims for unfair dismissal), and the detailed procedure (timing, etc.) envisaged.

Seen in a comparative context these provisions are of special interest. In a country such as the German Federal Republic which has a statutory works council the obligation imposed on an employer is,[57] in a situation of this nature, to consult the works council which represents all workers, union members and others. In the United States it is of course the union which is the "statutory bargaining representative" that can claim to be consulted, and again, in that capacity it represents not only its members but all workers in the plant. The interesting point is that this is a context in which a recognised union occupies in this country a place comparable to that of the American statutory bargaining representative: the duty to consult arises whenever an employee is to be dismissed who belongs to a description in respect of which a union is recognised, even if he is not a member of that union.

These provisions of the Employment Protection Act serve two different, but connected purposes: one—consultation with a recognised union—is to enable the union to exert its influence in decisions about redundancies, and perhaps particularly in the selection of those who have to go. At the same time, however, the object of the law is to protect the labour market against sudden changes in the supply and demand situation and also to prepare the ground for the redeployment of a redundant labour force. This explains the obligation to consult the union in good time before

---

[55] ss. 99(1) and 126(1). Recognition for representation on individual grievances falls outside the statutory concept of recognition for collective bargaining purposes: *USDAW* v. *Sketchley Ltd.* [1981] I.R.L.R. 290.
[56] s. 99(5), (6).
[57] Works Constitution Law, 1972, s. 111.

the intended mass dismissal, coupled with an obligation to notify the Secretary of State, *i.e.* the Department of Employment.[58] If the employer fails to notify the Secretary of State, he may be fined.[59] He may instead forfeit part of the "redundancy rebate"[60]: the redundancy rebate is paid out of a publicly administered fund to employers and it covers part of the amount the employer has to pay to a dismissed employee in the event of redundancy.[61]

If, however, the employer fails to consult the union—altogether or at the prescribed time—the union can, from an industrial tribunal, obtain a "protective award" under which the employer has to pay statutory remuneration for a "protected period" to each employee concerned.[62] The details—which are extremely complex—do not call for comment here, but it must be pointed out that it is the union and not the individual employee who is entitled to the protective award. This is a sanction for the violation of a collective interest, and therefore a remedy exclusively to be used by the union. On the basis of the protective award it is then for the individual employee to enforce his individual right in the industrial tribunal.[63] The union may support him there—if he is a member—but it cannot sue on the award in its own name. However, the facts that the sanction is for a violation of a collective interest, but that the beneficiary of the protective award is the individual employee have led to some difficulties about how the length of the protective award should be calculated (within the maxima set by the statute).[64] Initially, the E.A.T. seemed to stress the loss to the individual resulting from the failure to consult properly, and in particular seemed to be guided by the answer to the question of how much longer the employee would have been employed had the consultation procedure been properly implemented.[65] More recently, the Tribunal has stressed the need for industrial tribunals to have regard to the employer's default in complying with the

---

[58] s.100.

[59] s.105.

[60] s.104.

[61] Employment Protection (Consolidation) Act 1978, s. 104.

[62] Employment Protection Act 1975, s. 101. Again it can act as a statutory representative for non-members. This may give rise to difficult problems. See Wedderburn, 39 M.L.R. at pp. 175–176.

[63] ss. 102, 103. The details, especially the relation between the statutory right to payment for the protected period and the employee's contractual claims are of the most fearful complexity.

[64] s. 101(5): 90, 30 or 28 days according to the number of employees proposed to be dismissed.

[65] *Talke Fashions Ltd.* v. *Amalgamated Society of Textile Workers and Kindred Trades* [1977] I.C.R. 833.

consultation provisions when exercising their powers to determine the length of the protective award on a just and equitable basis.[66] On this basis, although the award is still seen to be aimed at compensating individual employees, the purpose is to compensate them for the failure properly to consult the union rather than for loss of days of employment as such. Consequently, a dismissed employee who immediately obtains another, equivalent job might nevertheless appropriately be the subject of a protective award. The Tribunal has not yet embarked upon the difficult task of quantifying the consequences of a failure properly to consult in terms of protective awards. This may be very problematic if, as has increasingly been the case in recent years, the economic pressures upon the employer were such that it is difficult to believe that he would have changed his mind in any respect as a result of full consultations. To make a protective award in such cases is, in effect, to use the consultation provisions to increase the amount of the employee's redundancy payment, and this seems remote from enforcing a duty to consult.

If arrangements for alternative employment or for the handling of redundancies are made by collective agreement, the Secretary of State may by order provide that the agreement takes the place of the statutory provisions.[67] This is quite similar to corresponding provisions about redundancy payments[68] and unfair dismissals.[69]

In spite of the (only qualified) success in adverse economic circumstances of the statutory duty to consult a recognised union in the case of proposed redundancies, there has been another EEC Directive[70] which has led to the introduction of another statutory consultation provision into the law of the U.K. Under the Transfer Regulations[71] made under the European Communities Act 1972, where a business or part of a business is transferred from one person to another, both the transferor and the transferee employer may come under a duty to independent unions recognised by them. That duty may be a duty simply to inform the representative of the union of the fact of the proposed transfer and its implications for the affected employees, but, where either transferor or transferee employer envisages that he will be "taking measures" in relation to the employees, the duty becomes a duty

---

[66] *Spillers-French (Holdings) Ltd.* v. *U.S.D.A.W.* [1980] I.C.R. 31.
[67] s. 107.
[68] Employment Protection (Consolidation) Act 1978, s. 96.
[69] s. 65.
[70] Council Directive No. 77/187/EEC.
[71] The Transfer of Undertakings (Protection of Employment) Regulations 1981 (S.I. 1981 No. 1794). See Hepple, (1982) 11 I.L.J. 29.

to consult. As with the obligation to consult over proposed redundancies the right of complaint over the employer's failure to inform or consult lies exclusively in the hands of the union, although the industrial tribunal's award will usually be for compensation to be paid to individual employees. However, the financial sanction is rather weak in this case: no more than two weeks' pay for each employee in respect of whom an award is made. More EEC initiatives requiring employer consultation with representatives of the employees may be expected in the future.

So much, then, for the role of the law in promoting collective bargaining. There is all the difference between legislation designed to do this, and legislation designed to promote agreement. Even a successful recommendation by the ACAS for union recognition and even a complete fulfilment of the duties of the employer to give information and to consult does not by itself produce agreement on wages, hours or anything else. It may produce a situation in which the parties sit around the bargaining table to discuss these things. In practice this may mean that the battle is half won; but it may not be over. There may still be deadlock and a stoppage. This however means that the law has further tasks to fulfil. It plays its role not only in promoting negotiation but also in promoting agreement, and this role of the law we must discuss in the next chapter.

CHAPTER 5

COLLECTIVE AGREEMENTS AND THE LAW:
PROMOTING AGREEMENT

1. VOLUNTARY METHODS

(a) Fundamental concepts

A collective agreement is a treaty between social powers. It is, as we have indicated, a peace treaty and at the same time a normative treaty. This being so, there is in every country a more or less well-defined line which separates the scope of the bilateral rule-making power of management and unions from the scope of what is often referred to as the " managerial prerogative." Subjects within the scope of bilateral power are matters for "negotiation"; subjects within the scope of the managerial prerogative used to be regarded as potential matters of "consultation." But "consultation" has lost much of whatever real significance it once had. Moreover the borderline between negotiation and consultation has always been fluid, and certainly as controversial as that between the Royal Prerogative and the legislative power of Parliament in the course of constitutional history. All this is, of course, intimately connected with the problem of workers' participation or union participation in managerial decision making and the inaugurated transformation of company law which may be linked with it. The scope of the managerial prerogative is, in this country, still comparatively wide, though in some respects it is shrinking. Thus, pensions, which in the United States are mandatory topics of collective bargaining,[1] *i.e.* matters on which the employer can be legally compelled to negotiate, are here still largely within the "managerial prerogative." However shadowy it may be, the difference between negotiation and consultation must be borne in mind when considering the role of the law in promoting collective agreements,

---

[1] Summers and Wellington, *Labor Law,* pp. 63 *et seq.* The leading case is *Inland Steel Co.* v. *N.L.R.B.,* 170 F. (2d) 247 (7th Circ. 1948). Wellington, *Labor and the Legal Process* (1968), p. 323, points out that the obligation of the employers to discuss pensions and welfare funds (which the NLRB imposed upon them) "was significant in the widespread establishment of such funds."

nor is this line likely to disappear under a system of union participation in managerial decisions.

A second distinction which is relevant in this context is that between substantive and procedural agreements. These are terms which the world of industrial relations has borrowed from the world of law. A substantive agreement is an agreement on wages or other conditions of employment, on the distribution of work among the members of the workforce, on access to jobs, in short on all the matters which determine the conditions under which relations between individual employers and workers can be and are created, and on the rights and obligations arising from the relationship once it has been created. A procedure agreement is an agreement on the relation between the collective bargaining partners as such, on the institutions and methods designed to be used for the prevention or settlement of disputes and thus for the making of substantive norms. These norms may include terms and conditions of employment as well as negotiating rights, facilities for officials of trade unions or other organisations of workers (such as shop stewards), procedures relating to dismissals and to other disciplinary matters and to individual grievance procedures generally. It thus refers to all procedures agreed between collective parties whether the procedures themselves are about collective or about individual disputes, and this expresses the well-known experience that a distinction between collective and individual disputes is very difficult in practice: every dispute about a disciplinary measure against an individual worker may become a dispute about freedom of organisation and the scope of union activities. It also includes consultation, both on negotiable matters (*i.e.* matters for bilateral settlement) and on matters within the unilateral power of management. Consultation about the exercise of unilateral power can of course be regulated through bilateral procedures. One notes further that procedure agreements cover what are called conflicts of right as well as conflicts of interest. We have already said[2] that the structure of British industrial relations makes this distinction particularly fluid and problematical.

And, thirdly, when considering what the law has done and what it can do to bring about agreements between mangement and labour, we ought to have a clear notion of what we mean by the "compulsory" as distinct from the "voluntary" nature of settlement machinery and of its intervention.[3] The word "compulsory"

---

[2] See Chap. 3.
[3] See Ramm, *The Legality of Industrial Action and the Method of Settlement Procedure,* in Aaron and Wedderburn (ed.), *Industrial Conflict* (1972) Chap. 5, esp. pp. 296 *et seq.*

may mean quite a number of different things, at least four. In the first place it may mean that the parties must use the procedure, that is, if the two sides of industry cannot come to terms they must appear before the relevant board or committee, office or individual, though they are free to reject whatever proposals are made by the officer, board or whatever it may be: in this sense compulsory conciliation exists in Canada,[4] and to some extent in France.[5] Secondly, however, it may mean, that whether the parties are or are not free to refuse to participate, the person or persons charged with the task of conciliating, arbitrating or investigating, can act at the request of either (or sometimes of neither) side to the dispute. In this country inquiries can be initiated *ex officio*, both by the ACAS[6] and, through formal Courts of Inquiry, by the Department of Employment,[7] and we have already met situations in which that which is coming to be known as "unilateral" arbitration can occur.[8] In this context, then, "voluntary" simply means that the procedure requires the consent of both sides. Thirdly, when we use the term "compulsory," especially in connection with arbitration, we may not refer to the procedure at all, but to its result, that is, to the award, and signify that, without being accepted, the award is binding on the parties; although this itself may mean very different things because the sanctions may be penal or civil, and again be civil sanctions as between the collective parties or between individual employers and employees through their contracts of employment. Lastly, the word "compulsory" sometimes connotes that during the intervention of a third party for the settlement of a dispute, or during a stated period, while intervention is pending, no industrial sanctions may be used by either side, that is no strike, go slow, etc., on the one side and no lockout on the other is permitted in connection with the particular dispute. The cooling-off or conciliation pause provisions applicable in the United States under the Taft-Hartley Act of 1947[9] have to be seen in this context.[10]

[4] Anton, *The Role of Government in the Settlement of Industrial Disputes in Canada* (1962), pp. 150 *et seq.;* Carrothers, *Collective Bargaining Law in Canada* (1965), Chap. 18.

[5] After the reforms made by the law of November 13, 1982, amending Title II of Book 5 of the *Code du Travail*, this statement remains true of the mediation process (new Art. L.524) but conciliation has become a voluntary matter (new Art. L.523).

[6] Employment Protection Act 1975, s.5.

[7] Industrial Courts Act 1919, s. 4. See Wedderburn and Davies, *Employment Grievances and Disputes Procedures in Britain* (1969), pp. 224 *et seq.*

[8] See above, Chap. 4.   [9] ss. 206–209.

[10] Also the repealed "emergency" provisions in ss. 138–145 of the Industrial Relations Act 1971.

We ought also—and here is a fourth point for conceptual clarification—to be clear about what we mean by conciliation, by mediation, by arbitration, by investigation and by inquiry.[11] Conciliation simply means that some third party—a conciliation officer designated by the ACAS,[12] a person without office but with personal prestige, or a statutory or agreed commission or board—seeks to get the parties together. If conciliation succeeds, the result is an agreement or the achievement of a sufficient degree of harmony between the parties that they can resume negotiations without the conciliator's help. Arbitration is quite different. The arbitrator listens to the parties and to the evidence and then makes a formulated award. If the aribitration is voluntary as to its outcome, this is a mere recommendation: if it is compulsory, the award binds the parties. Arbitration in this sense means the settlement of both conflicts on existing rights and on rights to be created. Unlike, *e.g.* in the German language,[13] the same word is in English applied to both activities—it symbolises the fact that they are especially difficult to distinguish in British industrial relations. It is significant that the Arbitration Act 1950, which governs arbitration on existing rights in commercial relations, is generally inapplicable.[14] Investigation or inquiry (in America often called "fact finding") is a procedure in which some third party (a commission, sometimes misleadingly known as a "court"[15]) is charged with finding the facts of a dispute, and sometimes (in this country usually[16]) also with the giving of advice or making of recommendations for its settlement. If conciliation produces an agreement, an arbitration produces an award while an investigation or inquiry produces a report which is often published. Oddly enough, a procedure of this type is known in France

---

[11] Wedderburn and Davies, *loc. cit.,* Pt. III; Sharp, *Industrial Conciliation and Arbitration in Great Britain* (1954), Pt. II; Ministry of Labour Evidence to Royal Commission, Third and Fourth Memoranda; ACAS, *Industrial Relations Handbook* (1980), pp. 25 *et seq.;* ACAS, *Annual Report 1978,* Chaps. 8–9; Davies, "Arbitration and the Role of Courts" U.K. National Report to the Ninth International Congress of the International Society for Labour Law and Social Security (Munich, 1978); Kessler, "The Prevention and Settlement of Collective Labour Disputes in the United Kingdom" I.R.J. March/April 1980, p.5; I.L.O., *Conciliation and Arbitration Procedures in Labour Disputes* (1980) (comparative).
[12] Employment Protection Act 1975, s.2.
[13] *Schiedsverfahren* and *Schlichtung.* The German equivalent of "award" covers both types. The French *arbitrage* covers both procedures.
[14] Employment Protection Act 1975, s. 3(5); Sched. 1, para. 26.
[15] Especially "Courts" of Inquiry under the Industrial Courts Act.
[16] Not in the United States: see Labor Management Relations Act, s. 296, but contrast Railway Labor Act 1926 (as amended), s.10.

as "*médiation*,"[17] but in English "mediation" and "conciliation" often seem to be synonymous; the former term is more frequently used in America, the latter in this country.[18] However, in ACAS practice mediation is distinguished from conciliation on the one hand and arbitration on the other. The position has been put as follows:

> "Mediation provides a further method of settling trade disputes and may be regarded as a 'half-way house' between conciliation and arbitration. The role of the conciliator is to assist the parties to reach their own negotiated settlement and he may make suggestions as appropriate. The mediator proceeds by way of conciliation but in addition is prepared and expected to make his own formal proposals or recommendations which may be accepted as they stand or provide the basis for further negotiations leading to a settlement. Such recommendations may be similar in form to an arbitrator's award but the crucial difference is that the parties do not undertake in advance to accept them."[19]

This passage also shows that ACAS regards arbitration awards as binding upon the parties in industrial relations terms even if such awards are not, in the U.K., legally binding. The Service will arrange arbitration only where the parties agree in advance to accept the arbitrator's award, which agreement probably does not create a legally binding commitment,[20] and if the parties do not feel able to give such a commitment, mediation is suggested.[21] Conciliation is the predominant form of ACAS intervention in trade disputes. In 1982, 1,716 conciliation cases were completed, 234 cases were referred to various forms of arbitration, in 16 cases arrangements were made for mediation, and there was one committee of inquiry.[22]

In principle, conciliation, arbitration and inquiry can be

---

[17] *Code du Travail*, 1974, Arts. L. 524–1 *et seq.*, See Camerlynck and Lyon-Caen, *loc. cit.* paras. 773 *et seq.*, pp. 816 *et seq.*; Sinay, *La Grève* (Camerlynck's *Traité*, Vol. 6), para. 205, p. 441.

[18] A purely technical distinction is drawn in Canada between "conciliation" by government-created organs, and "mediation" by a committee which is "a creature of the parties": see Carrothers, *Collective Bargaining Law in Canada*, pp. 306–307.

[19] ACAS *Annual Report 1978*, p. 70. The Employment Protection Act 1975, s. 2 permits the Service to offer assistance by way of conciliation "or by other means."

[20] Trade Union and Labour Relations Act 1974, s.18.

[21] ACAS *op. cit.*, pp. 68 and 70.

[22] ACAS, *Annual Report 1982*, Tables 1(b) and 7.

entrusted to a standing committee or person acting regularly, or to a committee or individual chosen ad hoc either by the parties or by an authority to which the parties delegate that choice. Generally one can say that in this country we have a comparatively highly developed mechanism for the settlement of disputes between labour and management concerning collective agreements, but that the settlement of individual grievance disputes is woefully under-developed, compared, *e.g.* with the United States.[23]

(b) Conciliation and other duties of the ACAS

This aspect of labour law has a fascinating history which goes back to the days of the younger Pitt.[24] A whole series of statutes were passed in the course of the nineteenth century with the object of providing settlement machinery, during the later stages very much with an eye to preventing or shortening stoppages (with which each generation always considers itself as being particularly cursed), but all of them ended in failure. It is doubtful whether this was due to the absence of a distinction between disputes about agreed wages and wages to be agreed—between disputes of right and interest—(this appears to have been the view of Sidney and Beatrice Webb),[25] to the element of compulsion which some of them introduced, or the unsuitable agencies to which some of these statutes entrusted these functions. The fact is that, as Lord Amulree clearly shows,[26] these statutes and the law altogether were simply by-passed by the development of industrial relations. There was a time, about the beginning of the last quarter of the nineteenth century, when many regarded industrial arbitration as a kind of panacea for industrial ills,[27] but this meant purely

---

[23] See Stieber, *Grievance Arbitration in the United States: An Analysis of its Functions and Effects* (1968): Royal Commission Research Paper No. 8 (*Three Studies in Collective Bargaining,* No. 1).

[24] Here and throughout this chapter, much reliance is placed on Amulree, *Industrial Arbitration in Great Britain* (1929). Lord Amulree—previously Sir William Mackenzie, K.C.—was the first President of the Industrial Court.

[25] *Industrial Democracy,* Pt. II, Chap. III, esp. p. 243. "The pretentious legislation" of 1867 and 1872 (repealed in 1896) failed because it sought to use the method of arbitration for the type of conflict of interest which requires conciliation. They also point out (p. 223, n. 2) that until well into the last quarter of the 19th century simple collective bargaining processes were often referred to as "arbitration." A very important point for the student of the history of labour law.

[26] Chaps. X and XI. In Henry Crompton's *Industrial Conciliation* (1876), p. 145, there is a most eloquent passage to the effect that "here, as in so many other parts of our social life, we find the legal system becoming inefficient and antiquated"—a thought developed in some detail.

[27] Henry Crompton's "classic" work (see Webb, *loc. cit.,* p. 223), quoted in the previous note, expresses this, but see above, n. 25.

voluntary and autonomous arbitration, and had nothing to do with the law.

All these statutes (in so far as they were still in force) were swept away by the Conciliation Act 1896, which was enacted as a result of the Report of the Royal Commission on Labour of 1894.[28] This, in turn, has now been repealed[29] and been replaced by the relevant provisions of the Employment Protection Act 1975 which deal with the powers and the duties of the ACAS.[30] The Conciliation Act was a statute of great importance: it was the legal basis of the conciliation services operated by the Department of Employment,[31] which are now, under the 1975 Act,[32] organised by the ACAS. These conciliation services (whether central or regional) are informal. The Service can intervene of its own motion or at the request of both of the parties to a trade dispute or of either.[33] The conciliation service is one of the important aspects of the practice of labour relations. ACAS has had a remarkable record of success, but it is perhaps essential to that success that all this is done quietly and is not often in the "news." Nor does the assistance which the Service offers for the purpose of settling a trade dispute necessarily consist of attempts by its own officers to conciliate. Instead of doing so, they may suggest that the parties entrust the attempt to find acceptable terms to an outside person enjoying their confidence,[34] or submit the dispute to arbitration, but no conciliation officer ever arbitrates himself: this old established and wise administrative practice has now been codified by law,[35] and been extended to the entire staff of the ACAS.

Like the legislation which it replaces, the Employment Protection Act gives effect to two cardinal principles which have traditionally permeated British labour legislation: the first is that whoever intervenes from outside (whether in an official capacity or not) has the task of helping the parties to achieve a settlement, but not of imposing it—the "voluntary" principle. The second is that the parties should, if possible, be encouraged to use their own

---

[28] Fifth and Final Report of the Royal Commission on Labour, C. 7421 (1894).
[29] Employment Protection Act 1975, Sched. 18.
[30] ss. 2, 3 and 5.
[31] For their description see Min. of Lab. Evidence to the Royal Commission, Third Memo., esp. paras. 6–15. See also Goodman and Krislov "Conciliation in Industrial Disputes in Great Britain: A Survey of the Attitude of the Parties" (1974) 12 Brit. J. of Ind. Rel. 327.
[32] s. 2.
[33] s. 2(1).
[34] s. 2(2).
[35] s. 3(1) (*a*).

settlement machinery,[36] and that in particular—special reasons to the contrary apart—a matter should not be referred to arbitration unless and until all possibilities of using the agreed procedures have been exhausted.[37] This is the principle of the priority of autonomous institutions. The "voluntary"principle must be understood in the light of the definition of the terms "compulsory" and "voluntary" given above. Conciliation[38] and inquiry[39] are voluntary only in the sense that the parties cannot be compelled to participate in the proceedings nor to accept their outcome whether it is a conciliator's suggestion or an investigator's advice[40] or report,[41] but they are not voluntary in the sense that the proceedings depend on the consent of the parties. But arbitration is just that: the Employment Protection Act says that a dispute may be referred to arbitration only "at the request of one or more parties to the dispute and with the consent of all the parties to the dispute,"[42] whilst an inquiry may be initiated by the Service "if it thinks fit"—and without anybody's request or consent.[43] An arbitration award does not bind the parties, but in practice those who have submitted their dispute to arbitration are normally willing to abide by its result. None of these procedures— conciliation, arbitration, or inquiry—restricts the right of either side to resort to industrial action, such as strike or lockout. Though one cannot prove it, one may guess that the success of these procedures, and especially of those of the conciliation services, is to no small extent due to the two cardinal principles we have mentioned: the absence of all compulsion and the respect for the autonomous institutions in the industry concerned.

Conciliation—in the sense under discussion—and arbitration always have, and inquiry often has, the purpose of achieving a collective agreement or regulation, at industry, enterprise, or plant level. If the parties arrive at an agreement—as they normally do—through unaided negotiation, none of these procedures is required. Hence conciliation and arbitration presuppose that a dispute either exists or is "apprehended."[44] We shall see in the last chapter what in detail is meant by a "trade dispute." Broadly it can

---

[36] s. 2(3).
[37] s. 3(2).
[38] s. 2.
[39] s. 5; Industrial Courts Act 1919, s. 4.
[40] Employment Protection Act 1975, s. 5.
[41] Industrial Courts Act 1919, s. 5.
[42] Employment Protection Act 1975, s. 3(1).
[43] s. 5(1).
[44] s. 2 and s. 3.

be described[45] as a dispute between employers and workers about employment and its termination, about its terms and conditions, about allocation of work, discipline, and union membership, and—very importantly—also about relations between employers and unions, including such things as facilities for shop stewards and union officials, and all the matters which can form the content of what we have learnt to know as a procedure agreement, which also includes recognition. These are the matters on which the Service has the power to conciliate and which may be referred to arbitration. It may conciliate *ex officio* or at the request of "one or more parties to the dispute," but of course refer to arbitration only on a joint request. This is here of importance, because the law considers the individual workers and employers as parties to the dispute[46] even if a trade union or employers' association is also a party. Hence the ACAS can conciliate in, and can refer to arbitration, "unofficial" as well as "official" disputes. The law does not prevent it from acting at the request of a union minority or an amorphous group involved in industrial action. It may be important that the Service should be able to settle wildcat strikes.

However, its power to inquire goes even futher: it extends "to any question relating to industrial relations generally or to industrial relations in any particular industry or in any particular undertaking or part of an undertaking."[47] This means that the Service can, even of its own motion, investigate, *e.g.* the possibilities of improving collective bargaining machinery or the co-operation between shop stewards of various unions or between them and management at any level, and without there being any actual or apprehended dispute. The power to inquire here merges into the power to advise, about which more is said below.

It would of course be ludicrous to assume that the ACAS has a monopoly of conciliation or of the organisation of arbitration. On the contrary: we have seen that its conciliation and arbitration services are in a sense subsidiary to those organised by the two sides of an industry on an autonomous basis. In fact anyone may, if he thinks he has the necessary authority and if he has the necessary courage, try his hand at settling a dispute, and it is anybody's guess how often this happens, especially in very small cases which the press may never report. Nor is there anything to prevent the parties from calling in a third party to assist them in their

---

[45] Employment Protection Act 1975, s. 126(1); Trade Union and Labour Relations Act 1974, s. 29(1) as amended by the Employment Act 1982, s. 18.
[46] *Ibid.* s. 29(1).
[47] Employment Protection Act 1975, s. 5(1).

negotiations, without consulting the Service at all and without there being any previously organised agreed negotiating machinery. In very vital cases of national importance it has occurred that a Minister, and even the Prime Minister himself, intervened to prevent or to terminate a stoppage. The ACAS offers to the two sides of industry certain facilities: the facility of conciliation and that of preparing arbitration. There is no other conciliation procedure organised on a statutory basis, nor is there any other statutory basis for voluntary industrial arbitration. We shall presently see that there is however an alternative basis for statutory inquiry.

(c) Arbitration by the CAC

Voluntary industrial arbitration may, under the Act, proceed on two different lines[48] (and these two lines can already be traced in the legislation which preceded, and which was displaced by, the present law.)[49] With the consent of the parties the ACAS may refer the dispute (or part of it) to ad hoc arbitrators (or one ad hoc arbitrator), or to the standing statutory organ for voluntary arbitration, the Central Arbitration Committee to which reference has been made in the previous chapter. Let it however be emphasised again that, whilst in the procedures there described the CAC acts as an organ of unilateral arbitration, *i.e.* without the consent of both parties, it can never act as an arbitration body on a reference by the ACAS in a trade dispute otherwise than by the consent of both sides.

There has been a considerable growth since the creation of ACAS in the willingness of parties to make use of arbitration arranged by the Service. In the early years of the previous decade the number of references to arbitration by the Department of Employment did not usually exceed 60 per annum. In 1975 and all subsequent years the number of references has always exceeded 200, although there has been a slight falling off since 1980 from the high points reached in 1978 and 1979. This growth has benefited, however, ad hoc forms of arbitration, and in particular single arbitrators. Thus, in 1982, a not untypical year, 194 cases were referred to single arbitrators, 26 to ad hoc boards of arbitration, and only 10 cases to the CAC. Indeed, during the nineteen-seventies the Committee and its predecessors heard each year fewer voluntary arbitrations than had been the case during the

---

[48] s. 3(1) (*a*) and (*b*).
[49] Industrial Courts Act 1919, s. 2(2)—now repealed.

preceding decade.[50] The reasons for the growth in the use of arbitration and for the popularity of single arbitrators are not entirely clear, but the Service regards single arbitrators as "especially suitable for the settlement of local disputes" and stresses that hearings by such arbitrators "are conducted in an informal atmosphere and normally take place in private."[51] Single arbitrators are not necessarily, or even usually, lawyers, but include academics with backgrounds in industrial relations, labour economics and so on, as well as former government officials.

Despite the decline of its voluntary jurisdiction the workload of the CAC nevertheless expanded enormously in the late 1970s because its "compulsory" role under various statutes, which its predecessors had had from the earliest days, was much increased. We have already noted[52] its role under the now-repealed recognition procedure and the still-operative disclosure provisions. We shall consider later its role in the enforcement of standards of wages and other terms and conditions of employment (including the question of equal pay).[53] Nevertheless, historically the main preoccupation of the CAC's predecessors was with voluntary arbitration, and public policy on the matter of arbitration has been most often discussed in relation to these bodies. It is not without interest, therefore, at this point to cast a further glance at the history of the CAC and its predecessor, the Industrial Court, which was created under the Industrial Courts Act 1919 and which was, in 1971, re-christened the Industrial Arbitration Board.

We have seen that the Conciliation Act of 1896, despite its insignificant appearance—Lord Amulree called it the "ridiculous mouse" to which the mountain of the Royal Commission of 1892 gave birth[54]—was of vital importance as the basis of the conciliation services of what came to be known as the Department of Employment.[55] It was, however, inadequate in one respect: it failed to create a permanent arbitration board, *i.e.* a body which would develop not only its own expertise, but possibly also a set of

---

[50] Davies, *op. cit.* pp. 304–313; ACAS, *Annual Report 1982*, Table 7.
[51] ACAS, *Annual Report 1975*, para. 4.2. In its *Annual Report 1980*, para. 3.11, the Service suggests that parties may prefer non-CAC arbitration because CAC Awards are published and the CAC procedure does not enable the parties to nominate the wingmen or be consulted about the choice of chairman.
[52] Chap. 4.
[53] Chap. 6.
[54] *loc. cit.* p. 107.
[55] See its Third Memo. to the Royal Commission, and Industrial Relations Handbook, Chap. 2.

principles that could be brought to bear on the settlement of industrial conflicts. In 1908 Winston Churchill, who, as President of the Board of Trade, was then in charge of these matters, tried to fill the gap through administrative arrangments for a permanent panel of arbitrators.[56] This does not appear to have been very successful during the brief spell between its creation and the First World War, but it paved the way for the recommendation to create a permanent Board which the Whitely Committee made during the War in one of its reports.[57] That report in turn was the basis of the Industrial Courts Act of 1919 which set up the Industrial Court, despite its name not a "court" in the usual sense at all, but a standing statutory tripartite tribunal for the settlement of industrial disputes by voluntary arbitration. Under its new name of Industrial Arbitration Board[58] it continued to operate under the Industrial Relations Act 1971, but when that Act was repealed by the Trade Union and Labour Relations Act 1974,[59] it was abolished (the relevant portions of the 1919 Act were repealed)[60] and the CAC inherited its functions.

We have already seen[61] that the tripartite structure of the Industrial Arbitration Board has been maintained in the organisation of the CAC and that, like its predecessor, it is not subject to directions from anyone, and, despite its organisational links with the ACAS, is as independent from the Service as the Industrial Arbitration Board was from the Department of Employment. Nevertheless, there has, under the Employment Protection Act, been one change in its position which raises a point of importance.

We have emphasised that arbitration is dominated by the twin principles of the need for consent by the parties and the priority of their own autonomous machinery. Under the Employment Protection Act, as under the previous law, the application of the second of these principles is guaranteed by the procedure which must be observed before a case can go to arbitration.[62] Exceptional cases apart,[63] no one can submit a case for arbitration directly. The CAC cannot arbitrate except upon a reference by the Service, just

---

[56] Amulree, *loc cit.*, p. 113; Askwith, *Industrial Problems and Disputes* (1920), p.127

[57] Fourth Report, Cd. 9099 (1918).

[58] Industrial Relations Act 1971. s. 124

[59] s. 1.

[60] Employment Protection Act 1975, Sched. 18.

[61] In Chap. 4.

[62] Employment Protection Act 1975, s. 3(1).

[63] *i.e.* where the Committee is asked to interpret one of its own awards: *Ibid.* Sched. 1, para. 24.

as its predecessor, the Industrial Arbitration Board, could not do so without a reference by the Department of Employment.[64] The change to which we have referred is the substitution of the autonomous ACAS for the Department of Employment as the organ which can open or block the way to arbitration. All a party to a dispute can do is to ask ("request") the Service to refer the matter to the CAC, and the Service, of course, cannot comply with this request unless all parties to the dispute agree. But the vital point is that such general agreement enables, but does not compel, the Service to make the reference. Before doing so, it must consider two matters: the first is whether the dispute cannot be settled by conciliation, and the second is whether there is autonomous settlement machinery and—special reasons for by-passing it apart—whether an attempt to use it has been made and failed. The mere agreement between the parties to the dispute does not relieve the Service of the duty to ensure that the intervention of statutory procedures is treated as subsidiary to autonomous regulation.[65]

The CAC is not of course a court. As a voluntary arbitration board it is its duty to promote agreements, *i.e.* to assist in the creation of rights and obligations between the parties, and not, as a court usually does, to determine what rights and obligations are already in existence. Nevertheless, its spirit is judicial and so is, to some extent, its procedure. It sits in public, but its chairman may, in his discretion, order that it should sit in private.[66] It hears the parties—the oral hearing is usually prepared by documents—and arrives at its award either by a unanimous decision or, if that cannot be reached, by that of the chairman who then acts as umpire.[67] What this means in practice is simply that the members of the Committee "representing" management and labour cannot outvote the chairman. Since the two sides are represented by equal numbers (usually one only) on either side, this is a most unlikely thing to happen. The decision must be published[68]—this is different where the matter goes before ad hoc arbitrators, when publication is optional.[69] It must be published, but the law does

---

[64] Industrial Courts Act 1919, s. 2(2)—now repealed.
[65] Employment Protection Act 1975, s. 3(2). For details of the operation of the previous law, see Min. of Lab. Evid., *loc. cit.*; Wedderburn and Davies, *loc. cit.*, pp. 182–192. For a desciption of the procedure of the CAC see its *First Annual Report* 1976, Chap. 3.
[66] Employment Protection Act 1975, Sched. 1, para. 18.
[67] *Ibid.* para 19 (in Scotland "oversman").
[68] *Ibid.* para. 24.
[69] s. 3(4). The possibility of avoiding publicity may be an inducement to adopt this procedure.

not say that, when acting as a voluntary arbitration body,[70] the CAC must give reasons for its award, and this raises a matter of principle, and indeed goes to the root of arbitration of trade disputes.

It was, in the early days of the Industrial Court, regarded as possible that, in the course of its extensive arbitration practice, it would develop a set of principles to be applied to trade disputes, a kind of "industrial case law." That this was going to happen was the expectation of its first President, Lord Amulree.[71] He thought that there would be developed something like an industrial common law; perhaps this was one of the reasons why the statutory arbitration board was at first called a "court."[72] Assuming the development of such a body of principles had been feasible, it could obviously have been achieved only if the reasons of the Board for its awards had been formulated and published. To some extent this was done during the very early years,[73] but—special cases apart—it has for decades been the normal practice to summarise in the award the proceedings and the principal arguments of the parites, but not to disclose the substantive considerations which led the Board—now the Committee—to its conclusion.[74] In retrospect this was inevitable.[75] The object of the proceedings is to put an end to a dispute. Unlike the report of an investigating commission, the award of an arbitrator or arbitration board is not intended to be the basis of further negotiations, but to take their place. As the President of the (then) Industrial Court pointed out in his evidence to the Donovan Commission, if reasons were given, this would "result in prolonging and possibly even exacerbating the differences between the parties, or in transferring the area of controversy from one topic or topics to another."[76] And, by the same token, a detailed

---

[70] Quite different in cases of unilateral arbitration on recognition issues. See Chap. 4.

[71] *loc. cit.,* pp. 190 *et seq.*

[72] On this nomenclature see the evidence of Sir Roy Wilson, Q.C., the President of the (then) Industrial Court, before the Donovan Commission: Minutes of Evidence No. 45 (July 26, 1966), Qu. 7207 *et seq.,* and Sir Roy Wilson's further evidence, p. 1965, No. 3.

[73] Amulree, *loc. cit.,* pp. 183 *et seq.* Lord Amulree was much in favour of this.

[74] On this and what follows, see the evidence to the Donovan Commission of Sir Roy Wilson, Q.C., No. 45 (July 26, 1966), paras. 4–8; and of Sir George Honeyman, Q.C., the Chairman of the Civil Service Arbitration Tribunal, *ibid.* No. 50 (Sept. 27, 1966), paras. 5–9.

[75] The Donovan Commission arrived at a different conclusion (paras. 284–286 of its Report).

[76] Para. 7(*a*) of his evidence.

allocation, say, of an awarded wage increase "for separate components" may be equally harmful.[77] But, perhaps even more importantly, the Committee is, as has been said, tripartite. The employer and the employee "side" members or "wingmen" are intended to be (and no doubt are) impartial towards the particular dispute, but they are supposed to bring to bear upon the decision the experience and the point of view of management and labour. This is true of all "tripartite" bodies. Where such a body is a judicial tribunal, called upon to apply existing law (such as the industrial tribunals which deal with individual disputes between employers and employees or even the Committee when acting under its compulsory jurisdictions), the difference between the experience and approach of the members of the court will mainly emerge in the appreciation of the evidence and the assessment of the facts, and on the legal questions the chairman's opinion will usually prevail. There is every reason why such a tribunal should publish the considerations which guided its decision. But where the body is formulating an award which, to some extent at least, reflects the power situation between the parties, that is, traces a line on which the parties can be expected to meet, and which, besides, incorporates policy considerations of comparability with other industries, and of the desirability of maintaning differentials or, conversely, of upgrading lower income groups, it would be injudicious to publish reasons.

If it did so, the Committee might create expectations for future cases, to be decided in different circumstances calling for a different assessment of the power situation and of the weight to be attached to different considerations. Moreover, a board of this nature is intended by its constitution to express in its decisions a line of policy on which, if possible, the representatives of the two sides of industry and the chairman can agree. Such agreement may often be in the nature of a compromise, but the reasons which induced its members to accept it may be very different. In his evidence to the Donovan Commission the Chairman of the Civil Service Arbitration Tribunal[78] reported that "on numerous occasions" there was in that body "no difficulty in reaching agreement on the conclusion but there would have been considerable difficulty in reaching agreement on the reasons." To publish "concurrent" opinions (as is done in collegiate courts in common

---

[77] See Sir G. Honeyman's evidence, para. 7.
[78] *Ibid.* para. 8. Though the CAC is organised by statute and the CSAT by collective agreement between the Treasury and the relevant unions, the problems are the same.

law countries) would be as disastrous as the publication of "dissenting" opinions of the members of a body deliberately designed to reflect divergent interests. The motives for not publishing the reasons for awards in labour relations are different from those which prompt arbitrators acting under the Arbitration Acts not to do so—motives connected with the law of arbitration as laid down in those statutes[79] which, as we have seen, do not apply to labour arbitration.[80] The sacrifice of the idea of an "industrial case law" stems from the fact that the conflict between capital and labour is permanent, a conflict in which there cannot be a decision on set principles, but only an adjustment from time to time in the light of the ever-varying power situation. The settlement of trade disputes (whether by arbitration or otherwise) is much more comparable with the making of an international treaty or even with a commercial transaction than with a legal decision. It is not "justiciable."

It is right to give so much emphasis to this point for two reasons. In the first place it is linked with the much debated problem whether a body such as the CAC should have the right and should have the obligation to take into account the incomes policy of the government of the day.[81] One may be tempted to argue that a statutory body should not give effect to policies at variance with those of the Government.[82] However, as the President of the (then) Industrial Court emphasised in his evidence to the Donovan Commission, this argument neglects a vital point: arbitration of the type here under discussion is valueless, and we shall come back to this in a moment when we talk about compulsory arbitration, unless the arbitrators are, and—this is essential—are believed to be, independent of the Government, and subject to no instructions at all.[83] They must be as independent as all collective bargaining parties are, with the exception of those who are or represent a government department. The collective bargaining parties may be

---

[79] Arbitration Act 1950, esp. ss. 21 *et seq.*, and its predecessor, the Arbitration Act 1889, as amended in 1934. But see now also Arbitration Act 1979, ss. 1(5), (6), 3 and 4.

[80] Employment Protection Act 1975, s. 3(5) and Sched. 1, para. 26.

[81] See Sir Roy Wilson's evidence, paras. 12 *et seq.*; evidence of the National Board of Prices and Incomes, PIB Report No. 19, Cmnd. 3087, Chap. 7, and the evidence to the Donovan Commission of the Rt. Hon. Aubrey Jones (then Chairman of the Board) (Minutes of Evidence No. 51, Oct 4, 1966, Questions 8253 *et seq.*). See now also the observations in the CAC's *First Annual Report.* 1976. Chap. 5.

[82] This was the view of the Donovan Commission. See its Report, paras. 284 and 285.

[83] Sir Roy Wilson's evidence, paras. 13 and 14.

impressed by the need for adhering to policies formulated by the Government because they believe their observance to be in the general interest, and so may the arbitrators. It is humanly impossible for the members of a body such as the CAC not to be influenced by what they read in the papers, and by their knowledge of the need for anti-inflationary measures; and if they are convinced that the Government is right in formulating policies accordingly, why should they not give effect to them, not because they are the policies of the Government but because they are right? But it would be very bad if this was expressed in anything savouring of a directive or instruction, or even if there was a mistaken impression that such directives or instructions existed. Such a suspicion appears to have existed in trade union quarters at one time, and to have done the arbitration system great harm, at least temporarily.[84] This situation provides additional grounds for not publishing the reasons prompting an award. The line between adopting a policy by reason of a belief that it is right and adopting it by reason of a suspected hidden "directive" may not always be as clear to all those concerned as in objective fact no doubt it is. It may be added that acceptance by government in recent years of the fact that arbitration can be effective only if truly independent has led to a reluctance on the part of government to include compulsory arbitration in the standing arrangements for the settlement of wages disputes with its own employees or those for whom it is in effect the paymaster.[85]

The second reason why we have said so much about this problem of "reasons" is that it demonstrates how much lawyers have to jettison their accustomed modes of thinking when handling problems of industrial relations, and it is perhaps significant in this context that, where the Industrial Arbitration Board did deal with what you may describe as a "legal" issue, *viz.*, the interpretation of one of its previous awards, it used to give reasons for the decision.[86] It is also significant in this context that

---

[84] *Ibid.* para. 14. During the period of the "Social Contract" incomes policy (1975–1978), ACAS sent copies of the relevant White Papers to arbitrators, but arbitration facilities continued to be freely available to the parties and arbitrators were recommended "to include in their awards, where appropriate, a statement that they were not empowered to give an authoritative ruling as to whether the award conformed with the pay policy and that if the parties had any doubts on that aspect they should seek the advice of the appropriate authorities." ACAS, *Annual Report 1976,* p. 14.

[85] See, *e.g.* Report of Inquiry into Civil Service Pay (Cmnd. 8590, 1982), paras. 263–272.

[86] *Ibid.* Oral answers to Questions 7241 *et seq.*; see Employment Protection Act 1975, Sched. 1, para. 23.

the CAC, whose workload has been dominated in recent years by its compulsory jurisdictions, which often involve interpreting and applying legislative provisions, has developed the practice of inserting in its published awards a statement of the "general considerations" which have guided it. This is not a full statement of the reasons for the award, but a description of the Committee's general approach to the problem and, in typical forward-looking arbitral manner, an indication of the Committee's view as to the best way for the parties to proceed in the future. Nevertheless, how misleading the lawyer's pattern of thought can be in this matter is cogently shown by the fact that even as experienced a lawyer as the late Lord Amulree, the first President of the Industrial Court, succumbed to the false analogy between the development of the common law through decided cases, and the development of labour relations through industrial arbitration.

(d) Investigation by the ACAS and by Courts of Inquiry

Statutory conciliation services and the statutory procedure for reference to arbitration are now, as we have seen, concentrated in the ACAS. In addition, the Service has the power,[87] "if it thinks fit," to "inquire into any question relating to industrial relations," generally, in an industry, in an undertaking or in part of an undertaking(*e.g.* a particular plant or workshop). These investigative powers the Service has inherited from the Department of Employment,[88] but they are much enlarged. However, the power to inquire into trade disputes in particular (which is comprised in the power to inquire into questions of industrial relations) is shared by the ACAS with so-called Courts of Inquiry. These are not permanent institutions, but are appointed ad hoc, *i.e.* a special "court" for each case, in his discretion by the Secretary of State for Employment under Part II of the Industrial Courts Act 1919, which is still in force.[89] Strictly speaking, it is the Secretary of State himself who has a residual power of inquiry by virtue of these provisions, a power which he may, but need not, exercise through the appointment of such an investigating committee, misnamed in the Act a "court" (which it certainly is not in any accepted sense of that word). That the Secretary of State has himself this residual power under the 1919 Act is not a merely academic observation: there is nothing to prevent him from exercising it by appointing a commission of investigation which is not a "court of inquiry"

---

[87] Employment Protection Act 1975, s. 5.
[88] Conciliation Act 1896, s. 2(1) (*a*)—now repealed.
[89] Industrial Courts Act 1919, s. 4.

within the meaning of the Act—its procedure may be less formal and its report need not be published. In the past it appears to have been usual for the Secretary of State, when using this residual power, not to rely on the 1919 Act, but on "his general powers, *i.e.* those which he enjoys by virtue of his Ministerial position."[90] One reason for using these was that they enabled the Secretary of State to set up an inquiry jointly with another Minister.

We have thus three types of investigative procedures: those initiated by the ACAS, those used by the Secretary of State under his residual powers (whether this be the residual power under the 1919 Act or the "general" ministerial power), and formal Courts of Inquiry. Courts of Inquiry have, in the past, been used sparingly, mainly in major cases of industrial conflict.[91] The Secretary of State may, and invariably on appointing a Court does, make rules regulating its procedure, and these usually give it powers to call for documents and to take evidence on oath.[92] What is, however, decisive is that the report of Court of Inquiry is always[93] published as a Command Paper[94] (unless security reasons stand in the way), and often debated in Parliament. The idea is that public opinion should be mobilised in favour of its recommendations. From all this it will be seen that this is, as it were, the "heavy artillery" in the arsenal of the authorities charged with the settlement of disputes. It is also very important that, apart from the ACAS, there is no permanent investigating body as there is a permanent arbitration body. Since a Court of Inquiry ceases to exist when it has made and published its recommendations, no false expectations can be aroused by publishing the reasons for making them. And since it is appointed and able to act without the consent of the parties and since it is the government which formulates its terms of reference, it may perhaps sometimes be easier for a secretary of a trade union or of an employer's association to persuade his organisation to accept such recommendations than it would have been to suggest that it should submit a dispute to arbitration and to accept an award. In the past,

---

[90] Min. of Lab. Evid., *loc. cit.,* para. 35.
[91] Wedderburn and Davies, *op. cit.,* pp. 224 *et seq.*; Sharp, *loc. cit.,* p. 362; Min. Of Lab. Fourth Memo., paras. 30 *et seq.* The best analysis is McCarthy and Clifford, "The Work of Industrial Courts of Inquiry. A Study of Existing Provisions and Past Practices" (1966) 4 Brit. J. of Ind. Rel. 39.
[92] Min. of Lab., *loc. cit.,* para. 31; Industrial Courts Act 1919, s. 4(4) and (5) (still in force); McCarthy and Clifford, *loc. cit.,* p. 40.
[93] Industrial Courts Act 1919, s. 5 (in force).
[94] McCarthy and Clifford, *loc. cit.,* p. 41; Sharp, *loc. cit.,* pp. 290 *et seq.* For an analysis of the past work of committees of investigation, see Wedderburn and Davies, *op. cit.,* pp. 232 *et seq.*

for a time at least, it seems to have been possible to settle through this kind of inquiry some disputes which defied handling in any other manner.[95]

The principal contrast between an inquiry by the ACAS and by a Court of Inquiry is in the element of publicity, both of the proceedings and of their result. Whilst a report and recommendations of a Court of Inquiry are always published—and indeed that may be its *raison d'être*,—the ACAS may also,[96] but it need not, publish the findings resulting from one of its inquiries or the advice it gives to the parties on the basis of them. It does so only if it is advisable in the interest of the improvement of industrial relations generally or in a particular respect, and after consulting all the parties concerned. It has a complete discretion in the matter. Such findings and advice are not laid before Parliament.

(e) The ACAS and the reform of labour relations

Conciliation and arbitration are principally substitutes for direct negotiation on substantive terms of employment, but, as we have seen, they, and especially conciliation, can also be used to settle disputes on bargaining machinery, on recognition, and quite generally on what can be the subject of a procedure agreement. More significantly, the ACAS can use its investigative powers to advise on the improvement of the mechanics of industrial relations, and the Employment Protection Act makes it very clear[97] that this can be done, no matter whether an entire industry or enterprise is concerned or "part of an undertaking," *e.g.* the bargaining methods as between the shop stewards and local management in a particular plant. This alone would mean that the ACAS would be able to help by its advice to improve the collective bargaining mechanism itself, and especially, because this is particularly necessary, the machinery and procedures for the settlement of disputes within a particular plant or enterprise. Courts of Inquiry too have in the past quite generally recommended improvement of disputes procedures on a large scale— sometimes indeed they were specially appointed to deal with recognition disputes.[98] In addition to all this, however, and quite apart from its task of settling disputes and making inquiries, the

---

[95] McCarthy and Clifford, *loc. cit.*, pp. 51, 56, and Wedderburn and Davies, *loc. cit.* Such courts have been used sparingly in recent years and none has been established since 1977 when Lord Scarman chaired an inquiry into the dispute at Grunwick Processing Laboratories (above, p. 100).

[96] Employment Protection Act 1975, s. 5(2)

[97] s. 5(1).

[98] McCarthy and Clifford, *loc. cit.*, pp. 45 *et seq.*

ACAS has expressly and most explicitly been given the function of advising employers and their organisations, trade unions and workers, on request or of its own motion, free of charge, "on any matter concerned with industrial relations or employment policies,"[99] and, if it sees fit, it may publish such advice if it is general,[1] which presumably means not concerned with a particular undertaking. The ACAS has thus the power—which means the duty—to play a central role in the reform not only of collective bargaining at all levels, from the highest to the lowest, of grievance procedures, and indeed of communication between employers and workers quite generally, but also of recognition practices, and facilities for union officials, such as shop stewards, at the workplace. It can and, where the need arises (and that need is very widespread), it must go further, and seek to help the parties to achieve better codes of discipline and disciplinary procedures,[2] and especially procedures for the termination of employment. It may and must assist management and organised labour in manpower planning, in developing methods of recruitment, of promotion, and—nothing more vital—training of workers, of payment systems, and—a matter now central in view of the provisions on "equal pay for work of equal value"—of job evaluation. All these are only examples of the many directions in which the advisory function of the Service is to be utilised for the so urgently necessary modernisation of the system of labour relations, that is relations between management and labour. But the organisation of the trade unions themselves is in equally great need of overhaul and so is that of the employers, and, at least in so far as it serves the "purpose of collective bargaining", advice on this has also been included in the list of tasks imposed upon the ACAS by law.[3] In this particular connection the tri-partite composition of its Council to which we referred in the previous chapter may prove to be of great value.

Hence the ACAS has been given a task which the previous law had not in so many words imposed upon the Department of Employment: the reform of the mechanics of labour relations. This function stems from the diagnosis of those relations in the Donovan Report, and especially from its finding that procedure

---

[99] Employment Protection Act 1975, s. 4 (1). For a description of the advisory work, see ACAS, *Annual Report 1979*, Chap. 8.

[1] s. 4(2).

[2] See its Code of Practice No. 1: "Disciplinary practice and procedures in employment."

[3] s. 4 (1) (a).

agreements were badly in need of reform[4] and that the "root of the evil" of wildcat strikes was the absence of "speedy, clear and effective" settlement and bargaining procedures especially, but not only, at plant level.[5] It recommended[6] that, for the first time,[7] a special institution should be created for the purpose of investigating industrial procedures and for recommending their improvement, and also for the solution of recognition problems. This recommendation was implemented by setting up the Commission on Industrial Relations, at first by Royal Warrant,[8] and then, under the Industrial Relations Act 1971,[9] as an independent statutory body. The CIR which, during its brief existence, published a long series of valuable reports, disappeared in 1974 with the repeal of the Industrial Relations Act, but its powers and duties were taken over by the ACAS and this is the background of its present advisory function: it is the direct successor of the CIR. The big difference is that whereas the CIR acted upon a reference by a minister or by several ministers, normally by the Secretary of State for Employment, the ACAS acts "if it thinks fit," of its own motion or on request. This is a significant change.

This statutory organisation dedicated to the improvement of the mechanics of labour relations is still something of very recent origin. In the past there were only vestiges of such arrangements, such as the tri-partite ad hoc commissions of inquiry set up under the Wages Councils Acts[10] to advise the Department of Employment on whether minimum wage machinery should be created, varied or abolished for a given category of workers. Their functions have now been taken over by the ACAS.[11]

(f) Conciliation in individual disputes

One common factor of all these activities, *i.e.* arbitration, inquiry, and also and especially, conciliation, is that they are designed and intended to promote collective agreements and to improve collective labour relations. There is, however, also another type of conciliation—it is that which refers to individual

---

[4] Paras. 59–74 of the Report. See also Flanders, *Industrial Relations: What is Wrong with the System?* (1965), esp. Chap. 6.
[5] Para. 475.
[6] Paras. 198 *et seq.*
[7] s. 4 of the Conciliation Act 1896 was a dead letter.
[8] See its First General Report, Cmnd. 4417.
[9] s. 120.
[10] Wages Councils Act 1959, s. 2—now repealed.
[11] Employment Protection Act 1975, s. 89, now replaced by Wages Councils Act 1979, ss. 3, 6, 7, 10, 12. See, *e.g.*, ACAS, *Annual Report 1979*, pp. 53–56.

disputes between an employer and a worker. For many of these disputes the industrial tribunals have jurisdiction under a number of statutes, and many of these statutes provide that the proceedings before the tribunal must be preceded by an attempt at conciliation. At the moment this jurisdiction covers only rights arising from statutes (*e.g.* in the event of unfair dismissal),[12] but the Lord Chancellor and the Secretary of State for Scotland may extend it (as a jurisdiction concurrent with that of the ordinary courts) to rights arising from contracts of employment at common law,[13] and if this happens, the enforcement of common law claims in the industrial tribunals will also have to be preceded by conciliation.[14] It is one of the functions of the ACAS to designate conciliation officers for this purpose.[15] They have to try to bring about an amicable settlement in all those cases in which the statute does not only confer jurisdiction on industrial tribunals, but also lays down that they must be preceded by conciliation, whether it is the Employment Protection (Consolidation) Act itself or any other statute passed before or after that Act.[16] Thus, the conciliation officers designated by the ACAS deal with unfair dismissal, with guarantee pay, maternity pay, violation of rights to union membership and activity, "time off," and other matters, including claims by individuals that they have been unreasonably excluded or expelled from a trade union. The main claim not covered is that for a redundancy payment.

In imposing this function on the ACAS the statute expressly refers not only to "matters which are . . . the subject of proceedings before an industrial tribunal," but also to those which are not, but "could be": hence this individual conciliation service has, from the procedural point of view, a preventive or prophylactic as well as a curative or therapeutic role.[17] It is designed to settle disputes, but also to prevent them.

In recent times over 40,000 applications to industrial tribunals a year have been referred to the Service for conciliation.[18] One third or more are settled by conciliation, and a further quarter do not

---

[12] Employment Protection (Consolidation) Act 1978, s. 128(1).
[13] s. 131.
[14] s. 133(1)(*c*).
[15] Employment Protection Act 1975, s. 2(4).
[16] This covers the Equal Pay Act 1970, the Sex Discrimination Act 1975 and the Race Relations Act 1976 and any Act specified under s. 133(7) (*b*).
[17] ss.133(3) and 134(3). In 1980 8,648 cases were handled under these provisions. See also *Duport Furniture Products Ltd.* v. *Moore* [1982] I.C.R. 84 (H.L.).
[18] For an account of the Service's work in this area see ACAS, *Annual Report 1978*, Chap. 10.

proceed to a tribunal hearing for other reasons. The conciliation officer has a duty to intervene if requested by the parties to do so or if, without such a request, he believes he could act with a reasonable prospect of success.[19] In practice, conciliation officers make at least initial approaches to the parties under this latter provision in all cases referred to them, so that over half the operational staff resources in the ACAS regions are devoted to individual conciliation. This high rate of settlement is prima facie evidence of the success of individual conciliation, but there has been criticism of the quality of the settlements achieved. There is a tension here between two views of the conciliation process in individual disputes. The Service has stated that it sees individual conciliation as akin to collective conciliation, so that the achievement of a settlement which both parties accept—or at least acquiesce in—is the goal of the process. Conciliation in individual claims is "a completely voluntary process based on the underlying tradition in British industrial relations of voluntary bargaining and agreement."[20] On the other hand, one might see the tribunal process, of which conciliation is an integral part, as a means of vindicating individuals' rights, so that the nature of any settlement achieved becomes a matter of concern.[21] To some extent the statute itself adopts the second perspective, because in unfair dismissal claims—the majority of cases—the conciliator is under a statutory duty to promote the reinstatement or re-engagement of a dismissed employee or, failing that, the payment to him of a sum by way of compensation.[22] If a settlement is achieved between the parties, it is formally recorded and is effective to prevent the employee subsequently pursuing his claim before a tribunal, *i.e.* a conciliated settlement is an exception to the general rule than an employee cannot contract out of his statutory rights under the employment protection legislation.[23]

Our law is careful to separate the conciliation service from the judicial service itself. In other counties, *e.g.* France and Germany, the judicial officers themselves are called upon to conciliate, in

---

[19] Employment Protection (Consolidation) Act 1978, s. 134(1).

[20] ACAS, *op. cit.,* p. 84. In one respect at least the statute reinforces this view, for s. 134(4) requires conciliators to have regard to the desirability of encouraging the use of voluntary procedures, rather than of tribunals, to settle the grievance.

[21] This view would identify the decision of the House of Lords in *Duport Furniture Products Ltd.* v. *Moore* as a disappointing one—see above, n. 17 and below, n. 22.

[22] s. 134(2), although the concilator is not, it seems, under a duty to produce a settlement that is fair: *Duport Furniture Products Ltd.* v. *Moore* (above).

[23] s. 140(2) (*g*).

Germany the magistrate who will have to preside if conciliation fails, in France different members of the *conseil de prud'hommes* which is the equivalent of an industrial tribunal. After a few years it will be interesting to compare notes on the experience derived from these different procedural methods of giving effect to the policy of reducing litigation to a minimum.

2. COMPULSORY METHODS

None of the rules and institutions so far described in this chapter is backed by any legal compulsion. This is an important difference between the present law and the Industrial Relations Act 1971,[24] under which the National Industrial Relations Court had jurisdiction to impose a procedure agreement. It is, however, useful to cast a glance at the role which compulsory arbitration plays in other countries and which it has played in this country in the past, and at the conditions under which it can function.

"Agreement" and "compulsion" seem to be antithetic terms. We are nevertheless dealing with compulsory arbitration under the heading of "promoting agreement" because in practice the line between voluntary bargaining and compulsory arbitration may, as the Australian example shows,[25] be far more fluid than it appears to be in conceptual scheme, and, secondly, because even in a conceptual scheme compulsory methods are sometimes designed to produce a decision or award which the law treats as an agreement[26] or voluntary agreements are treated as if they were a compulsory award.[27]

We are concerned only with compulsory arbitration. Conciliation and investigation can be compulsory only in the sense that the parties may be compelled to attend or that the procedure does not depend on their consent or that their freedom to take industrial action is restricted.[28] With the problem of restrictions on the freedom to strike or to lock out we shall deal later.[29] Compulsion to attend and proceedings without the parties' consent cannot in themselves impose a settlement or a procedure agreement. This

---

[24] ss. 37 *et seq.*

[25] See *infra.*

[26] For examples of the compulsory order or award as an imputed contract: German Arbitration Decree of October 30, 1923, Art I, s. 5, para. 4 and s. 6, para. 3.

[27] For an example of a voluntary agreement treated as if it was an award: Australian Commonwealth Conciliation and Arbitration Acts 1904–1976, s. 28. Consent awards are very important in practice. See Mills and Sorrell, *Federal Industrial Law* (1975), pp. 73 *et seq.* See further below.

[28] *e.g.* under the provisions of the Taft-Hartley Act discussed below in Chap. 8.

[29] Chap. 8.

however is what matters in the present context: that the parties are in one form or another bound by a regulation which is not of their own choosing, a regulation of conditions of employment or a regulation of the machinery for settling disputes and for determining conditions of employment. This subjection of the parties to regulation imposed from outside is the result of compulsory arbitration, compulsory in the sense that arbitration does not depend on the consent of both sides and that the award is binding on them, whether they accept or reject it. If one of these two elements, *i.e.* the compulsory proceedings or the compulsory award is absent, either side can prevent the compulsory operation of the system, either by not participating in the proceedings or by rejecting the award.

This legal definition of compulsory arbitration does not however touch the core of the matter, that is, the social and political significance of this form of settlement. This depends first and foremost on the status of the arbitrator in relation to the Government. If he is bound by general directives or specific instructions issued by the Government, then compulsory arbitration is to a smaller or larger degree a mechanism for the fixing of wages and other conditions by governmental order in accordance with the economic and social policies of the government—it is the system of the "political wage," and industrial pressures are replaced by political pressures. It depends on the political constitution whether this means that parliamentary procedures take the place of industrial procedures or whether the decisions emanate from the internal and invisible relations of power groups inside an executive. The classical example is the compulsory arbitration system of the Weimar Republic in Germany in which in effect the Minister of Labour was the chief arbitrator and all others acted in accordance with his general directives.[30] The awards were part and parcel of the (at the critical time deflationary) economic policy of the Government. The relevant decree provided however that the imposed award was a fictitious collective agreement, and the two sides of industry had to observe and to enforce it as if it had been a freely concluded contract.[31] This system of compulsory arbitration paved the way to the regulation of wages and other

---

[30] Arbitration Decree of October 30, 1923, Art. 1, s. 7.

[31] *Ibid.* s. 5, para. 4. By this an award which was binding by virtue of a statute had "the effect of a written collective agreement." Also *ibid.* s. 6, para. 3, by which the order making the award binding was deemed to replace (*"ersetzt"*) its acceptance by the parties. See R. Lewis and J. Clark (eds.), *Labour Law and Politics in the Weimar Republic by Otto Kahn-Freund*, (1981), Chap. 4.

conditions of employment by governmental order which Hitler introduced after he had destroyed the trade unions.

The classical examples, on the other hand, of systems of compulsory arbitration by independent arbitrators are those of Australia[32] and New Zealand.[33] Since 1904 wages and other conditions of employment have, to the extent to which the Federal Constitution allowed it,[34] been settled in this manner in the Commonwealth of Australia, and for many decades a similar system has been in operation in four of the six Australian States[35] whilst in New Zealand it goes back to 1894.[36] Nothing is more difficult than to understand, from the other side of the globe, systems of industrial relations as subtle and complex as those of Australia and that of New Zealand (which differ widely between each other). Still, as far as one can venture to form a judgment, it seems that in the words of the former President of the Commonwealth Conciliation and Arbitration Commission, "arbitration and collective bargaining are not mutually exclusive." In his view "they go hand in hand to some extent in collective bargaining countries and to a greater extent in this country," *i.e.* in Australia.[37] If, in the course of the conciliation proceedings, the parties do arrive at an agreement, a memorandum is drawn up, and, subject to a number of conditions, this memorandum, if certified by the Commission, "has the same effect as, and shall be deemed to be, an award of the Commission for all purposes of this Act."[38] In very numerous cases the parties arrive at an agreement, and, having done so, consent to ask the Commission to make an

---

[32] Commonwealth Conciliation and Arbitration Acts 1904–79; Mills and Sorrell, *Federal Industrial Law* (5th ed. 1975); Sykes and Glasbeek, *Labour Law in Australia* (1972), p. 369.

[33] Mathieson, *Industrial Law in New Zealand,* Vol. I (1970) and supp. (1975).

[34] s. 51 (xxxv): "conciliation and arbitration for the prevention and settlement of industrial disputes extending beyond the limits of one State." The federal "trade and commerce" power (s. 51 (*i*)) is not—except for certain industries— regarded as a constitutional basis for labour legislation, a fundamental difference from the modern interpretation of the "interstate commerce power" under the Constitution of the United States.

[35] The exceptions are Victoria and Tasmania which have "wage board systems."

[36] Industrial Conciliation and Arbitration Act 1894, often amended, and replaced by subsequent statutes. The present statute is the Industrial Relations Act 1973, again subsequently amended.

[37] Kirby, "Some Comparisons between Compulsory Arbitration and Collective Bargaining" (1965) 24 *Public Administration* 200, cited in Mathieson, *supra,* pp. 240–241. This is still true despite the procedural separation of conciliation and arbitration since the Amending Act of 1972. See ss. 28–30 of the present Act, and Mills and Sorrell, *loc. cit.*, p. 77.

[38] s. 28(3).

award incorporating its terms. Whilst in other countries we sometimes find that an award is treated as a fictitious agreement, Australia treats the agreement as a fictitious award; it illustrates not only a legislative technique, but it seems to an observer from far away to symbolise the extent to which this system of arbitration has become part of the mores of the country. It is clear that to an appreciable extent the Australian system of compulsory arbitration is used as an opportunity for the parties to make collective agreements which are then given "teeth" through being incorporated in a consent award or "certified" by the Commission. The Commission can, but rarely does,[39] refuse to do so if, in its opinion, this would be against the public interest; the "public interest" is here not synonymous with the policy of the Government. This feature that collective bargaining and arbitration are closely intertwined is shared by the New Zealand system,[40] however different it may be in other respects from that of Australia. In neither country has compulsory arbitration suppressed the freedom of the two sides of industry. Like our centrally agreed wage rates, all wages determined in Australia and New Zealand by arbitration are minima, not standard, even where there are "margins" for skill, or other additions to the "basic" wage. Hence much is left to local or enterprise or plant bargaining on actual wages as distinct from minimum rates,[41] and it appears that at times of a high level of employment this becomes as important as in this country or elsewhere in Europe. How could it fail to be? No doubt the arbitration authorities have a very strong influence on wages, standard hours, and other conditions of employment. Yet, despite their formidable legal carapace, the Australian and New Zealand methods of compulsory arbitration are, seen across a distance of thousands of miles, far less different from our familiar collective bargaining systems than one would have expected. The difference lies in the enforcement.

There could thus be no greater contrast than that between the Australian and New Zealand variants of compulsory arbitration and the Weimar system to which we have briefly referred. However, these Australian and New Zealand systems are almost

---

[39] Sykes, "Labor Arbitration in Australia" (1964) 13 Am. J. of Comp. Law 216, 226, n. 18.

[40] Mathieson, *loc. cit.*, pp. 239 *et seq.*

[41] See Grunfeld, "Australian Compulsory Arbitration: Appearance and Reality" (1971) 9 Brit. J. of Ind. Rel. 330; I. E. Issac, "Compulsory Arbitration and Collective Bargaining Reconsidered" (1974) 16 (Australian) J. of Ind. Rel. No. 1. Perhaps for this reason the system has been prone to high levels of industrial conflict in recent years.

equally different from those which were in force in this country during the two World Wars, and for a number of years after the Second War. Nothing need be said about the Munitions of War Acts of the First World War,[42] and one can concentrate on the scheme of things developed in and after 1940, which still has repercussions today. The Conditions of Employment and National Arbitration Order of 1940, the famous Order No. 1305, was made by the Minister of Labour and National Service in virtue of powers conferred upon him by a Defence Regulation[43] made under the Emergency Powers Act.[44] In the vital interest of uninterrupted production, strikes and lockouts in connection with trade disputes were conditionally forbidden, *i.e.* forbidden unless three weeks' notice of the dispute had been given to the Ministry of Labour and the Ministry had within these three weeks failed to take any steps towards a settlement.[45] The first duty of the Ministry was to settle the dispute through the autonomous institutions of the industry concerned, and, failing this, through conciliation or voluntary arbitration,[46] and only in the last resort to refer it to the compulsory arbitration body set up by the Order which was known as the National Arbitration Tribunal (NAT).[47] The NAT, after having heard the parties, made an award whose content was compulsorily incorporated in the relevant contracts of employment. This system was in operation from 1940–1951. As a matter of law, it rested on the Order; in fact it rested on an agreement between the top organisations of management and labour.[48] In so far as it worked at all, it worked as a result of this understanding, and one government after another emphasised that it would be terminated if either side of industry desired this. Without this political background the system cannot be understood.[49]

---

[42] For a very good analysis, see Sharp, *Industrial Conciliation and Arbitration in Great Britain* (1954), pp. 309–319 and G. R. Rubin "The Origins of Industrial Tribunals: Munitions Tribunals during the First World War" (1977) 6 I.L.J. 149.

[43] Defence (General) Regulation 58AA (S.R. & O. 1940 No. 1217).

[44] Especially the Emergency Powers (Defence) Act 1940.

[45] Art. 4. See Sharp. *loc. cit.*, pp. 419 *et seq.*

[46] Art. 2.

[47] Art. 1.

[48] The late Lord Terrington, the very successful Chairman of the NAT, deprecated on this ground the use of the term "compulsory arbitration" for what he was doing. Politically, if not legally, he was right. On Bevin's policy in making the Order, see Bullock. *The Life and Times of Ernest Bevin* (1967) Vol. II, pp. 266 *et seq.*

[49] See for the history and effect on industrial relations of Order 1305/1940 and of Order 1376/1951: Flanders, *The Tradition of Voluntarism* (1974) 12 Brit. J. of Ind. Rel. 359 *et. seq.*

In our present context its most interesting aspect is that it operated only in marginal cases, and that it left the customary system of collective bargaining quite undisturbed.[50] It failed to prevent strikes[51]—about this we shall say something in another context. What is important is that a scheme so alien to the British tradition should have had so small an impact on industrial relations. In 1951 the utter failure of the penal provisions of the Order became obvious in a dramatic case arising from a dock strike,[52] and the Order was revoked. Its place was taken by the Industrial Disputes Order which was in force from 1951–1959. There were no longer any prohibitions against industrial action, but compulsory arbitration continued, now (because of the absence of restrictions on strikes) called "unilateral arbitration." The Tribunal, now re-christened Industrial Disputes Tribunal (IDT),[53] still acted upon a reference by the Minister to which only one party, usually the union, had consented, and its award was still compulsorily implied in the contracts of employment.[54] If this system had been more important in practice than it was, it would have been inconceivable for the employers to put up with it for more than seven years. This system of "unilateral" arbitration is the one which, as has been mentioned, the Employment Protection Act 1975 uses as a sanction for the employer's obligation to furnish to recognised unions certain information with a view to promoting the bargaining process.[55]

The principal lesson we can draw from this bird's-eye view comparison of various schemes of compulsory arbitration is first of all that the independence of the arbitration body from the Government is the neuralgic point. To some extent this explains why compulsory arbitration did not destroy (but perhaps helped to stimulate) a free collective bargaining system in Australia and in New Zealand, and also in this country, and why it had an utterly destructive effect on collective bargaining and on the trade unions in the dying Weimar Republic. A further lesson is that compulsory arbitration may have one effect if it is used as an *ultima ratio* and quite another if it supersedes bargaining and is intended to do so.

---

[50] See for the statistics extracted from the Reports of the Ministry of Labour: Flanders and Clegg, *System of Industrial Relations in Great Britain* (1954), p. 96.

[51] Donovan Report, para. 486.

[52] For the Seven Dockers' Trial at the Old Bailey, see *Annual Register 1951*, p. 34.

[53] S.I. 1951 No. 1376. See McCarthy, *Compulsory Arbitration in Britain: The Work of the Industrial Disputes Tribunal,* Royal Commission Research Paper No. 8: (*Three Studies in Collective Bargaining,* No. 2).

[54] Art 10.

[55] s. 21.

But what may be equally or even more important is that things which may have a disastrous effect in a declining labour market can be absorbed by a buoyant economy, and that a healthy union movement can "take" a great deal of legal intervention, whilst weak unions may be its victim.

As has been indicated, the Industrial Relations Act of 1971 tried to introduce in this country a novel system of compulsory arbitration, applicable only to the regulation of "procedure," *i.e.* of those aspects of labour relations which form the subject-matter of procedure agreements.[56] During the short life of the Act there does not seem to have been a single case in which these provisions were applied.[57] They were a failure.[58]

---

[56] ss. 37–41.
[57] In *Writers' Guild of Great Britain* v. *B.B.C.* [1974] I.C.R. 234 (N.I.R.C.) an application to do so failed.
[58] See the First Edition of this book, pp. 120 *et seq.*

CHAPTER 6

COLLECTIVE AGREEMENTS AND THE LAW:
OBSERVANCE OF AGREEMENTS

1. INTRODUCTION

A collective agreement is an industrial peace treaty and at the
same time a source of rules for terms and conditions of
employment, for the distribution of work and for the stability of
jobs. Its two functions express the principal expectations of the
two sides, and it is through reconciling their expectations that a
system of industrial relations is able to achieve that balance of
power which is one of its main objectives. What can the law do to
protect these expectations?

To the two social functions of a collective agreement there
correspond two actual or potential legal characteristics.[1] The
agreement may be, and in many counties is, a contract between
those who made it, *i.e.* between an employer or employers or their
association or associations on the one side and a trade union or
unions on the other. At the same time the agreement is also
potentially, and in many countries actually, a legal code. In this
country it is generally neither a legally enforceable contract, nor
(exceptions apart) a legally enforceable code.[2]

The contractual function is mainly, but not exclusively, subservient to the maintenance of industrial peace. The "peace
obligation" has received different interpretations at different times
and places.[3] Does it mean that a union party to the agreement
undertakes during its currency not to strike at all or only that it will
not strike in order to change the terms of the agreement, *i.e.* is the

---

[1] This view of the dual effect of collective agreements (see Flanders and Clegg,
System of Industrial Relations, p. 55) is now widely accepted. It is generally
accepted in most Continental countries, but, surprisingly this elementary
distinction is still sometimes ignored by English courts: see *Loman* v. *Merseyside
Transport Services Ltd.* (1968) 3 I.T.R. 108, and *Gascol Conversions Ltd.* v.
Mercer [1974] I.C.R. 420, and the comments on these cases by Professors
Wedderburn (1969) 32 M.L.R. 99 and Hepple (1974) 31 I.L.J. 164.
[2] But its terms normally become, through voluntary incorporation, enforceable
terms of the contracts of employment. See below.
[3] See C.E.C.A., *Collection du Droit du Travail,* Vol. V: *"La Grève,"* 1961.

"peace obligation" absolute or relative?[4] Does it bind the members of the union as well as the union itself?[5] Does it impose on the organisations an obligation to press their members to apply the terms of the agreement, or only an obligation to make an effort in this direction? Or does it go so far as to impose on them a guarantee that their members will act in accordance with these terms?[6] Do the parties make themselves legally liable to maintain common institutions, such as joint committees, or pensions funds, or a holiday scheme such as that which exists in some (including this) countries in the building industry?[7] These are some of the very difficult legal problems attaching to the "contractual function" of collective agreements.

The normative, *i.e.* the codifying and rule-making function, of a collective agreement serves to ensure that the agreed conditions are applied in the plant, enterprise or industry to which the agreement refers, *i.e.* applied by individual employers and workers. Many of them prescribe the terms of the individual employment relationship, others the conditions under which that relationship may or may not be created. A clause on wages or holidays or overtime belongs to the first, a clause on the reservation of jobs for skilled workers or on the employment of non-union members belongs to the second category. Still others prescribe the mutual rights and duties between union representatives, such as shop stewards, and employers. The comprehensiveness of the code varies from industry to industry, sometimes from enterprise to enterprise. As has already been indicated,[8] agreements are generally more comprehensive and "rich" in the well-organised American industries than they are likely to be in Europe where so much more is left to legislation. In this country the parties are free to shape the content of the agreement

---

[4] See, *e.g.* for France: Javillier, *Droit du Travail* (2nd. ed., 1981) pp. 573–575; for Germany: Hueck-Nipperdey, *Lehrbuch des Arbeitsrechts,* Vol II (7th ed., 1966), pp. 313 *et seq.*; Ramm, *Kampfmassnahme und Friedenspflicht* (1962); for the very much more complex situation in Italy: *International Encyclopaedia for Labour Law and Industrial Relations*, Vol. 5, "Italy" pp. 143–144. For Sweden: F. Schmidt, *Law and Industrial Relations in Sweden,* Chap. 11, pp. 160 *et seq.*

[5] As it does under the Swedish Act on the Joint Regulation of Working Life, 1976, s. 26.

[6] See for France: *Code du Travail*, Art. L 135–3 (*"Ne rien faire qui soit de nature à en compromettre l'exécution loyale"*), and by contrast the much more far-reaching German *Einwirkungspflicht* (see Hueck-Nipperdey, *loc. cit.*, pp. 329 *et seq.*).

[7] See *Building and Civil Engineering Holidays Scheme Management Ltd.* v. *Post Office* [1966] 1 Q.B. 247 (C.A.).

[8] See Chap. 4.

according to their pleasure. The law does not require them to include[9] or not to include anything, except that no collective agreement may contain a term which expresses a discrimination against either sex. Such a term can be eliminated through an elaborate procedure.[10]

As a code, then, a collective agreement determines the content of existing and predetermines that of future contracts of employment. Often, usually, it prescribes only minima; sometimes, especially if it is a plant agreement, it sets a standard not to be departed from downwards or upwards. It determines the substance of the contract of employment, but not its existence. As a matter of law, the individual employer and worker decide whether or not to enter into a contract; once they have done so, it is the collective agreement which says what are their rights and obligations under the contract. The contract of employment is typically that which we call a "standard" contract[11] and that which the French call a "contract of adhesion,"[12] that is, an act by which either one party or both sign on the "dotted line," and thus "adhere" to conditions not of their own making. One party may simply submit to terms made by the other—we all have to do this when we make insurance or hire-purchase or transport contracts. Alternatively both may submit to terms made by a third, *e.g.* a trade association. In the case of the contract of employment the parties submit to terms made by an agreement betwen others (the organisations of the two sides) or between one of the parties to the contract of employment (the employer) and a third party (the union).

With his usual felicity and lucidity the late Mr. Justice Jackson of the United States Supreme Court expressed it in this way[13]:

> "Collective bargaining between an employer and representatives of a unit, usually a union, results in an accord as to terms which will govern hiring and work and pay in that unit. The

---

[9] This is different in France for all collective agreements which are to be "extended." See *Code du Travail*, Art. L 133–5, as amended in 1982 so as to expand the *contenu obligatoire* of a collective agreement which is capable of being extended. See J. C. Javillier, *Les Reformes du Droit du Travail Depuis Le 10 Mai 1981*, 1982, p. 330. Moreover, all collective agreements must contain a conciliation clause, *ibid.*

[10] Equal Pay Act 1970, s. 3. See Davies "The Central Arbitration Comittee and Equal Pay" [1980] C.L.P. 165.

[11] Treitel, *Law of Contract* (5th ed.), Chap. 7, p. 151. Prausnitz, *The Standardisation of Commercial Contracts,* 1937.

[12] See *e.g.* Carbonnier, *Droit Civil* (10th. ed., 1979), Vol. 4, paras. 13, 16, 17, 18.

[13] *J. I. Case Co.* v. *N.L.R.B.,* 321 U.S. 332 at p. 335 (1944).

result is not, however, a contract of employment except in rare cases; no one has a job by reason of it and no obligation to any individual comes into existence from it alone. The negotiations between union and management result in what often has been called a trade agreement, rather than in a contract of employment. Without pushing the analogy too far, the agreement may be likened to the tariffs established by a carrier, to standard provisions prescribed by supervising authorities for insurance policies, or to utility schedules of rates and rules for service, which do not of themselves establish any relationships but which do govern the terms of the shipper or insurer or customer relationship whenever and with whomever it may be established. . . . After the collective trade agreement is made the individuals who shall benefit by it are identified by individual hirings. The employer, except as restricted by the collective agreement itself . . . is free to select those he will employ or discharge. But the terms of employment already have been traded out. There is little left to agreement except the act of hiring. . . . "

If we substitute for Mr. Justice Jackson's examples of, *e.g.* provisions prescribed by insurance authorities, English examples such as conditions of insurance policies formulated by the Institute of Underwriters,[14] then we have here a very helpful description of the relation between the collective agreement and the contract of employment. It is however a factual description which also illustrates the contrast between collective plant agreements in America and industry-wide collective agreements in Europe, including this country. The American plant agreement leaves to the employer "little . . . except the act of hiring." In this country collective agreements leave a very wide scope to the managerial power of unilateral rule-making, expressed in works rules and similar regulations which the worker has to accept and to sign "on the dotted line." The contract of employment is therefore an act of submission or adhesion in a dual sense. Both sides submit to the collective agreement which expresses the combined or bilateral rule-making power of management and organised labour, but in addition the worker also submits to works rules which emanate from the unilateral rule-making power of management.[15] This

---

[14] *Arnould on Marine Insurance and Average* (16th ed., 1981) by Mustill and Gilman, Vol. 2, pp. 1163 *et seq.*

[15] In Germany this has to a limited extent been made bilateral through the "works agreement" between the works council and the employer; Works Constitution Law of 1972, s. 77.

raises a problem of the hierarchy of these rules, a problem of legal priority to which we must soon return.

2. THE COLLECTIVE AGREEMENT AS CONTRACT

Before doing so, however, we must ask ourselves what the law does about the contractual side of collective bargaining, that is, how far the agreement is a legally binding contract, In the late 1960s and early 1970s this was a central area of acute controversy in British labour law and recent government proposals have to some extent revived the debate.[16]

As it stood before the coming into force of the Industrial Relations Act 1971, the law was silent.[17] It did not say that collective agreements were contracts, nor did it say that they were not. There was nothing in the law to say that they could not be contracts if the parties wanted this and gave the agreement a wording which a court could interpret. What we call the doctrine of "consideration" certainly did not stand in the way: the parties' mutual promises to observe the standards and the mutual "peace" undertakings supported each other as that which we call "executory consideration." There was no difficulty here, nor would the legal characteristics of the organisations on both sides have stood in the way of regarding the agreement as a contract. True, as we shall still have to explain, it was doubtful how far unions had corporate personality,[18] but this is beside the point because an unincorporated association can make a contract, and contracts (other than collective agreements) were often enforced against unions in the courts.[19] If they were registered they could sue and be sued in contract in their own name,[20] and whether registered or not, they could sue and be sued in certain types of cases through their trustees,[21] in other cases through a technical device known as

---

[16] For an excellent analysis of this controversy see Roy Lewis, "The Legal Enforceability of Collective Agreements" (1970) 8 Brit. J. of Ind. Rel. 313, with reference to further literature. For the recent proposals see nn. 61–63 below.

[17] See Donovan Report, para. 470; Wedderburn, *The Worker and the Law* (2nd ed.), pp. 171 *et seq.*

[18] Chap. 7. See now Trade Union and Labour Relations Act 1974, s. 2 (and, on employers' associations, s. 3.)

[19] *e.g.* in *Bonsor* v. *Musicians' Union* [1956] A.C. 104.

[20] *e.g. National Union of General and Municipal Workers* v. *Gillian* [1946] K.B. 81 (C.A.); *Taff Vale Railway* v. *Amalgamated Society of Railway Servants* [1901] A.C. 426.

[21] Trade Union Act 1871, s. 9 (registered unions); for unregistered unions, see Citrine-Hickling, *Trade Union Law* (3rd ed.), pp. 197 *et seq.* The Act of 1871 was repealed by the Industrial Relations Act 1971, Sched. 9.

a "representative action."[22] Clearly unions and employers' associations could make contracts; the contract of membership was only one very important example. It had in fact happened in the past that an employers' association and a trade union did give their agreement the force of a contract. The best known examples were the famous Terms of Settlement in the Boot and Shoe Industry of 1895,[23] drafted by Sir Courtenay Boyle, Permanent Secretary of the Board of Trade.

There was thus nothing in the law itself[24] to explain the fact that, before the Act of 1971 went into operation, British collective agreements were generally not contracts. This can only be explained by the lack of that intent to conclude a legally binding contract which is an indispensable element of contract-making as much as offer and acceptance and consideration.[25] That this intent did not exist and that for this reason collective agreements were not as a rule contracts in the legal sense was the conclusion at which the Donovan Commission arrived in its Report.[26] It was based on the general view of all those who had given evidence; the (then) Ministry of Labour[27] was explicit on the point, and so were the trade unions (including the TUC)[28] and the employers' associations (including the Confederation of British Industry).[29] The controversy was all about whether all or some collective agreements should in future be made into contracts by law—a very different matter. In 1969 the question whether collective agreements were contracts had, for the first time, to be faced explicitly

---

[22] Citrine-Hickling, *loc. cit.*, pp. 177 *et seq.* For the present law see Trade Union and Labour Relations Act 1974, s. 2(1) (*c*), s. 3(1) (*c*), and below Chap. 7.

[23] Clegg, Fox and Thomson, *History of British Trade Unions since 1889*, pp. 200 *et seq.*; Sidney and Beatrice Webb, *Industrial Democracy*, p. 241; Sharp, *loc. cit.*, pp. 221 *et seq.*; for this and some other examples, Wedderburn and Davies, *loc. cit.*, pp. 65 *et seq.*

[24] Especially not in the much discussed s. 4(4) of the Trade Union Act 1871 (see Cmnd. 3623, para. 470; Wedderburn, *The Worker and the Law* (2nd ed., 1971), pp. 179–180), repealed by the Industrial Relations Act 1971, Sched. 9, and not revived by the repeal of that Act in 1974 (Interpretation Act 1889, s. 11(1) and s. 38 (2) (*a*); now ss. 15 and 16(1) of the Interpretation Act 1978).

[25] Treitel, *loc. cit.*, pp. 107 *et seq.*

[26] Donovan Report, para. 471. See *contra*, Cronin and Grime, *Labour Law,* Chap. X; Selwyn, "Collective Agreements and the Law" (1969) 32 M.L.R. 377; and, as regards the theory of "contractual intent" in general, Hepple, "Intention to Create Legal Relations" (1970) 28 C.L.J. 122.

[27] Second Memo., paras. 26 *et seq.*

[28] "Trade Unionism"—the evidence of the TUC to the Donovan Commission, para. 339.

[29] See paras. 172–175 of the CBI's First and Principal Memorandum, containing a cautious discussion of the problem whether collective agreements should be made legally enforceable, on the assumption that they are not so enforceable.

by a court. In *Ford Motor Co.* v. *Amalgamated Union of Engineering and Foundry Workers*[30] Geoffrey Lane J. held that an agreement between the Ford Motor Co. and a number of unions could not be enforced as a contract. The decision was based on the factual finding that there was no contractual intent.

This lack of contractual intent is not due to the caprice of the parties. It is rooted in the history, and, more importantly, in the structure of British collective bargaining, and especially in the "institutional" or "dynamic" method of bargaining, the impact of "custom and practice," and also the multiplicity of bargaining levels.[31] Owing to these (and perhaps other) factors it would, quite irrespective of the law, be very difficult to press collective agreements into the mould of legal contracts.

Even if the parties intended to give contractual force to their agreements, they could not in many cases do so unless they changed their bargaining methods. The language of many agreements is so vague that a court may have to hold them to be "void for uncertainty."[32] It is to be hoped that their style may in future be improved and this would remove the obstacle of "uncertainty," but a great deal will still be incomprehensible without reference to semi-articulate or inarticulate practices.[33] Evidence of these can probably be given in court, but to disentangle them will be a formidable task. Interpretation will remain a major headache.[34]

From a practical point of view the contractual nature of collective agreements has given rise to problems mainly in connection with those procedure agreements whose non-observance has often contributed to interruptions of production. The style and the content of some of the major procedure agreements then in force which were studied by the Donovan Commission[35] (*e.g.* in engineering and in building) showed that

---

[30] [1969] 2 Q.B. 303; see also *Stuart* v. *Ministry of Defence* [1973] I.R.L.R. 143 (N.I.R.C.).

[31] See above, Chap. 3.

[32] *Scammell* v. *Ouston* [1941] A.C. 251 is directly in point. Countless phrases in collective agreements are at least as vague as the words "on hire-purchase terms."

[33] As with regard to trade union rules: see *Heatons Transport (St. Helens) Ltd.* v. *T.G.W.U.* [1972] I.C.R. 308 (H.L.), and *supra,* Chap. 3, p. 77, text to nn. 38 and 39.

[34] This also applies to the interpretation of collectively agreed terms incorporated in contracts of employment (see below). On the cases on "compulsory overtime" under the redundancy payments legislation, see Grunfeld, *Law of Redundancy* (2nd. ed., 1980) pp. 366–376. They show the difficulty.

[35] Para. 473.

they could not have been intended to be binding contracts, any more than substantive agreements on wages, etc.

This diagnosis of the situation does not answer the question whether collective agreements should be enforceable as contracts. Only an extreme conservative justifies a social institution by its existence. That collective agreements are not contracts is due to the structure of bargaining, but if social necessities required it, such difficulties would have to be faced and, if possible, overcome. It is a matter of social expediency, not of social ethics. There is nothing morally reprehensible in treating collective agreements as contracts, any more than in treating them as being outside the law. To bring the rule *pacta sunt servanda* in the legal sense to bear on collective agreements (or any agreements) has no moral virtue, any more than there is moral virtue in keeping the law out of labour relations. The question, it must be emphasised, is not whether collective agreements are "binding"—of course they are and many say so in explicit terms—but whether the application of legal sanctions, damages, injunctions, etc., is an expedient technique to give effect to this binding force. There is no moral ethos in this problem.[35a]

Some countries enforce collective agreements as binding contracts,[36] others do not.[37] Not all those which do treat the agreement as a contract take the view that it implies a peace

---

[35a] [This concluding statement, which the editors have reproduced out of faithfulness to the original argument, nevertheless seems slightly to over-state the case that is being made. There does not seem to be any special reason for regarding the question of legal enforceability of collective agreements as a question free of ethical connotations. There seems a much stronger case for the more limited proposition, yet the more important one in this context, that there is no reason to regard legal enforceability as ethically superior to social enforceability.]

[36] *e.g.* the United States under s. 301 of the Taft-Hartley Act: see Summers and Wellington, *Labor Law,* Chap. 5, pp. 658 (where, in a very perceptive introductory note the authors point out that bargaining and agreement could take a form different from the American pattern, *viz.* a system of joint administration). Also Germany, see Hueck-Nipperdey, *loc. cit.,* Vol. II, p. 208; Sweden, see Folke Schmidt, *loc. cit.* (1977), Chaps. 9 and 11; France, see Despax, *Les Conventions Collectives* (Camerlynck's *Traité,* Vol. VII) para. 170.

[37] *e.g.* not Belgium before the Law on Collective Agreements etc. of December 5, 1968. Even today Art. 4 of the 1968 Act to some extent reduplicates the pattern of the British Act of 1974 by providing that damages for breach of the collective agreement are payable only where the agreement expressly so provides, and in practice such provision is not made. See *International Encyclopaedia for Labour Law and Industrial Relations*, Vol. 2, "Belgium," p. 214. See, generally, Giugni, "The Peace Obligation", Chap. 3 of Aaron and Wedderburn (ed.), *Industrial Conflict: A Comparative Legal Survey* (1972).

obligation.[38]There are the most extraordinary variations of attitudes to these problems. It has nothing to do with "common law" and "civil law" traditions, but it may have a great deal to do with economic history and with the bargaining methods which result from it.[39]

The question of social expediency is: are the social purposes of collective agreements more likely to be helped or to be hindered if they are enforceable in courts of law? On this the Donovan Commission[40] was divided, perhaps less deeply than a superficial reading of its report seems to have suggested, and on this there was a profound divergence between the policy of the (then) Labour Government (as expressed in the White Paper "In Place of Strife"[41] and in its Industrial Relations Bill[42]) and that of the subsequent Conservative Government, foreshadowed by the pamphlet "Fair Deal at Work,"[43] and expressed in the Industrial Relations Act 1971.[44]

The emphasis in this country is on procedure agreements, that is, on the "peace obligation" which they impose. This is, as we have said, the principal—not the only—aspect of the "contractual" function of collective agreements. The peace obligation applies to both sides: it restricts strikes, go slows, overtime bans, etc., but also lockouts. But important as these latter may be at times of a falling labour market, their social significance cannot be compared to that of strikes. It is not a gross exaggeration to say that the contractual function of collective agreements is mainly for the benefit of management, and its normative function mainly for the benefit of labour.

With one exception[45] all the members of the Donovan Commission dealt with the problem as one affecting procedure agreements only. Eight out of 12 thought that on principle they should not be made into contracts,[46] but that procedures should be reformed so as to make them more effective and comprehensive, speedier and

---

[38] It seems that some opinion in Italy would consider a binding peace obligation as an infringement of the constitutionally guaranteed right to strike. The matter is, however, highly controversial. See *International Encyclopaedia for Labour Law and Industrial Relations*, Vol. 6, "Italy," pp. 151–4.

[39] As pointed out in Chap. 3, the pattern of collective bargaining in Belgium is in some respects similar to the British pattern.

[40] Cmnd. 3623, Chap. VIII, see para. 519.

[41] Cmnd. 3888, para. 46 (1969).

[42] Industrial Relations Bill 1970, cl. 29.

[43] *Fair Deal at Work*, p. 32.

[44] ss. 34 *et seq.*

[45] See the Note of Reservation by Mr. Andrew Shonfield, Report, pp. 288 *et seq.*

[46] Paras. 500 *et seq.*

clearer.[47] The Industrial Court, as it then was,[48] should, in case of necessity, have the power to make an agreed reformed procedure legally enforceable, but only ad hoc and for a particular establishment or undertaking in which unconstitutional strikes, *i.e.* strikes in breach of procedure, continued to be a serious problem, and provided the Court was satisfied that this threat of legal sanctions could be expected to lead to a reduction in the number or magnitude of these stoppages.[49] This seems to be a clear expression of an insight that this is a question of expediency and nothing more. Four members of the Commission would have made reformed (not existing) procedures enforceable on principle in a variety of ways.[50]

Under the Industrial Relations Act 1971, however, a written collective agreement was conclusively presumed to be a legally enforceable contract, unless the parties had by an express term agreed that it, or part of it, was not intended to be legally enforceable.[51] A very complicated provision[52] tried to apply the concept of the binding contract to institutional collective bargaining, *i.e.* to decisions of joint negotiating bodies. Breach of a legally binding agreement (or decision) would, as an "unfair industrial practice"[53] have been visited with the equivalent of orders for damages and injunctions.[54] Moreover, a trade union or employers' association, party to such an agreement or decision, would have had to take all reasonably practicable steps to prevent its members and anyone purporting to act on its behalf from acting or from continuing to act contrary to the agreement.[55]

If these provisions had ever been applied in practice, they could have produced an extraordinary situation: an agreement could have been a legally enforceable contract, although one party had expressly informed the other that it did not want to be legally bound—a situation incompatible with the most elementary rules of the law of contract.

---

[47] Para. 504.
[48] Now the Central Arbitration Committee (see *supra*, Chap. 5).
[49] Paras. 511 *et seq.*
[50] See para. 519; Supplementary Note by Lord Tangley, pp. 282 *et seq.*, esp. p. 286; Supplementary Note by Lord Robens, Sir George Pollock and Mr. John Thomson, p. 287; Note of Reservation by Mr. Andrew Shonfield, pp. 288 *et seq.*, esp. paras. 34 *et seq.*
[51] s. 34.
[52] s. 35.
[53] s. 36(1).
[54] s. 101(3) (*b*) and (*c*).
[55] s. 36(2).

All this, however, was purely academic. What happened in fact was that "disclaimer" clauses became "common form" in collective bargaining, much like arbitration clauses in many types of commercial contracts and in deeds of partnership. Words such as: "this is not a legally enforeable agreement" were generally inserted at the request of the union. Employers did not resist it—they did not "make an issue of this question"[56] so as to secure any bargaining advantage. Many employers did not and do not seem to feel that the legal enforceability of collective agreements is of any advantage to them. It would seem that where no "disclaimer clause" was put into an agreement, this was most likely due to the forgetfulness or carelessness of a union representative.[57] The attitude of most employers is easy to explain: they are disinclined to use the law against their own workers. Even before 1971 most employers could have sued many of their workers for damages for breach of contract[58] during, or (in most cases) after a wildcat strike, but they hardly ever did, and they were, it seems, equally reluctant to use the weapons given them by the 1971 Act. These were rights against the union, rather than against its members, but experience has shown that employers adopt this attitude not so much in order not to throw good money after bad, as in order not to kindle afresh a flame which has died down.[59] How many employers want to revive a settled conflict with a union?

Whatever the explanation, the provisions of the 1971 Act on the legal enforcement of collective agreements as contracts were a complete failure. They were resisted by the unions and not suported by management. They had no effect on the improvement of labour relations at all.

The Trade Union and Labour Relations Act 1974[60] has put in their place a series of provisions which give legal form to—and at the same time clarify—the situation as it was before the 1971 Act. That Act—repealed by the 1974 Act—had, as it were, made the

---

[56] Weekes, Mellish, Dickens and Lloyd, *loc. cit.,* p. 158.

[57] See the impressive evidence collected by Weekes, Mellish, Dickens and Lloyd, *loc cit.,* pp. 156 *et seq.—N.U.B.E.* v. *Mitsubishi Ltd.* [1974] I.C.R. 200 (C.A.) was a freakish case in which (see Lord Denning M.R. at p. 207) the parties had concluded a collective agreement without (probably) realising that they were doing so.

[58] See the Donovan Report, Cmnd. 3623, para. 463. The reason was the non-observance of the contractual or statutory notice to terminate the contract.

[59] See the evidence of the CBI to the Donovan Commission, First and Principal Memorandum, para. 170.

[60] s. 18 (1)–(3); s. 18(4) and (5) deal with an entirely different problem, which is discussed below.

law of collective agreements stand on its head, and the 1974 Act put it back on its feet. This it did by reversing the "conclusive presumption." This is now—in accordance with the facts of life—to the effect that the agreement is not "intended by the parties to be legally enforceable," except to the extent to which the contrary is expressed in writing (in which—improbable—case it is to that extent conclusively presumed to be an enforceable contract). Such an "enforcement" clause may cover the whole or part of the agreement. These provisions, and especially the need for the written form of the "enforcement" clause, should eliminate all further doubt or dispute about this matter.

Rather curiously in view of the decisiveness of the experience afforded by the working of the 1971 Act, the debate about legal enforcement of collective agreements and, in particular, peace obligations was to enjoy a revival in the aftermath of the Employment Act 1980. That Act represented a more permissive treatment of industrial action than would have been favoured by important sectors of the government of the day, and emerged in the form that it did only at the price of a commitment to the formulation of a further programme of legislation to be put into effect if the 1980 Act failed to achieve the desired degree of restriction upon industrial action. In the event there appeared, not so much the sword of Damocles which had been thus fore-shadowed, but rather a less committed discussion paper about the available options for further legislation. This was the Green Paper on Trade Union Immunities.[61] Its political background explains why it was concentrated to a significant extent upon possible bases for limiting the immunity in the law of tort of trade unions (which we shall examine in Chapter 8), though it ranged far wider than that. One of the possible bases taken up for discussion was an idea, apparently originating in the deliberations of the Confederation of British Industry, that immunity might be removed from industrial action taken in breach of the provisions of a collective agreement. In the Green Paper it was argued with some cogency that this proposal could not be evaluated in isolation from the whole idea of legal enforcement of collective agreements as contracts, for otherwise the suggestion would lack the fundamental quality of mutuality necessary to make it an even remotely feasible reality.[62] Thus committed to the general discussion of legal enforceability, the Green Paper in fact pursues a cautious line in relation thereto, stressing that, whatever merits seem to attach to the proposal on

---

[61] Cmnd. 8128, presented by the Secretary of State for Employment, January 1981.
[62] *Ibid.* paras. 222–223.

the basis of comparative observation of other labour law systems, the adaptations to our own system of collective bargaining necessary to purchase those advantages seem exceedingly difficult to bring about in the short term or at all.[63] This must be the correct conclusion; above all, it could only further damage an already precarious collective bargaining framework to seek to make it the basis for new liabilities placed upon the organisers of industrial action.

We must now turn or return to the second—and very much more important—role played by collective agreements in labour relations.

3. THE COLLECTIVE AGREEMENT AS A CODE

(a) Automatic effect

The substantive rules or norms of collective agreements are mainly designed to protect the expectation of the workers that their standard of living will be maintained. If one says "mainly," not "exclusively," it is because many agreements also contain rules seeking to impose obligations on workers, *e.g.* to work overtime at the employer's request, or to work certain shifts. In a highly competitive market they may have the side-effect of protecting employers against undercutting by commercial rivals. Indeed, many years ago the highest German court held a firm in breach of a collective agreement to be liable for the tort of "unfair competition."[64]

Yet the principal social function of the agreement as a code is the maintenance of wage and other standards in the interests of the workers. Our question must be: what can the law do and what does it do to give effect to this "normative function"? In asking this question we are chiefly concerned with rules regulating terms of existing contracts of employment (wages, hours, holidays, terms of discipline, notice, etc.) and less with rules regulating labour supply and job allocation which affect the conditions for the making of contracts of employment. The effect of rules designed to shape the mutual obligations of employers and workers under their individual contracts may or may not be automatic, and it may or may not be compulsory. These two things are different. In our law the effect may be automatic, but in so far as it is, it is not compulsory. It may also be compulsory, but in so far as it is, it is not automatic.

---

[63] *Ibid.* paras. 242–243.
[64] Decision of April 12, 1927, R.G.Z., Vol. 117, p. 16; it was an agreement which the Minister of Labour had declared to be binding as a "common rule."

Let us explain. We are discussing the central issue of how the law defines the borderline between the unilateral rule-making power of management and the bilateral rule-making power of the combined two sides of industry. Or, in legal terms: how far is the exercise of the freedom of contract of employers and employees influenced or restrained by collective agreements applying in the plant, enterprise, or industry? It may be so influenced without being restrained. To see how this happens one has to realise on what principles a court or tribunal has to act when asked to determine the mutual obligations of the parties to a contract of employment where they have not expressed any intention as to what these are to be. These of course are, in law, terms "voluntarily" undertaken, and somewhere an intention must be found tacitly to agree on something. In fact, despite the growing habit of incorporating terms in written employees' handbooks and similar documents (to which we shall refer in a moment), there will always be numerous and critical cases in which the parties never dreamt of agreeing on what was to happen in a situation which they simply did not contemplate (as was pointed out above,[65] it is that sort of situation which is most likely to confront a court). The common law has certain rules, or at least forms of words, to cope with this problem. In default of an "express" agreement it looks for an "implied" agreement and in the absence of that it holds the parties liable to do what is "reasonable," *i.e.* the judge holds them liable to do what in his view they should have agreed to do. This gives less scope for arbitrary decisions and produces less uncertainty than one might assume because of the sensible rule that the parties are deemed to have intended to incorporate in their contract that which is customary in the trade and locality or undertaking.[66] The courts have never gone so far as to treat the terms "normal" and "normative" as synonymous: they will not apply a custom which is "unreasonable." But this is not important from our point of view. What matters is that existing custom and practice are normally read into the contract, and thus allowed to circumscribe the range of the managerial prerogative. This attitude to "custom" is not of course peculiar to the contract of employment—it is especially important in commercial law where it has been the matrix of momentous developments. It is however of particular significance in an area in which millions of contracts are made every year which are necessarily inarticulate (though decreasingly so). It is moreover especially important as regards

---

[65] Chap. 2.
[66] Treitel, *loc. cit.,* p. 149.

labour law because it is through this rule as to "custom" that a legal link can be found between collective agreements and contracts of employment.

Kahn-Freund adhered strongly to the view that the results of collective bargaining affected individual contracts of employment as "crystallised custom". This theory has the great merit that, like Kahn-Freund's other suggestion that the non-enforceability of collective agreements as contracts could be attributed to the absence of an intention to create legal relations, it explains a phenomenon peculiar to the employment situation in terms of the general principles of the law of contract. No doubt it was also attractive to Kahn-Freund to be able to suggest a path of development for the common law which maximised its responsiveness to the patterns of industrial relations and employment practice in the workplace. We must nevertheless admit to some degree of scepticism as to whether the crystallised custom theory can be made to work, at least as the law and the practice have now developed. There are two main problems about applying the theory. First, the industrial tribunals and the courts simply do not in practice apply to collective agreements the sorts of tests that the general principles of the law of contract impose as the criteria for binding customs; and if they did, these rather exacting requirements would be unlikely to be met in any given case. Secondly, if one regards the relevant social phenomenon as being workplace custom and practice, and if one regards collective bargaining as a codification of that custom and practice, one would have to admit that the deliberately and consciously non-normative or even anti-normative character of a good deal of that custom and practice would cast severe doubt on the appropriateness of terms derived from it for incorporation into the individual contract of employment. The reality seems to be that the tribunals and courts sidestep difficulties of that kind. They do not particularly demand a theory for incorporation of terms from collective agreements; they simply treat or hold terms to be so incorporated in the circumstances where they regard it as appropriate to do so. One may validly deploy various theories to provide a critique of the results of this process; but it should not be supposed that one is thereby explaining how those results are actually reached.

Whatever, then, the theoretical basis for so doing, the terms of a collective agreement are likely[67] to be automatically implied in the

---

[67] Likely, but not certain: see *Singh* v. *British Steel Corporation* [1974] I.R.L.R. 131 (where at the time of a new collective agreement the worker had left the union).

relevant contracts of employment. "Automatically"—this means that there is no need for anything being said by either side. Unless something to the contrary has been (in the legal sense) "agreed" upon between employer and worker, the wage rates, the pre-scribed and permitted hours, the holidays, etc., laid down in the collective agreement thus become terms of the contracts of employment and may, as such, have to be interpreted by a court or tribunal called upon to enforce that contract.[68] It is still good for clarification if the parties expressly refer to the collective agree-ment, but there is no need for this to be done. This is the effect which, on general principles of the common law, must be attached to the collective agreement as a source of custom. Its terms will continue to operate as terms of the contracts of employment in which they are incorporated even after the collective agreement itself has expired unless and until it has been displaced by another agreement.[69] There are countries, *e.g.* formerly Belgium,[70] where the same effect is produced by a statutory provision giving the force of a "supplementary" or "optional" source of norms to the agreement as such. This means almost, but as we shall point out in a moment, not quite, the same thing in practice. This rule as to custom then is in practice the way the bilateral rule-making power influences the exercise of the unilateral rule-making power of management which is in fact subordinated to it.

In fact, but not in law. In law (but not necessarily in fact) management may insist on the exercise of its unfettered power to lay down the rules of employment, that is, to refuse to observe the collective agreement, to "contract out" of it, and to employ its workers on its own terms. Thus the employer may announce to his workmen that their wages will be 10 per cent. below those fixed by a relevant joint industrial council or negotiating committee.[71] To prevent the employer from doing so, a special procedure before

---

[68] If and when the appropriate Ministers make the orders envisaged in the Employment Protection (Consolidation) Act 1978, s. 131, the industrial tribunals will thus play a decisive role in the interpretation of the terms of collective agreements, see esp. s. 131 (7).

[69] *Morris* v. *C. H. Bailey Ltd.* [1969] 2 Lloyd's Rep. 215 (C.A.); compare also *Burroughs Machines Ltd.* v. *Timmoney* [1977] I.R.L.R. 404 (Ct. of Sess.).

[70] Laws of March 4 & 11, 1954, amending Art. 3 of the Law of March 10, 1900, and Art 3 of the Law of August 7, 1922. See Horion, *loc. cit.*, (1st ed.) para. 186, p. 145. Now Art. 26 of the Law of December 5, 1968, which provides that the terms of a collective agreement shall have supplementary binding effect in respect of employers not contractually bound by it but who are within the scope of the joint body which concluded it.

[71] As in *Hulland* v. *Saunders* [1945] K.B. 78 (C.A.).

the Central Arbitration Committee[72] could formerly, but can no longer, be set in motion by which the terms of the collective agreement were made binding on him. They then became "compulsory," but this compulsory effect was not automatic. By a similar procedure the CAC may, on a reference to it by any of the parties or by the Secretary of Employment, compulsorily amend a collective agreement so as to remove any express discrimination between men and women.[73]

In practice the non-compulsory effect of collective bargaining is what really matters. The provisions allowing the terms of the agreement to be imposed upon the employer were not often applied. We shall have to say a little more presently about them and about other possible ways of giving compulsory effect to substantive collective agreements as codes of terms of employment. For the moment we must concentrate on what is most important in actual industrial relations, that is, on the normal situation in which, without any legal compulsion, collective agreements shape the terms of employment, as they do for something like 65 per cent. of the labour force.

As we have said, there may be an automatic link between collective agreement and contract of employment. But it is becoming more and more usual to dispense with the automatic link and to make an express reference to the collective agreement, a practice which should be encouraged. The express reference may be in a written contract as in the leading case of *National Coal Board* v. *Galley*[74] where the employee agreed that his

> "wages shall be regulated by such national agreement and the county wage agreement for the time being in force and that this contract of service shall be subject to those agreements and to any other agreements relating to or subsidiary to the wages agreement and to statutory provisions for the time being in force affecting the same."

The employee was a man in a supervisory position—a deputy employed by the National Coal Board. Here you would expect to find a formal contract of employment. You would not expect to

---

[72] Employment Protection Act 1975, s. 89 and Sched. XI.—repealed by the Employment Act 1980.

[73] Equal Pay Act 1970 (as amended by Sex Discrimination Act 1975, Sched. 1), s. 3.

[74] [1958] 1 W.L.R. 16 (C.A.). On incorporation of collective agreements in contracts of employment, see the excellent analysis in Hepple and O'Higgins, *Employment Law* (4th ed.), Chap. 8.

find a document of this kind in the case of an ordinary manual worker. An increasing number of employers seem however to adopt the wise practice of formulating a set of "work rules"[75] or a "handbook"—a "codification" of terms—and of handing a copy of this document to each worker on engagement, sometimes of having it signed by him.[76] This may, and no doubt often does, refer to the relevant collective agreement or agreements. If well drafted, it will, like the contract between Mr. Galley and the National Coal Board, contain a reference to these agreements as they are "for the time being," and thus expressly give the contract of employment a content variable with the changing agreements of the industry. Thus in *Pearson* v. *William Jones Ltd.*[77] the employer had a "works rule" which said:

> "Any overtime working is in accordance with the provisions of the national agreements currently in force between the Engineering Employers' Federation and the Confederation of Shipbuilding and Engineering Unions."

This is an express reference which, on established legal principles, leaves no doubt that the collective terms are incorporated in the contract.[78] It may of course happen, but it is not very likely, that the rules laid down by the employer contain another express term at variance with the collective agreement, and such a term would probably have priority, just as the handwritten or typed clauses of a commercial standard contract (charterparty, insurance policy, etc.) generally prevail over the printed terms.

One of the main reasons why such express references have become very much more important is to be found in what was originally the Contracts of Employment Act 1963.[79] Under this enactment the employer must give to an employee within the first 13 weeks of his employment, and later keep up to date, a written statement of some of the fundamental terms ("particulars") of that employment, or, which is decisive for us here, refer him for such "particulars" to a document which he "has reasonable opportuni-

---

[75] Such work rules may have a vital significance under a statute, *e.g.* the Truck Act 1896.

[76] See Wedderburn, *loc. cit.,* pp. 71 *et seq.*; Hepple and O'Higgins, *loc. cit.,* Chap. 7, paras. 225 *et seq.*

[77] [1967] 1 W.L.R. 1140; [1967] 2 All E.R. 1062.

[78] The advantage of the reference in the works rule to the collective agreement is shown by the contrast between this works rule and that in *Camden Exhibition and Display Ltd.* v. *Lynott* [1966] 1 Q.B. 555 which was obscure.

[79] Now Pt. I of the Employment Protection (Consolidation) Act 1978.

ties of reading in the course of his employment, or which is made reasonably accessible to him in some other way." This will often be a collective agreement the terms of which will thus be expressly incorporated in the contract. This has been affirmed by the courts in a number of cases.[80] However, the matter is not always unproblematical. Thus, in the case of *Pearson* v. *William Jones Ltd.* to which we have just referred, the statement given by the employer said: "your normal working hours and the terms and conditions relating to such hours are in accordance with the works rules" and these rules in turn, as we have seen, referred to the relevant collective agreements; this is, as it were, private legislation by reference. One may wonder whether an employee, a lorry driver in this case, has a "reasonable opportunity" of reading the three documents he is invited to consult and to collate, still more whether they are made "reasonably accessible" to him, but this is not the point in the present context. The point is that the Act of 1963 somewhat reduced the importance of the "automatic effect" of collective agreements.

Still, the elementary rule of contractual construction,[81] in fact no more than a rule of common sense and almost a platitude, that the parties are, in the absence of an express term to the contrary, deemed implicitly to have incorporated the substance of the prevailing usages or customs, remains the principal link between collective agreements and contracts of employment.[82] In connection with the "Uniform List of Prices" of the Lancashire cotton weaving industry this principle was applied by the Court of Appeal more than forty years ago in *Hart* v. *Riversdale Mill Co.*[83] and in *Sagar* v. *Ridehalgh.*[84] It has since been acted upon again and again.

The principle does not however apply to the agreement as such but to the custom or usage it creates.[85] Agreements are generally acted upon, and this may be assumed, but not necessarily. If either party can show that an agreement (without having been formally abrogated) was widely ignored, its terms may not qualify as

---

[80] *Camden Exhibition and Display Ltd.* v. *Lynott, supra.* For further cases, see Davies and Freedland, *op. cit.,* pp. 225 *et. seq.*. For a case in which this had the opposite effect of frustrating the effect of a collective agreement see *Gascol Conversions Ltd.* v. *Mercer* [1974] I.C.R. 420 (C.A.). *Cf.* also *Robertson* v. *British Gas Corporation* [1983] I.C.R. 351, discussed below in n. 91a.

[81] *Supra,* p. 167, n. 66.

[82] The reader is referred to the paragraph in square brackets on p. 168.

[83] [1928] 1 K.B. 176.

[84] [1931] 1 Ch. 301.

[85] The reader is referred to the paragraph in square brackets on p. 168.

custom or usage. On the other hand, they may do so, even if the agreement is of recent origin and intended to innovate rather than to codify, provided the terms are generally observed. It is for the court to say on the facts whether an agreement or any given term of it must or, as, *e.g.* in *Rodwell* v. *Thomas*,[86] must not be considered as incorporated in the contract. Here one sees how different is a system where a statute elevates the terms of the agreement to the status of "optional" legislation which, it is true, may still be contracted out of, but which, if this is not done, applies as law and not merely by virtue of the intent of the parties. The practical importance of this theoretical difference must not be overrated. Collective agreements are generally observed in this country, and cases must be rare in which their terms cannot be considered as custom or usage.

"Custom and practice" may however have this "automatic" effect although it is not codified or crystallised in a collective agreement—this "non-codification" responds to a deep-seated instinct,[87] an aversion against "tidiness." That an uncodified custom can have this effect is shown by the decision of the Court of Appeal in *Marshall* v. *English Electric*[88] where the employer's practice of suspending workmen for breaches of discipline (a penalty unknown to the common law)[89] was by a majority held to have been tacitly incorporated in the contract of employment—in more realistic and less legalistic terms, that it was one of the rules made by management to which the worker had submitted. But the dissenting judgment of du Parq L. J.[90] shows that this factual finding was—to say the least of it—open to very considerable doubt, and it is the doubt which illustrates the difference between incorporating an uncodified usage and incorporating the terms of a collective agreement. It is difficult to establish the practice, and especially to do so through evidence admissible in a court. The defendants in *Marshall's* case succeeded in doing so, but the first judge heard "a mass of evidence on five or six days."[91] Had there been an agreement specifiying the employer's right to suspend,

---

[86] [1944] 1 All E.R. 700.
[87] See Chap. 3, *supra.*
[88] [1945] 1 All E.R. 653, a custom established by management and held to have been accepted by the workers. *Mutatis mutandis* the same applies to the frequent case of a custom established by the workers and tacitly accepted by management.
[89] *Hanley* v. *Pease and Partners Ltd.* [1915] 1 K.B. 698.
[90] [1945] 1 All E.R. 653 at p. 657.
[91] See MacKinnon L. J. at p. 656E.

this part of the case would have been over in five or six minutes.[91a]
In this case a custom was invoked against the worker—indeed in
most of the older cases that reached the law reports it was the
employer who relied on the incorporation of customary or
collective terms in the contract of employment, but this shows no
more than that the unions were disinclined to use the courts in
order to establish the rights of their members. It does not touch
the principle.

That principle—automatic incorporation—applies whether or
not the worker concerned is a member of any or of a particular
union. In this country the unions never acquired the habit of
seeking to reserve benefits or privileges conferred by collective
agreements for their own members.[92] Their practice has been to
operate through the reservation of jobs, not through the reservation of favourable terms of employment.[93] This is different in some
Continental countries where the closed shop has always or has for
some time been illegal,[94] but benefit reservation has also been
declared illegal, in France by statute,[95] in Germany by the

---

[91a] It is interesting to consider from this standpoint the recent case in the Court of
Appeal of *Robertson* v. *British Gas Corporation* [1983] I.C.R. 351, where the
issue was whether a bonus scheme embodied in a collective agreement was
entrenched in the individual contracts of employment of the workers covered by
the agreement, despite the fact that the corporation had given the requisite
notice to terminate that part of the agreement at the collective level. The
employees succeeded in this claim not least because their counsel, having
originally sought to show implied or "automatic" incorporation, shifted their
ground to that of express incorporation via the statutory statement of terms and
the original letter of appointment. But the case was still not "over in five or six
minutes"; it is indeed instructive as to the complexity of the arguments that may
arise even as to express incorporation.

[92] It was already pointed out by the Webbs (*Industrial Democracy*, 1926 ed., p.
178) that "collective bargaining . . . extends over a much larger part of the
industrial field than trade unionism." It is an essential characteristic of British
industrial relations.

[93] A custom of this type (this must have been a very exceptional case) was rightly
held to be unreasonable by the Mayor's Court of the City of London in the case
of *Hooker* v. *Lange Bell & Co.* (1937) 4. L.J.N.C.C.R. 199, which Prof.
Wedderburn's diligence has rescued from oblivion (*Cases and Materials on
Labour Law*, p. 290, n.).

[94] As it was held to be in Germany by the highest court as early as 1922: R.G.Z.,
Vol. 104, p. 327, and as it is still held to be: Hueck-Nipperdey, *Grundriss* (4th
ed.), pp. 182 *et seq.*, and as it is in France under the law of April 27, 1956, now
Code du Travail, 1974, Art. L412–2; (Camerlynck et Lyon-Caen, *loc. cit.*, (10th
ed.) para. 540, p. 630; Verdier, *Syndicats*, in Camerlynck's *Traité*, Vol. 5, para.
155, p. 327 and *Mise à jour 1976* p. 43.

[95] *Code du Travail*, 1974, Art. L412–2.

courts.[96] The importance of all this for the structure of industrial relations is fundamental. The Donovan Commission found[97] that, whilst only 10 out of 24 million employees were union members, the wages and conditions of more than 15 million were directly affected by collective agreements.

But all this applies only to those collective terms which are capable of being, and intended to be, terms of the contracts of employment, and as terms of those contracts to give rise to rights and obligations which can be enforced through the remedies of the law of contract. This is true of many terms of collective agreements, but of many others it is not. Obligations to make or not to make contracts cannot be terms of those contracts—this applies to the whole corpus of terms on job allocation and on job reservations, or, to take another example, whilst an obligation to "re-instate"[98] in a certain event, *e.g.* after a strike, would be a term of the contract (it would refer to its own termination or continuation), an obligation to "re-engage" would not.[99] It would not belong to the terms governing the content of contracts of employment, but to those determining the making of such contracts. These however cannot become terms of the contracts of employment themselves.

[The view that terms in collective agreements which pertained to the making of contracts of employment rather than to their content could not be incorporated into individual contracts was clearly one that Kahn-Freund had held strongly over many years; but it is to be doubted whether the courts would now be very much influenced by the principle that English law knows no contract to make a contract—a principle that commands far less adherence in the law of contract generally than it once did. For instance, it is respectfully suggested that the courts would not be much more troubled by the prospect of a contractual obligation to re-engage in

---

[96] See the highly controversial decision of the Great Senate of the Federal Labour Court of November 29, 1967 (*Arbeitsrechts-Praxis*, Art. 9, No. 13). The only European country in which such clauses appear to be of some importance is Belgium. See *International Encyclopaedia for Labour Law and Industrial Relations*, Vol. 2, "Belgium," paras. 35 and 198.

[97] Cmnd. 3623, para. 38.

[98] One of the reasons for the decision in *R.* v. *N.A.T., ex p. Crowther* [1948] 1 K.B. 424 (though differently expressed). English law knows no "contract to make a contract" (*pactum de contrahendo*).

[99] For a definition of the difference between re-instatement (continuing a contract) and re-engagement (making a new contract) see Employment Protection (Consolidation) Act 1978, s. 69 (3)–(5).

suitable alternative employment than by a contractual obligation to reinstate].

Nor can terms of collective agreements which for other reasons can only be implemented by organisations, not by individual employers or employees, such as the setting up of joint institutions (conciliation or negotiation committees) as between employers or their organisations and unions, or joint holiday schemes such as that which exists in the building industry, become terms of the individual contract of employment. Above all—and here is a matter of major importance—procedure agreements, and "no strike" or "peace" obligations are obligations of trade unions, and not obligations of their members. An individual cannot as such finance or organise a strike or other industrial action. As we shall see, it is the essence of industrial action, including a strike, that it is concerted action, and hence a peace obligation is a collective obligation. Participation in a strike is another matter, and it is conceivable that, by formulating a "peace" or "no strike" obligation, the parties to a collective agreement intended to impose on each individual employee, in relation to his employer, an undertaking not to participate in a strike. Such an interpretation of a "peace" or "no strike" clause is not inconceivable, but it is very artificial and strained. Nevertheless, apparently owing to very special circumstances, this strained interpretation was admitted by the defendants in *Rookes* v. *Barnard*[1] to be applicable to the agreement before the court, and this admission bound the court which never found as a fact that this was its meaning. The normal situation in this country is that peace clauses appear within the framework of procedure agreements which create collective, not individual, obligations.

To eliminate all doubts, however, and to prevent a repetition of a situation such as that in *Rookes* v. *Barnard,* the Trade Union and Labour Relations Act 1974[2] provides that, in order to "form part" of a contract of employment a peace clause in a collective agreement must not only be in writing, but expressly say that it shall or may be incorporated in the contract (*i.e.* have "normative" effect). It must also be "reasonably accessible" to the workers concerned at the place of work during working hours. This is therefore a case in which the normative effect, *i.e.* the effect on the contracts of employment, of a clause in a collective agreement is deliberately restricted by law. Moreover, to prevent what the Americans call "sweetheart agreements" it is also

---

[1] [1964] A.C. 1129.
[2] s. 18(4) and (5).

provided that in no event can a peace clause in a collective agreement have normative effect, unless each union party to the agreement is "independent."[3] None of these requirements can be contracted out, either by collective agreement or by contract of employment.

(b) Compulsory effect

Such, then, is the effect which collective agreements have on the terms of employment, but, as we have already said, there is nothing in the law to prevent the employer from refusing to apply it, even if it was signed by him or his organisation, provided, of course, the workers submit to less favourable terms. The individual worker is not a party to the collective agreement; from his point of view it is, to use the legal term, *res inter alios acta,* and his submission to the employer's less favourable terms is in law his consent to an express term in the contract of employment which makes it impossible to imply a term at variance with it. Here again is a rule of the law of contract so obvious as to be almost platitudinous: you cannot—in the absence of an express statutory provision to this effect—imply that people who have expressed one thing intended to agree on something else. More than thirty years ago, in *Hulland* v. *Saunders & Co.,*[4] the Court of Appeal assumed (there was no need to decide the point) that if the worker agreed to less than the collective wage, he could not claim the difference; that is, that the employer can validly contract out of the collective agreement. What is remarkable is that the trade unions never seem to have pressed for legislation to change this; that no one gave evidence to the Donovan Commission in this sense[5]; and that no such provision was included in the legislation of 1974 and 1975.

This is remarkable and all the more so because this is an almost unique feature of British law. In most Continental countries the terms of collective agreements are legally binding.[6] This means

---

[3] *i.e.* (see s. 30(1)) not dominated or controlled, or liable to be interfered with, by an employer, group of employers, or employers' association. The Certification Officer has exclusive jurisdicition to determine whether a union is independent. See below, Chap. 7.

[4] [1945] K.B. 78 (C.A.).   [5] Report, para. 468.

[6] France: *Code du Travail,* Art. L135–2, as re-stated in 1982 (which in its origin goes back to a law of March 19, 1919, the present formulation stems from the law of Feb. 11, 1950). Western Germany: Law of April 9, 1949, s. 4 (in the amended version now republished on Aug. 25, 1969; in its origins, and disregarding the Nazi period, this goes back to Decree of Dec. 23, 1918). In Switzerland such legislation has been in force since 1912 (Code of Obligations, Art. 322), in the Netherlands since a law of December 24, 1927, in Belgium since the law of December 5, 1968.

that they are mandatory law; and that an employer who is a party to the agreement, or member of an organisation which is, cannot to the detriment of his employees validly contract out of its terms; and in many countries it does not matter whether the employee concerned is or is not a union member. Thus the bilateral rule-making power of the parties to the collective agreement does not only influence but restrains the unilateral rule-making power of management. A term of the contract of employment which is less favourable to the worker than the corresponding collective term is automatically void, and the collective term is deemed to have been agreed by the parties to the individual contract. It is a compulsory effect which is automatic (in most Continental countries) as regards employers who are parties or members of parties to the agreement, but not as regards "outsiders," "non-federated firms." They can also be subjected to this compulsory effect, but this is not automatic. To "extend" it to them an order of some authority is needed, generally the Ministry of Labour.[7] This, however, is done only on proof that the agreement is of widespread or general application or covers a minimum percentage of workers (Germany) or has been concluded by "the most representative" organisations (a highly technical term of French law), and also sometimes that it is in the "public interest" to make it into a "common rule" for an industry. Moreover it must comply with certain requirements of substance and form, and in some countries an elaborate procedure, including the co-operation of the two sides of industry, must be observed. The individual worker can enforce the "common rule" as part of his contract of employment.[8]

Two further points should be made about the compulsory effect of the collective code under foreign systems (whether automatic or not). The first is techncial and refers to the nature of the worker's claim against the employer. It is a claim based on the contract of employment, not of course on the collective agreement nor on the

---

[7] France: *Code du Travail*, Arts. L133–1 *et seq.*, going back to a law of June 24, 1936; Western Germany, *ubi supra*, s. 5; Switzerland: Law of Sept. 23, 1956; Netherlands: Law of May 24, 1937.

[8] The expression "common rule" was, it seems, coined by Sidney and Beatrice Webb (*Industrial Democracy*, pp. 560 *et seq.*). It has become part of the vocabulary of labour law and labour relations in Australia: see Higgins, *New Province of Law and Order*, pp. 21 *et seq.* However, s. 41 of the original Commonwealth Conciliation and Arbitration Act was declared unconstitutional by the High Court in *Australian Boot Trade Employers' Federation* v. *Whybrow* (1910) 11 C.L.R. 311. The present "common rule" enactment applies only to the Federal Territories (s. 49). The States are, of course, free to use their conciliation and arbitration procedures for the formulation of common rules.

statute which makes it enforceable in this way. The contractual right is shaped by the collective agreement as a result of the statute. This, as we have seen, is the same with minimum wage laws in this country,[9] and, until recently,[10] with awards of the Central Arbitration Committee giving effect to collective agreements (as it is also in cases of awards based on the provisions of the Employment Protection Act on unilateral arbitration).[11] Awards under the Australian[12] and New Zealand[13] systems are, broadly speaking, enforced in the same way, but much depends on the particular legislation which may be different (as it was in the case of the Western Australian statute before the Privy Council in *True* v. *Amalgamated Collieries of Western Australia Ltd.*).[14]

The second point has much wider implications. The object of these provisions is, as we have said, to delimit the power of management as against the combined rule-making power of management and labour. Hence the general rule is that the collective terms are a "floor," not a "ceiling" and can be contracted out for the benefit of the worker, and at times of a high level of employment this is of course what happens in practice. The compulsory nature of the collective code is mainly important where the supply of labour exceeds the demand. The law as a countervailing force is called upon to support the weaker side in industrial relations. But, as already emphasised in another context,[15] the law is impotent as a countervailing force against the combined forces of labour and mangement. This is why it is so difficult to lay down that the collective terms are not only minima but also maxima—that is, one can lay it down, but how does one legally enforce it? If an employer is willing, that is, presumably compelled by scarcity of labour, to pay a higher wage than that laid down in the agreement, who will prevent him? If the market reduces the power of management, can the law restore it? It can try, as we have pointed out, but such attempts can only succeed where they are backed by a very determined policy of organised labour itself. During the Second World War the Government of the United States tried to counteract inflation through wage controls, and the Government of the United Kingdom tried to do

---

[9] See Chap. 2.
[10] *i.e.* until the repeal of Schedule XI of the Employment Protection Act 1975 by the Employment Act 1980—see below, pp. 183–184.
[11] s. 16 and s. 21, above Chap. 4.
[12] Commonwealth Conciliation and Arbitration Act 1904, s. 123.
[13] See Mathieson, *loc. cit.,* pp. 20 *et seq.*
[14] [1940] A.C. 537.
[15] Chap. 3.

the same through labour market controls. Neither Government succeeded in curbing inflation, that twin of war, but a comparative investigation organised by the ILO after the War suggested that the drastic labour market controls resulting in this country, *e.g.* from the Essential Work Orders, worked better than the wage controls of the American War Labor Board.[16] To regulate demand is perhaps more within the reach of governmental power than to regulate wage levels. A lawyer makes a point like this with diffidence, but it is a point relevant when considering potential functions of legislation on collective agreements. The function of legislation in an anti-inflationary wages policy can only be ancillary. If organised labour is determined to curb inflation by restraining wage demands it neither needs nor has it much use for legislation to achieve this purpose. The most important aspect of collective bargaining in this country at the end of the 1970s was its restraint through the "social contract" between Government and the TUC under the Labour government of 1974–1979. This was of course not a "contract" in the legal sense, but a political compact—a significant new factor as regards the long-term development of collective bargaining in this country.

There are however other reasons for which trade unions may be interested in treating collective terms not only as minima but also as maxima. This happens when employers offer to workers terms more favourable than those obtainable by a union with a view to inducing them not to join it. This practice seems to be well known among militant anti-union employers in the United States or outside the United States but influenced by American practice. The United States Supreme Court has laid down[17] that this is an "unfair labor practice" which can be suppressed by the National Labor Relations Board, if necessary through court injunctions. A similar principle has been adopted in Sweden.[18]

Seen in a European context, the typical pattern of legislation is, as we have said, that employers who are parties or members of parties to collective agreements are automatically bound by their terms, but that outside employers can be bound by an act of subordinate legislation which makes the agreement into a common rule for an industry. In this country no employer is bound by (*i.e.* precluded from contracting out of) the agreement (except where

---

[16] *Labour-Management Co-operation in United States War Production,* (Montreal, 1948), pp. 323 *et seq.*

[17] *J. I. Case Co.* v. *N.L.R.B.,* 321 U.S. 332 (1944). See also the rather different circumstances of *Emporium Capwell Co.* v. *Western Addition Community Org'n.* 420 U.S. 50 (1975).

[18] See below, Chap. 7.

its terms had been made binding upon him by a compulsory award of the Central Arbitration Committee prior to 1980). That which in many Continental countries is achieved through a general rule imposed on an industry by a quasi-legislative procedure was until 1980 done in this country through a quasi-judicial act creating a common rule ad hoc, not for an industry, but for an enterprise.

The relevant provisions originated in war-time legislation, in that same Order 1305 of 1940[19] which created compulsory arbitration on new terms. For the purpose of preventing stoppages it was necessary not only to have machinery for the making of new terms, but—and this is what we are now considering—machinery to prevent friction arising from non-observance of existing terms. In a modified form this machinery was taken over in the Industrial Disputes Order of 1951.[20] When this was revoked in 1958 and went out of force in 1959, and when unilateral arbitration disappeared, it was urged in many quarters, especially by white collar unions, that the machinery designed to compel employers to observe collective agreements should be retained and made permanent. This was first done by the Terms and Conditions of Employment Act 1959,[21] and later by the Employment Protection Act 1975[22] by which the Act of 1959 was repealed.[23]

Under this statute the Central Arbitration Committee could make an award requiring an employer to observe the—minimum or standard—terms of a collective agreement (or, which amounts to much the same thing, of an award accepted by both sides), provided these terms covered workers in an employment comparable to that of one or more of his own workers. In theory it did not matter whether the employer was a member of an organisation party to the agreement, but in practice this was intended to be, and it was, applied to "outsiders."[24] Whilst in theory it could be used to make collective agreements binding on those employers who in many foreign countries are automatically bound, it was in practice used to enforce the agreement against those employers who are not bound in any country unless they have been made subject to it

---

[19] Conditions of Employment and National Arbitration Order 1940, art. 5.

[20] S.I. 1951 No. 1376, Art. 10.

[21] s. 8, amended by the Industrial Relations Act 1971, see its Sched. 7 (now repealed). For a very informative analysis of its operation in practice see Latta, "The Legal Extension of Collective Bargaining: A Study of Section 8 of the Terms and Conditions of Employment Act 1959" (1974) 3 I.L.J. 215.

[22] s. 98 and Sched. 11.

[23] By Sched. 18 to the Employment Protection Act 1975. It had not been repealed by the Trade Union and Labour Relations Act 1974.

[24] The words "whether represented as aforesaid or not" in s. 8(1) (c) of the 1959 Act were omitted from the 1975 statute, but this had no material effect.

by a governmental act, and this is the reason why the procedure was known as "extension" of terms and conditions.[25] Insiders are generally more inclined to apply collective agreements; if they were not, they would hardly be members of any employers' association; and normally the association will, in its own interest and in that of the other members, seek to ensure that each member abides by the agreements it has made.

Not every collective agreement or award could thus be made enforceable. This could only be done if the parties to it on both sides were organisations (or federations of organisations)[26] which represented a substantial proportion of the employers and workers to whom the agreement or award related, and if, on the workers' side, they were "independent" unions.[27] That is: the terms to be enforced had to be what are called "recognised terms and conditions."[28] As such they might be established for the entire trade or industry, or for a section of that trade or industry in which the employer was engaged, and their scope might be national or it might be the employer's district, and whether an organisation was substantially representative depended on its membership in the trade, industry, or section, and in the district to which the agreement applied. In an important case[29] it was decided that the word "section" must here be understood in the occupational and not in the geographical sense (*e.g.* the carpenters in the building industry, not the building workers in a town or county), so that an employer's undertaking was not a "section" and the terms could be made binding on him, even though only a minority of his own workers (or none at all) were members of the union. This requirement that, to be imposed, the collectively agreed terms must be "recognised terms and conditions" corresponded to the condition which foreign systems attach to the "extension" of an agreement, *e.g.* that it must cover more than half the workers or

---

[25] The title of Sched. 11 to the Employment Protection Act 1975 was "Extension of Terms and Conditions," an interesting case of the influence of Continental, especially French, nomenclature on British statute law.

[26] See s. 126(1) and Trade Unions and Labour Relations Act 1974, s. 28(1) (*b*) and s. 30(1).

[27] See below Chap. 7.

[28] Employment Protection Act 1975, Sched. 11, Pt. I, para. 2 (*a*). The terms and conditions must have been "settled" by the agreement or award. The 1959 Act (s. 8(1) (*a*)) also said that they had to be "established," but, as Dr. Bercusson pointed out in his annotation to Sched. 11, para 2 in the *Current Law Statutes,* this made no difference.

[29] *R.* v. *I.D.T., ex p. Courage & Co., Ltd.* [1956] 1 W.L.R. 1062; [1956] 3 All E.R. 411, decided under S.I. 1951 No. 1376, but its principle was still applicable under Sched. 11 of the 1975 Act.

have been concluded by the "most representative" organisations. Only, whilst, *e.g.* French or German law[30] defines this in minute terms, our concept of a "substantial" proportion of the workers and employers was deliberately (and wisely) left in an aura of vagueness.

As we see, only certain collective agreements could be made enforceable. But conversely, that which was made enforceable did not need to be a collective agreement or award. Here the Employment Protection Act 1975[31] introduced a significant innovation. Where there were no recognised terms and conditions, no normative rules, there might still be a general practice, something which, though not normative, was normal. The law spoke of "the general level" of terms and conditions observed for comparable workers by employers in the trade or industry (or section of it) and the district in which the employer was engaged and "whose circumstances are similar to those of the employer in question."[32] This—as is easy to see—was as vague as any statutory formula can be, and it left a great deal to interpretation, but a similar definition of the normal standard of good employers in the Fair Wages Resolution of the House of Commons of 1946[33] which was the model of this and which we shall discuss presently was not known to have led to much difficulty in practice. The main point is that employers whose treatment of their workers fell below normal standards could be made to improve conditions, although these standards had not been crystallised in a collective agreement or award.

Ironically enough, this innovation introduced by the 1975 Act was, by 1980, to have toppled the entire structure of legal extension of collectively bargained terms of employment. The Conservative opposition was in 1975 loud in its criticisms of the inflationary consequences of the "general level" provisions of Schedule 11; and when returned to Government, they were quick

---

[30] *Supra*, n. 7, p. 178.
[31] Sched. 11, para. 1. See Bercusson, "The New Fair Wages Policy: Schedule 11 of the Employment Protection Act" (1976) 5 I.L.J. 129.
[32] *Ibid.* para. 2 (*b*).
[33] See below. The decision of Griffiths J. in *Racal Communications Ltd.* v. *Pay Board* [1974] I.R.C. 590, on the subsidiary nature of the "general level" standard as against a collective agreement—though its terms may be exceeded by general practice—referred to the Fair Wages Resolution, but is relevant here. The Industrial Arbitration Board came to the opposite conclusion in its Awards nos. 3290 and 3296. See Bercusson, *loc. cit.,* pp. 130–131; and compare *R.* v. *C.A.C., ex p. Deltaflow Ltd.* [1978] I.C.R. 534 (Div. Ct.) where the point was decided in relation to Schedule XI itself. (see below).

to repeal not just the 1975 extension but the whole of Schedule 11. They thus dismantled an entire structure of statutory support for collective bargaining that had existed in some form or other from the time of the Second World War onwards. The irony is all the greater in that the legislators in 1975 had been careful to preserve the primacy of the old provisions for extension of collective bargaining over the new provisions concerning "general levels", as had been affirmed in a judicial decision in 1978.[34] Why was it then that the Employment Act 1980 could throw the baby of legal extension of collectively bargained terms out with the bathwater of the "general level" provisions, with no significant debate or opposition in Parliament or even from the TUC? Part of the answer must be found in the sheer predominance of the newly returned government in Parliament, and in a political climate which strongly favoured any measures having a counter-inflationary aspect. But one must also allow for the fact that the extension provisions had by 1975 been revealed as of very limited effectiveness when standing by themselves because of the decline in importance of national or district-level bargaining, so that a return to those provisions alone would not have been significantly more attractive to the TUC than the repeal of the whole of Schedule 11 which actually took place. Moreover one slightly suspects that many TUC unions must have regarded the general level provisions rather as the sorcerer's apprentice regarded the multiplying brooms, given the capacity of the general level provisions to cut across existing pay structures and differentials, however beneficially at the tactical level. That, however, is mere speculation. The fact remains that the 1980 repeal swept away a piece of machinery which, whatever its practical consequences, was at least of some conceptual significance for its pattern of statutory importation of the results of collective bargaining into individual contracts of employment not otherwise covered by the collective bargaining process.

(c) Minimum wage laws

Despite the temporary prominence of the "general level" provisions of Schedule XI between 1975 and 1980, the system of minimum wage legislation[35] may in fact have been a much more powerful instrument for the observance of collective terms than

---

[34] R. v. *CAC ex p. Deltaflow Ltd.*, *supra*.

[35] Wages Councils Act 1979, Agricultural Wages Act 1948, Agricultural Wages Act (Scotland) 1949, the latter two as amended by the Employment Protection Act 1975—See Bayliss, *British Wages Councils* (1962).

the procedure before the Central Arbitration Committee. Those procedures presupposed that some sort of collective bargaining existed or at least that there was a union or unions strong enough to enforce the observance of a general level of good employment practice. But minimum wage legislation—to which we have already referred in other contexts[36]—must be understood as a substitute for collective bargaining where, owing to weak organisation or (as in agriculture) owing to the dispersal of the labour force, collective bargaining cannot work. Under the Wages Councils Act minimum remuneration, minimum holidays, and now other terms and conditions,[37] are fixed by a tripartite wages council which, to some extent, is a statutory replica of a voluntary negotiation board. It consists of representatives of the two sides of industry—they are now appointed and no longer, as they used to be until 1975, only nominated by the organisations on both sides[38]—and a number of independent members (academics, lawyers etc.) whose role becomes decisive if the two "sides" cannot agree.[39] The Agricultural Wages Boards for England and Scotland are similarly composed, and their powers are practically identical with those of wages councils.[40] Wages councils as well as Agricultural Wages Boards make their own orders—without consulting any government department[41]—fixing remuneration, requiring holidays to be allowed, and fixing other terms and conditions autonomously. This however means that in practice the difference between these statutory minimum wage orders and collective agreements is not nearly as great as appears at first sight. When the two sides agree, as they often do in wages councils, even if the independent members have the decisive say, the order made by a wages council is in fact an emanation of the autonomous forces of the two sides of industry, and in substance not all that different from a collective agreement, though in law it is of course something miles apart from it. *Mutatis mutandis* the same can be said of the Agricultural Wages Boards, though agreement between

---

[36] Chap. 3.

[37] Wages Councils Act 1979, s. 14.

[38] Wages Councils Act 1979, Sched. 2, para 1.

[39] *Ibid.* and Agricultural Wages Acts 1948 and 1949, Sched. 1; Bayliss, *loc cit.,* Chap. 7.

[40] Agricultural Wages Acts 1948 and 1949, s. 3, both as amended by Scheds. 9, Pt. I and 10, Pt. I of the 1975 Act.

[41] Under the 1975 Act the power of wages councils to make proposals to the Secretary of State was transormed into a power to make orders. The councils have now the same power of passing subordinate legislation that the Agricultural Wages Boards had had for a long time, and the Secretary of State is no longer concerned.

the two sides is here very infrequent.[42] However, what results is enforceable through legal sanctions. The orders made by a wages council[43] or by one of the two Agricultural Wages Boards[44] are enforced through inspection, if necessary through criminal prosecution. In order to enable the Secretary of State, *i.e.* the Department of Employment, to enforce an order made by a wages council, an employer must furnish to the Department such information as it demands.[45] As we have seen,[46] the terms of such orders are compulsorily implied in the relevant contracts of employment and can thus be enforced in the civil courts, in future possibly in the industrial tribunals.[47] Within certain limits the inspector can also enforce the contract on behalf of the worker by obtaining an order for the payment of the difference between wages paid and wages due under an order made by a wages council or Agricultural Wages Board—up to two years back.[48] But whilst the employer is contractually liable not only to grant the prescribed minimum wages, holidays, and holiday remuneration, but also the other prescribed minimum conditions, it is not a criminal offence for him to act contrary to an order as regards any terms other than those referring to wages, holiday remuneration and holidays.[49] In spite of the formidable enforcement mechanisms contained in the statutes, there have been persistent complaints in recent years alleging high rates of failure by employers to meet the statutory minima and low rates of inspection and prosecution by the wages inspectors.[50]

Is it fanciful to say that minimum wage legislation plays in this country to some extent the role which in other countries is played by the binding effect of collective agreements as codes? That

---

[42] See the evidence of Sir George Honeyman (Chairman of the Agricultural Wages Board for England and Wales) to the Donovan Commission: Minutes of Evidence, Sept. 27, 1966 (No. 50) Qu. 8191. From this it is clear that the independent members play a much greater role in the Agricultural Wages Board than they generally do in a wages council.

[43] Wages Councils Act 1979, s. 15.

[44] Agricultural Wages Acts 1948 and 1959, s. 4 (as amended by Sched. 9, Pt II, para. 1 and Sched. 10, Pt. II, para 1 of the 1975 Act), and s. 12.

[45] 1979 Act. s. 24.

[46] In Chap. 3.

[47] Employment Protection Act 1975, s. 109(8) (*a*) and (*b*).

[48] Wages Councils Act 1979, s. 15; Agricultural Wages Acts 1948 and 1949, s. 4.

[49] See 1979 Act, s. 15(2) and (3), and the addititon to s. 11 of the 1948 and 1949 Acts, inserted by Sched. 9, Pt. II, para. 3, of the 9th and 10th Schedules of the 1975 Act.

[50] See the evidence collected in Low Pay Unit, *Minimum Wages for Women* (1980), pp. 26–28.

binding effect is of course of practical importance mainly in situations in which the unions are too weak to enforce the observance of collective agreements by their own methods, and have to resort to legal sanctions. Those situations are most likely to arise in the trades and industries covered by our minimum wage laws. It is the presence and operation of those laws which helps to explain why the automatic compulsory enforcement of collective agreements has, in this country, been considered as unnecessary.

This, however, is true only to some extent. As we have pointed out before,[51] the standards enforced under minimum wage laws are generally (not always) much lower than those created by collective agreements. After all, the Wages Councils Act operates in branches of the economy in which the wage level is generally low, for economic reasons, or as a result of bad organisation of the workers, and largely owing to the prevalence of badly paid female labour. And, further, statutory levels may be fixed to temper the wind to the shorn lamb, *i.e.* the less efficient employer.[52] This is why statutory machinery cannot be a substitute in the full sense for collective bargaining. It must however be taken into account that in wages council industries (not in agriculture) very often the two sources of regulation exist side by side: the statutory minimum wage is only the ground floor of a sometimes impressive structure of wages and conditions built up through collective bargaining for the benefit of those employed by the better and the more efficient (often the larger) employers.[53] The co-existence of statutory and voluntary machinery cannot be entirely avoided.

One of the objects of wages councils legislation has always been to stimulate collective bargaining, to provide a training ground for voluntary procedure, and to this extent to make the statutory procedure superfluous. This did not happen extensively in practice. Even where collective bargaining had developed, employers' associations, especially those representing small firms, tended to be in favour of retention of the wages council, and with it the system of enforcement of wages, as a protection against

---

[51] Chap. 3.

[52] In spite of this, wages councils have come under Parliamentary criticism for fixing rates, especially for young workers, that are too high and which, it is alleged, operate to reduce employment opportunities. In consequence the future of the wages councils is in some doubt. See n. 54, above p. 57.

[53] The Donovan Commission (see Cmnd. 3623, paras. 225 *et seq.*, esp. para. 261) found that the minimum wages fixed by the Agricultural Wages Boards were generally closer to the real level of earnings than many of those fixed by wages councils.

undercutting on the product market.[54] Consequently, the law was changed in 1971 so as to allow the Secretary of State, after consultations with employers, to abolish wages councils on the application of a representative trade union alone,[55] trade unions tending to see the continuation of statutory minimum wages as causing the perpetuation of low pay. An even more fundamental criticism of wages councils was developed in some quarters, to the effect that their existence actually discouraged the development of collective bargaining, by providing the parties with no incentive to develop voluntary machinery, especially at plant or company level. In recent years government has responded to these views by adopting a more active policy of abolishing or reducing the scope of wages councils. Whereas before 1962 only a handful of wages councils had been abolished, since that date more than 20 have been abolished or merged. However, from the beginning this new policy has been subject to the contrary criticism that abolition might not by itself encourage collective bargaining on a sufficiently extensive scale, and that some vulnerable groups of workers would suffer as a result of the removal of the statutory minima. Recent research has tended to show that these fears were justified.[56]

An alternative approach to the problem was introduced in the Employment Protection Act 1975,[57] the relevant provisions of which are now re-enacted in the 1979 Wages Councils Act. The 1975 Act created a "half way house." A wages council can be transformed by the Secretary of State for Employment into a "statutory joint industrial council," a hybrid creature, sharing some features with a statutory wages council and some with a voluntary negotiating body. It has no independent members, and is entirely composed of representatives of the two sides,[58] just like a voluntary council. But it makes statutory orders which are enforceable like orders made by a wages council.[59] This form of organisation is adjusted to trades or industries in which there are, on both sides, organisations strong enough to achieve a regulation by bargaining, but not yet strong enough to prevent undercutting by outsiders, and therefore in need of the support of the law. If they do not come to terms in a statutory joint industrial council,

---

[54] See Craig, Rubery, Tarling and Wilkinson, *Abolition and After: the Cutlery Wages Council* (D.E. Research Paper No. 18, 1980), pp. 1–2.

[55] Now the 1979 Act, s. 5(1) (c).

[56] Craig, etc., *Labour Market Structure, Industrial Organisation and Low Pay* (1982) esp. Chap. 4.

[57] ss. 90–94, and Sched. 8.

[58] s. 90 and Sched. 8; now s. 10 and Sched. 4 of the 1979 Act.

[59] s. 91; now ss. 10 and 15 of the 1979 Act.

they may request the ACAS to settle the matter—it takes, as it were, the place of the independent members of a wages council.[60] If it does not succeed, it must refer the matter to arbitration by the CAC or by an arbitrator, and the award is "final and binding." This means that the statutory joint industrial council is then under a duty to make an order accordingly, and that duty is, on general principles, ultimately enforceable through an order of mandamus by the Queen's Bench Division of the High Court. Although the matter goes to the ACAS only on the request of the statutory joint industrial council itself, once it has gone there the further progress of the proceedings is no longer in the council's hands. In a sense therefore this is a case—in fact, the only case—of genuine compulsory arbitration in our law. All this is intended to be transitory, and as soon as possible, *i.e.* as soon as adequate voluntary machinery exists, such a council will be abolished by the Secretary of State who has created it.[61]

(d) Equal pay

From its inception in 1909 until the present day it has been the major object of minimum wage legislation to level up the wages of the lowest paid categories of workers. We have seen that this was not done—as in the United States and in France—by laying down a statutory minimum guaranteed to every worker, but by selecting for statutory regulation of their wages and other conditions those groups of workers who were most in need of it. This, however, has from the beginning necessarily meant that the large majority of workers covered by this legislation were women.[62] The discrepancy between male and female wages is one of the dominant features of labour relations, indeed of economic and social life in this country, as in other similar countries. Any measure designed to raise the wages of women to the level of the wages of men doing

---

[60] s. 92; now s. 11 of the 1979 Act.

[61] s. 93; now s. 12 of the 1979 Act. In fact, the Secretary of State has not, as yet, had occasion to create a S.J.I.C.

[62] Of those employees who were covered by the original Trade Boards Act 1909, "the vast majority were women," Bayliss, *loc. cit.,* p. 10. After the Trade Boards Act 1918, *i.e.* in 1920, "seventy per cent. of the workers involved were women." (*ibid.* p. 17). After the reform of the system through the Wages Councils Act 1945 (and the Catering Wages Act 1943) the large majority of employees within the system were in retail distribution and catering. Taking all wages councils together, the average proportion of women workers was now "about 75 per cent. of the labour force of the trades as a whole" (*ibid.* p. 73). Bayliss estimates that "not far short of one woman worker in two is within the Councils' scope." There is the closest possible social connection between minimum wage and equal pay legislation.

work of the same value must of necessity be a most far reaching, almost revolutionary piece of legislation. The Equal Pay Act of 1970[63] is such a measure. Its potentialities are greater than that of any other statute we have considered so far: no statute could, if implemented, contribute more towards achieving justice in society, but perhaps no statute could contribute more towards raising the cost of production or distribution in labour-intensive industries or trades. One does not get the impression that the boldness of the underlying conception, that the social promises this statute holds out and the economic risks it may involve have as yet been fully appreciated. There is a case for saying that it is the most important statute on labour law passed by Parliament since the Second World War.

The policy of the 1970 Act—like that of the relevant Convention No. 100 of the ILO and that of the European Social Charter[64]— goes beyond the simple rule of "equal pay for equal work." It is possible, indeed probable, that the major problem in this country is one of job distribution and—a different thing—of job evaluation. That is: whilst no doubt there are cases, perhaps there are many cases, in which a woman doing precisely the same work as a man is paid less, the principal problem seems to be that women have far inferior opportunities of access to the better paid job (the problem of job distribution) and that the jobs mainly done by women are remunerated at a lower level than possibly similar jobs mainly done by men (the problem of job evaluation). We shall return presently to the complex problems associated with the question of job evaluation; let us at this stage look a little further into the question of job distribution, or, as it is known by reference to the obverse side of the coin, job segregation. Since the problem of job distribution is inseparable from that of equal pay, the Equal Pay Act of 1970 must be seen in conjunction with the Sex Discrimination Act 1975. This provides, *inter alia*, that[65] an employer may not discriminate against a woman in the arrange-

---

[63] Now as amended by the Sex Discrimination Act 1975, Sched. 1, Pt. I, and printed in its amended form in Sched. 1, Pt. II, which in its turn was amended by the Employment Protection Act 1975, Sched. 16, para. 13 and para. 18(2), and is about to be amended by the important Equal Pay (Amendment) Regulations 1983.

[64] Convention concerning Equal Remuneration for Men and Women for Work of Equal Value, in force since May 23, 1953, as also the corresponding Recommendation No. 90. Convention No. 100 has now been ratified by the United Kingdom, not however the corresponding Art. 4(3) of the European Social Charter. On the difference between the Convention and the Charter: Kahn-Freund, *The European Social Charter*, in *European Law and the Individual*, ed. by F. G. Jacobs (1976), p. 189.

[65] s. 6(1).

ments he makes for the purpose of determining who should be offered a given employment, or refuse or deliberately omit to offer it to a woman; and similar and at least equally important rules apply to promotion[66] and training. Access to better paid jobs does not, however, depend only on the recruiting policy adopted by employers, but equally on training opportunities offered by vocational training bodies (whether the training be through apprenticeship or institutional), on employment agencies and their practice, and—very important—on trade unions and their admission policies. All this is subject to detailed regulation in the Sex Discrimination Act.[67]

It may take a very long time before sex discrimination ceases to be a major factor in job distribution and therefore in income distribution, and before the job expectations of a girl begin to approach those of a boy. This is a major attempt to change the social mores of a nation. Once this has been achieved—if ever it will be—the Equal Pay Act will still be important, but not nearly as important as it is now. Is not one of the main reasons, perhaps the main reason, why women are paid so badly that they have so little chance of competing with men for the better paid jobs? Is this not also one of the reasons why women have to put up with low valuation of such jobs as they can get? To carry out the policy of the Sex Discrimination Act will mean no less than to eliminate the instinctive differentiation in people's minds between "men's jobs" and "women's jobs." This distinction is psychologically deep seated. To get rid of it would be a great social achievement, but it will take a long time. During that time the levelling up of the remuneration paid for "women's jobs" must be a major preoccupation of the law, and the Equal Pay Act will have to do a great deal of work which an implementation of the Sex Discrimination Act may make less necessary.

We have already seen[68] that the Equal Pay Act has an important impact on the law governing collective agreements. Any collective agreement which involves express discrimination between men and women can be amended by the Central Arbitration Committee, and the procedure can, if necessary, be set in motion by the Department of Employment, though neither the management nor the labour side wants it to go there. The principles of autonomy and of voluntary regulation—the very foundations of British

---

[66] s. 6(2) (*a*).
[67] ss. 12–16. See Henry Phelps Brown, *The Inequality of Pay* (1977) and Peter J. Sloane (ed.), *Women and Low Pay* (1980).
[68] Above, text to n. 73, p. 170.

collective labour law—have been sacrificed to this most urgent need for counteracting discrimination in conditions of employment. This is a public policy which may have to be enforced against the combined forces of both sides of industry, and this means that collective agreements can by compulsion of law be changed through a procedure not initiated by either.[69] However, in view of what we have said about the actual significance for women's wages of minimum wage laws, and especially of the Wages Councils Act, it is easy to see that in practice it may be even more essential that orders made by wages councils or statutory joint industrial councils, and also those of one of the Agricultural Wages Boards, can be adjusted to the principle of non-discrimination.[70] The Secretary of State (*i.e.* the Department of Employment) can refer to the Central Arbitration Committee any of these orders, just as he can refer a collective agreement, either at the request of either side of the council or Board or of his own motion. If the CAC decides that the order has to be amended, it becomes the duty of the wages council or statutory joint industrial council or Agricultural Wages Board to amend it accordingly, or to make a new order complying with the decision of the CAC. If this is not done, the Queen's Bench Division of the High Court can issue an order of mandamus enforcing this obligation.[71]

These principles apply not only to the bilateral regulation of wages and other terms in collective agreements and orders made by wages councils, etc., but also to a unilaterally imposed "pay structure,"[72] *i.e.* "any arrangements adopted by an employer . . . which fix common terms and conditions of employment for his employees or any class of employees, and of which the provisions are generally known or open to be known by the employees concerned." This seems to be the first time that the law openly recognises the unilateral rule-making power of management as the

[69] Equal Pay Act 1970, s. 3. Note, however, the limitations placed on the C.A.C. by the decision in *Ex p. Hy-Mac* [1979] I.R.L.R. 461 (D.C.). Note also that any complaint arising from an alleged violation of the Act through an individual contract of employment (see s. 1) goes to an industrial tribunal (s. 2), while complaints arising from collective regulations go to the CAC (ss. 3–5).

[70] Equal Pay Act 1970, s. 4 and s. 5.

[71] The Act (as amended by the Employment Protection Act 1975) says in s. 4 that "it shall be the *duty*" of a wages council or statutory joint industrial council to take the requisite action. The same form of words had already been used in the original text of the Act (s. 5) as regards the Agricultural Wages Boards. The amendment of s. 4 was necessary because until the coming into force of the Employment Protection Act this was the duty of the Secretary of State.

[72] Equal Pay Act 1970, s. 3(6). Note the distinction between a contract of employment (s. 2) and a pay structure.

exercise of a law giving, and in that sense, a legislative function. It is a case of adjusting legal concepts to social realities, and it is no coincidence that the Federal Labour Court of the German Federal Republic performed an almost identical operation in this very context of implementing a policy directed against sex discrimination. Any employer was held to be bound by the constitutional guarantee[73] of equal treatment of the sexes when making a unilateral and general decision on conditions of employment,[74] because in doing so he exercised a rule-making power.

So much, then, for the procedures for the direct reformulation of the results of collective bargaining to accord with equal pay criteria. Let us revert for a moment to the wider question of what the impact has been of equal pay legislation as a whole upon the practices and products of the collective bargaining system. One cannot escape the feeling that the Equal Pay Act itself has by now had its main impact, an impact which while great and significant stops short of the fundamentals of the problem.[75] Is it entirely a coincidence that in these circumstances the scene of the action should have shifted to Luxembourg where several important references from the British courts to the European Court of Justice on equal pay have recently been adjudicated?[76] Essentially, there have been several attempts to invoke article 119 of the Treaty of Rome as a basis for breaking out of the restrictions upon the concept of equal pay under the British legislation. Article 119 was significantly amplified by an EEC Directive of 1975,[77] article 1 of which stated that the principle of equal pay means for the same work or work to which equal value is attributed the elimination of all discrimination on grounds of sex with regard to all aspects and conditions of remuneration. The nature and extent of the direct applicability of this Directive as between individuals in Britain is still uncertain[78]; but the European Court of Justice is showing some inclination to read the provisions of the Directive back into the Treaty article itself and to take a fairly aggressive stance on the direct applicability of the Treaty article as thus interpreted. This positive stance on the direct applicability of the equal pay principle could be seen to be taken in different contexts in each of three

---

[73] Bonn Basic Law, Art. 3, para. 2.
[74] Decision of the Federal Labour Court of May 10, 1962, [1962] N.J.W. 1537.
[75] See Chiplin and Sloane, *Tackling Discrimination at the Workplace* (1982), pp. 16–19.
[76] *Macarthys Ltd.* v. *Smith* [1980] I.C.R. 672; *Worringham* v. *Lloyds Bank Ltd* [1981] I.C.R. 558; *Jenkins* v. *Kingsgate Ltd.* [1981] I.C.R. 592.
[77] EEC Council Directive No. 75/117 of February 10, 1975.
[78] See Schofield (1980) 9 I.L.J. 173.

equal pay cases recently decided on reference from the United Kingdom.[79] But courts everywhere tend to be more assertive of their own jurisdiction than of specific policies, and on the crucial substantive issue of lower hourly rates for part-time workers as compared with full-time workers, the European Court seems to have displayed much the same caution as the British courts towards classifying this differentiation in terms of discrimination against women workers.[80] Again, they have recently taken a cautious approach to the question of how far pension provisions and the conditions relating to them came within the ambit of the equal pay concept.[81] Progress in these matters is necessarily slow, and no doubt the courts are reluctant to engage in administering fundamental shocks to employers' payment structures; but, and this is the crucial point, it is only by means of an expansion of the equal pay principle that patterns of collective bargaining and of managerial determination of terms and conditions of employment can be significantly changed so far as the equal treatment of men and women at work is concerned.

However, if both the European Court and the courts of the United Kingdom have been relatively cautious in their development of the equal pay measures, the EEC Commission has been rather more aggressive, and there are currently some indications that a significant expansion of the equal pay principle may be on the point of taking place. In order to explain this, we have to return to the question, which we mentioned briefly earlier, of job evaluation. Although it is a truism in one sense, it is nevertheless a statement of great practical consequence that in order to move from a narrow principle of equal pay for the same or similar work to a broad principle of equal pay for work of equal value—which is, of course, the crucial change in kind and not just degree—you have to engage in some kind of process of evaluating jobs in relation to each other. Yet not only would it need the philosopher's stone to find a universally acceptable method of relative job evaluation, but it is all too clear that existing labour

---

[79] *Supra,* note 76.

[80] Compare the ECJ decision in *Jenkins* v. *Kingsgate Ltd.* (Note 76, *supra*), with the decisions of the EAT in *Handley* v. *Mono Ltd.* [1979] I.C.R. 147; but contrast, on the other hand, the more positive approach of the EAT in *Jenkins* v. *Kingsgate* [1981] I.C.R. 715 on the reference back from the ECJ.

[81] *Worringham* v. *Lloyds Bank* (*supra,* note 76). The ECJ treated payments made to male workers to recompense them for their contributions to an occupational pension scheme as coming within the concept of pay because those sums were taken into account for quantifying other entitlements based on a calculation of gross salary. If that is a *sine qua non* for including such payments within the equal pay concept, the result would be a restrictive one in relation to pension schemes.

costs would be inflated and existing pay structures would be seriously threatened by such a method even if it could be found and operated. The contemplation of this apparently yawning abyss gave the framers of the Equal Pay Act vertigo, and they contented themselves with making equal pay for work of equal value mandatory only (apart of course from comparisons between like work) where equality of value was in fact established by a job evaluation study already carried out in relation to jobs within an undertaking or group of undertakings.[82] Despite judicial construction in the United Kingdom courts tending to maximise the application of this rule,[83] the rule palpably falls short of a fully developed equal value principle in that it is confined to such job evaluation studies as employers voluntarily choose to undertake or at least permit to take place. It was therefore not difficult for the EEC Commission, ultimately moved to take enforcement proceedings against the British Government in respect of this matter,[84] to obtain a declaration from the European Court that the Equal Pay Act failed to implement the EEC equal pay requirements so far as the equal value principle was concerned, and that the government was accordingly failing to carry out its treaty obligations towards the EEC. The Department of Employment accordingly brought forward a set of regulations[85] made under the European Communities Act 1972 (a further example of the capacity of that Act to be the source of departmental legislation of major importance to Labour Law) to amend the Equal Pay Act in favour of a fuller implementation of the equal value principle and promised a set of Regulations making consequential changes to the procedure of Industrial Tribunals.[86] The Regulations essentially provide for industrial tribunals to hear equal pay claims on the equal value basis as well as on the existing like work basis,[87] and for them to refer equal value issues to an expert assessor, on the basis of whose reports they can then adjudicate such issues.[88] An extremely important aspect of this process from our present point of view is that of how

---

[82] s. 1(2)(*b*), (5).
[83] *O'Brien* v. *Sim-Chem Ltd.* [1980] I.C.R. 573 (H.L.); *Arnold* v. *Beecham Group Ltd.* [1982] I.C.R. 744 (E.A.T.).
[84] *Commission of the European Communities* v. *United Kingdom (Case 61/81)* [1982] I.C.R. 578.
[85] Draft Equal Pay (Amendment) Regulations 1983, to come into force on January 1, 1984.
[86] See Department of Employment, *Specification for amending the Equal Pay Act* (August 1982).
[87] Equal Pay (Amendment) Regulations. Reg. 2, amending s. 1(2) of the 1970 Act.
[88] *Ibid.* Reg. 3, introducing a new s. 2A into the 1970 Act.

far there will be provisions[89] designed to maximise the opportunities for voluntary settlements of equal value issues, and to ensure that such voluntary settlements are not narrowly confined, as the adjudicated settlement of the issue will necessarily be, to a simple direct equal value comparison between particular cases, but can extend to a more wide-ranging treatment of the consequences for a whole pay structure of a particular equal value claim. How far such provisions will prove to be merely aspirational cannot yet be clear for some time to come; what is quite clear is that these regulations as a whole offer the prospect of quite a major change in pay structures, and accordingly quite a major new challenge for the collective bargaining system in relation to managerial rule-making powers.

(e) Fair wages clauses

Minimum wage legislation as well as the Equal Pay Act are instruments for the creation of new and the improvement of existing collective standards, and they seek to guarantee their observance. But there is an additional method for achieving this purpose. This is an administrative device which the governments of many countries (including the British) have found to be at least as effective for this purpose as statutes, courts, and penal or civil sanctions. Its use is based on the elementary principle that as a tool for creating what are now called "motivations" the carrot is normally far preferable to the stick. In our society the government has a large store of carrots: government contracts, statutory licences, subsidies. Hence for many years the British Government made it a condition of government contracts that the contractor and his subcontractors and their subcontractors should comply with collective agreements. Similar policies have (under relevant legislation) for a long time been in operation, *e.g.* in France[90]— and in the United States.[91] It is a policy which was applied in this country not only by the central Government, but also by many local authorities, and by corporations administering publicly owned industries. It was also used in a number of statutes as a condition for obtaining and maintaining licences (*e.g.* in road

---

[89] *Cf.* D.E. Specification, *supra*, n. 86.

[90] On the *Décrets Millerand* of August 10, 1899, revised in 1937, see Brun et Galland, *Droit du Travail* (1958), Pt II, paras. 208 and 209, p. 459. This development is not discussed in the same detail in the second edition of this work (1978).

[91] For an analysis of the Walsh-Healey (Public Contracts) Act of 1936, as amended, and of the Davis-Bacon Act of 1931, see Aaron and Mathews, *The Employment Relation and the Law* (1957), pp. 406 *et seq.*

transport)[92] and also, in various industries, subsidies. But the most important aspect of these "fair wages clauses" was their application to contracts made with central government authorities. This policy goes back to the first "Fair Wages Resolution" of the House of Commons, most recently re-formulated in the Fair Wages Resolution of 1946.[93]

This was a resolution of the House of Commons; and it was not a statute, and not part of the "law." Legally it was merely a set of directives addressed to government departments, and requiring them to insert certain clauses into their contracts. The most important of these was to the effect that the contractor must pay wages and observe hours and conditions of labour not less favourable to the workers than those laid down in the relevant collective agreements made by substantially representative organisations on both sides, *i.e.* what later came to be known as "recognised terms and conditions," and, failing these,[94] comply at least with the standards generally applied by comparable employers. He must also guarantee that his subcontractors do the same, and must exhibit the Resolution at the work place. Obviously the terms "fair wages resolution" and "fair wages clause" were misnomers, because these cover all conditions of employment and not only wages.

What were the sanctions in the event of non-compliance? Legally the fair wages clause operated as a condition of a contract the breach of which entitled the other party, here the Government, to rescind the contract and to claim damages. This was the theory; it was of no importance. It was obvious too that, this being part of a contract between the Government, *i.e.* the Crown, and the contractor, no one else could claim rights under it, and in particular neither the worker affected by underpayment, nor his union. A forlorn attempt was made many years ago[95] by a workman to enforce a fair wages clause against an employer. It had to fail. The real sanction was not legal at all, but administrative: it was the threat of being taken off the list of government

---

[92] Public Passenger Vehicle Act 1981, s.28.

[93] Fair Wages Resolution of the House of Commons, printed in *Industrial Relations Handbook,* p. 151. Previous Resolutions were passed in 1891 and in 1909. For the history, see Kahn-Freund, "Legislation through Adjudication" (1948) 11 M.L.R. 269 and 429.

[94] In *Racal Communications Ltd.* v. *Pay Board* [1974] 3 All E.R. 263, Griffiths J. held that, if a collective agreement existed for the district, the Fair Wages Resolution did not oblige the employer to apply a standard higher than that of the agreement though such might be generally applied by comparable employers in the district. The matter was controversial: see above n. 33, p. 183.

[95] *Simpson* v. *Kodak* [1948] 2 K.B. 184.

contractors. If a complaint was made against a contractor of having failed to comply with the clause (the complaint was most likely to emanate from a trade union) and could not be settled by the department concerned (which might be anything from the Ministry of Defence to H.M. Stationery Office) the matter would be taken in hand by the Department of Employment and if this could not settle it, it would be referred to "an independent tribunal for decision." In practice this meant the members of the Central Arbitration Committee who, however, if acting in this capacity did not do so as the Arbitration Committee, but as an arbitral tribunal under the contract, *i.e.* not as a statutory body.[96]

The fact is that by what seemed to be general consent no governmental measure had over the last three quarters of a century done more to spread the habit of observing collective agreements than these Fair Wages resolutions, covering as they did a very wide sector of the economy, especially through the inclusion of sub-contractors. It was, therefore, particularly significant when Parliament, at the instigation of the government, resolved at the end of 1982 that the Fair Wages Resolution should be rescinded as from September 21, 1983.[97] This removed a resolution which Parliament had adopted as long ago as 1891 and which had been a continuous part of the law of collective bargaining since that time. The effect of the rescission was also to render inoperative those clauses in statutes which incorporated the Fair Wages Resolution by reference.[98] Although the practice of public, nationalised and, especially, local authorities is not necessarily affected by the rescission of the Resolution *vis-à-vis* the contractors of central government, it does seem likely that at least some of these bodies will follow the lead of central government. At a more fundamental level than the mere removal of a long-standing part of our law stand two further points. It was a momentous event that, in order to be able to rescind the Resolution, the government had to denounce the United Kingdom's adherence to ILO Convention No. 94 concerning labour clauses in public contracts. This was the first time the United Kingdom had denounced an ILO convention it had previously ratified because of disagreement with the policy underlying the convention, and it was a remarkable twist of events

---

[96] *R.* v.*Industrial Court, ex p. A.S.S.E.T.* [1965] 1 Q.B. 377, but not so as to create a submission to arbitration within the meaning of the Arbitration Acts: *I.M.I. (Kynoch) Ltd.* v. *A.U.E.W.* [1979] I.C.R. 23 (C.A.).

[97] See H.C. Deb., Cols. 499–568, December 16, 1982.

[98] See, *e.g.* Public Passenger Vehicles Act 1981, s.28; Broadcasting Act 1981, s.25; Films Act 1960, s.42.

that this should occur in relation to a convention which British practice had so much influenced at the time of its formulation.[99] Secondly, the reasons the government gave for rescinding the Resolution, which were essentially the same as those given for the repeal of Schedule 11 to the Employment Protection Act in 1980, indicated a fundamental shift in government policy. The extension of terms and conditions of employment to create a common rule for an industry was now seen as "external interference" in matters that should be regulated by individual employers and their employees in the light of their particular circumstances, and it was denied that the Resolution played a significant role in dealing with low pay.[1] Thus, the law has virtually shed its role of giving compulsory effect to the code of terms and conditions of employment contained in collective agreements. Although membership of another international organisation, the European Community, is currently sustaining and even expanding the United Kingdom's commitment to equality of pay in collective agreements, it must be wondered how much more of the law which aims to promote the observance of collective agreements, especially the minimum wage legislation,[2] is under threat of execution.

---

[99] Art. 2 of Convention 94 of 1949 is clearly closely based on clause 1 of the Fair Wages Resolution 1946.

[1] See n. 97, *supra*.

[2] ILO Convention No. 26 of 1928 concerning minimum wage-fixing machinery, which the U.K. has ratified, currently protects the domestic law. It can be denounced in 1985.

CHAPTER 7

TRADE UNIONS AND THE LAW

LABOUR law, as we pointed out in the first chapter, deals with the power of management and with the power of labour, and with their adjustment. A firm, a government department, a local authority, co-ordinates human and material resources and thereby becomes a managerial unit and as such a bearer of power. On the workers' side the analogous process is association in trade unions. The formation of unions, that is the organisation of labour, is the counterpart of the accumulation of capital. There can be labour relations without employers' associations—though this would be difficult and very undesirable—but there cannot be labour relations without trade unions. The analogy between employers' associations and trade unions is useful to the lawyer, but a distortion of social reality. We have seen the importance of this when looking into the question whether either of them acts as principal or agent in the process of collective bargaining.[1]

We are dealing with labour law, and the accumulation of capital and its legal aspect are not its concern. They belong to the sphere of company law and of administrative law. The association of workers however is our business here. We cannot discuss all its legal aspects,[2] and we have singled out the problems of freedom of organisation, of the closed shop, and of "trade union democracy."

1. FREEDOM OF ORGANISATION

Workers' organisations cannot exist if workers are not free to join them, to work for them, and to remain in them. This is a fundamental human right, a civil liberty, which as such appears in the catalogues of fundamental rights in a number of constitutions.[3]

---

[1] In Chap. 3, p. 83.
[2] Not, for example the problems arising from inter-union relations and amalgamations. For a general survey see Kidner, *Trade Union Law* (2nd. ed., 1983).
[3] Such as the Preamble to the French Constitution of 1946 (which is incorporated in the present Constitution of 1958), Art. 9 of the Basic Law of the German Federal Republic, Art. 39 of the Italian Constitution. Frequently (*e.g.* in Austria, in Belgium, in the Netherlands and Switzerland) the Constitution guarantees the general freedom to form occupational and professional associations without specifically referring to those operating in labour relations: Spyropoulos, *La Liberté Syndicale*, p. 21.

It appears in the international declarations and covenants which express the aspirations of mankind,[4] and as such it ranks with freedom of speech, freedom of religion, and freedom from arbitrary arrest and seizure. It is, however, also complementary to collective bargaining; that is, it is a *conditio sine qua non* of industrial relations in all except totalitarian societies. It is therefore in accordance with political and social reality that it should also appear in those conventions and treaties which deal with labour relations. Outstanding among these are the ILO Conventions of 1948 concerning freedom of association and protection of the right to organise[5] and of 1949 concerning the application of the principles of the right to organise and to bargain collectively,[6] both of which have been ratified by the United Kingdom, as has the equally important Article 5 of the European Social Charter made under the auspices of the Council of Europe.[7] The ILO has built up an important organisation for the international protection of trade union freedom.[8] Its Committee on Freedom of Association has investigated and continues to investigate and to report on many cases in which a complaint is made against an infringement of the principles of the Conventions of 1948 and 1949. The United Kingdom was involved in a number of such cases.[9]

When we talk about "freedom of organisation" we really mean two different things: the absence of prohibitions or restraints, and the presence of positive guarantees for its exercise. For an

---

[4] Universal Declaration of Human Rights 1948, Art. 23(4); International Covenant on Economic, Social and Cultural Rights 1966, Art. 8; European Convention for the Protection of Human Rights and Fundamental Freedoms, Art. 11.

[5] Convention No. 87.

[6] Convention No. 98.

[7] Under it the Contracting Parties undertake that national law shall not impair nor shall it be so applied as to impair the freedom of workers and employers to form and join local, national and international organisations for the protection of their economic and social interests. There is a limited exception regarding the police and a more far reaching exception regarding the armed forces.

[8] On this, see Jenks, *The International Protection of Trade Union Freedom* (1975); Valticos, *Droit International du Travail*, Vol. 8 of Camerlynck's *Traité*, pp. 587 *et seq.*, and especially Valticos, *Un Système de Contrôle International: La Mise en Oeuvre des Conventions Internationales du Travail*, Recueil des Cours de l'Académie de Droit International, 1968—I, 314–407; von Potobsky, (1972) 105 *International Labour Review* 69.

[9] See the Report of the Inquiry by Lord Cameron into the Complaint made by the National Union of Bank Employees, Cmnd. 2202 (1963), and see App. III thereof for the case of the Aeronautical Engineers' Association.

understanding of English law it is important that we should distinguish between them.

(a) Absence of restraint

The "negative" aspect of freedom of association is something primitive and simple: the State does not prevent a man or woman from helping to form a union, or from joining or working for an existing union and from remaining its member. This is a freedom "from" something, from criminal prosecution, from administrative measures. It is not a guarantee that its exercise will not be impeded by social forces, *e.g.* by an employer or by the unions themselves. Such a guarantee requires positive measures, the use of judicial sanctions against those who seek to encroach upon this freedom. For the moment we shall concentrate on the negative aspect.

Britain was one of the first, possibly the first, country in Europe to lift the ban on trade unions. This happened in 1824[10]; in France it did not (at least in form) happen until 1884,[11] in large parts of Germany not until 1869.[12] Behind all this there is a complex history of political events and political ideas, of apprehensions and misapprehensions, of fears and favours. One of the most surprising features is the vigour and the tenacity of the ideas of Jean Jacques Rousseau in France, as expressed in the Loi Le Chapelier[13] passed in 1791 by the Assemblée Constituante and remaining on the French statute book until 1884. It enacted the principle that there were to be no "mediators" between the individual and the *volonté générale* manifested in the State. Wages and hours were to be left to individual bargaining (*aux conventions libres d'individu à individu*)—those who drafted this celebrated document knew about the link between freedom of association and what we call collective bargaining. Nor, as J. M. Thompson rightly emphasises,[14] did it single out the workers for special adverse treatment. It was hostile to employers' associations as

---

[10] Combination Laws Repeal Act 1824.

[11] Law of March 21, 1884, as amended. Its substantive part is now condsolidated in *Code du Travail,* 1974, Art. L 411–2. For a detailed analysis, see Spyropoulos, *loc. cit.,* pp. 15 *et seq.*

[12] Para. 152 of the *Bundes-* (afterwards *Reichs-*) *Gewerbeordnung* of 1869, but this applied only to industry, not to agriculture or domestic service. This had to wait until 1918.

[13] Law of June 14 to 17, 1791 which prohibited temporary (*"coalition"*) as well as permanent (*"syndicat"*) combinations of employers and workers.

[14] J. M. Thompson, *The French Revolution* (1944), pp. 166 *et seq.,* gives an admirable brief account of the Loi Le Chapelier and its background. On the present point, see p. 169.

well, indeed to all associations. The practical effect is another matter. If this is the pure milk of Rousseau's doctrine, it is also a classical case of that false identification of workers' and employers' associations to which we have referred—perhaps it was less false in the France of 1791 than it is today.

In this country the story is very involved, and it is possible only to give a few hints.[15] One must go back to the Elizabethan[16] legislation by which the system of maximum wages inherited from the Statute of Edward III[17] was developed into an administrative structure.[18] If it was an offence to demand wages higher than those fixed by the justices of the peace, then it was a conspiracy to agree to ask for higher wages. Besides, numerous statutes were passed, even before, but especially in the eighteenth century, for trade after trade, threatening with imprisonment journeymen and labourers who entered into agreements for advancing their wages or lessening their hours of work.[19] The suppression of such "agreements" was complementary to the rudimentary anti-inflationary wages policy of the statute of Elizabeth I. Pitt's Combination Acts of 1799[20] and 1800[21] were, in a sense, only the generalisation of many earlier special statutes. When Pitt's statutes were passed, wage fixing by the justices of the peace had long fallen into disuse, as emerges from Adam Smith's testimony.[22] It was almost dead when in 1811 the Court of King's Bench gave it the *coup de grâce* by holding that mandamus would not lie to force the justices to exercise their powers under the Statute of Apprentices.[23] It was formally abolished in 1813.[24] But the

---

[15] The literature is prodigious. As outstandingly important one can mention S. and B. Webb, *History of Trade Unionism*; Hedges and Winterbottom, *Legal History of Trade Unionism* (1930); Stephen, *History of the Criminal Law of England*, Vol. 3; a very good account is in the "Historical Introduction" to Landis and Manoff, *Cases on Labor Law* (1942). Reference should also be made to Wright, *Law of Criminal Conspiracy* (1873) and to the important article by Sayre, "Criminal Conspiracy" (1922) 35 Harv. L. Rev. 393.

[16] Statute of Apprentices 1562. See Holdsworth, *History of English Law,* Vol IV. pp. 340 *et seq.*, pp. 379 *et seq.*

[17] Statutes of Labourers 1349 and 1350. See Stephen, *loc. cit.*, p. 203.

[18] Holdsworth, *History of English Law,* Vol IV, pp. 340 *et seq.*, pp. 379 *et seq.*, for a useful account of the Elizabethan system. One does not have to share his view of its social consequences.

[19] Stephen, *loc. cit.*, p. 206.

[20] Combinations of Workmen Act 1799.

[21] Combinations of Workmen Act 1800.

[22] *Wealth of Nations,* Bk. I, Chap. X, Pt. 2 (1776) (Ed. by Edwin Cannan, 5th ed., 1930, Vol. I, p. 142): "The practice has now gone entirely into disuse."

[23] *R.* v. *Justices of Kent* (1811) 14 East 395.

[24] Wages of Artificers Act 1813.

legislation against workers' organisations (nominally also against employers' associations) remained on the statute book, however imperfectly it was enforced.

The Combination Acts were repealed by the famous statute of 1824,[25] soon replaced by another statute of 1825.[26] One of the most ironic features of this repeal is that Francis Place, the promoter behind the scenes of this legislation, and his friends in the House of Commons, were Benthamites and hostile to the unions. They thought that what held them together was their illegality, and that, once they were legal, they would evaporate.[27] For some reason—was it owing to Place's superb manipulative skill?—the House passed this decisive and historic statute almost without a debate,[28] in a fit of absent-mindedness from which it recovered when a wave of strikes swept the country during the winter 1824–1825. The result was the Act of 1825. This curtailed the freedom to strike, but it did not revive the prohibitions against associations. For half a century, from 1825 until the enactment of Disraeli's Conspiracy and Protection of Property Act of 1875, during the first formative era of trade unionism, this country provided an object lesson in the difference between freedom of organisation and freedom to strike.

At no time since, either in peace or in war, has the freedom of organisation of civilians been impaired—with two exceptions, both in the "public" sector. The first was only temporary, the other is still with us. From 1927[29] until 1946[30] established civil servants were not allowed to be members of an organisation unless its membership was restricted to Crown servants and unless it was unaffiliated to any federation such as the TUC which comprises organisations of employees other than civil servants. And secondly, since 1919,[31] members of the police force have not been free to join unions: they have a statutory federation which exercises some of the functions of a collective bargaining body, but which is not a trade union. Its disability to associate with a body outside the police service was mitigated by the Police Act 1972, but the statutory disability of the police to belong to unions has come

---

[25] Combination Laws Repeal Act 1824.
[26] Combination Laws Repeal Act Amendment Act 1825.
[27] Graham Wallas, *The Life of Francis Place* (4th ed., 1925), p. 217.
[28] Stephen, *History of the Criminal Law of England*, Vol. 3, p. 212
[29] Trade Disputes and Trade Unions Act 1927, s. 5.
[30] Trade Disputes and Trade Unions Act 1946.
[31] Police Act 1919, now Police Act 1964, s. 47.

under increasing social scrutiny in recent years.[32] Otherwise public, like private, employees have since 1824 been free to form and join unions,[33] and none of the doctrinal and other difficulties encountered, *e.g.* in the United States and in Germany, have in this country stood in the way of trade unionism, collective bargaining, or the freedom to strike[33a] in the public sector of the economy.

This negative freedom is no more than, in the words of the relevant ILO Convention[34]: "the right to establish and . . . to join organisations of their own choosing without previous authorisation." We call it a freedom and not a right because it does not involve any power to set in motion the judicial or administrative machinery of government. All it means is that the government does not intervene (on its legislative, administrative, or judicial side) so as to impede a certain type of human activity.

(b) Positive guarantees

(i) Against employers
Until recently there was a glaring contrast between the wide scope of this freedom and the absence of any legislation seeking to guarantee its exercise. There was no vestige in legislation (as distinct from administrative practice) of an "adequate protection" of workers "against acts of anti-union discrimination in their employment"[35] nor of "protection of workers' and employers' organisations . . . against any acts of interference by each other or each other's agents or members in their establishment, functioning or administration."[36] The only legal protection was through the operation of fair wages clauses[37] in government contracts and in

---

[32] See for instance the Report of the Committee of Inquiry on the Police, Cmnd. 7283, July 1978.
[33] See the series "Comparative Studies in Public Employment Relations," published in 1971 by the Ann Arbor Institute of Labor and Inustrial Relations in connection with an International Symposium on Public Employment Labour Relations organised in New York by the New York State Public Employment Relations Board in May 1971. The three volumes referring to the United Kingdom are: Hepple and O'Higgins, *Public Employee Trade Unionism in the United Kingdom, The Legal Framework*; Levinson, *Collective Bargaining by British Local Authority Employees*; Loveridge, *Collective Bargaining by National Employees in the United Kingdom*.
[33a] On the problem of industrial action in "essential services", a category that overlaps but is not coterminous with the public sector, see Chap. 8, below.
[34] No. 87. Art. 2.
[35] ILO Convention No. 98, Art. 1.
[36] *Ibid.* Art. 2.
[37] The Fair Wages Resolution is now rescinded. See Chap. 6 *ad finem*.

statutes which made it a condition of a contract or licence or subsidy that an employer and his sub-contractors should respect their workpeople's freedom of organisation.[38] In 1952 the long-standing practice of a large printing firm to exact from its workers an undertaking not to be or remain members of a union led to a strike, and this led to the appointment of a Court of Inquiry.[39] The first thing counsel for the union did was to assure counsel for the firm that he would not argue that this practice was illegal—and he was right. The "yellow-dog" contract (as it is known in America), the "document" (as it used to be known in British nineteenth century history), that is the signing away of a fundamental right, was not obnoxious to the law. Nor was it, until very recently,[40] illegal for a union arbitrarily to exclude a person from membership, however irrelevant the reasons. On the other hand even before the intervention of Parliament the common law for some time had given a union member in certain situations a measure of protection against deprivation of membership by unreasonable expulsion.

What can the law do to ensure that the freedom of organisation is not only proclaimed on paper but protected against adverse social forces? The law can refuse to enforce any contracts or other measures intended or calculated to abridge this freedom, and it does so in some countries.[41] This expresses a fundamental principle but it means little in terms of social policy. If a person is in so dependent a position that he or she must promise an employer not to join a union, he is likely to be also too weak to be able to rely on the invalidity of the promise. The validity or voidness of a contract is relevant only between parties who are "at arm's length." The mere withholding of civil sanctions, *i.e.* the invalidity of contractual promises, has little social effect.

But the law can go further and take positive measures to suppress such practices. The most important pattern of legislation is that created in the United States by the National Labor Relations Act of 1935. This threatens with positive sanctions those who seek to use their economic power to curtail the exercise of

---

[38] See ACAS, *Industrial Relations Handbook* (1980), pp. 29–30.

[39] Report of a Court of Inquiry into a Dispute between D. C. Thomson & Co. Ltd. and certain workpeople, members of the National Society of Operative Printers and Assistants, Cmd. 8607, 1952.

[40] By reason of the new remedy introduced (in the closed shop situation only) by ss. 4 and 5 of the Employment Act 1980. See below, pp. 235–236.

[41] *e.g.* under Art. 9 of the Bonn Basic Law, as already under Art. 159 of the Weimar Constitution in Germany, and under the Swedish Act on the Joint Regulation of Working Life, 1976. s. 4.

other persons' freedom to organise. It lists types of encroachment by employers upon the exercise of their employees' freedom of organisation which are characterised as "unfair labor practices."[42] To this the Taft-Hartley Act of 1947 added a corresponding catalogue of "unfair labor practices" which can be committed by trade unions.[43] Employers' unfair labor practices include acts by which employers "interfere with, restrain, or coerce employees" in the exercise of the right of self-organisation, the right to form, join or assist labour organisations, etc.[44] For an employer it is also an unfair labor practice "by discrimination in regard to hire or tenure of employment or any term or condition of employment to encourage or discourage membership in any labor organisation."[45] These are two examples from a comprehensive list. The point is that, if it can be proved that such practices have been committed by any person, the National Labor Relations Board can make[46] "an order requiring such person to cease and desist from such unfair labor practice, and to take such affirmative action including reinstatement of employees with or without back pay as will effectuate the policies of this Act." If disobeyed, the Board can ask the appropriate federal court to enforce the order through injunctions.[47] The ultimate sanction protecting the exercise of a person's freedom of association is thus the law of contempt of court. The effectiveness of all this depends on the ability of the unions to enforce it—but it depends on the union, not, like the assertion of the mere invalidity of a contract, on the individual.

This American pattern of legislation can be compared with the Swedish provisions[48] which protect the right of association. These have been invoked not only against discriminatory dismissals, but also[49] against discriminatory refusals to promote an employee, an offer of a wage increase or of better facilities to earn overtime on condition of non-membership in the union, a refusal to reinstate after a temporary lay-off or seasonal break, and also of course

---

[42] s. 8(*a*).
[43] s. 8(*b*).
[44] s. 8(*a*) (1)
[45] s. 8(*a*) (3).
[46] s. 10(*c*).
[47] s. 10(*e*).
[48] Act on the Joint Regulation of Working Life, 1976, ss. 7–9, taking the place of, and being largely identical with, the Act respecting the Right of Association and the Right of Collective Bargaining of Sept. 11, 1936, as amended. For what follows we are heavily indebted to Folke Schmidt, *Law and Industrial Relations in Sweden*, 1977, especially Chap. 5 (The Right of Association).
[49] Schmidt, *loc. cit.*, p. 72.

against the yellow-dog contract itself.[50] All this resembles to some extent the American practice, but the difference is that, unlike the United States, Sweden does not have a public authority to act as the guardian of the freedom to organise. The sanction in Sweden is an action against the employer for damages[51] or for enforcement of the contract, *e.g.* for the reason that a dismissal in violation of the freedom of association is void.[52] This may be brought by the organisation concerned, whether or not it is in collective bargaining relations with the employer.[53] An employers' association may be liable if it has failed to try to induce its members to abstain from or to terminate a violation of the right of association.[54] The difference from the American situation may not be all that important in practice, because even in the United States someone must "charge" the employer before the National Labor Relations Board.

Perhaps the most explicit protection to be found anywhere in Europe is that enacted in the Italian *Statuto dei Lavoratori* of 1970[55]—one of the most remarkable enactments in labour law. This guarantees[56] the right to form and to join unions and to be active on their behalf. Agreements by which the employment of a worker is made conditional on membership or non-membership of a union are void, and so are acts by which a worker is dismissed or otherwise discriminated against by reason of union membership or activity or participation in a strike.[57] As in the United States, discriminatory acts are usually controlled by means of cease and desist orders made under the emergency procedures of the statute.[57a] But where the employer has influenced the employees in the exercise of their trade union rights by the discriminatory distribution of benefits, the judge may impose a penalty equivalent to the economic value of the benefit (up to one year back) unlawfully withheld from the victim of discrimination, imposed on the application of the union and payable to a publicly administered pensions fund.[58]

---

[50] *Ibid.* p. 67.
[51] s. 54 of the Law of 1976.
[52] *Ibid.* s. 8(3).
[53] Act on Litigation in Labour Disputes of May 31, 1974, Chap. IV, s. 5. For the union's right of representation see Folke Schmidt, *loc. cit.*, pp. 41–43; pp. 56–58.
[54] s. 9 of the Law of 1976.
[55] Freni and Giugni, *Lo Statuto dei Lavoratori* (Milan (Giuffre), 1971—an annotated text).
[56] Art. 14.
[57] Art. 15.
[57a] Art. 28.
[58] Art. 16.

The Donovan Commission did not recommend the enactment of such measures as those adopted in these countries, except that to a certain degree its proposals for protection against unfair dismissal were intended to cover this ground.[59] Nor did the Commission deal with the problem as one of a fundamental civil right—had it done so it would have recommended the invalidity of all contracts inimical to its exercise—but rather in terms of the need for extending collective bargaining and in connection with union recognition.[60] A hostile attitude on the part of the employer may, especially in the white collar field, deter workers from joining a union and thus reduce the union's chance of being recognised. The Commission found that discrimination against union members still existed in this country, mainly but not exclusively in the case of white collar workers, and it identified two types of practice which it recommended be put down. The first was the crude yellow-dog contract, and the Commission recommended that (except in the police force and in the armed forces) a stipulation that an employee should not belong to a union was to be null and void.[61] The second was a rule book of a benefit society financed by the employers, offering substantial advantages to supervisory employees joining it, and declaring membership incompatible with that in a union.[62] The Commission recommended that no friendly society should be allowed to make membership conditional on non-membership of a union.[63]

The problem of the organisation of employees exercising supervisory and other managerial functions has arisen not only in this country—the Donovan Report showed this—but also abroad. Here we see one of the practical consequences of the overlap of the spheres of labour and management to which we referred previously.[64] Should, *e.g.* a foreman be free not only to join unions in general, but in particular to remain or become a member of the union organising those whom he supervises? He has probably "risen from the ranks" and, if so, may wish to remain in the union to which he belonged during the whole of his working life. In the United States "any individual employed as a supervisor" was by the Taft-Hartley Act of 1947 completely excluded from the

---

[59] Chap. 9, esp. para. 540.
[60] Para. 219.
[61] Para. 245.
[62] The Foremen and Staff Mutual Benefit Society. See paras. 247–252.
[63] Para. 252. The offending clause was deleted, but the friendly societies legislation has not been changed in this respect.
[64] In Chap. 1.

protective provisions to which we have referred.[65] In Sweden it used to be the law[66] that, whilst a foreman enjoyed the guarantees we have mentioned, it might be stipulated in his individual contract of employment or in a collective agreement that he should not belong to the union of those supervised by him—a clause apparently never much used in practice and now omitted from the Law of 1976. No such provision appears to exist in Italy, nor does it in this country[67] where, especially in the engineering industry, this would give rise to very formidable problems.

In many countries attempts (frequently successful) have been made by employers to organise and finance bodies outwardly appearing as trade unions, but in fact dominated by employers—a fact sometimes difficult to prove. This is the most invidious form of interference with freedom of organisation, a denial of the foundation of labour relations—that is the regulation of labour through the combined action of the independent forces of labour and management. It has been an unfair labor practice in the United States since 1935[68] and the Italian statute of 1970 has a similar clause.[69] The relevant ILO Convention[70] seeks to protect both workers' and employers' organisations "against acts of interference by each other or each other's agents in their establishment, functioning or administration." The matter is of great importance, especially as a result of the growth of the white collar sector in advanced economies and the tendency on the part of some employers to strangle the growth of trade unionism among white collar workers through organising staff or house associations.[71] The boot may, of course, be on the other foot—the

---

[65] s. 2(3)

[66] Act of 1936, s. 3(5); Folke Schmidt, *Law and Industrial Relations in Sweden*, pp. 75 *et seq.*

[67] Compare the "overlap" situation in *Boulting* v. *ACTAT* [1963] 2 Q.B. 606 (C.A.) where the view of the majority of the Court shows the extent to which anything like the "supervisor" clause of the Taft-Hartley Act is alien to the principles applied in this country. It may nevertheless be asked whether Lord Denning's dissent was not much closer to social reality than the majority view. Compare also *Yeshiva University* v. *NLRB* 444 U.S. 672 (1980) where the U.S. Supreme Court held that full-time faculty members in a private university were managerial employees, and thus excluded from the scope of the National Labor Relations Act, because of the absolute authority they exercised in academic (though not in other) matters.

[68] It is "an unfair labor practice for an employer to dominate or interfere with the formation or administration of any labor organisation or contribute financial or other support to it": National Labor Relations Act 1935, s. 8(*a*) (2).

[69] Art. 17.   [70] No. 98, Art. 2.

[71] See Bain, *Trade Union Growth and Recognition,* Royal Commission Research Paper No. 6, para. 228

ILO Convention we have quoted seems to assume that employers' organisations may be interfered with by workers' organistions, though it is not easy to see how. The Taft-Hartley Act and the Landrum-Griffin Act of 1959 added to the United States National Labor Relations Act list of unfair labor practices that can be committed by labour organisations or their agents. Most of these are not relevant in the present context, but there is[72] among them a prohibition upon restraining an employer in the selection of his own representatives for collective bargaining and grievance adjustment. Although this is far less important than the prohibition of sham trade unions, it is based on the same principle. The principle is the need for complete mutual independence of management and labour. We shall see presently how our law now seeks to cope with this problem.

The Industrial Relations Act 1971 was the first statute in this country to proclaim freedom of organisation as a legal principle,[73] *i.e.* the freedom to be a member of a union, to participate in its activities, and to stand for, or to hold, office in it. If an employer discriminated against, or penalised, a worker because he had exercised this freedom, *e.g.* if he refused to engage or to promote him or if he dismissed him for that reason, this was—on the American pattern—an "unfair industrial practice."[74] But, unlike American law, the Act did not say that discrimination could be directly suppressed by an injunction. The worst that could happen to the employer was that he had to pay a very restricted sum by way of damages, and, if he so chose, he could thus "buy out" an active unionist.[75] All this, however, did not matter in practice. The Act limited the worker's freedom of organisation to registered unions. Since the overwhelming majority of unions and all the large unions refused to be on the register, the proclamation of the freedom of organisation was a dead, one might say a still-born, letter. In this, as in many other respects, the 1971 Act was an ephemeral episode which failed to make any major difference in practice. Still there were cases in which it led to strange situations. If a minority union which the employer did not recognise got itself on to the register, its members could insist on a legal right to engage in union activities at the work place and to use facilities there to which the only union to bargain collectively with the employer, not being registered, could lay no legal claim.[76] The

---

[72] s. 8(*b*)(1)(B).   [74] s. 5.
[73] s. 1(1)(*c*).   [75] ss. 106, 118.
[76] The leading, but not the only, case is *Post Office* v. *Union of Post Office Workers* [1974] I.C.R. 378. For a good summary of the relevant cases, see Weekes, Mellish, Dickens and Lloyd, *loc. cit.*, Appendix VIII, pp. 295 *et seq.*

privileges of registered unions have now disappeared, and the Employment Protection Act sought, as we shall see, to avoid this grotesque discrepancy between negotiating rights and organising rights.[77]

The Act of 1975 did not, in abstract terms, proclaim the principle of freedom of organisation. But, together with the Trade Union and Labour Relations Act 1974, it protected by detailed provisions[78]: the freedom (a) to join, and to be a member of, a union which is independent,[79] (b) to take part in its activities, (c) to refuse to join, or to remain in, a union which was not "independent," *i.e.* which was dominated or controlled by the employer or, *e.g.* owing to financial support, liable to managerial interference tending towards such control. Our law, differing from the laws, *e.g.* of the United States or of Italy, does not forbid the setting up of sham unions, but protects workers against attempts to compel them to join or remain in them,[80] which may be equivalent to a compulsion not to join or to leave a genuine union.

Unlike Swedish or German law, and despite the Donovan recommendation, the present law does not say that the "yellow-dog" contract by which a worker promises not to become or to remain a union member is void, perhaps because such terms are not imposed much in practice.[81] In this respect our law pursues the policy embodied in ILO Convention No. 98 of condemning interference by either side of labour relations with the other side's organisations. The individual employee's right not to be dismissed or to have action short of dismissal taken against him for refusal to belong to an employer-dominated union has not, as far as is

---

[77] "Organising rights" include the right to represent an employee in individiual grievance proceedings. Thus, a registered but unrecognised union had no right to participate in a negotiating body, but did have a right to appear before a grievance committee. See the contrast between the decisions of the NIRC in *Central Electricity Board* v. *Coleman* [1973] I.C.R. 230 and in *Howle* v. *G.E.C Power Engineering Ltd.* [1974] I.C.R. 13.

[78] Now Employment Protection (Consolidation) Act 1978, ss. 58(1), 23(1) as amended. Section 15 of the Employment Act 1980 provided protection against action short of dismissal to compel membership not only of non-independent unions but also of independent unions in the absence of a union membership agreement satisfying the statutory conditions. This extended the function of the provision concerned from that of protecting freedom of association in the strict sense to that of protecting freedom to dissociate also. s. 3 of the Employment Act 1982 inserted a new s. 58(1) of the 1978 Act which makes the same change in respect of protection against dismissal—see below pp. 259 and 264.

[79] s. 30(1) of the 1974 Act; s. 126(1) of the 1975 Act.

[80] See above, n. 78.

[81] Though for a prime example of a true yellow dog contract see *Camellia Tankers Ltd.* v. *International Transport Workers Federation* [1976] I.C.R. 274.

known, been invoked in practice, presumably because employers
do not in practice seek to coerce particular employees into
belonging to non-independent staff associations, however detrimental the presence of the latter may be to the development of
meaningful collective bargaining. The legal challenge to non-
independent unions was therefore in practice confined to denying
them access to the statutory recognition provisions of the Employment Protection Act 1975.[82] This produced an interesting crop of
cases in which the Employment Appeal Tribunal tended increasingly to deflect the Certification Officer's caution in accepting
that once dependent staff associations had attained the character
of truly independent unions.[83] The Certification Officer's discretion was eventually restored by the Court of Appeal,[84] but the
repeal of the statutory recognition provisions by the Employment
Act 1980 removed the principal focus of concern on the part of the
state with the independence of unions.

What is more important is that the present law, differing from
the Industrial Relations Act 1971,[85] does nothing to protect an
applicant for a job against anti-union discrimination, nothing to
prevent an employer from systematically rejecting union members, or, more significantly, union members known to be "active,"
nothing to counteract blacklists.[86] The law protects "employees"
only, *i.e.*[87] those who have entered into a contract of employment,
not those who seek to do so. It is not as if "hiring" was any more
beyond the reach of the law than "firing"—the law forbids racial[88]
and sex[89] discrimination in engaging workers, why not anti-union
discrimination? It is little short of astonishing that, in view of the
advances made in the law concerning discrimination generally, the
law of freedom of association should still be limited by the refusal
to extend it to cover refusals to hire.[90]

---

[82] Now repealed. See above pp. 96–106.
[83] *Blue Circle Staff Association* v. *C.O.* [1977] I.C.R. 224; *Association of H.S.D. Employees* v. *C.O.* [1978] I.C.R. 21; *Squibb U.K. Staff Association* v. *C.O.* [1978] I.C.R. 115 (E.A.T.).
[84] *Squibb U.K. Staff Association* v. *C.O.* [1979] I.C.R. 235 which, when applied by the E.A.T. in *A. Monk & Co. Staff Association* v. *C.O.* [1981] I.R.L.R. 431, produced a result in favour of the staff association concerned.
[85] s. 5(2) (*c*).
[86] Contrast the French *Code du Travail*, 1974, Art L 412–2.
[87] See above, n. 79, p. 212
[88] Race Relations Act 1976, s. 4(1).
[89] Sex Discrimination Act 1975, s. 6(1).
[90] The E.A.T. has been unwilling to allow the law of unfair dismissal to be used to counteract this refusal—*City of Birmingham D.C.* v. *Beyer* [1978] 1 All E.R. 910.

While he is employed the worker enjoys a threefold protection. First: he must not[91] because he is a member of a union—whether recognised or not—or, *e.g.* because he is a shop steward, be put at a disadvantage in the conditions of his employment, assigned to less well paid jobs, refused opportunities for overtime, be put in an unfavourable place on a holiday roster, passed over for promotion, etc. And if he alleges that any such things were done by reason of his union membership or activity, then the employer must show what were the reasons for doing it, *i.e.* the employer must prove that it was not done for discriminatory reasons.[92]

Second: he must not be "prevented or deterred" from union activity. This is important. It means in the first place that no worker must suffer a disadvantage in the terms of his employment by reason of what he does in the interest of his union, whether at the place of employment or outside. But it means more; if an employee representing the union in the plant, *e.g.* a shop steward, is denied the facilities which are indispensable for the exercise of this function, he is prevented from exercising it. Hence the employer is under an obligation to provide him with these facilities, such as the use of a notice board, a desk, a telephone, and, if the size of the plant justifies this, an office.[93] This applies to every independent union, whether or not the employer has recognised it: indeed a shop steward or other representative of a non-recognised union may need this protection of the law particularly because in order to obtain recognition he may first of all have to recruit a minimum number of workers at the workplace. All this, however, has to be done outside working hours, unless an arrangement for union activity during working time has been made with the employer or the employer has given his consent,[94] or unless the union official represents a recognised union. In the latter case he is entitled to a certain amount of release at full pay during working hours, but only for purposes

---

[91] Employment Protection Act (Consolidation) Act 1978, s. 23.

[92] *Ibid.* s. 25(1).

[93] See ILO Convention 135 Concerning Protection and Facilities to be afforded to Workers' Representatives in the Undertaking, ratified by the United Kingdom on March 15, 1972, and Recommendation 143. The ACAS Code of Practice on Time Off (see p. 62) contains at the end a note of the facilities that an employer ought to afford to shop stewards.

[94] Employment Protection (Consolidation) Act 1978, s. 23(1) (*b*) and (2). The Court of Appeal held in *Marley Tile Company* v. *Shaw* [1980] I.C.R. 72 that consent to the calling of a meeting of maintenance men by a shop steward during working time could not be inferred merely from the fact that the meeting arose out of a grievance falling within the province of the shop steward.

connected with industrial relations in the plant or enterprise (*e.g.* negotiations or their preparation) or in order to undergo such training as he needs to carry out these duties and as has been approved by his union or by the TUC.[95] In everybody's interest there is—as the Donovan Commission said[96]—an "immense" need for better trained shop stewards, and "everybody" includes the employer himself—the law now recognises this. Of course, any member of a recognised union—official or not—may wish to get free time to participate in outside union activities—conferences, committee meetings etc.—or in activities of bodies such as trades councils or the TUC in which he wishes to represent his union. Within reason he can get such free time, but at his own expense, not that of the employer.[97] The minute details of all this are partly regulated by the Act and partly taken care of by the Code of Practice.[98]

Third: an employee must not be dismissed by reason of his membership in, or his activity for, an independent union, or his refusal to be a member of a dependent (sham) union.[99] If the employer dismisses one of his employees mainly or entirely for one of these reasons,[1] it is an "unfair dismissal," but an unfair dismissal with a difference. It is unfair *per se.* Normally, when an employee complains to an industrial tribunal on the ground that he was unfairly dismissed, the employer may show what was his principal reason for dismissing him—lack of capability or qualification, conduct, redundancy, etc.—and then the Tribunal will consider the circumstances of the case (its "equity and substantial merits") and decide whether the employer has proved that the dismissal was reasonable.[2] But if it is proved that, by dismissing him, the employer encroached on the employee's freedom of

---

[95] *Ibid.* s. 27. See *Beal* v. *Beecham Group Ltd.* [1982] I.C.R. 460.

[96] Cmnd. 3623, para. 712.

[97] Employment Protection (Consolidation) Act 1978, s. 28(1) and (2). The Act also provides for release without pay for certain public duties, *e.g.* as justice of the peace, member of a local authority, of a statutory tribunal (*e.g.* an industrial tribunal), etc., (s. 29), and for time off with pay during notice by reason of redundancy in order to look for a new job or for retraining facilities (s. 31).

[98] *Ibid.* s. 27(2)–(7), s. 28(3) and (4); ACAS, Code of Practice No. 3, Time Off for Trade Union Duties and Activities.

[99] See n. 78 *supra.* And now, of course, for refusal to be a member of an *independent* union also. See below, p. 264.

[1] Employment Protection (Consolidation) Act 1978, s. 58. The wording of s. 58(1)(*a*) suggests that under the present law a worker, in order to be protected, does not have to specify the union he proposes to join.

[2] *Ibid.* s. 57.

organisation, then there can be no discretionary appraisal of individual circumstances.[3] This is excluded. There can be no individual circumstances which make a violation of a person's freedom to organise appear as "fair," not even if this was not the only reason for dismissal, but the main reason. It is for the employer to prove why he dismissed an employee, and especially that none of the main reasons contravened the employee's freedom to organise."[4] To this there are exceptions. Suppose the employer dismisses 100 men by reason of redundancy, and among them there is a shop steward who alleges that his union activity was the main reason why he was included among those declared redundant. If he can prove this, he will succeed, but in the face of redundancy he will have to prove it.[5] Another exceptional situation in which the contravention of the freedom to organise must be proved by the employee arises where the employee has either been employed for less than 52 weeks or has reached retiring age, *i.e.* in the absence of a special arrangement, 65 in the case of a man and 60 in the case of a woman. Those belonging to these categories are protected against unfair dismissal only if it is a dismissal on these grounds[6] and this the employee must prove.[7] Those who have been holding a job only for a short time and also those who are beyond retiring age have, in the eyes of the law, a tenuous expectation of job security and cannot therefore complain that, on general grounds, a dismissal was unfair. But they, like every one else, have their freedom of organisation and the right to have it protected, only that it has been violated must in this case be proved by the claimant.

Probably the most important aspect of the protection against dismissal is that it gives a measure of security to active union representatives at the workplace, *e.g.* to shop stewards, a matter of increasing importance with the growth of plant bargaining. In

---

[3] *Ibid.* s. 58. None of this applies to a dismissal during a strike or lockout. For this see below, Chap. 8.

[4] *Ibid.* s. 57(1). In this connection it is most important that the 1978 Act, s. 53, gives to the employee a right to a written statement by the employer, on request, of the reasons for his dismissal.

[5] *Ibid.* s. 59. For an illustration see *Taylor* v. *Butler Machine Tool Co. Ltd.* [1976] I.R.L.R. 113.

[6] *Ibid.* s. 64. Note that under s. 53 of the Act an employee who has been employed for less than 26 weeks is not entitled to a written statement of the reasons for his dismissal.

[7] See *Smith* v. *Hayle Town Council* [1978] I.C.R. 996; *cf. Maund* v. *Penwith D.C.* [1982] I.R.L.R. 399.

France and in Germany[8] the statutorily elected representatives of the workers, and in France also the equivalent of our shop stewards, enjoy much stronger safeguards against dismissal. Our protection against a dismissal which infringes an employee's freedom of association fulfils to some extent a similar function.

In all these respects, including dismissal protection, it is irrelevant whether the union is or is not recognised by the employer, except as regards time off during working hours, and this even if the employer has recognised one union and the employee concerned is a member of, or active for, another independent union. In the absence of a closed shop ("union membership agreement")[9] and, as we shall see shortly, since 1980 to some extent even in the presence of such an agreement, a recognised union has no monopoly of membership or activity in a plant or enterprise. Employees other than members of a recognised union may wish to become or already be members of a rival union (which is independent), or actively seek to establish it at the workplace. The employer must not prevent them from being or doing any of these things nor dismiss them or otherwise discriminate against them for it. This is not the way to solve inter-union disputes. If the union which the employer has recognised has not agreed with him on a closed shop, rival unionism can, however deplorable, legitimately exist in the plant, and the employer must not suppress it. This, however, is, at least potentially, an explosive situation: the employer may find himself threatened by a strike or other industrial action on the part of one group if he tolerates organising activities of the other and by that other group if he refuses to do so. Nevertheless the law says that for him it is no excuse or adequate explanation to allege and to prove that in such a situation he prevented an employee from union activities or that he dismissed him under the pressure of threatened or actual strike or other industrial action.[10] He is thus placed between the devil

---

[8] Germany: *Kündigungsschutz-Gesetz,* 1969, para. 15, as amended by the *Betriebsverfassungsgesetz,* 1972, para. 123. France: *Code du Travail,* Art. L 412–15, Art. L 420–22, Art. L 436–1. The protection afforded to the *délégués syndicaux,* to the *délégués du personnel* and to members of the *comités d'entreprise* has recently been extended. See J.-M. Verdier, *Droit Social,* January 1983, p. 37 and H. Sinay, *ibid.,* June 1983, p. 413.

[9] Where there is a union membership agreement, freedom to take part in the activities of a union is confined to unions specified in the agreement: Employment Protection (Consolidation) Act 1978, s. 23 (2A) (*a*) as inserted by Employment Act 1980, s. 15(2).

[10] s. 25(2), s. 74(5) of the 1978 Act. [Kahn-Freund was firmly of the view that this provision was unjustifiable. Its presence in the unfair dismissal legislation is historically explicable in terms of the provision of the Industrial Relations Act

and the deep sea: either he yields to pressure, in which case he may have to pay heavy compensation which may not even be reduced on this ground,[11] or he resists it, in which case he may have a strike on his hands. Complaints that inter-union disputes are fought out on the back of employers are not always justified. In this case they are.

[While accepting this conclusion so far as the freedom of association provisions require exact parity of facilities as between unions, the editors would not see this argument as justifying the total confinement of the right to take part in union activities to recognised unions.]

All this used to be quite different if and when the recognised union entered into a "union membership agreement," *i.e.* a closed shop agreement with the employer. In sharp distinction to the 1971 Act the law in force from 1974 to 1980 was not opposed to the closed shop. The legislation recognised an agreement or arrangement by which employees of an identifiable class were in practice to be or to become members of a specified union.[12] An employer who made such an agreement was entitled to suppress activities of a union not so specified or accepted by the parties to the agreement as if specified.[13] As long as an employee who was not a member of a union covered by a closed shop was still employed the employer could not discriminate against him in his wages or other terms of employment, but he was allowed to prevent him from being active for a rival union.[14] The rival union could still try to get a foothold at the workplace but if it wanted to do that it had to refer the recognition issue to ACAS.[15] As long as the reference was pending, or once the Service had made an "operative" recommendation for the recognition of that union, the right to trade union membership and activity applied fully in respect of

---

1971, ss. 33, which, as a corollary to the provision complained of, gave the employer a right of recourse against those exercising the pressure. From 1974 to 1980 there was no such recourse provision. The Employment Act 1982, s. 7, makes a new recourse provision (new Employment Protection (Consolidation) Act 1978, s. 76(A)) where the pressure was exercised because the employee was not a member of a union. The new provision would, however, hardly meet Kahn-Freund's main concern, which was that the statutory protection of freedom of association should not offer a means of support to inter-union rivalry.]

[11] See *ibid.* s. 26(4).
[12] The definition of a "union membership agreement" in s. 30(1) of the 1974 Act, as amended by the 1976 Act, also applied to the 1975 Act (see its s. 126(1)) and adopted for the 1978 Act (s. 153(1)).
[13] s. 23(3)–(6) of the 1978 Act.
[14] s. 23(4) of the 1978 Act referring to s. 23(1) (*b*) but not to s. 23(1) (*a*).
[15] See above, pp. 96–106.

that union.[16] This represented a solution to the problem of the relation between negotiating and organising rights (including rights to represent an employee in individual grievance procedures) which led to such absurd situations under the 1971 Act. Recognition entailed organising rights which the law protected. The individual right to freedom of association was not confined to recognised unions and it could apply in favour of one union even if another was recognised, but once a recognised union had entered into a union membership agreement with the employer, another union could acquire the benefits of the individual right of freedom of association only by setting in motion the appropriate procedure in ACAS.

Much of this structure was changed by the Employment Acts 1980 to 1982. The closed shop is now tolerated much more narrowly and the law is broadly opposed to it. The establishment of a closed shop no longer provides the employer and the specified trade unions with a complete protection from activities on behalf of a non-recognised trade union (subject to the initiation of a reference to ACAS) as the law in force from 1974 to 1980 did. An employee will have the right to take part in the activities of an unrecognised trade union unless the closed shop agreement has received the necessary approval in a ballot of the employees covered by it and, even where this is the case, the activity will still be protected if dismissal in the circumstances would be unfair, *e.g.* because the employee was not a member of a specified trade union when the closed shop was introduced.[17] On the other hand a rival union excluded from the benefit of the individual right to trade union activity by the presence of a union membership agreement no longer has the opportunity to refer the recognition issue to ACAS because the statutory recognition provisions have been repealed.[18] Hence, this solution to the problem of the relation between negotiating and organising rights which prevailed between 1975 and 1980 has ceased to be available.

The ultimate sanction to protect the freedom of organisation is always the payment of a sum of money by way of compensation to the individual concerned, not to the union. On a complaint of discriminatory action short of dismissal the industrial tribunal may

---

[16] ss. 23(5) (*b*), 58(4) of the 1978 Act.

[17] s. 23(2A) and (2B) of the 1978 Act, as added by s. 15 of the 1980 Act and amended by s. 10 of the 1982 Act. In addition these provisions apply only to specified unions and not to unions accepted by the parties as specified as well. See further below pp. 252 *et seq.*

[18] See above, pp. 96–106.

make an appropriate declaration[19] and award compensation.[20] This is assessed on broad principles of justice and equity, and not restricted to the employee's pecuniary loss, such as loss of wages.[21] It is, however, reduced in so far as the employee, *e.g.* by provocative conduct, contributed to it.[22]

On a complaint on the ground that the claimant was dismissed for an inadmissible reason the tribunal can, as in all cases of unfair dismissal, order that he should be re-instated,[23] *i.e.* that he should be treated as if he had not been dismissed. Alternatively it can order the employer or his successor to re-engage the employee,[24] *i.e.* to make a new contract of employment with him, similar to the old contract. And thirdly,[25] the tribunal can, instead of doing either of these things, award compensation to the employee. The provisions relating to the amount of compensation have been altered dramatically as a result of the Employment Act 1982.[26] In addition to the usual compensatory award the employee dismissed for union membership or activities is entitled to a specially enhanced basic award and to a new special award. These provisions were introduced mainly with those dismissed for non-membership of a union in mind[27] but they apply also where the employee's freedom of association has been infringed. The tribunal will presumably (and indeed it should) normally order the employee to be reinstated or re-engaged if he has been dismissed for union membership or activities. But even here it cannot directly compel the employer to reinstate. If the order is disobeyed by the employer he becomes liable[28] to pay compensation at a higher rate, notably a higher special award,[29] than if the tribunal had initially decided to award compensation rather than

---

[19] 1978 Act, s. 24.

[20] *Ibid.* s. 26, see also, s. 30(2).

[21] In *Brassington* v. *Cauldon Wholesale Ltd.* [1978] I.C.R. 405, the E.A.T. restricted the award by insisting that it must relate to specific loss and that it could not include a penal element. This further emphasises that the remedy is a personal rather than a collective one.

[22] *Ibid.* s. 26(5).

[23] *Ibid.* ss. 68, 69.

[24] *Ibid.* ss. 68, 69.

[25] *Ibid.* s. 68, ss. 72–74.

[26] Employment Act 1982, ss. 4–5, amending ss. 71–73 of the 1978 Act and introducing a new s. 75A.

[27] See below, p. 265.

[28] New s. 75A(2) of the 1978 Act: "Unless the employer satisfies the tribunal that it was not practicable to comply with the order."

[29] *Ibid.* A minimum of £15,000 instead of a minimum of £10,000.

reinstatement.[30] Such is the precarious compromise between the policies of avoiding direct compulsion through the ultimate sanctions of contempt of court, and of making it as expensive as possible for employers to encroach upon their employees' freedom of organisation.

None of this, however, could do much good if, by dismissing a worker in violation of that freedom, *e.g.* an active shop steward, the employer could create a *fait accompli* for the whole period of the tribunal (and possibly appeal) proceedings, *i.e.* for weeks, perhaps for months. To cope with this decisive problem of the status quo a special interlocutory procedure is available,[31] if necessary before the chairman alone without employer and employee members,[32] to be used if the complaint is based on a dismissal by reasons of actual or intended union membership or activity. The dismissed employee must set it in motion within seven days of the termination of his employment and he must arm himself with a certificate by his union that he is or wants to become a member and that there are reasonable grounds for supposing that he was dismissed for the alleged reason.[33] The tribunal must treat this as a matter of urgency.[34] If it finds that the employee is likely to succeed it must suggest to the employer that he reinstate or re-engage him immediately, and, if he does not do so, order the continuation of the contract, *i.e.* restore the status quo for the duration of the proceedings.[35] Or rather, it must try to do so. If the employer is sufficiently recalcitrant or determined not to comply with the order, all the tribunal can do is to order him to pay to the employee an extra amount for arrears of remuneration and extra compensation.[36] In the last resort all safeguards are pecuniary; and in practice, those concerned tend to view the remedies in that light from the very outset.

---

[30] The old higher additional award is now payable only if the dismissal was an act of race or sex discrimination.

[31] *Ibid.* s. 77. See Benedictus, "Employment Protection: New Institutions and Trade Union Rights" (1976) 5 I.L.J. 12, 21. On the status quo problem in general see Anderman, "The Status Quo Issue and Industrial Disputes Procedures" (1975) 4 I.L.J. 131; on dismissal in particular, pp. 149–150. By s. 8 of the Employment Act 1982 (amending s. 77 of the 1978 Act) the interlocutory provisions are also made applicable to dismissal on grounds of non-membership of a union. See below.

[32] 1978 Act, Sched. 9, para. 8.

[33] *Ibid.* s. 77(2). See *Farneary* v. *Veterinary Drug Co. Ltd.* [1976] I.R.L.R. 322.

[34] *Ibid.* s. 77(3) and (4).

[35] *Ibid.* s. 77(5)–(9), s. 78; see also s. 79(2).

[36] *Ibid.* s. 79(3).

(ii) Against trade unions

Freedom of organisation needs to be protected against high-handed action by employers. It also needs to be protected against high-handed action by trade unions. In this respect the statutes of 1974, 1975, and 1976 were ultimately silent.[37] They gave a measure of protection against discriminatory action by employers, but none against discriminatory action by unions, except where it was racial or sex discrimination. The gap was to some extent filled by rules of the common law and by action taken by the unions themselves outside the law. The Employment Act 1980[38] provides a new statutory right of complaint to industrial tribunals in respect of unreasonable exclusion or expulsion from a trade union in relation to cases where a union membership agreement applies.

The problem which we are now approaching arises from the position which trade unions occupy in our society. It is a problem of conflict between autonomy and responsibility. On the one hand, trade unions are voluntary and autonomous bodies, and if they were not they could not fulfil the important role of being the counterpart of management in industrial relations. The law forces no one to be or not to be a member: compulsory unionism—in the legal sense—has never been tried and will not, it is supposed, ever be tried in this country. Not only is membership voluntary, as far as the law is concerned, but the union is and must be free in laying down the conditions of admission to membership. It is also free and autonomous in determining its own constitution, that is the election or appointment to offices, the distribution of functions among the various organs of the union, the qualification for office and so on. In these respects a trade union is, and must on principle be, as autonomous as a sports club or, to take a more appropriate analogy, any professional organisation, trade association or other similar body. This is one side of the coin.

The other side of the coin is that trade unions are voluntary associations which fulfil vital functions in the public interest. They are or can, if they choose, be represented on an untold number of governmental committees, some created by purely administrative practice, others by statute: wages councils, Agricultural Wages Boards and committees and the Central Arbitration Committee are some examples, to say nothing of all the administrative and judicial organs which handle our social security and other social legislation. The industrial tribunals whose functions have now been greatly enlarged are another example. In short, the unions,

---

[37] See below, p. 233.
[38] Employment Act 1980, ss. 4 and 5.

though voluntary bodies, are an indispensable element in the process of government in many of its aspects, most of which there is not even the space to mention here. Nor is this all. Whatever may be the legal aspect of collective bargaining, its social effect is indistinguishable from that of legislation. The unions as well as the employers' associations participate in the making of rules or norms which are intended to be applied or obeyed by more than half of the population of this country. This is a feature of trade unions (and they share it with employers' associations) which singles them out from other voluntary bodies. There is here a difference not only in quantity but in quality from a football club or a commercial trade association or a college. There is also here a difference between organisations of workers and organisations of employers which is based in the nature of industrial relations. From the point of view of an employer, especially a small employer, his association may be so vitally important that he would (probably quite rightly) feel lost without it. But in the case of the worker the existence and availability of the union is much more than this: without it he cannot be an active participant in labour relations. His right to membership is as essential to him as his right to vote at a parliamentary election. His membership is the only way open to a worker in our kind of society of being an active participant in the shaping of his own occupational existence. It may—in a closed shop—also be his only access to the labour market.[39]

This is where the problem lies. Is it possible to leave the control over their own membership to the unfettered discretion of the unions themselves without encroaching upon that freedom of the individual worker to be a member of a union which is, and must be, the foundation of any system of industrial relations in a democratic society? Is it, on the other hand, possible to restrict this control without depriving the unions of that autonomy without which they cannot perform their vital role in industrial relations?

One might have assumed that a union was always interested in recruiting and retaining the maximum number of members so that its self-interest was a sufficient safeguard against exclusions or expulsions which would deprive an individual of his freedom to

---

[39] [This passage sets out Kahn-Freund's thesis that the legal control of union admissions and expulsions is a necessary corollary of the legal protection of freedom of association as against employers. The passage, however, concludes by identifying the justification for legal control over trade union admissions and expulsions as a corollary not of freedom of association but of the role of the union in collective bargaining or of the union's control over access to employment where there is a closed shop. These two narrower propositions seem stronger than the general one.]

become or remain a member. But this is not entirely the case. We must not forget that, especially in this country and in other English speaking countries such as the United States, Australia and the major part of Canada, the unions have assumed (perhaps inherited from much earlier forms of social organisation) an important market regulating function. To some extent this is exercised through control of admission to the union or to a particular section of it (*e.g.* the "skilled" section) and especially through stringent conditions of age, apprenticeship, etc., imposed by them.[40] These restrictions can be very detrimental to the economy—and very often they are—but they exist, the process of getting rid of them is bound to be slow, and at times of rising unemployment one should at least understand why they are so strenuously defended. It is to be hoped that gradually they may be reduced and eventually disappear, but this cannot be achieved through legal sanctions.[41] Inasmuch as the practice of a union of admitting or rejecting members emanates from its policy of controlling the labour market, the law cannot achieve anything. These are not the cases which one has in mind when one thinks of the protection of the freedom to organise against arbitrary union practices. The labour market regulating practices may be undesirable in the economic sense, but they are not arbitrary in the legal sense.

An applicant for membership may be rejected and a member may be expelled for reasons which have nothing to do with the labour market at all. They may be prompted by irrelevant motives: race, religion, personal animosities, factional disputes. Above all, they may be prompted by nepotism and other manifestations of group preferences.[42] We are facing a very complex legislative problem. Let us see how it was approached in Australia and in the United States.[43]

The Commonwealth Conciliation and Arbitration Act[44] provides for the registration of organisations of both sides which

---

[40] See on this Chap. VI of the Donovan Report, esp. paras. 335 *et seq.*

[41] See, for a different view, Mr. Andrew Shonfield's Note of Reservation to the Donovan Report, esp. paras. 23 *et seq.,* pp. 296 *et seq.*

[42] As seems to happen in the docks. See McCarthy, *The Closed Shop in Britain,* p. 18.

[43] On the Continent of Europe these problems seem to have been completely neglected, almost ignored. It can perhaps be explained from the fact that they do not in this form play a significant role, owing to the small importance of "union security" practices. See for this and what follows, Kahn-Freund, "Trade Unions, The Law, and Society" (1970) 33 M.L.R. 241; and Kay, "The Settlement of Membership Disputes in Trade Unions" in Carby-Hall (ed.), *Studies in Labour Law* (1976), p. 160.

[44] Pt. VIII, s. 132.

desire to represent their members in arbitration proceedings and to exercise other functions within the arbitration system—a vital matter in Australia where arbitration has traditionally been at the centre of industrial relations. Once an association of employees is registered as an organisation under the Act, it must, irrespective of its rules, admit any person employed or usually employed or qualified to be employed in connnection with the relevant industry, "unless he is of general bad character" and provided he pays such amounts as are "properly payable," and allow him to remain a member as long as he complies with the rules.[45] This is what we call the principle of the "open union." Its Australian formulation goes very far inasmuch as it is not restricted to the prohibition of arbitrary, discriminatory or unreasonable exclusions or expulsions, but it must be remembered that an employer can, by an award, be compelled to give preference to members of an organisation.[46] The preference clause is technically different from a closed shop, but its effect is similar, and where something resembling the closed shop is not only permitted, but may be imposed, it is particularly important to protect the individual's freedom of association and, for this purpose, give effect to the rule of the "open union."

This link between the closed shop and the open union can also be seen in the United States, but there it operates, as it were, in reverse. American Federal law has no general principle of the "open union" such as exists in Australia, and the Landrum-Griffin Act of 1959,[47] however deep the inroads it makes into union autonomy in other respects, is silent about admissions. It does, however, forbid expulsions unless those elementary rules of decency are observed which the Americans call "procedural due process" and we call "natural justice."[48] No union is under any obligation to admit anyone (except under the Civil Rights Act about which we shall say something in a moment), but if it does not act on the "open union" principle it cannot insist on the observance of the "union shop," *i.e.* that form of the post-entry closed shop[49] which is, under certain conditions, permitted.[50] Unless the union is "open" the employer may not act on the union

---

[45] s. 144.
[46] s. 47.
[47] Labor-Management Reporting and Disclosure Act 1959.
[48] s. 101(5).
[49] See below.
[50] National Labor Relations Act, s. 8(*a*)(3), proviso (2).

shop agreement. If the union discriminates in admission or expulsion, the employer may not discriminate in employment. This, almost inexcusably simplified, is the American system.

If the worker cannot get or hold a job without being a union member, his protection against arbitrary exclusion or expulsion is particularly important. It does not follow that, in the absence of a closed shop, he is not in need of such protection.

For us, however, American law has a much more important lesson: it is that the need for eliminating race discrimination overrides everything: union "autonomy," managerial "prerogatives" and whatever else you can think of. Here we are up against the fundamentals of civilisation. The Federal Civil Rights Act of 1964[51] forbids (as "unfair employment practices") discrimination against any individual "by reason of such individual's race, color, religion, sex, or national origin," and this includes discrimination by employers and potential employers, labour organisations, and employment agencies. The Act protects (or seeks to protect) members of minorities in getting and in holding jobs, in their terms of employment, and in their training opportunities, as well as in their admissions to unions, the maintenance of their membership, and—most important[52]—their treatment in and by the union, and, equally important, it seeks to suppress sex discrimination. Our Race Relations Act 1968[53] was strongly influenced by this American statute and so is the present Race Relations Act 1976,[54] and the Sex Discrimination Act 1975.[55]

The Donovan Commission[56] was of course aware of the foreign legislative patterns. With the help of an elaborate fact and opinion survey[57] it scrutinised past experience in this country and concluded: "It is unlikely that abuse of power by trade unions is widespread," but: "There can be little doubt that occasionally it

---

[51] s. 703.
[52] How important, one can see from the famous decision of the United States Supreme Court in *Steele* v. *Louisville and Nashville R.R.*, 323 U.S. 192 (1944).
[53] ss. 3, 4; see Hepple, *Race, Jobs and the Law* (2nd ed., 1970); Lester and Bindman, *Race Relations* (1972).
[54] s. 11.
[55] ss. 9, 12.
[56] Report, Chap. XI.
[57] Conducted by the Government Social Survey. The findings relevant in the present context are summarised in *Workplace Industrial Relations* (1968) pp. 123–125. See also the surveys by Rideout, "The Content of Trade Union Disciplinary Rules" and "The Content of Trade Union Rules Regulating Admission" (1965) 3 Brit. J. of Ind. Rel. 153; (1966) 4 Brit. J. of Ind. Rel. 77.

does happen."[58] Cases which arise in connection with expulsions can be seen reflected in the law reports.[59] The Donovan Commission proposed that the measures to be taken should be analogous to those recommended to protect the individual against abuse of managerial power through unfair dismissal. An unsuccessful applicant for membership in a union or union section and an expelled member should have a right to complain first to a higher body in the union, and then to an independent outside review body which, if it found the action of the union to be arbitrary, would be able so to declare and thereby replace the refusal of admission or cancel the expulsion, and also to fix a limited compensation.[60] No recommendation was made to prohibit the closed shop.[61] These unanimous recommendations were accepted by the Labour Government in the White Paper "In Place of Strife," published early in 1969,[62] but they did not appear in the Industrial Relations Bill presented by the Labour Government in the spring of 1970.

The reason why the law was in need of reform (just as it was in Australia and in America and maybe elsewhere) is that the courts cannot in their arsenal of legal concepts and institutions find any weapon to attack an arbitrary refusal by a voluntary body to admit a new member. There is no contract between him and the organisation he wants to join—so where is the breach of contract?—nor is there (on orthodox reasoning) a tort. All this was thrashed out and laid down in a much discussed and much attacked decision of the House of Lords dealing with the refusal of the Stock Exchange during and after the First World War to re-admit members with German-sounding names.[63] All the same, much more recently the Court of Appeal[64] held that the Jockey Club could be compelled to give up its discriminatory practice of refusing to grant licences to women horse trainers, thus preventing them from entering horses for races in their own name. It was said that there was a "right to work" and that its infringement was against public policy and could be checked by injunction—a bold

---

[58] Cmnd. 3623, paras. 602, 603. The L.S.E. research survey of the practice of 79 trade unions, whose results are set out in the D.E. Gazette of June 1980 at pp. 591 *et seq.,* concludes that there are probably few instances "of injustice to individual members by trade unions."

[59] See Rideout, *The Right to Membership of a Trade Union,* 1963; Citrine-Hickling, *loc. cit.,* pp. 265 *et seq.;* Grunfeld, *Modern Trade Union Law,* Chap. 9.

[60] Paras. 609 *et seq.;* paras. 625 *et seq.*

[61] See below p. 244.

[62] Cmnd. 3888, paras 114–116.

[63] *Weinberger* v. *Inglis* [1919] A.C. 606.

[64] *Nagle* v. *Fielden* [1966] 2 Q.B. 633, long before the Sex Discrimination Act 1975.

and somewhat isolated decision.[65] If the law did know a "right to work," this could of course be infringed by a rule of a union giving it the power to refuse admission in its unfettered discretion or making eligibility for membership dependent on irrelevant considerations. In a decision of 1963, however, the House of Lords declined to nullify a rule of the Film Artistes' Association by which no person who had ever been convicted in a court of law of a criminal offence (one insignificant exception apart) was eligible for or able to retain membership in the union. Lord Evershed emphasised that no "principle of natural justice" could prevent this arbitrary rule on admissions from being applied, because the case was "in no sense analogous" to one of expulsion where, as we shall presently explain, rules of "natural justice" do apply.[66] Since then, Lord Denning has, in a case decided in 1970,[67] reiterated his view, expressed previously in the *Jockey Club* case, that, whilst a refusal to admit (and *a fortiori* to re-admit) may sometimes be justified "as when the trade is oversupplied with labour," "it will not be justified if it is exercised in an arbitrary or capricious manner or with unfair discrimination." Much as one may be inclined to sympathise with Lord Denning's attitude, it could represent the actual law only if a person applying for a job and rejected "in an arbitrary or capricious manner or with unfair discrimination" also had an actionable "right to work." There is no law against unfair refusal to employ[68] as there is a law against unfair dismissal, and if the common law gave a person a right against irrelevant rejection of an application for a job, would not large portions of the Race Relations and Sex Discrimination Acts have been superfluous? Yet, on the question of admission to unions there is obviously a rift in judicial opinion. Nothing short of a clear statute[69] could establish a power of the courts to check a

---

[65] There have since been other straws in the wind. Compare Slade J. in *Greig* v. *Insole* [1978] 3 All E.R. 449, 509 and Megarry V.C.'s judgment in *McInnes* v. *Onslow-Fane* [1978] 3 All E.R. 211 (noted by Elias (1979) 8 I.L.J. 111).

[66] *Faramus* v. *Film Artistes' Association* [1964] A.C. 925. See on this and related problems Kahn-Freund, "Trade Unions, The Law, and Society" (1970) 33 M.L.R. 241.

[67] *Edwards* v. *Society of Graphical and Allied Trades* [1971] Ch. 354.

[68] There are exceptional cases in which an employer is under an obligation not only to pay, but actually go give specific work to, an employee. This is an entirely different matter because where such an obligation exists, it is based on an existing contract of employment. We are concerned with an alleged obligation to enter into a contract of employment. On the "right to work" in general, see Hepple, (1981) 10 I.L.J. 65.

[69] Such as now exists in the special situation where a union membership agreement applies: Employment Act 1980, ss. 4–5; see below, pp. 235–236.

union's decision to exclude an applicant from membership, *i.e.* not to admit him in the first place or not to re-admit him if his membership has lapsed, *e.g.* for non-payment of dues. It is possible—not certain—that at common law a rule permitting arbitrary refusal to admit, especially in a closed shop situation, might have constituted an illegal "restraint of trade," but the Trade Union and Labour Relations Act 1974[70] clarifies the law[71] by saying that a union rule cannot be "unlawful or unenforceable" on this ground.

With expulsions the courts have always been on safer ground. Here the claim can be based on the existing contract of membership.[72] This "contract of membership" is of course precisely the same sort of legal tool of thought as the "contract of employment." Both are a necessary legal cloak for the social essence of acts of submission. The rules of the union are the terms of that contract, but, in addition, the law implies in the contract of membership two terms which are imperative, *i.e.* incapable of being contracted out. The first is formulated in the Trade Union and Labour Relations Act 1974,[73] and is to the effect that each member is entitled, on giving reasonable notice and complying with any reasonable conditions, to terminate his membership. The other—which is relevant here—is that the union is not entitled to terminate membership except in so far as this is expressly provided for in the contract, *i.e.* in the rule book. This is a rule of the common law. It has two aspects, a procedural and a substantive aspect. No expulsion is valid unless the procedure provided for in the rules has been strictly observed, *e.g.* as regards the timing and

---

[70] s. 2(5). The same applies to employers' associations: s. 3(5). The Trade Union Act 1971, s. 3, and subsequently the Industrial Relations Act 1971, s. 135 (*b*)—the 1971 Act repealed that of 1871—provided that the purposes of a trade union shall not, by reason merely that they are in restraint of trade, be unlawful so as to make any agreement or trust void or voidable; and having in its turn repealed the 1971 Act, the Trade Union and Labour Relations Act 1974 re-enacted these words in s. 2(5), with the addition, however, that a trade union rule shall not "be unlawful or unenforceable by reason only that it is in restraint of trade," and similarly with rules of employers' associations (s. 3(5)).

[71] The addition was occasioned by the judgment of Sachs L.J. in the *Edwards* case (*supra*, n. 67) who interpreted s. 3 of the 1871 Act as not applicable to a union rule on expulsion. This interpretation was, however, incorrect, and incompatible with the decision of the House of Lords in the *Faramus* case (*supra*, n. 66). The additions in s. 2(5) and s. 3(5) of the 1974 Act were unnecessary, but useful in removing a doubt.

[72] *Bonsor* v. *Musicians' Union* [1956] A.C. 104.

[73] s. 7, as amended by Trade Union and Labour Relations (Amendment) Act 1976, s. 3(1).

the place of the committee meeting, the form and content of notice, and the composition of the committee. This is the procedural aspect.[74] The substantive aspect is that no member can be validly expelled except on the grounds formulated in the rule book.[75] In itself, and apart from what we must say presently, this does not mean much because many, probably most, union rule books contain an "omnibus" clause mentioning as grounds for expulsion things such as "conduct detrimental to the union," or "conduct contrary to the union's interest," or "conduct which renders the member unfit for membership."[76] Frequently it is said that a member can—or must—be expelled if he is guilty of one of these things "in the opinion of the committee." This would appear—apart from the procedure—to give the union an almost unlimited discretion. But, as we shall see, appearance is not reality.

Let us go back to the minimum procedural requirements for a valid expulsion. These are not exhausted by what the rule book says. They are decisively supplemented by what is in this country called "natural justice" and, as we have seen, in America "procedural due process." The rules of natural justice[77] can be summarised in the two old tags: *audi alteram partem* and *nemo judex in sua causa*. In other words: whatever the rules say, the member to be expelled must be given a reasonable chance of stating his case and producing his evidence, and the hearing should be reasonably impartial. These rules of natural justice are mandatory, *i.e.* they cannot be abrogated by the rules of the union. The best way of explaining them is to consider them as terms of the contract of membership compulsorily implied by the common law. Others would regard them as a "higher law"; this is merely a battle of words. What is more important is this: unless a union handles its business carelessly or foregetfully, it is no more difficult to comply with these procedural rules of natural justice

---

[74] The cases are legion, see, *e.g.* the *Bonsor* case, *supra*. Recent cases: *Hiles* v. *Amalg. Soc. of Woodworkers* [1968] Ch. 440; *Braithwaite* v. *E.E.T.P.U.* [1969] 2 All E.R. 859 (C.A.); *Santer* v. *National Graphical Association* [1973] I.C.R. 60; *Radford* v. *National Society of Printers etc.* [1972] I.C.R. 484; *McLelland* v. *National Union of Journalists* [1975] I.C.R. 116.

[75] *Amalgamated Society of Carpenters* v. *Braithwaite* [1922] 2 A.C. 440; *Lee* v. *Showmen's Guild* [1952] 2 Q.B. 329 (C.A.); *Esterman* v. *N.A.L.G.O.* [1974] I.C.R. 625.

[76] See Rideout, "The Content of Trade Union Rules as to Discipline" (1965) 3 Brit. J. of Ind. Rel. 153.

[77] *Annamunthodo* v. *Oilfield Workers' Union* [1961] A.C. 945 (P.C.); *Lawlor* v. *U.P.W.* [1965] Ch. 718; *Taylor* v. *Nat. Union of Seamen* [1967] 1 W.L.R. 532; *Leary* v. *Nat. Union of Vehicle Builders* [1970] 2 All. E.R. 713.

than it is to comply with the procedural rules of the rule book itself. The power of intervening to check arbitrary expulsion which the courts seem to have assumed with the formulation of these rules sounds much more grandiose than it is.

This, however, is not quite the end of the story. The substantive aspect is becoming more important than the procedural aspect. The reason is that in a series of decisions in the course of the last quarter of a century[78] the courts have established that it is for them, and not for the unions, ultimately to interpret those "omnibus clauses" to which we have referred, and that this is the case even if words such as "in the opinion of he committee" appear in the rule. In that case the court will decide whether on the facts a committee, acting reasonably, could have come to the conclusion that, *e.g.* by his conduct the member had rendered himself unfit for membership. This is to quote from a recent judgment which contains a clear and cautious formulation of this significant extension of the power of the courts to counteract an abuse of union power[79]:

> "It is well established that this court (*i.e.* the Chancery Division of the High Court) will not interfere with the decision of a domestic tribunal which is bona fide arrived at. . . . *a fortiori* this court will not . . . interfere to prevent a domestic tribunal from hearing and adjudicating a complaint unless the court is satisfied that no reasonable tribunal acting bona fide could uphold the complaint. Only in the most exceptional circumstances will it be right for the court to interfere. It is agreed that the question I have to determine is, has the plaintiff established a prima facie case that no committee applying itself correctly as to the law and obeying the principles of natural justice could arrive at the finding that the plaintiff had been guilty of conduct rendering her unfit to be a member of [the union]".

---

[78] See the cases in n. 75, *supra,* and also *Lawlor* v. *U.P.W., supra,* n. 77; *Leigh* v. *N.U.R.* [1970] Ch. 326.

[79] *Esterman* v. *N.A.L.G.O.* [1974] I.C.R. 625 at p. 632, *per* Templeman J. However, in applying this principle Templeman J. tended to ask himself, not whether the committee could reasonably conclude that the individual had acted contrary to the union's interests, but whether the individual could reasonably conclude that the union's instruction was unlawful or, even, merely unwise—a rather different test. The words "in the opinion of the committee" in the rule book cannot oust the jurisdiction of the courts: in so far as they purport to do so, they are against public policy.

It will be observed that "natural justice" has here acquired a new practical importance, but not perhaps a new meaning. The decision of the committee of the union may be such as to be explicable only on the assumption that it did not pay proper attention to the facts adduced and the arguments developed by the person charged. A substantive injustice is—effectively if artificially–explained as a procedural error. In this way, the weapons that the courts have in recent years fashioned for the control of administrative action are turned to the service of controlling trade union action. Hence the restraints of the public law of judicial review are combined with those of the private law of contract. The cumulative effect is potentially—and at times actually—considerable.

However, even thus expanded, the power of the courts in these matters is circumscribed. Frequently the problem arises from what is in substance an expulsion but in form a refusal to re-admit after a lapse of membership through non-payment of subscriptions.[80] In this situtation the courts are (as we have seen)—probably—powerless.[81] They can do no more—outside the fields of operation of the Race Relations and Sex Discrimination Acts—to check arbitrary, discriminatory or unfair refusals to admit to a union than they can do to check similar refusals to admit to a job. And even the elaborate and voluminous body of case law on unlawful union expulsions gives only limited protection to an individual unjustly deprived of membership, nothing comparable to the protection against unfair dismissal, especially after its reform by the Employment Protection Act 1975. It is of course obvious that, as a social phenomenon, unfair dismissal is infinitely more frequent than unfair expulsion. But it is elementary that statistical evidence is irrelevant to an argument about abuse of power in marginal cases.

This is one of the most controversial issues in our labour law. The Industrial Relations Act 1971,[82] passed by a Conservative majority, contained an elaborate code to be observed by the unions, part of which was not more than a codification of good practice whilst other parts saddled the unions with an impossible burden. The Act went much too far in encroaching upon the

---

[80] See, *e.g. Edwards* v. *S.O.G.A.T.*, *supra*, n. 67, p. 228, and, generally, Rideout, *The Right to Membership of a Trade Union* (1965), pp. 8–9.
[81] Unless— as in *Radford* v. *N.A.T.S.O.P.A.* [1972] I.C.R. 484—the automatic forfeiture clause is itself considered as void which it is most unlikely to be under the present law, whatever may have been the position under the 1971 Act.
[82] s. 65.

self-determination of the unions. In this as in other respects it was predictably doomed to failure. The Trade Union and Labour Relations Act 1974, passed under a Labour government, repealed the 1971 Act,[83] but it also contained a clause,[84] inserted by the opposition against the intentions of the Government, directed against "arbitrary or unreasonable" exclusion or expulsion from membership and providing for a procedure before industrial tribunals and, if necessary, the ordinary courts, to redress the situation. This clause was, one may think, acceptable in principle, but not as it stood : it still overshot the mark very considerably by enabling the tribunals to apply the law of restraint of trade.[85] This could (and probably would) have meant that the tribunals had arrogated to themselves the power of revising decisions of the unions based on labour market or other economic considerations. The question became academic, because this section was repealed by the Amendment Act of 1976.[86]

However, as part of the political settlement which permitted the enactment of the 1976 Act, the TUC was committed to the provision of a voluntary process to afford some remedy to those aggrieved by the operation of closed shops by TUC unions. In accordance with an undertaking it had given it established an Independent Review Committee. In doing so, the General Council of the TUC acted in consultation with the Secretary of State for Employment and with the Chairman of the ACAS.[87] This is of course an arrangement outside the law, but the unions affiliated to the TUC have promised to abide by the decisions of the Committee. Its terms of reference however are limited. True, they cover appeals by individuals who have been expelled, and also of individuals who have been excluded (*i.e.* been refused admission), but since they are confined to cases where exclusion denies access to specific job opportunities, they do not extend to the normal pre-entry closed shop situation where the exclusion from membership has the result that the applicant for a job is never given a specific job opportunity in the first place. These terms of reference also ignore the fact that exclusion or expulsion from a union can be a most serious matter for the individual even

---

[83] s. 1(1).

[84] s. 5. For a trenchant criticism of its wording see Wedderburn (1974) 37 M.L.R. 533–534, but this criticism does not touch the principle.

[85] s. 5(4). The crucial words were "or section 2(5) above." These were decisive.

[86] Trade Union and Labour Relations (Amendment) Act 1976, s. 1(1). For a balanced presentation of the problem see Kidner, "The Individual and the Collective Interest in Trade Union Law" (1976) 5 I.L.J. 90.

[87] TUC Press Release of July 27, 1976.

in the absence of a closed shop. Still, what is essential is that the composition of the Committee guarantees its independence and that it is probably much more competent to handle such cases than many industrial tribunals. Moreover, a statement made by the chairman at the first hearing[88] showed that the Committee was determined to be impartial. It has always had to walk a tight-rope, on the one hand vindicating its independence of the TUC unions and on the other hand sufficiently securing their confidence in its decisions to make them effective. It is a natural consequence of these constrictions that the Committee should increasingly have perceived its role in terms of conciliation rather than simple adjudication.

The first case which came before the Committee illustrates an important point. It was a case—by no means the first of its kind to occur—in which a union had bona fide terminated a man's membership on the ground that he had been admitted in error and as a result of an oversight: according to an inter-union agreement he should have belonged to another union. This is a situation which can and must almost inevitably result from the complexities of our union structure. A union affiliated to the TUC must apply the decisions of the Disputes Committee of the TUC concerning the proper affiliation of any workers to one union or the other.[89] But if it does, the termination of the membership of these workers who are to join another union is not justified by the fact that, in terminating the membership, the union did its own duty under the principles of the TUC[90]—the "Bridlington principles." These principles may be part of the Constitution of the TUC, but they are not "law," not at any rate as between any union an its members, unless the union has incorporated them in its own rules so as to make them terms of the "contract" with its members and thus make them respectable in the eyes of a court.[91] It is one of the best illustrations available to show the co-existence and, in some cases, the incompatibility of norms of social conduct without legal force and legal norms with little support in social mores. Very few trade unionists would probably even understand how the law could support a union member insisting on his "contract" of membership

---

[88] On July 19, 1976.

[89] See Ball (1980) 9 I.L.J. 13.

[90] *Spring* v. *National Amalgamated Society of Stevedores* [1956] 1 W.L.R. 385.

[91] As many unions have done in the course of the last 20 years as a result of the decision in the *Spring* case, *supra*. See the evidence of the TUC to the Donovan Commission, para. 74. Even then the expulsion has been held liable to successful challenge: *Rothwell* v. *A.P.E.X.* [1976] I.C.R. 211; *cf. Cheall* v. *A.P.E.X.* [1983] I.C.R. 398.

as against the observance of the Bridlington rules, which are an indispensable element of our system of industrial relations,[92] and very few lawyers would probably even understand how anyone could support the reliance by a party to a contract (here the union) on a *res inter alios acta*.

Whatever the extent of success the Independent Review Committee has had in achieving its declared goals—and that has been a subject of argument[93]—it was predictable that, as a political solution to the problems posed by the closed shop, such a system would remain vulnerable to a demand for hard legal rights for individuals against unions where exclusions or expulsions resulted in loss of job opportunities or of actual jobs. It is indeed a measure of the extent to which the closed shop has come to dominate the whole discussion of the relationship between the individual and the trade union that when the legislature returned in 1980 to the theme of statutory protection for the individual against arbitrary exclusion or expulsion by trade unions, they did so—in sections 4 and 5 of the Employment Act 1980—only for the situation in which a union membership agreement is in operation.[94]

This statutory protection takes the form of an individual right where there is a union membership agreement in operation not to be unreasonably refused membership of or expelled from a trade union.[95] It is a right enjoyed cumulatively with common law rights[96] and is justiciable by complaint to an industrial tribunal[97] which must give a declaration where a complaint is well-founded[98] and must on application award compensation for loss up to the amount of the basic and compensatory unfair dismissal awards where the complainant has been admitted or readmitted to the union[99] Where he has not been, the Employment Appeal Tribunal

---

[92] *Rothwell* v. *A.P.E.X., supra,* shows the deplorable results of fighting inter-union disputes in the courts. A union was held to be unable to expel a member in reliance on a "Bridlington" clause in its rules unless the Disputes Committee had, in the judge's view, acted within the powers conferred by the TUC Rules and properly applied the Bridlington principles. *Phillips* v. *N.A.L.G.O. and N.U.P.E.* [1973] I.R.L.R. 19 decided that the union cannot rely on the Bridlington clause in the absence of a prior decision of the TUC Disputes Committee. See generally Ball, "The Resolution of Inter-union Conflict" (1980) 9 I.L.J. 13.

[93] See Ewing and Rees, "The TUC Independent Review Committee and the Closed Shop," (1981) 10 I.L.J. 84.

[94] s. 4(1).

[95] s. 4(2).

[96] s. 4(3).

[97] s. 4(4)

[98] s. 4(7).

[99] s. 5(1), (2), (4)(*a*), (7).

must on application award compensation such as it considers just
and equitable up to the same amount plus a further year's pay.[1] It
is thought likely that the criteria of unreasonable action on the part
of trade unions will correspond with those developed by the courts
in common law actions against trade unions, and the Code of
Practice on the closed shop contains some guidance on this point
which we shall consider in the context of the closed shop below.

It must indeed be stressed that the Employment Act 1980 deals
with exclusion and expulsion from trade union membership as a
function of the closed shop issue rather than as a general problem
in its own right. It might be thought that provisions of this kind are
desirable, whether or not the trade union's action has consequences in terms of access to employment. It might be thought that
this was a necessary corollary of legal protection of freedom of
association as against employers. The closed shop is envisaged in
this scheme of things as a distinct (and essentially narrower) issue
to the consideration of which we now turn.

2. THE CLOSED SHOP

In many countries the freedom not to organise is put on a par with
the freedom to organise. If everyone, so it is argued, has the
fundamental right to join a union, he has the equally fundamental
right not to do so.[2] The law should not prevent anyone from being
a union member, nor should it compel him to enter a union. But
this is not enough. Just as the law must see that people can
effectively exercise their freedom of association, and take positive
steps to ensure this, so it is not enough to reject the principle of
legally compulsory unionism (which in this country no one has
ever advocated). The law must also protect people from being in
fact constrained or pressed to join. No one must be exposed to the
dilemma between joining a union he does not want to join, and not
obtaining or holding a job he wants to obtain or to hold. This is as
obnoxious as exposing him to the dilemma between getting or

---

[1] s. 5(4) (*b*), (8).
[2] See, *e.g.* European Commission on Human Rights in X v.*Belgium Applic.* No.
4972/69, Decision, February 3, 1970, 13 *Year Book of the European Convention
on Human Rights* [1971], p. 708. The Commission was recently faced with this
problem of whether freedom of association implies a corresponding freedom to
dissociate, in relation to the closed shop in British Rail. Their report in the cases
of *Young and James* v. *U.K., Webster* v. *U.K.* (1980) managed however to avoid
this general issue of principle, and found a violation of article 11 of the European
Convention on the narrower basis that the closed shop in question involved a
denial of the freedom to choose which union to join or in certain circumstances
to form a new one. See below, p. 238 and n. 13a.

holding a job and joining or remaining in the union of his choice. For many people this reasoning appears to be intellectually attractive. Its symmetry is superficially satisfying. Let us see how far it has been accepted in our own and other legal systems.

The closed shop has been banned in all or in some of its numerous manifestations in a large part of the world, but it is not possible to discern any intelligible principle which would explain the widely divergent attitudes of countries with similar social structures and legal traditions. Thus in the United States it is illegal collectively to agree on union membership as a pre-condition of engagement of a worker, but legal to agree on union membership as a term of the contract of employment itself.[3] In Canada the provincial statutes generally permit the closed shop in all its manifestations, subject to safeguards which vary from province to province.[4] In Australia[5] the "union preference clause"—which is one manifestation of the closed shop principle—is commonly included in compulsory arbitration awards. There is no visible common policy among the English-speaking nations with a common law background.

We find a similar picture on the European continent. The closed shop has been banned in France,[6] in Western Germany,[7] in Italy,[8]

---

[3] National Labor Relations Act 1935, s. 8 (*a*) (3) and (*b*) (2) under which the "pre-entry closed shop" is forbidden, but (subject to state legislation, see s. 14 (*b*)) the "post-entry closed shop" is allowed. For these terms see below.

[4] See *International Encyclopaedia for Labour Law and Industrial Relations*, Vol. 3, "Canada," pp. 189–190.

[5] Commonwealth Conciliation and Arbitration Act, 1904, s. 47; Mills and Sorrell, *loc. cit.* pp. 214 *et seq.*

[6] Law of April 27, 1956, now *Code du Travail*, 1974, Art. L 412–2 and see also Art. L 413. See for details (also comparative) the admirable analysis in Verdier, *Syndicats* (Camerlynck's *Traité*, Vol. 5), pp. 313 *et seq.* Prof. Verdier emphasises that (p. 317) closed shop agreements of any kind have always been rare in France. The pre-1956 case law is scanty.

[7] The matter is probably more important in Germany than in France, but about the illegality of the closed shop agreement there can be no doubt. See the decision of the *Reichsgericht*, R.G.Z., Vol. 104, p. 327 (1922) referred to above, note 94, p. 174. Prevailing opinion is to the effect that Art. 9, para. 3, of the Bonn Basic Law which protects the freedom to organise also protects the freedom not to organise. This is the view of the Federal Labour Court. For a full discussion and display of the controversy: Hueck-Nipperdey, *Lehrbuch des Arbeitsrechts* (7th ed., 1966), Vol. 2, pp. 154 *et seq.*

[8] Art. 15 of the *Statuto dei Lavoratori* of 1970 declares null and void any agreement or act which has the object of making the employment of a worker conditional on his membership or non-membership in a union. It seems that even before the *Statuto dei Lavoratori* the freedom not to belong to a union was considered as inherent in the constitutionally guaranteed freedom of association (Art. 39). See Riva Sanseverino, *Diritto Sindacale* (1964), pp. 163 & 165.

in Switzerland,[9] in Belgium,[10] but not in the Netherlands[11] or in Sweden.[12] One must however remember that there is no continental country in which "job control" by the unions has ever played the crucial role it has played in this country, and in other English speaking countries, including the United States. The restrictions on the closed shop in countries with this "guild" tradition of trade unionism have a very different character from those *en vogue* on the Continent: American law is a good example. The same reasons which make it unnecessary for the law on the Continent to insist on the open union make it unnecessary for the unions there to resist the banning of the closed shop. It does not mean that the unions do not everywhere, by "unilateral enforcement,"[13] seek to achieve 100 per cent. unionism nor that they refrain from pressure in this direction. It may be, and no doubt it is in fact, impossible in many places for a man to get or hold a job without holding a union card, but the employer has nothing to do with this arrangement, though he may have to tolerate it.

The diversity of legal and industrial relations traditions within Europe in relation to the closed shop was vividly displayed when the legality of the closed shop among employees of British Rail was successfully challenged before the European Court of Human Rights in the case of *Young, James and Webster* v. *U.K.* (1981).[13a] The applicants successfully claimed that their dismissal for refusal to belong to one of the three rail unions party to the union membership agreement with British Rail constituted a violation of their rights under the European Convention on Human Rights and in particular Article 11 which guarantees to everyone the right to

---

[9] Art. 322 *bis,* para. 4 of the Code of Obligations (introduced by Federal Law of September 28, 1956). See Schweingruber-Bigler, *Kommentar zum Gesamtarbeitsvertrag* (1963), p. 51.

[10] The interpretation of Arts. 1–4 of the law of May 24, 1921 is not, however, free from doubt.

[11] So, however, that (Law on Collective Agreements of 1927, Art 1(3)) the closed shop agreement is only valid in so far as it requires union membership in general, not membership of a particular union (which can easily be understood in view of the Dutch union structure). Nor can a closed shop clause be "extended" (Law on Extension of Collective Agreements of 1937, Art. 2(5) (*b*) and (*c*)).

[12] Folke Schmidt, *loc. cit.,* pp. 69 *et seq.* However, if the employer who has a closed shop agreement with union A dismisses a worker because he belongs to union B and not to A, he acts in violation of the law of 1976, not because that law is opposed to the requirement that the worker should join A but because it protects his right to join B. This does not operate in favour of the non-unionist, but the Employment Protection Law of 1974 may now protect him against unfair dismissal.

[13] McCarthy's expression, *The Closed Shop in Britain,* p. 21.

[13a] [1981] I.R.L.R. 408 (see Forde, (1982) 11 I.L.J. 1).

"freedom of association with others, including the right to form and join trade unions for the protection of his interests." The crucial question was whether this right includes a right not to belong to a trade union. The judgment of the majority of the Court, while denying that any and every compulsion to join a trade union necessarily involved a violation of Article 11, came very close to recognising the correlative freedom to dissociate, for they recognised that a compulsion to join consisting in the threat of dismissal for not joining could, and in this case did, "strike at the very substance of the freedom guaranteed by Art 11."[13b] The basis for this proposition seemed to be that the compulsion to join, while not *per se* a violation of Art 11, amounted to such a violation because it restricted the freedom to choose to join a different union or indeed to form a union oneself. This seems to be a conclusion formed in the context of the European continental tradition of industrial relations in which trade union structure reflects a political and ideological pluralism hitherto virtually absent in Great Britain. If the applicants in this case were asserting a claim to political and ideological pluralism, it was certainly not a claim which involved an interest in joining or forming a different union, for they represented the phenomenon far more typical (though not universal) in Great Britain whereby the objector to the closed shop is a non-unionist. It is significant that all the members of the dissenting minority in this case, to whom the equation favoured by the majority between compulsion to join Union A and denial of freedom to join or form Union B did not appeal, came from Scandinavian countries where trade union structure far more closely resembles that of Great Britain than that of continental Europe in this respect. But it would be idle to deny that the majority judgment in this case has not only (as we shall shortly see) been envisaged as necessitating or justifying changes in statute law designed to restrict the conditions on which a closed shop may be maintained, but has also fostered a sense that freedom to dissociate is, to all intents and purposes, a logical corollary of freedom to associate. Indeed, one almost begins to speculate that the decision contributes to a growing tendency on the part of government to identify political and ideological pluralism as a goal in relation to the British trade union movement. If so, great changes are indeed under way. But it is time to turn our attention to arguments about the law and the closed shop other than those narrowly dependent on the connection between freedom to associate and freedom to dissociate.

[13b] *Ibid.* at p. 417.

There are strong arguments in favour of banning or at least restricting the closed shop—arguments far stronger than the shallow legalism of the reasoning from analogy with the freedom to organise. Access to jobs should be free. This is in the interest of the development of the economy and of the optimal use of manpower. To exclude the non-unionist may mean to exclude the best man for the job. And if there are to be restrictions of access they should be imposed by organs of government responsible through democratic processes, and not by private organisations who are not publicly responsible. The closed shop is, if not a relic, then an image of the medieval guild organisation, or, if you like, of the Elizabethan Statute of Apprentices and it may produce job reservations for privileged minorities. This may not only restrict the supply of (especially skilled) labour, it may also, exactly like educational privileges, cause waste and frustration by robbing people of their opportunities, and it may subject the individual too much to the power of trade union officials. Where several unions compete, it may mean that minorities are suppressed by majorities, or the other way. In France the closed shop was banned in 1956, partly to protect minority unions against the powerful *Confédération Générale du Travail.*[14] Lastly—the evidence received by the Donovan Commission was to this effect[15]—there are small groups of people who have conscientious objections to joining unions, mainly on religious grounds.

Arguments such as these are used to support a policy of suppressing the closed shop or alternatively of merely restricting it. To see what this involves—and especially what possible restrictions can be contemplated—it is advisable to get a somewhat clearer idea of what a "closed shop" actually means, because it is in fact a term of many meanings. We must make a few intersecting distinctions.

In the first place we must distinguish the pre-entry and the post-entry closed shop[16] (called "union shop" in America). The pre-entry closed shop is the agreed practice whereby no one can apply for a job unless he is a member of a particular union. This may (but need not) mean that the union actually supplies the applicants.[17] Here, if this is formalised, union membership is a

---

[14] J. C. Javillier, *Droit du Travail* (2nd. ed., 1981) pp. 196–197.

[15] Cmnd. 3623, para. 604.

[16] McCarthy, *loc. cit.,* p. 16; Weekes, Mellish, Dickens and Lloyd, *loc. cit.* p. 33 point out that this distinction may be blurred, where the time for joining the union after taking up employment is very short.

[17] McCarthy, *loc cit.,* p. 38, calls this the "labour supply shop" which is more or less what in the United States at one time was called the "hiring hall."

condition for the making of the contract of employment. The post-entry closed shop arrangement imposes no restriction on application for jobs and no condition on the making of the contract of employment, but makes it incumbent on every worker to join the union (or a specified union) within a stated period after having taken up the job: union membership is a term of the contract of employment, not a condition of its making.

Secondly, we must distinguish between a requirement that the worker should be or become a member of a union in general, and a requirement that he should be or become a member of a union of a particular description (*e.g.* affiliated to the TUC), or that—the most important in practice—he should be or become a member of a particular union, or—more stringent—of a particular section of a particular union, *e.g.* Section 1, the skilled section of the Amalgamated Union of Engineering Workers.

Thirdly, as Lord McCarthy has shown (to whose book on the closed shop we are heavily indebted[18]) there is the vital difference between a formal closed shop agreement between a union and an employer or employers' association, and an informal closed shop practice observed by the workers and tolerated by the employer, but not articulated.

Fourthly, there is a distinction which cuts across all the previous categories and is in its way as important as they are. This is the distinction between the open union closed shop and the closed union closed shop. An open union is one which, in relation to a particular occupational group, does not restrict the categories of persons whom it will admit to membership, while a closed union is one which does place such restrictions. Many of the older craft unions provide examples of closed unionism by virtue of their requirements to complete an apprenticeship in the craft as a pre-condition of full membership. The closed union closed shop will tend to take the form of a pre-entry closed shop because, where it exists, the employer will in practice wish to ascertain the acceptability to the union of a potential employee before employing him; and the best way of ensuring his acceptability is to insist that he should already belong to the union. But it should not be thought that the distinction between the open and the closed union closed shop coincides completely with that between the pre- and post- entry closed shop. There can, for instance, be an open union pre-entry closed shop. Indeed, one can say that the pre- and post- entry distinction is ultimately one which relates merely to the

---

[18] *Loc. cit.,* pp. 20 *et seq.* For an older presentation, see V. L. Allen, *Power in Trade Unions,* Chap. 4.

method of administration; it is the open union versus closed union distinction that expresses a fundamental difference of type. Sometimes a legal system will deliberately accord a harsher regime to the pre-entry than to the post-entry closed shop.[19] This was the case under the Industrial Relations Act 1971 which by section 7 made pre-entry closed shop agreements altogether void while providing in other sections for an admittedly limited degree of validity for post-entry closed shop agreements. Where this kind of differentiation is made, one may well conclude that it is really the closed union closed shop that is being primarily aimed at. If so, it is understandable, but perhaps in the end misleading, that the legislation should appear to distinguish between types of closed shop while underlyingly differentiating between types of unionism.

There are many varieties of what the Americans call "union security" arrangements; we have referred to the "preference for unionists" undertaking by employers which may be imposed by award under Australian law[20]—there are many others. Those who want to know about them should read Lord McCarthy's book.[21]

In this country the informal closed shop understanding may at one time have been more common than formal agreements, but latterly formal agreements have come to pre-dominate,[22] perhaps by way of response to the pressure to conform to legislative models which has been exerted by successive statutes since 1971, as we shall shortly see. The pre-entry closed shop is relatively rare— rarer than it was at one time in the United States—and the post-entry closed shop is the rule. It relates normally to membership of a particular union.[23] The usual manifestation of the closed shop in British practice is, thus, that the worker is expected under a formal agreement, to join the union soon after taking on the job. Formal arrangements are sometimes explicable from the particular conditions of an industry, *e.g.* high labour turnover[24] or, as in merchant shipping,[25] difficulty for the union in contacting the workers, and in campaigning for membership. Sometimes, as in

---

[19] As in the U.S. See above, p. 237.

[20] See n. 5, p. 237.

[21] Esp. Chap. 2.

[22] See Gennard, Dunn & Wright, 1979 *Employment Gazette* 1088 at p. 1089 and below, p. 249, n. 55.

[23] See the definition of a union membership agreement in Trade Union and Labour Relations Act 1974, s. 30(1) (as amended by the 1976 Act).

[24] Building workers, entertainment workers. See McCarthy, *loc. cit.*, pp. 108, 157, 159.

[25] *Ibid.* p. 109. See *Reynolds* v. *Shipping Federation* [1924] 1 Ch. 28. Private road haulage is another example: see McCarthy, *loc. cit.*, p. 154.

the case of the formal post-entry closed shop arrangement between the Transport and General Workers' Union and the authority running the London buses, it can be explained from past events—in this case a dramatic breakaway 40 years ago: it led to an equally dramatic law case which went up to the House of Lords.[26] The other, no longer predominant but still significant, form of the closed shop is the informal understanding[27] which may or may not involve an informal recognition of the closed shop by management. If not, the closed shop is a unilateral union rule, based on union power, which means the possibility of a strike to eliminate a non-unionist. In practice, the borderlines between these types of arrangement are less neat than they are on paper.[28] Even if the closed shop is recognised by management, its enforcement may still depend on the union's power to strike. As McCarthy says: "The threat of unilateral enforcement lies behind bilateral enforcement and co-operation."[29]

In view of the complexity of the closed shop as a social phenomenon, and of the multiplicity of its manifestations, there may well be a case for differentiation: that is, a case for allowing it in some conditions but not in others, or, as in the federal law of the United States, in some of its manifestations, but not in others. This approach may be reinforced by the consideration that in some respects, but not in others, action against some, but not all, of the manifestations of the closed shop may be within the factual possibilities of the law. This is, however, an argument accpetable only to those who share the view that what legislation should avoid at almost any cost is to pretend to regulate what is outside its reach. Those less preoccupied with the problems of the competence and the effectiveness of labour legislation will more readily tend, as we shall see, to adopt an "all or nothing" approach to legal regulation of the closed shop.

The argument which is most frequently advanced in favour of the closed shop is: "he who does not sow, neither shall he reap." The non-unionist enjoys the fruit of the union's negotiations with the employer—it is neither desirable nor practicable for the employer to differentiate between union members and others—but he does not pay his share of the cost. The main significance of

---

[26] *Ibid.* p. 57. See *London Passenger Transport Board* v. *Moscrop* [1942] 1 All E.R. 97.
[27] The amendment of the definition of a union membership agreement in s. 30 (1) of the 1974 Act by s. 3(3) (*a*) of the 1976 Act (see below) takes account of this.
[28] See McCarthy, *loc. cit.,* pp. 20 *et seq.*
[29] *Ibid.* p. 22.

this argument is that it is so widely maintained, and that it has an emotional appeal. It is not a very strong argument in itself because foreign experience (the "solidarity contribution" system in Switzerland,[30] and the "agency shop" in America), shows that one can substitute for the obligation to join the union a contribution to its funds, not involving membership. Moreover, though the analogy may not be strong, it is, as McCarthy points out,[31] a fact that people constantly reap the benefit of voluntary efforts to which they make no contribution: not only those who pay their annual subscription to the National Trust enjoy the scenery and the architecture it preserves.

The case for the closed shop can only be made in terms of the need for an equilibrium of power. It cannot in the end be sustained or refuted in terms of general ethical sentiments, but only in terms of social expediency.[31a] Moreover—and this is not the same point—the case for legislation against it can also only be made in these terms: strictly in terms of utility and nothing else. It was for reasons of expediency that, after weighing the arguments *pro* and *contra,* the Donovan Commission[32] decided not to recommend legislation against it. In the view of at least some employers it was in the mutual interest: it reduces friction on the shop floor and thus a whole range of causes of disputes and it ensures that the union represents the whole of the work force. The scene of the struggle between groups among the workers, between militant and less militant wings, is shifted away from the workplace. Further, there are branches of the economy where there can be no equilibrium without a closed shop, either because (as with seamen, road haulage workers and others) recruitment for membership is technically impossible, or because (as in large parts of the building industry) no collective regulation can be made effective without the entire work force being subject to union discipline. Even the Industrial Relations Act 1971, which on principle prohibited the closed shop, permitted it under very restricted conditions in order to take account of the needs of some of the unions facing the first of these situations.[33] Moreover the experience of the Industrial Relations Act has shown that the law cannot suppress practices

---

[30] See Schweingruber-Bigler, *loc. cit.,* p. 48. This "agency shop" practice is apparently very common in Switzerland.

[31] *Loc. cit.,* p. 180.

[31a] [This proposition is central to Kahn-Freund's thesis about legal toleration of the closed shop; but it is fair to add that many would see the case for toleration as having a greater claim to ethicality than he is prepared to concede here.]

[32] Cmnd. 3623, paras. 592, 593.

[33] Industrial Relations Act 1971, ss. 17, 18; Sched. 1—the approved closed shop.

based on informal and generally shared understandings of the workers, and for good reasons tolerated, and sometimes even welcomed, by employers.[34]

There is a case for the closed shop, not necessarily the pre-entry closed shop, in the interest of creating or maintaining that equilibrium of power on which the system of labour relations rests. But there may be a case for it in the interest of management as well as of labour, and indeed of the public in general. This is especially the case where the closed shop prevents secession, the formation of breakaway unions. That this may be a vital matter was shown by the facts of a case decided by the Court of Appeal in 1968, called *Morgan* v. *Fry*.[35] The case was about the 650 lockmen in the Ports of London and Tilbury who held what Lord Denning M.R. called a "key position." "Without them the ports could be brought to a standstill." All were members of the Transport and General Workers' Union. There was no formal closed shop, *i.e.* the employer (the Port of London Authority) did not make union membership a condition of employment, but, to quote the judge at first instance[36]:

> "At all material times the bulk of the men so employed were members of the T. & G.W.U. . . . . The P.L.A. welcomed this because, although they do not wish to insist on what is popularly called a closed shop, it is a convenience to them to be able to negotiate with a single union on behalf of the lockmen as a whole."

For quite a long time there had been an informal understanding between the PLA and the TGWU that the PLA would not negotiate with any other union as regards the lockmen in their employment. There arose dissension inside the union because a minority did not think the union was sufficiently militant in its

---

[34] As mentioned in *Sarvent* v. *Central Electricity Generating Board* [1976] I.R.L.R. 66 at p. 68, the Board are convinced that a formalised shop agreement concluded in 1969 has "brought peaceful industrial relations within the industry, coupled with dramatic improvements in efficiency and mobility." More recently, a survey carried out by the Warwick University Industrial Relations Research Unit has indicated a considerable measure of positive support for closed shops among managers at establishments where a closed shop is in force, on the grounds that its presence reduces some aspects at least of their problems of industrial relations. See Moira Hart, "Why bosses love the closed shop" *New Society*, February 15, 1979. See also below p. 250, n. 56.

[35] [1968] 2 Q.B. 710. The facts retain their illustrative value despite any doubts as to the legal conclusions at which the Court arrived: see *Simmons* v. *Hoover Ltd.* [1976] I.R.L.R. 266 (E.A.T.).

[36] Widgery J. (as he then was) [1967] 2 All E.R. 386 at p. 388.

demands. Finally there was a secession, and the formation of a breakaway union. After long negotiations the TGWU informed the PLA that if by a certain time the members of the breakaway had not rejoined the TGWU, the members of the TGWU would refuse to work alongside them. The plaintiff who was a secessionist refused to rejoin the TGWU and was dismissed. He sued the union representatives for damages by reason of "intimidation."[37] Here an informal understanding that all workers should belong to the same union was a vital instrument of union discipline and thus of industrial peace where a stoppage would have quickly become a national disaster.

Yet, it is said, the protection of human freedom comes first. If, during the Second World War, conscientious objectors were exempt from joining the Forces, then surely, whatever the general interest, no one should, as a condition for getting or holding a job, be made to join a voluntary association, if he does not wish to do so. No one has, it seems, ever suggested that a closed shop agreement should be legally enforceable so as to order a worker into a union by means of a mandatory injunction. This would be absurd, and it is not the point. Compulsory unionism is as undesirable as compulsory voting at elections which exists in some countries, but will not, one hopes, ever be introduced here. The analogy is valid. In the occupational existence of most people trade unions are, as we have said,[38] the equivalent of the franchise in their political existence. The law should encourage, but not compel, men and women to take an active part in determining the conditions in which they and their fellows live and work—to say the least it should neither discourage them nor allow others to do so. Conscientious objectors should be given the chance of staying outside without disadvantage but also without benefit to themselves, and, as we shall see, the law takes account of this consideration. Beyond this, it is suggested that it is not the office of the law to discourage union membership. We proceed to consider the successive legislative approaches to this issue from the Industrial Relations Act 1971 to the Employment Acts 1980–1982.

There is, however, an additional aspect. For many years most of

---

[37] Such a claim would now be impossible to the extent that it would be met by the Trade Union and Labour Relations Act 1974, s. 13(1)(*b*). The restrictions placed upon that provision by s. 17 of the Employment Act 1980 would not be relevant because the contract in question was a contract of employment, and the dispute had probably developed beyond the stage of a pure worker and worker dispute. See below p. 339.

[38] See Chap. 1.

the larger unions have given financial support to the Labour Party. In 1909, in the case of *Amalgamated Society of Railway Servants* v. *Osborne*[39] the House of Lords held this to be unlawful; the reasons are today of purely historical interest. This decision could not stand because it was incompatible with the financial basis of parliamentary government. Like other bodies representative of sectional interests the unions must be able to give financial support to a political party which they expect to promote their interest. But if the consequences of the *Osborne* decision were incompatible with democratic principles, so would have been the restoration of an unqualified power of the unions to spend their funds for political purposes. If in part of the economy the closed shop or something similar to it is one of the facts of life, if, to earn a living in a number of occupations, a man must be a member of a union, then he must be able to prevent what he himself contributes from being spent on a political object which he rejects. No one must be faced with a choice between his job and the pursuit of his political convictions. The Trade Union Act 1913[40] gives effect to this. It is a compromise between two democratic necessities: to enable the unions (after compliance with certain formalities) to spend funds for political purposes, and to enable the union member, without thereby suffering any disability or disadvantage,[41] to refuse to pay that part of his subscription which would go into the union's political fund out of which all political payments must be financed. The principles of the 1913 Act have been in force for more than 60 years.[42] They have hitherto been generally accepted, and the legislation has left them substantially unchanged.[43] This is the reason this is mentioned here. The "political fund" and the ceremony of "contracting out" have become part of the pattern of

---

[39] [1910] A.C. 87.

[40] Trade Union Act 1913, s. 3, as amended by the Trade Union and Labour Relations Act 1974, Sched. 3, and Employment Protection Act 1975, Sched. 16, Pt. IV. For significant recent applications of its provisions, see *Parkin* v. *ASTMS* [1980] I.C.R. 662 (Q.B.D.) where the executive of the union successfully resisted an attempt by a branch to use the political fund for donation to the Conservative Party; and *Richards* v. *NUM* [1981] I.R.L.R. 247 (C.O.) where the Certification Officer upheld complaints that general funds were being used for purposes for which only the political fund was properly available, being purposes in support of the Labour Party.

[41] See *Reeves* v. *TGWU* [1980] I.C.R. 728 (E.A.T.).

[42] Under s. 4 of the Trade Disputes and Trade Union Act 1927, enacted as a result of the General Stike of 1926, and repealed under the first post-war Labour Government by the Trade Disputes and Trade Unions Act 1946, the rule of "contracting in" was substituted for the "contracting out" rule.

[43] The amendments referred to in n. 40 do not touch the principle.

British social life.[44] They have been taken for granted. But if something like a closed shop had not been also taken for granted in 1913 and ever since, this would be incomprehensible. The history of the political fund demonstrates how deeply the principle of the closed shop is rooted in this country. In a sense the political fund is an institution complementary to the closed shop. It is no coincidence that, as we shall see later in this Chapter, the legal regime governing trade union political funds should have been brought into question by way of a continuation of the initiative which gave rise to a new restrictiveness towards the closed shop in 1980 and 1982.

The Industrial Relations Act 1971 adopted, with important modifications, the policy of stamping out the closed shop which had been formulated in the pamphlet *A Fair Deal at Work*, published by the Conservative Political Centre in April 1968.[45] The modification resulted in part from consultations between the Government and management as well as union representatives from which it emerged that a total prohibition of the closed shop was in the interest of neither side of industry.[46] The pre-entry closed shop was entirely forbidden, but the post-entry closed shop was (in theory) allowed either in the form of the "agency shop," *i.e.* an agreement permitting each worker to choose between becoming a union member, or, without doing so, paying the subscriptions, or, in very exceptional circumstances, as an "approved closed shop." Since, however, only registered unions could enter either into an agency shop or into an approved closed shop agreement, these exceptions to the prohibition were not of any decisive importance in practice. Some unions, however, remained on the Register, and were temporarily expelled from the TUC. Among them were the National Union of Seamen and the British Actors' Equity Association because to them it was vital to be able to conclude an agreement for an approved closed shop.[47] Except in those circumstances in which an agency or approved closed shop agreement was in operation, an employer dismissing an employee for non-membership could be made to pay com-

---

[44] A recent article by Keith Ewing ((1980) 9 I.L.J. 137) suggests that adjudication of issues arising under trade union political fund rules originally by the Chief Registrar of Friendly Societies and latterly by the Certification Officer has made a positive contribution to the successful operation of the political fund provisions of the 1913 Act.

[45] *Fair Deal at Work, the Conservative approach to modern industrial relations* (1968), p. 24.

[46] See Weekes, Mellish, Dickens and Lloyd, *loc cit.*, pp. 35 *et seq.*

[47] *Loc. cit.* p. 54, pp. 259 *et seq.*

pensation to him,[48] and any attempt by a union to enforce through strike or other industrial action any agreement for a closed shop could be visited by injunctions or orders for damages emanating from the National Industrial Relations Court.[49]

Despite this formidable array of legal sanctions, the Act had practically no effect on the closed shop as an industrial custom. This is now common knowledge and borne out by detailed factual investigations[50] into the actual events that occurred during the period when the relevant provisions of the Act were in operation, *i.e.* December 1, 1971 (and partly March 1, 1972), and August 1, 1974.[51] The Donovan Commission had in 1968 arrived at the conclusion that about two-fifths of all union members were covered by some sort of closed shop practice,[52] the same estimate as that made by McCarthy in his book published in 1964.[53] It is possible that this proportion grew during the period between the publication of the Donovan Report and the coming into force of the 1971 Act,[54] largely owing to the unionisation of the white collar sector and the spread of closed shop agreements or customs among white collar workers.[55] There does not appear to be the

---

[48] s. 5(2)–(5), s. 106, s. 116.   [49] s. 33(2) and (3), s. 101.

[50] For an excellent and detailed analysis see Weekes, Mellish, Dickens and Lloyd, *loc. cit.*, Chap. 2.

[51] Industrial Relations Act 1971 (Commencement No. 3 and No. 4) Orders, S. I. 1971 No. 1761, and S. I. 1972 No. 36; Trade Union and Labour Relations Act 1974 (Commencement) Order, S. I. 1974 No. 1385.

[52] Cmnd. 3623, paras. 588, 589

[53] McCarthy, *loc. cit.*, pp. 30 *et seq.* A survey carried out by the Industrial Relations Department of the L.S.E. from 1978 to 1979 showed that closed shop arrangements by then covered at least 23 per cent. of all workers compared with McCarthy's ratio of one in six in 1964, (see Gennard, Dunn and Wright, "The extent of closed shop arrangements in British industry" 1980 *Employment Gazette* 16). As a proportion of all union members at that date, the coverage of closed shop arrangements was nearly half. This growth may have been slowed down during the 1971 to 1974 period but is unlikely to have been reversed.

[54] See Weekes, Mellish, Dickens and Lloyd, *loc. cit.*, pp. 38 *et seq.*

[55] The L.S.E. survey found that by 1978 about 11 per cent. of the white collar workforce were covered by closed shop practices whereas 15 years before the proportion had been 3.5 per cent. (Gennard, Dunn and Wright, *loc. cit.*, p. 18. Kahn-Freund, in the second edition of this book posed the question how far the unionisation of white collar workers and the spread of the closed shop in the white collar sector had led to an increasing formalisation of closed shop agreements. Both the L.S.E. survey and a survey conducted at the same period by the Industrial Relations Research Unit at Warwick University suggest that a marked degree of formalisation has occurred since the time of the Donovan Report, though neither survey specially links that with the white collar sector in particular. See respectively Gennard, Dunn and Wright, "The content of British closed shop agreements," 1979 *Employment Gazette* 1089, and Moira Hart, "Why bosses love the closed shop" 1979 *New Society* 352.

slightest evidence that the Act had any appreciable impact on the existing scope and extent of closed shop practice.[56] It is a conspicuous example of the failure of a policy and of a failure of the law.

This failure was predictable and it is very easy to understand. The TUC and the unions affiliated to it were determined to maintain their opposition to the Act, and, more important in this context, to maintain the existing closed shop agreements and practices whatever the legal consequences. In a labour market in which the unions were strong—stronger than they are today—what did this mean from the employers' point of view? The best answer is given by the events at the Chrysler motor works at Coventry which were caused by a dispute between a welder called Joseph Langston and the AUEW.[57] The union operated a closed shop at Chryslers, and when Langston left the union, the other workers objected to his presence at the works—it was clear to everybody, including the Chrysler management, that, Act or no Act, that presence would result in a stoppage at a time when the order books were full. In order to avoid this—and at the same time the payment of compensation to which Langston would have been entitled, if he had been dismissed by reason of his refusal to remain a member of the union—the firm paid him his wages without requiring him to work for them. A number of cases did in fact develop out of this situation. What matters, however, is the illustrative significance of the facts. This was probably not the only case of this kind.[58]

Thus, when the entire closed shop legislation fell to the ground with the repeal of the 1971 Act by the Trade Union and Labour Relations Act 1974, the actual change which resulted was infinitesimal. From the legal point of view (and this, though obvious, deserves emphasis) what the 1974 Act did was no more than to restore the position as it had been until less than three years before. It did not introduce any law by which the closed shop

---

[56] Weekes, Mellish, Dickens and Lloyd, pp. 62 *et seq.* The authors add the significant observation: "The main reason was that the employers defended it almost as tenaciously as did workers." The stamping out of the closed shop was a policy promoted by politicians and by lawyers. This observation was very much borne out by the subsequent Warwick survey; see Moira Hart, *loc. cit.*

[57] *Langston* v. *A.U.E.W.* [1974] I.C.R. 180 (C.A.), reversing [1973] I.C.R. 211 (N.I.R.C.); *Langston* v. *A.U.E.W. (No. 2)* [1974] I.C.R. 510 (N.I.R.C.). See for an account of the Langston saga, Weekes, Mellish, Dickens and Lloyd, *loc. cit.*, pp. 58 *et seq.*, also Kahn-Freund "The Industrial Relations Act 1971—Some retrospective reflections" (1974) 3 I.L.J. 186, pp. 194 *et. seq.*, and especially the comments by Prof. Hepple (1974) 37 M.L.R. 681 *et. seq.*

[58] See Weekes, Mellish, Dickens and Lloyd, *loc. cit.*, p. 47.

was expressly legalised or permitted, but it withdrew a temporary prohibition which had been in operation for a short time, and during that short time had been quite ineffective.

Yet, this is subject to one important exception, and it is this exception which gave rise to the battles raging around the 1974 Act. The Industrial Relations Act had for the first time introduced a protection against unfair dismissal,[59] and the 1974 Act had to make it clear that an employer could not be ordered to re-instate or re-engage, or pay compensation to, an employee who, in a closed shop situation, refused to join, or insisted on leaving, or was excluded or expelled from the union concerned and was dismissed on that ground.[60] It was for this reason, and for this reason only, that the 1974 Act[61] had to define a "union membership agreement" and also to define the conditions under which the dismissal of a conscientious objector who refused to join the union would have to be regarded as unfair despite the closed shop.

The original 1974 Act,[62] as amended against the intentions of the then Labour Government, defined a conscientious objector as an employee who "genuinely objects on grounds of religious belief to being a member of any trade union whatsoever or on any reasonable grounds to being a member of a particular union." The last 13 words of this definition were crucial. They gave rise to a very bitter and protracted struggle in Parliament, and this can easily be understood. What they involved was that in each case of a violation of the closed shop agreement or practice the industrial tribunal would have had to weigh in the light of the particular circumstances whether it was objectively reasonable to request a worker to be or to become a member of a particular union.[63] And since it was not a question of an objection to unions in general (as in the case of the religious objection) but to the particular union, this opened up an unattractive vista of a fighting out of inter-union disputes and animosities in a court of law.

Eventually the 13 words which formed the apple of discord were deleted by the 1976 Act,[64] and religious objections to unions as

---

[59] ss. 22 *et seq.*
[60] Trade Union and Labour Relations Act 1974, Sched. 1, para. 6(5), (5A), as subsequently amended; see the remainder of this section.
[61] s. 30(1) as amended by, and s. 30(5A) inserted by, s. 3(3) and (4) of the Amendment Act 1976.
[62] Sched. 1, para. 6(5).
[63] This is well illustrated by *Stover* v. *Chrysler U.K. Ltd.* [1975] I.R.L.R. 66, and by *McColm* v. *Agnew and Lithgow* [1976] I.R.L.R. 13.
[64] s. 1(*e*).

such, not a non-religious objection and not an objection to a particular union, became until 1980 the exclusive basis for a claim for unfair dismissal by reason of non-union membership in a closed shop.

It was then, however, alleged in some quarters (and denied in others) that a closed shop operated by the National Union of Journalists would menace the freedom of the press, although the Act did not make this any more legal—in Fleet Street or anywhere else—than it had been three years before. After a fierce Parliamentary struggle the 1974 Act was amended by a provision[65] inviting the organisations of journalists and the employers or their organisations to agree on a "charter" safeguarding the freedom of expression of editors, employed journalists and outside contributors to the press, which, if approved by both Houses of Parliament, was to be issued by the Employment Secretary as a statutory instrument. Failing agreement within a year[66] it was to be drafted by the Employment Secretary. A charter was never in the event prepared, and in 1980 the enabling provision was quietly repealed, the whole notion of a charter having been submerged in a major new political and legislative initiative conerning the closed shop, to which we must now turn our attention. The Conservative government which came to power in 1979 proclaimed an intention from the outset to give effect to libertarian objections to the practice of the closed shop. Early in their term of office they issued a Working Paper on the Closed Shop which not only contained the proposals which were to form the basis of the closed shop provisions of the Employment Act 1980, but which also declared more directly than any government had previously done an outright hostility to the closed shop and a reluctant tolerance of it only because it was so deeply entrenched in the industrial relations system. (The traditional discourse of governmental policy towards industrial relations has accorded quite a degree of legitimacy to the closed shop, given a degree of protection for the dissenting individual. Even the Industrial Relations Act itself was committed to establishing an acceptable form of closed shop rather than to simply curtailing the practice as a whole.)

The 1980 Act therefore introduced a markedly more severe and restrictive approach to the closed shop, though, as we shall see, this stopped short of a direct and outright onslaught upon the practice of the closed shop. Of the changes made, undoubtedly

---

[65] s. 1A, inserted by s. 2 of the Amendment Act of 1976. See Royal Commission on the Press, Final Report, Cmnd. 6810 (1977), Chap. 17.
[66] See Cmnd. 6810, para. 17.14.

one of the most important, if not the most important, consisted in
widening the category of those protected from dismissal by reason
of their refusal on conscientious grounds to belong to a union
where a union membership agreement is in force. As we have
seen, this exemption had from 1976 onwards been confined to
those objecting on the grounds of religious belief to belonging to
any trade union at all. It was now extended to anyone genuinely
objecting on grounds of conscience or other deeply-held personal
conviction to being a member of any trade union whatsoever or of
a particular trade union.[67] The re-introduction of the right to
object to being a member of a particular union, though not an
objector to trade union membership in general, re-opens that
unattractive vista that presented itself between the passing of the
1974 Act with its rearguard amendments to the like effect, and the
striking out of those amendments by the 1976 Act.[68] And of the
new concept of deeply held personal conviction, one finds it hard
to read the phrase without hearing in one's mind's ear the fine
irony with which some trade unionists pronounce the grand
phrases which Parliament sees fit from time to time to inject into
labour law. It is understood that industrial tribunals are somewhat
nervous of being called upon to apply this concept, and so far they
have not been placed in the position of having to do so. Less
eye-catching and contentious and possibly more important in
practice is the next of the new provisions relating to the closed
shop,[69] by which unfair dismissal protection is extended to
employees who were already in post when a union membership
agreement first came in principle to require them to belong to a
union and who have not so belonged since that time; so the
position of the pre-agreement continuing non-member becomes a
protected one. This provision has the advantage of, apparently,
reflecting normal voluntary practice under many union membership agreements.[70]

The third of the new provisions relating to the closed shop[71] did
not affect union membership agreements already in being in
August 1980 when the Act came into effect; it introduced an

---

[67] Employment Act 1980, s. 7(2), now after the changes made by the Employment
Act 1982 contained in Employment Protection (Consolidation) Act 1978, s.
58(4).
[68] See above, p. 251.
[69] EA 1980, s. 7(2), now EPCA 1978, s. 58(5).
[70] See R. W. Benedictus, "Closed Shop Exemptions and Their Wording," (1979) 8
I.L.J. 160.
[71] Employment Act 1980, s. 7(2), now EPCA 1978, ss. 58(3)(c) and 58A(1) and
(2).

altogether more stringent set of requirements for agreements made after that date, requirements which had to be observed if the employer was to be protected when carrying out a dismissal in implementation of the agreement. The Act thus distinguished sharply between new agreements and already existing agreements; as we shall see, that may be a difficult line to draw in practice. Moreover, it is possible that a change in their closed shop arrangements which the employer and the unions would not for a moment envisage as constituting a whole new agreement may nevertheless turn out to have that effect in law, with consequences not especially welcome to the parties to the agreement—though of course the framers of the legislation would admit and indeed positively maintain that they did not have the interests solely of the parties to the collective agreement in mind (for that after all is what a union membership agreement is) when framing this provision. The new requirement was that at least 80 per cent. of the employees who would be covered by the agreement should have voted for its application to them in a secret ballot.[72] Even where approval for the agreement was obtained in the ballot, a personal right was given to become, as it were, an entrenched non-member from the date of the ballot.[73] This would give in theory at least an opportunity to establish oneself as a non-member before the ballot took place even if one had been a member of the union when the agreement came into effect.

But the most important thing about the new provision is the statement it made about the very high level of support for a closed shop which was deemed to be necessary before dismissal in pursuance of it could be justified. The new provision repeated a pattern found in the Industrial Relations Act in relation to the agency shop and the approved closed shop whereby the required level of support (in that case a simple majority) was expressed as a proportion of the whole workforce involved rather than as a proportion of those voting, so that failure to vote operates as a negative vote.[74] One can see why that approach might be though specially appropriate in relation to the closed shop because of the

---

[72] Employment Act 1980, s. 7(3), now EPCA 1978, s. 58A(2).

[73] Employment Act 1980, s. 7(2), now EPCA 1978, s. 58(6).

[74] See section 11(3), making ballotted support a condition of the employer's duty to enter into an agreement for an agency shop; and section 17 and Schedule I whereby a CIR report recommending an approved closed shop could on application be subjected to a ballot. In both cases the alternative standard was provided of two thirds of those voting being in favour: see s. 13(1) and Sched. 1, para. 14.

personal detriment potentially involved for individuals ceasing for whatever reasons to belong to the union after the ballot. But it is always necessary in relation to workplace ballots to preserve a strong sense of the social and industrial relations context in which such ballots take place; and such a sense would remind one what a formidably stiff requirement this is, in view of the apathy about voting that often attends these ballots. One wonders how far the legislators of 1980 really were, as they maintained, accepting that the closed shop had an established place in the industrial relations system.

We have not yet completed our narrative of the various ways in which the 1980 legislation sought to limit and control the closed shop; we have only described how this was done in relation to the law of unfair dismissal. Before pursuing the story further, it is necessary to examine in some detail how the legislators have gone about defining the union membership agreement.

Although the legal provisions on the closed shop were between 1974 and 1980 no more than a series of exceptions to the law of unfair dismissal (or, in the case of conscientious objectors, exceptions to the exceptions), it was necessary to define the closed shop, *i.e.* the "union membership agreement" and in particular the types of workers and the types of unions to which it applied.[75] The definition in the 1974 Act[76] was in some important respects changed by the amending Act of 1976.[77] Some of its dominant characteristics reflect the peculiar features of the closed shop as it exists in this country. Thus, the so-called "union membership agreement" (the term is a misnomer) does not really have to be an "agreement" at all, as that word is understood by a lawyer. It may be an "arrangement," a term which would cover the completely informal practices to which we have referred. The "parties" to it (if one may use that expression in relating to something which may be so amorphous and intangible) may, on the workers' side, be one union or several unions—nothing could more vividly illustrate the impact of multi-unionism on industrial practice—and on the employers' side one or more employers or their associations.

---

[75] In the absence of a union membership agreement a dismissal caused by the worker having left the union could be unfair; see *Dunbar* v. *Ford Motor Co. Ltd.* [1975] I.R.L.R. 176. After 1982 dismissal for non-membership of a union is automatically unfair in the absence of a union membership agreement. See Employment Act 1982, s. 3, introducing into the EPCA 1978 a new s. 58(1)(c) and see below n. 5, p. 264. Hence, the law of unfair dismissal may re-inforce the interest of management in formal closed shop agreements.

[76] s. 30(1).

[77] s. 3(3) and (4).

Again our definition shows how uneasily the law moves in a sphere of life in which all clear contours of legal institutions are often dissolved in the aura of "custom and practice": it says that the "agreement or arrangement" must be "made by or on behalf of, or otherwise exist between," these parties. What else could it say about "arrangements" the origin of which may be as mysterious and as lost in the dark recesses of the past as that of a corporation by prescription? Even an informal "arrangement", however, and *a fortiori* something that can be identified as an "agreement" must be clear in one respect (otherwise it cannot create an exception to any statutory provisions on non-discrimination or unfair dismissal); it must identify the class of workers to whom it relates.[78] If this class is not clearly defined, an industrial tribunal cannot know whether the employer was within his rights in refusing to tolerate activities for a rival union by a particular employee or in dismissing him for non-membership of one of the unions specified in or tolerated by the union membership agreement.

The definition covers the pre-entry as well as the post-entry closed shop. At any rate it does so as amended by the 1976 Act. Under the original 1974 Act a union membership agreement had to require the terms and conditions of employment of every employee of the relevant class to include a condition that he must be or become a member. This could have been interpreted as not covering the pre-entry closed shop because the pre-conditions for making a contract cannot be terms of the contract itself. Now, however, under the amended definition, the "union membership agreement" is an agreement or arrangement the effect of which is a "practice." The practice is that employees of the relevant class[79] are required to be or to become members of one of the unions parties to the agreement or arrangement. It does not matter whether there is a condition to that effect in their contracts of employment. This elimination of the "condition" in the individual contracts of employment as an element of the closed shop has the further important result that it is no longer necessary to prove that such a condition was expressly agreed between individual employer and employee or implied in the legal sense—which might

---

[78] The Act of 1974 simply referred to an "identifiable" class, but the new section 30 (5A), inserted by the 1976 Act, makes it clear that the "class" is to be identified "by the parties to the agreement," and this may be done "by reference to any characteristics or circumstances whatsoever." Note, however, the qualification as to ballots in EPCA 1978, s. 58A(6).

[79] But not, after the 1976 Amendment, necessarily all employees of the relevant class without exception. See *Taylor* v. *Co-operative Retail Services Ltd.* [1982] I.C.R. 600 (C.A.).

have given rise to great difficulties. An "arrangement" creating a "practice" suffices. There can hardly ever have been on the statute book a legal definition which is so much at variance with the traditional desire of lawyers for clear outlines of concepts. Only by adopting these vague notions of "arrangement" and "practice" could the draftsman do justice to the nature of the industrial relations which the definition was intended to reflect.

This last observation extends even to the designation of the unions, membership of which is required. Such are the complexities of our union structure that membership of any of a number of unions may satisfy the requirements of the closed shop. This is not only the case where two or more unions participate in the agreement or arrangement. The definition in the 1974 Act was to the effect that the employee could, under a union membership agreement, become a member of one of the unions parties to it, but also of "another appropriate independent trade union"[80]—an ambiguous wording which might have been interpreted as leaving the choice of the union entirely to the employee so that in fact the closed shop would have become an arrangement to belong not to a particular union or particular unions, but to be a union member. This interpretation was rightly rejected by an industrial tribunal when the matter became acute in the so-called *Ferrybridge* case,[81] and this view was approved by the Employment Appeal Tribunal.[82] The doubt was however eliminated by the 1976 Amendment Act which has replaced the reference to an "appropriate" union by a reference to a "specified" union. We now have two situations in which a worker may, in a closed shop, choose to remain in, or to join, a union which is not party to it. One is where it is expressly "specified"—which presumably it can only be if there is a formal closed shop "agreement." The other situation is where it is "accepted by the parties . . . as being equivalent" to a specified union. This can mean that in an informal arrangement it is tacitly tolerated, but such toleration is also possible (though perhaps less likely) where the arrangement has been formalised.

The definition of a "union membership agreement" is of general interest beyond its actual scope of application and purpose. It demonstrates the immense difficulties inherent in giving legal expression to the intangible and formless customs which govern so

---

[80] See Wedderburn (1974) 37 M.L.R. 529–30.
[81] *Sarvent* v. *Central Electricity Generating Board* [1976] I.R.L.R. 66.
[82] *Home Counties Dairies* v. *Woods* [1977] I.C.R. 463, dealing with a situation in which the 1974 Act did, but the 1976 Act did not yet, apply.

much of British industry. As we have said, the need for this arose exclusively from the creation of a body of principles designed to prevent discrimination and unfair dismissal. Such principles also exist in other countries—rules against unfair dismissal in the German Federal Republic, rules against discrimination in the United States—but the situation in this country is unique. It is unique because in other countries the closed shop is either illegal (*e.g.* in the Federal Republic) or formalised (*e.g.* in the United States). It is not easy to marry a system of industrial relations which is imbued with the spirit of empiricism and the horror of abstract norms of conduct with the requirements of the law, the function of which is to give clear guidance to parties and judges. The definition of the union membership agreement is placed at the point of intersection. This gives it its special significance for an understanding of the relation between labour and the law. Before the legislation of 1980, one could indeed virtually equate the law concerning the closed shop with the legal regime of positive toleration accorded to the union membership agreement. But that equation is no longer maintainable, and some further account of the events of 1980 and 1982 is needed to show why.

We have already seen how the Employment Act 1980 modified the treatment of the union membership agreement in various ways in relation to the law of unfair dismissal: how it extended the categories of protected and entrenched non-members of unions and how it introduced the crucial new requirement of balloted support for new union membership agreements. It is easy to lose sight of the fact that the 1980 Act did a number of other things in relation to the closed shop which lie outside the confines of the law of unfair dismissal, at least in the sense hitherto discussed. A number of new controls were introduced upon various types of acts done to compel others to belong to trade unions. First, provision was made whereby an employer who complained that he had been induced to dismiss a worker for not belonging to a union, by industrial action or the threat thereof, might join the inducer as a party to unfair dismissal proceedings against the employer and obtain contribution from him towards any compensation he had to pay the worker concerned.[83] This joinder provision revived a pattern followed in the Industrial Relations Act, but it is significant that, unlike the 1971 Act, the 1980 Act confined joinder to the particular case of acts done because the employee was not a member of a union. Secondly, there was a rather complex double joinder provision whereby an employer might join for contribution

---

[83] Employment Act 1980, s. 10, creating new EPCA 1978, s. 76A.

in unfair dismissal proceedings a contractor who had caused the dismissal by enforcing a requirement that only trade union members should be provided to work on the contract concerned; and whereby that contractor might in turn join any person who induced him by industrial action or the threat of it to refuse to allow the claimant employee to work on the contract. The situation aimed at here is that in which employees of, for example, a labour-only sub-contractor in the building industry have to be dismissed because of pressure on the head contractor to compel him to accept only trade union labour on the contract work. The double joinder provision is now, however, of only historical interest, because it was repealed by the Employment Act 1982, which adopted instead the approach of making the industrial pressure itself unlawful.[84]

Thirdly, and we shall return to this when we consider the law relating to industrial conflict,[85] there was a new provision withdrawing the trade dispute immunity in the law of tort where secondary action was taken or threatened by or in respect of employees of a certain employer for the purpose of compelling workers employed by a different employer to join a particular union or group of unions.[86] This was directed at refusal to handle non-union work for the purpose of compelling non-union establishments to become unionised. Instances of this in the printing industry had been found in an official report to be abuses.[87] The fourth, last, and much the most important of this group of provisions concerned with the control of acts done to compel trade union membership is section 15(1) of the 1980 Act, which amended section 23 of the 1978 Act by giving employees an important new right not to have action short of dismissal taken against them by their employers for the purpose of compelling them to belong to a trade union. This provision was previously limited to compulsion to belong to non-independent trade unions, and has been entirely transformed by the removal of that limitation. It now covers all sorts of action falling short of

---

[84] The double joinder provisions were created by s. 10 of the 1980 Act, inserting new ss. 76 B and C into the 1978 Act, and were repealed by Sched. 4 to the 1982 Act. The provisions on the legality of the industrial action are contained in s. 14 of the 1982 Act. See below p. 321.

[85] See below, p. 321.

[86] Employment Act 1980, s. 18. This section was also repealed by the 1982 Act, its operation being absorbed by the provisions of s. 14 of the 1982 Act. See the previous note.

[87] The Report by Andrew Leggatt Q.C. into Certain Trade-Union Recruitment Activities, Cmnd. 7706, 1979 (often known as the SLADE inquiry).

dismissal, such as restricting overtime opportunities to union members. This provision was then[88] linked up with the provisions about union membership agreements, so that where such an agreement is in force, the new right applied only in those circumstances in which a dismissal for non-membership of a union would be unfair, *i.e.* where the employee is a protected non-member or an entrenched non-member or where the agreement came into effect after section 7 of the 1980 did, and has not had 80 per cent. balloted approval. In general, then, the law about the closed shop, although originally a by-product of the new law of unfair dismissal, was extended far beyond the confines of unfair dismissal.

Even now we have not completed the account of the changes made in 1980 to the legal treatment of the closed shop. So far we have described the measures designed to reconcile closed shop practice with the law of unfair dismissal; and measures designed to control acts done to compel union membership outside the acceptable limits of closed shop practice. There is now a third distinct strand to governmental policy towards the closed shop, which is subtly but significantly different from the two so far considered. Hitherto successive governments have been, broadly speaking, engaged in recognising and making allowance for existing closed shop practice, albeit subject to some differentiation between acceptable and unacceptable versions of the practice. The Industrial Relations Act started off on quite a different tack; it sought to impose its own model of acceptable closed shop practice in the shape of the agency shop, which gave workers the alternatives of paying contributions to the union instead of belonging to it or of making equivalent payments to charity if they were conscientious objectors to union membership.[89] But the lack of interest of the trade union movement in taking up this option went beyond even their general reluctance to operate the machinery of the Act, so that the small handful of unions that felt forced against their political inclinations to work within the scheme of the legislation went not for the agency shop but for the very restricted provision that had also been made in the Act for the approved closed shop.[90] From 1974 onwards the legislation was concerned not to impose a normative model *ab extra* but rather to

---

[88] Employment Act 1980, s. 15(2) creating new EPCA, s. 23(2A) and (2B). The joinder provisions were also extended to action short of dismissal, *ibid.* s. 15(4) creating new EPCA 1978, s. 26A. The 1982 Act further amended ss. 23 and 26A.
[89] Sections 7–10.
[90] *Ibid.* sections 17–18.

identify, in the form of the union membership agreement, a descriptive model of the acceptable versions of the closed shop as it was actually to be found in industrial relations practice. The 1980 legislation moved from that position into a more normative stance, while stopping short of the directly normative approach of the 1971 Act. We have already seen the main example of this in the imposition of the requirement of balloted support upon new union membership agreements. Let it be noted in passing that this balloted support is also now required of new union membership agreements where those agreements are relied on (as has been possible since 1975[91]) to confine the right to trade union activity on the employer's premises to the activities of unions specified in the union membership agreement.[92]

However, while the policy of requiring compliance with a legislative model of the closed shop is evident in the 1980 Act, it was far more prominently displayed in the Code of Practice on Closed Shop Agreements and Arrangements issued under the Act by the Department of Employment in August 1980. There has been a good deal of debate about whether this Code stayed within its proper constitutional function, a debate seeking to distinguish between the proper function of explaining and filling out the details of the statutory provisions and the improper function of legislating distinctly from the statute.[93] What the Code does in essence is to declare a policy of getting existing closed shop practice to adapt itself to conform to a normative model. The features of this model were expressly spelt out in paragraph 3 of the Code:

> "Any agreement or practice on union membership should protect basic individual rights; should enjoy the overwhelming support of those affected; and should be flexibly and tolerantly applied."

The 1980 Act no doubt pursued all three of these aims; the first by widening the category of protected non-membership, the second by the requirements of balloted support for new agreements, and the third by introducing the concept of entrenched non-members.[94] The Code pursued these aims further; it made the model more specific; and ultimately it built into the model features which had no direct counterpart in the statute itself. Into the first

---

[91] Under EPA 1975, s. 53(3); later EPCA 1978, s. 23(3). See above p. 219.
[92] EA 1980, s. 15(2), creating new EPCA 1978, s. 23(2A) (*a*) & (2B).
[93] See McCarthy, "Closed Minds and Closed Shops," (1980) *Federation News* 145.
[94] See above, pp. 252 *et seq*.

of these three categories would fall the provisions of the code which remind employers of their freedoms not to agree to a closed shop at all, to agree subject only to a higher percentage of support than the 80 per cent. standard adopted by the statute, or to agree with payment to a charity by individual non-unionists of sums equivalent to union subscriptions as an alternative to membership.[95] Into the second of these categories would come the suggestion that a new closed shop agreement might well exclude professional or managerial personnel or part-time employees.[96]

The third category is of course the most contentious. Into it would come the statement in the Code that no new pre-entry closed shops should be contemplated.[97] There also would come the statement that new closed shop agreements should provide that an employee will not be dismissed if expelled from his union for refusal to take part in industrial action.[98] But most important, within the third category was the statement that all closed shop agreements, whether new or existing, should be subject to periodic review.[99] The periodic review was basically designed to add a dimension of continuity to the policy of requiring the overwhelming support of workers affected. But the legislation itself clearly contemplated that balloted approval would be only an initial hurdle to be surmounted by new agreements. The Code seemed to be making a radical new departure in this respect, as is evidenced by the fact that the Green Paper on Trade Union Immunities canvassed the suggestion of new legislation requiring periodic review.[1] The Green Paper rehearsed the argument that the case for periodic review as a statutory requirement consists precisely in the threat to the individual worker posed by the closed shop.

That the Code is envisaged as a vehicle for legislative initiative in all but name is indicated by the statement made by the Secretary of State for Employment when introducing the draft of a revised Code at the end of 1982, when he made it clear that it was regarded as necessary to strengthen the provisions of the Code to cope with what were seen as substantial injustices to individuals still arising out of closed shop practice. In particular it was regarded as abusive that trade unions were using the threat of expulsion and consequent dismissal to ensure participation in

---

[95] Respectively paras. 20, 35, 31.
[96] Para. 30.
[97] Para. 46.
[98] Para. 30.
[99] Para. 42.
[1] Cmnd. 8128 (1981), paras. 276–279.

industrial action, which might be unlawful—the TUC's Day of Action of 1982 was instanced[1a] and accordingly the Code was strengthened so that unions are enjoined not to discipline members for refusal to take part in industrial action, whatever the reason for that refusal, where: (i) the industrial action has not been affirmed in a secret ballot; or (ii) is in breach of a procedure agreement; or (iii) where the member believed that the industrial action contravened his professional or other code of ethics; or (iv) where it involved a breach of statutory duty or the criminal law or constituted a serious risk to public safety, health or property or—and here is the new extension—where the members had reasonable grounds for believing that any of those conditions was fulfilled or that the industrial action was unlawful in the sense of lacking immunity in tort.[1b] This extension, as the Departmental statement itself predicted, greatly increases the likelihood that a member expelled from his union for refusing to take industrial action will be able successfully to complain to an industrial tribunal under the provisions of sections 4 and 5 of the 1980 Act.[1c] Hence the Code as revised makes an important modification to the law relating to the closed shop by substantially restricting the use of the closed shop as a means of ensuring comprehensive participation in industrial action. But even before this change, the legal constraints upon the closed shop had been further increased by some provisions of the Employment Act 1982 to which we should now turn our attention.

In 1982 there was yet another set of changes to the law of the closed shop, in the Employment Act 1982. Between 1980 and 1982, the Government seemed to have come to view the closed shop even more directly than before as an intolerable encroachment upon individual liberties. This was a particular tenet of Mr. Tebbit who had replaced the more moderate Mr. Prior as Secretary of State for Employment. It was reflected in the text of the Working Paper in which the proposals for the 1982 Act were introduced.[2] The previous references to the need to work within

---

[1a] This was a day of industrial action called in protest against the Government's proposals for labour legislation and against their employment policies. The suggestion was that it would accordingly be unlawful in the sense of falling outside the ambit of the trade dispute formula. See below, p. 315.

[1b] Para. 61 of the Revised Code of Practice on Closed Shop Agreements and Arrangements (1983). The corresponding paragraph in the original Code of 1980 is Para. 54.

[1c] See above, p. 235.

[2] "Proposals for industrial relations legislation" Department of Employment, November 23, 1981; set out *in extenso* in *The Times*, November 24, 1981.

the existing framework of industrial relations were not repeated here. The whole emphasis was on the need to enhance the protection of individuals.[3] There was specific reference to the public concern over two *causes célèbres*[4] where employees of two local authorites had been dismissed in pursuance of closed shops maintained by those local authorites despite the remedies available under the unfair dismissal legislation as amended in 1980.

The 1982 Act in fact contains a large number of new measures against the closed shop both within and beyond the law of unfair dismissal. We shall describe first those lying within the law of unfair dismissal. A general principle of much importance is laid down to the effect that any dismissal on the ground of non-membership of a union is unfair,[5] subject only to the provision[6] that such a dismissal is fair if it comes within the specially protected case of the dismissal in pursuance of a union membership agreement (a case which is, as we shall see, increasingly hedged about with qualifications and restrictions). This general principle testifies to the growth of hostility towards the closed shop on the part of those responsible for the legislation; hitherto it had been viewed as appropriate to leave cases of dismissal for refusal of union membership where there was no union membership agreeement in force to be determined by the ordinary law of unfair dismissal, except in the special case of refusal of membership of a *non-independent* trade union. By making this change the legislators of 1982 indicated that in their view the protection of the freedom to dissociate should go hand in hand with the previously conferred protection of the freedom to associate. They also took steps to ensure that the protection of the freedom to dissociate included protection against being obliged to make payments or submit to deductions from wages instead of belonging to a trade union by treating such obligations in the same way as obligations to join a union.[7]

The second major change made by the 1982 Act consisted in making balloted approval of a union membership agreement a

---

[3] See in particular para. 3 thereof.

[4] See para. 4 thereof. The incidents referred to were those of the dismissal of a poultry inspector by Sandwell Council and of a number of dinner-ladies by Walsall Council in 1981.

[5] EA 1982 s. 3 substituting new EPCA 1978 s. 58(1)(*c*). This complements the similar change already made in respect of action short of dismissal by the 1980 Act. See above p. 259.

[6] EA 1982 s. 3 substituting new EPCA 1978 s. 58(3)–(14).

[7] EA 1982 s. 3 substituting new EPCA 1978 s. 58(13). Such action is also made remediable as action short of dismissal—EA 1982 s. 10(3) inserting new EPCA 1978 23(1A)–(1B).

necessary condition for reliance on it as justifying a dismissal in relation to all union membership agreements[8] and not just, as hitherto, agreements made after the coming into force of the 1980 Act on August 14, 1980. Moreover this measure embodies the notion of periodic review which was foreshadowed, as we have seen, in the Code of Practice on the Closed Shop[9]; for in any given case where balloted approval is invoked to make good a union membership agreement as a justification for a dismissal, that approval has to have been manifested not more than five years before the dismissal in question.[10] As a slight concession to the argument that abstentions should not be treated as negative votes, it is provided that pre-1980 agreements can be effectively approved by an 85 per cent. majority of those voting as well as by an 80 per cent. majority of the whole constituency[11]; but a ballot in which neither of these levels of support is attained is treated as cancelling out any previous balloted approval,[12] so that there is a distinct gamble involved in holding a ballot at any time short of five years after a ballot in which approval is obtained.

A further set of measures concerns compensation for dismissal on the grounds of trade union membership, non-membership or activity. The aim of these measures was to ensure that there would be a really effective deterrent against dismissals for non-membership of trade unions outside the circumstances in which that is permitted by the statute. To this end, the following steps were taken in relation to unfair dismissal on the ground of, or involving selection on the ground of, trade union membership, non-membership or activity:

(1) the basic award is subjected to a minimum of £2,000[13]

(2) a new special award is provided in addition to the compensatory award, which is subject to a minimum of £10,000 where the employee asks to be reinstated but the tribunal decides it would

---

[8] EA 1982 s. 3 substituting new EPCA 1978 s. 58(3)(*c*). The law relating to action short of dismissal follows suit—EA 1982 s. 10(2) substituting new EPCA 1978 s. 23(2B) However, the extended balloting requirement has not yet been brought into force. This will happen in November 1984 unless the Secretary of State decides to bring the provisions into operation earlier. See s. 22(4) of the 1982 Act.

[9] See above, p. 262.

[10] EA 1982 s. 3 substituting new EPCA 1978 s. 58(3)(*c*).

[11] EA 1982 s. 3 substituting new EPCA 1978 s. 58A(1)–(2). The same concession is made for second and subsequent ballots of post-1980 agreements.

[12] EA 1982 s. 3 substituting new EPCA 1978 s. 58A(7).

[13] EA 1982 s. 4(1) substituting new EPCA 1978 s. 73(4A).

not be practicable or just to do so[14]; and of £15,000 where an order for reinstatement is not complied with.[15]

These measures attach a formidable premium to unfair dismissal on these particular grounds as distinct from other sorts of unfair dismissal. Furthermore, it is provided that compensation for dismissals of the kind under discussion may not be reduced by reference to the conduct of the employee in question in so far as his conduct consists in his resisting the imposition upon him of a requirement that he should belong to, not belong to or not take part in the activities of a trade union.[16] This seems to be directed against the possibility that the employer could plead the employee's refusal to comply with the operation of the Bridlington principles (in so far as their operation required him to belong to one TUC union and not to another) as a ground for reduction of compensation.

This seems a rather over-elaborate reaction to a slightly fanciful contingency, and perhaps indicates the way in which legislating against the closed shop has become a sort of moral crusade rather than a practical exercise. There are, as we shall see, other indications to the same effect. For instance, there is a complex new provision, inserted during the passage of the 1982 Bill through the House of Lords and no doubt in response to concerns raised by the then current industrial dispute in the National Health Service, to the effect that a union membership agreement cannot be invoked to justify a dismissal in pursuance of it where the dismissal stems from the employee's refusal to take part in industrial action in breach of a professional code to which he is subject, or from his refusal to belong to a union on the ground that he would be required so to act if he did belong.[17] However much one deplores the mischief at which this provision is aimed, surely one must recognise that it is exceedingly difficult for unions and employers alike to operate in practice according to such a multiplicity of legal rules. What one is really seeing here is another form of the breakdown of legal regulation of industrial relations; a form, that is, in which there is the outward appearance of a compromise between the state of affairs desired by the legislators and the state of affairs actually prevailing, but in which the compromise depends on such a labyrinthine pattern of rules that it exists solely on a theoretical plane quite remote from reality.

---

[14] EA 1982 s. 5(3) substituting new EPCA 1978 s. 75A(1).
[15] *Ibid.* new s. 75A(2).
[16] EA 1982 s. 6 substituting new EPCA s. 72A.
[17] EA 1982 s. 3 substituting new EPCA 1978 s. 58(8).

The element of moral crusading in the provisions of the 1982 Act concerning the closed shop is, however, at its most marked in the case of a provision directed not so much against those now running closed shops as against the legislators who devised the legal regime of tolerance towards the closed shop, which, as we have seen, existed between the repeal of the Industrial Relations Act in 1974 and the coming into effect of the Employment Act of 1980. In an almost unprecedented exercise in the retrospective reversal of the consequences of previous legislation, the 1982 Act provides[18] in effect that where dismissals in pursuance of union membership agreements were fair according to the law then in force but would have been unfair according to the law in force between 1980 and 1982, then the dismissed individual may claim compensation for his dismissal, the compensation to be assessed according to the law in force between 1976 and 1980 and to be paid, not by the employer but out of public funds at the discretion of the Secretary of State for Employment. The Government in making this provision seems to have been convinced by research findings that there was an identifiable category of beneficiaries of this provision amounting to about 400 persons, and by the decision of the European Court of Human Rights in the case concerning the British Rail closed shop[19] that this provision was ethically appropriate; but with its apparatus of inquiry into particular cases by a referee appointed by the Department of Employment, the whole provision smacks of a sort of self-inflicted exercise in post-war reparations and indicates the frightening degree of polarisation, in the perceptions of the legislators of 1982, between their goals and the previously existing legislation.

That provision is however singular within the 1982 Act in its concentration upon the collective public responsibility owed in the view of its formulators to the victims of the closed shop. Elsewhere, the 1982 Act is concerned to enhance the joint and several liabilities of employers and unions to those adversely affected by the operation of closed shops, and to stress the inter-connection between closed shop activity on the part not only of unions on the one hand but also on the part of employers on the other. Thus, lest the employer in carrying out a dismissal in pursuance of a union membership agreement should be isolated from the consequences of unreasonable exclusionary activity on the part of the union, it is now provided[20] that the employer

---

[18] EA 1982 s. 2 and Sched. 1.
[19] See above, p. 238.
[20] EA 1982, s. 3 substituting new EPCA 1978, s. 58(7).

cannot invoke the agreement to justify the dismissal where the employee has obtained, or even just applied for, an industrial tribunal declaration of unreasonabe exclusion or expulsion from a trade union.[21] Moreover the employee faced with dismissal by reason of non-membership of a trade union is now accorded[22] the same special possibility of obtaining interim relief against the employer as had hitherto been accorded only to the employee faced with dismissal for trade union membership or activity—a protection previously deemed appropriate for the particular purpose of safeguarding the collective interest in freedom of association at the work-place.[23]

These measures are concentrated upon the complicity of the employer in the enforcement of the closed shop. Other measures stress the primary responsibility of the union in bringing about action short of dismissal taken by employers for the purpose of compelling union membership, or in bringing about dismissal by reason of non-membership. The 1980 Act, as we have seen,[24] enabled the employer to bring the union in as a contributor when remedies were sought against him for action of these kinds; but that was an option available only to the defendant employer. Employers in practice would have little incentive to exercise this option; the 1982 Act takes the potentially more significant step of giving the complainant also the option of joining the third party who has induced the employer's action as a party to the proceedings against whom an award of compensation may be made instead of against the employer.[25] (How, incidentally, will industrial tribunals make that allocation? What considerations of justice and equity will enable that apportionment to be made?) This measure might appear at first sight to be merely procedural; but its fundamental substantive significance should not be over-looked. For the first time, the individual worker is given a cause of action of a tortious nature against the union before industrial tribunals; and the union enjoys neither immunity as such nor trade dispute protection, even heavily qualified as those protections now are as the result of other provisions of the 1982 Act. Hitherto only the "willing unionist" has been allowed recourse to the union in industrial tribunals; now that this recourse has been accorded to the non-unionist also, the industrial tribunals must in consequence

---

[21] Under s. 4 of the E.A. 1980; see above, p. 235.
[22] EA 1982 s. 8, amending EPCA 1978, s. 77.
[23] See above, p. 221.
[24] See above, p. 258.
[25] EA 1982 s. 7 substituing new EPCA 1978, s. 76A (dismissal); E.A. 1982, s. 11 substituting new EPCA 1978, s. 26A (action short of dismissal).

face an ever more politically delicate and controversial task, in which their reputation for impartiality becomes harder to maintain.

There is a further and highly important set of variants on the theme of the joint and several responsibility of employers and unions for closed shop activity in the 1982 Act. Already in the 1980 Act, as we have seen[26] there was the extension of that responsibility to the case where the contractor (typically himself an employer) at the behest of a union imposes upon an employer with whom he is contracting (typically a sub-contractor) a requirement of union membership on the part of the employees who will be engaged on the work contracted. In the 1980 Act that responsibility was expressed as an elaborate system of contribution whereby the employer could bring the contractor in as a contributory to unfair dismissal proceedings, and the contractor could in turn join the union as a contributory.[27] In the 1982 Act this idea is enormously extended and elaborated. Firstly, the contractual terms by which union membership requirements are sought to be imposed via commercial contracts are rendered void by statute.[28] Secondly, the activity of terminating or, even more significantly, of not entering into commercial contracts by way of imposing a union membership requirement is prohibited by statute and made into the breach of a statutory duty owed to the aggrieved contractor or potential contractor (*e.g.* the contractor excluded on the ground of a union-labour only requirement from a list from whom tenders are invited) and to any other person adversely affected by the contravention (*e.g.* presumably the non-unionist employee of the excluded potential contractor).[29] These measures intrude a very important labour law element into the process of commercial contracting and represent an important structural extension of the ambit of labour law.

Moreover—and this is one of the most important of the conceptual developments in the legislation—it was decided at a late stage in the passage of the 1982 Bill through Parliament to extend this type of prohibition to the case where union *recognition* requirements are sought to be imposed via the process of commercial contracting.[30] This was probably envisaged as little

---

[26] See above, p. 258.
[27] EA 1980, s. 10 adding new EPCA 1978, ss. 76B, 76C, provisions repealed by the 1982 Act.
[28] EA 1982, s. 12(1).
[29] EA 1982, s. 12(2)—(7).
[30] EA 1982, s. 13.

more than a way of controlling back-door evasion of the provisions concerning union labour only requirements; but its significance for the process of dismantling the structure of legislative support for collective bargaining is inescapable. This whole new edifice of prohibitions is buttressed by a corresponding further diminution of trade dispute immunity for unions and others in bringing pressure to impose union membership or recognition requirements[31]—a process already embarked upon in the 1980 Act.[32] So the preoccupation with the closed shop continues to eat ever deeper into the traditional fabric of Labour Law, and so the debate about the proper legal regime for the closed shop goes on. It is in the end a debate about the proper reconciliation, not between the partisan interests of capital and labour, but between the personal and individual freedoms of the worker and the collective interests of workers organised into unions. It seems we must accept the inevitability, and arguably the desirability, of a continuing tension between these two. A factor which has some influence on the course of this debate is the extent to which unions are perceived to be democratic organisations in which the interests and preferences of the members as individuals are effectively expressed and represented. This is a matter upon which the law may have a direct bearing and we therefore conclude our discussion of trade union law by turning to some consideration of democracy and autonomy.

3. DEMOCRACY AND AUTONOMY[33]

Trade unions are bearers of power. They must have power in order to play the role in society without which there can be no labour relations. These are truisms. But they may be misleading truisms. To speak about a collective unit—a business enterprise, a government department, a municipal authority, a trade union—as a bearer of power is misleading, because it is always individuals who make rules and decisions, and influence other people's

---

[31] EA 1982, s. 14.

[32] EA 1980, s. 18—see above, p. 259.

[33] The literature on this subject is gigantic. For systematic factual information, see especially B. C. Roberts, *Trade Union Government and Administration in Great Britain* (1957); V. L. Allen, *Power in Trade Unions* (1954), and more up to date, John Hughes, *Trade Union Structure and Government* (1968, Royal Commission Research Paper No. 5), Pt. 2; Clegg, *Changing System of Industrial Relations in Great Britain,* (1979) Chap. 5. Milne-Bailey *Trade Unions and the State* (1934) is still interesting, irrespective of his political theory. For a very useful comparative analysis see Folke Schmidt, "Industrial Action, the Role of Trade Unions and Employers' Associations" in *Industrial Conflict* (1972) Chap. 1, (Aaron and Wedderburn ed.).

thoughts and actions; and we must know who inside the collective unit can and will do that. It is as important to know how power is allocated inside trade unions as to know how it is distributed between unions, management, and government. The same question must be asked about government and management; but this is not our concern in this book. The question is what the law can and should do about power inside unions.

Trade unions represent the collective interest of the workers. This is the purpose of their existence. Does it follow that the constitution of the union should guarantee to the rank and file a minimum or a maximum of influence on the making of rules and decisions? Or should it, which is more realistic and practicable, at least ensure that the rank and file have a minimum or maximum of influence on the selection of those who make the decisions and the rules? How strong is the case for "trade union democracy"? What offices should be filled by election and what offices by appointment? How frequently should elections be held? What decisions should be left to branch meetings, regional conferences, annual or biennial union conferences? To ballots of the members? To delegate conferences or committees elected ad hoc?

There is no doubt a case for trade union democracy. It is, to use modern slang, the case for "integration" against "alienation." Especially at times of a fairly good chance of getting jobs, the interest of members in union affairs is liable to flag; everywhere (not only in this country) one reads complaints about poor attendance at branch meetings. Can such interest be retained or revived if the individual union member cannot feel that his voice or his vote counts in the making of decision? What is more: is the alternative to democracy not oligarchy; rule of a self-perpetuating group of union leaders; or clique of union bosses—choose the terms according to your prejudices? How can the union do its job of representing the members if the members do not have a decisive say in the definition of their interests and in the priorities of union objectives? These are formidable questions. They cannot be brushed aside.

However, there is also a case against trade union democracy. That case stems partly, but only partly, from the antithesis between efficiency and democracy which besets trade unions no less than commercial companies, local authorities, political parties, and the State itself. That antithesis may be false if it is put as between efficiency and democracy in general; it becomes real when put in terms of democratic decision-making. Masses can perhaps prevent, but they cannot make, decisions, let alone carry them into effect. Power is always exercised by the few, not by the many, and if union democracy is understood as giving effective rule- and decision-making powers to mass meetings then it will, like that superannuated idea of a "shareholders' democracy," produce a smile or a smirk on the faces of the augurs—the Soames Forsytes of this world.

The test of democracy is not who makes the decisions, but who chooses those who make them, and who can be chosen. Can the union rank and file effectively choose their leaders, and, apart from the leaders, their minor office holders? Here we have the great problem of election versus appointment, a fundamental problem of union constitution-making. Which is the better way of getting the best man for the job? This is a very real question. It is not the only question: it is also important to get the man who is believed to be the best man for the job. The two may not be identical.

There is, however, lurking behind these questions another issue which, somewhat surprisingly, does not seem to have been discussed very much in this country or elsewhere in Europe and which has for years been the subject of a fascinating and voluminous discussion in the United States.[34] As we in our present world understand "democracy," it presupposes parties. This means that there must inside the body politic be groups representing different interests and ideas, promoting different programmes, and competing for power. This again is a truism, as true of a parliamentary as of a presidential democracy, and as true of the Government of the United Kingdom as of any local authority. It is only through this organised competition for power that the elective processes of a democracy can work. The alternative would be a fight between persons as persons—feasible in the Greek Polis or in the ancient communities of Switzerland or of New England in which "direct democracy" is alleged to have flourished long ago and in which something like a *volonté générale* may have emerged from the *agora* or town meeting, and everyone knew everyone else. In our world no such thing can exist. Political parties are the inevitable answer to the question of how democracy can work in the anonymous mass society of today. The Transport and General Workers Union or the United Automobile Workers of America or the German Metal Workers' Union are no less mass societies than the United Kingdom, the United States of America or the German

---

[34] See for some references to this extensive literature, Kahn-Freund "Trade Unions, the Law, and Society" (1970) 33 M.L.R. 241.

Federal Republic themselves. There is no more guarantee that people inside gigantic voluntary organisations like these "know" their propective leaders than there is in the higher sphere of government. How can there be democracy, how can there be democratic selection of leaders and office holders inside modern unions without parties inside the union?

But why should there be no parties inside the unions if there are parties in central and even local government? Though one (it seems not unsuccessful) attempt at party government has been made in one big American union,[35] this has remained an isolated example even in the United States. As far as we know, no such experiment has ever been made in this country or elsewhere in Europe. We suggest that it cannot be made. Why not? Apart from the type of behaviour known as treason, the Government, the State, does not have to reckon with secession, split, breakaway, and neither does a municipal corporation. They can afford to have political parties as long as they are not threatened with a civil war. However violently a member of the opposition may disagree with those in office, the government remains his government; he cannot quit. His party cannot "secede" and form a fresh Kingdom or urban district council. But a union opposition can secede. The formation of organised groups with different programmes is a mortal threat to a voluntary association such as a political party or a trade union. There cannot in a union or other voluntary association be "parties"—there can only be "factions" or "coteries" who do not operate at the hustings or in the market place, but in a backroom or an antechamber. This is vital. It explains why, for example, electioneering,[36] the most normal and legitimate form of political agitation, is frowned upon by many union constitutions; why participation in union elections is so poor (there is no fight between groups with which the voter can identify himself); why it is so easy for minorities representing outside interests or creeds to dominate elections. There is a formidable case against an overdose of elective democracy in a voluntary body, and especially in a body always and inevitably threatened by

---

[35] The International Typographical Union. See the detailed analysis in Lipset, Trow and Coleman, *Union Democracy* (1956).

[36] Allen, *loc. cit.,* pp. 306 *et seq.* Hughes, *loc. cit.,* para. 101, shows how this is linked with "the problem" of "ensuring that the conduct of the election (and allegations surrounding it) does not become a tactic used in the struggle between rival groups within the union." Pt. I, Rule 2, paras. 9 and 10, of the AEU Rules of 1960, restricting electioneering to one address of no more than 750 words and distributed through the General Office, illustrates the point.

disruption because it is a fighting body which may be attacked by outside hostile interests working from inside.[37]

Is not all this fairly obvious? Why mention it here? Because it teaches a very important lesson on the role the law can or cannot play in these matters. It is impracticable, or at least inadvisable, for the law to lay down minimum rules of "democracy" to be followed by all unions, irrespective of the constitutions they themselves have adopted. To this extent, then, the *pouvoir constituant* of each union should remain inviolate and not be transferred to the State and its law. In fact the comparison of any given set of union constitutions in this country—take the two largest, the TGWU and the AUEW[38]—shows the wide differences in the dose of "democracy" injected into these constitutions. Here autonomy is better than uniformity. If ever there was what Professor Chafee of Harvard,[39] in a memorable article on these matters many years ago, called a "hot potato"—this is it.

Nevertheless, since 1959, the federal legislation of the United States[40] has included a formidable list of minimum requirements of democracy with which each union must comply. This does not only cover matters such as who is entitled to nominate candidates, to stand for elections, to vote at elections and on other occasions, but also the methods of assessing contributions, the frequency of elections, the methods of holding them (including the conduct of ballots and their scrutiny) and, most surprisingly, what offices have to be filled through elections. In this country it has, on the whole, been common ground that in this dilemma between imposing standards of democracy and protecting union autonomy the law must come down on the side of autonomy.[41] It certainly did so in the trade union legislation which was in force until the Act of 1971[42] came into operation, it continued to do so to some extent

---

[37] In Allen, *loc. cit.*, p. 10, the argument appears in reverse: trade union democracy is guaranteed because the members can vote with their feet, by leaving. How realistic is this?

[38] Compare Prof. Roberts's excellent diagrams, *loc. cit.*, pp. 489 and 522.

[39] Zechariah Chafee Jr., "The Internal Affairs of Associations Not for Profit" (1930) 43 Harv. L. R. 993.

[40] Labor Management Reporting and Disclosure Act 1959, s. 401.

[41] The Trade Unions (Amalgamations, etc.) Act 1964 is, in a sense, an exception. For reasons connected with the need for promoting amalgamations, the Act imposes certain procedural requirements, but it leaves as much as possible to autonomy. So is the Trade Union Act 1913 (political fund). See above. p. 247.

[42] The Trade Union Acts 1871–1876.

under that Act,[43] and the law in operation between 1974 and 1980 went further[44] in giving effect to the principle of autonomy.

The legislators of 1980, while continuing to observe the primacy of trade union autonomy over the imposition of trade union democracy (probably out of a disinclination to repeat the confrontations that followed the passing of the 1971 Act), nevertheless engaged in quite an elaborate attempt to encourage the use of secret ballots as the method by which unions should take decisions and make elections. This initiative proceeded on the basis of an assumption that in many or most unions there was a silent majority of moderate or conservative disposition which, if it could be persuaded to participate in union decisions, would act as a control upon the adoption of militant policies and the selection of militant leaders. The main thrust of this initiative was contained in section 1 of the Employment Act 1980, and regulations made thereunder,[44a] which between them provide a scheme for payments from public funds to trade unions by way of subsidy of secret ballots. The administration of the scheme was entrusted to the Certification Officer, and access to it was confined to independent trade unions. The scheme is at present confined to secret postal[44b] ballots held for the purposes of deciding whether to call or end industrial action, whether to accept an employer's offer, electing to the executive of the union or electing its main officers and employed officials, amending the rules or carrying out an amalgamation or transfer of engagements. The Certification Officer has under the scheme to satisfy himself, before making payments, of the fulfillment of a number of conditions which address themselves on the one hand to due observance of union rules and on the other hand to independent criteria such as that of the voters having a fair opportunity of voting without interference or constraint. Much of course depends on the manner of interpretation of such a concept, but one wonders how far the legislators' preferred model of union decision-making seeks to exclude the influence of group opinions and group perceptions, as well as the obviously undesirable features of direct interference or constraint.

---

[43] With the exception of the "compulsory strike ballot" (s. 141) which has, temporarily at least, ceased to exist.

[44] Especially through the repeal of Trade Union and Labour Relations Act 1974, s. 6, and the amendment of s. 8(6) by the Amendment Act 1976, s. 1(*b*) and (*c*).

[44a] Funds for Trade Union Ballots Regulations, S.I. 1980 No. 1252, as amended by S.I. 1982 Nos. 953 and 1108.

[44b] Reg. 6.

Although the proposals contained in section 1 of the 1980 Act did much to meet the demand from the supporters of the government for measures to promote the secret postal ballot, there remained a degree of pressure on the government to do more to promote secret ballots at the workplace also. The promotion of workplace secret balloting was seen as providing a positive alternative to the decision to take or prolong industrial action which the supporters of the government would tend to characterise as the impulsive and ill-considered outcome of the mass meeting at the workplace, where the crowd might be over-responsive to pressures brought to bear by shop stewards. The government was in no hurry to include workplace ballots in its scheme for subsidising ballots, still less to yield to the pressure for compulsory workplace secret ballots; but they did during the passage of the Bill through Parliament accept an amendment which now figures as section 2 of the 1980 Act and gives independent unions a right, as against employers, to be permitted so far as is reasonably practicable to hold secret ballots on the employer's premises. This right is confined to ballots for those purposes for which subsidy may be given to postal ballots under section 1. The right is also confined to recognised unions and arises only against employers of more than twenty workers. It is sanctioned by awards of compensation to the union by an industrial tribunal. It is not clear that this provision has been much invoked nor that it has met any real social demand. Indeed, and this is more significant, the scheme for subsidising ballots has been viewed by the TUC unions and the TUC itself as requiring of them a submission to the aims of the 1980 legislation which they are politically unwilling to make, so that even those unions, such as the Engineering Workers, who already make extensive use of the postal ballot (in their case for elections) have with varying degrees of reluctance decided not to make use of the Government's scheme. This gives an indication of the extent to which political polarisation in relation to labour law generally, and the suspicion with which trade unions have come to view any attempt to shape the conduct of their affairs by legislation, place obstacles in the path of those wishing to use the law to promote or require any given pattern of trade union democracy. As we shall shortly see, the Government has at the time of writing indicated a firm intention to tread that path by introducing new legislation to implement certain requirements relating to democracy within trade unions. But leaving aside for the moment the question of legislative promotion of particular patterns of trade union government, we must first ask the more general question of what legal framework is provided for trade unions and what impact does that framework have on the way they conduct their affairs.

It has been the traditional policy of the law in this country to lay down that a trade union must give itself a constitution, or, more correctly, that certain elements of its constitution must be formulated in writing through "rules," and the same policy has been applied to employers' associations.[45] The rule book, normally very voluminous, and not always very systematically organised, is not, however, the constitution of the union in the sense that it is self-contained and a complete codification of the principles which govern the distribution of functions and of powers inside the union. "Custom and practice" may have given rise to rules which are not to be found in the rule book and which may supplement or modify it, and may create procedures which vary from place to place.[46] "It is not to be assumed, as in the case of a commercial contract which has been reduced into writing, that all the terms of the agreement are to be found in the rule book alone: particularly as respects the discretion conferred by the members on committees or officials of the union as to the way in which they may act on the union's behalf. If authority to take a particular type of action is not excluded by the rules, and if such authority is reasonably to be implied from custom and practice, such authority will contine to exist until unequivocally withdrawn."[47] Thus the Trade Union Act 1871, which was repealed by the Industrial Relations Act 1971, made it incumbent on a registered union to make, by its rules, "a provision for the appointment and removal of a general committee of management, of a trustee or trustees, and other officers."[48] It did not, of course, having been enacted in 1871, say anything about rules on the credentials or the powers of shop stewards, and in fact the Donovan Commission found[49] that "in many rule books shop stewards, or their counterparts, are mentioned only because the union relies on them to collect subscriptions. The representative functions of shop stewards are referred to with surprising infrequency." Shop stewards are an essential element in the living constitution of many unions, and, especially, a democratic element of those constitutions. One does not exaggerate by saying that, in relation to that living constitution, the rule book may be no more

---

[45] Trade Union Act 1871, s. 14 and First Sched.—now repealed.
[46] See the TUC Handbook on the Industrial Relations Act, quoted by Lord Wilberforce in *Heatons Transport (St. Helens) Ltd.,* v. *T.G.W.U.* [1972] I.C.R. 308 at p. 394.
[47] Lord Wilberforce, *ibid.* at p. 393. See also above, Chap. 3.
[48] See above, n. 45.
[49] Cmnd. 3623, para. 698.

than the tip of the iceberg. This is what the House of Lords recognised in 1972 in its decision in *Heaton's Transport (St. Helens) Ltd.* v. *T.G.W.U.*[50] The relation between the written rules and "custom and practice" illustrates the fundamental difference between the meaning of documents in industrial relations and in commercial practice: it is a point of general significance.

The policy, then, was to prescribe that on certain fundamental matters unions and employers' associations had to exercise their constitution-making power by adopting written rules. But the object of this was to compel the unions to articulate these matters, and to make it possible for each of their members, and for outsiders, to see what the rule was. It was never the policy of the law in this country to prescribe to the union how it was to exercise this power, *i.e.* to prescribe the content as distinct from the form of those elements of the constitution which had to be regulated by formal rules. The situation was thus comparable with that created by an enactment conferring a discretionary authority on some inferior court or administrative agency; that inferior court or agency can be compelled to exercise its discretion, but it cannot be compelled to exercise it in a certain way.[51] This was, to some extent, also the policy of the Industrial Relations Act 1971, by which the Act of 1871 was replaced.[52]

Nevertheless, the 1971 Act had in this matter in reality a completely different effect. Under the Trade Union Act 1871, as under the Industrial Relations Act 1971, the obligation to adopt rules was exclusively imposed on trade unions and employers' associations which were registered.[53] Registration was voluntary under both statutes, but here the similarity ends. Under the 1871 Act in connection with various Finance Acts and eventually the Income and Corporation Taxes Act 1970,[54] registration carried with it a very vital income tax privilege, important for trade unions, but not for employers' associations. For this reason, and probably also for other reasons,[55] it was the normal thing for unions to register under the 1871 Act, at least for all the larger

---

[50] See above, n. 46. This point is not affected by the subsequent decision of the House of Lords in *General Aviation Services* v. *T.G.W.U.* [1976] I.R.L.R. 225.

[51] de Smith, *Judicial Review of Administrative Action* (4th ed., 1980), pp. 285 *et seq.*

[52] Sched. 4, whose para. 10 however imposed on registered unions the burden of "specifying" what, in the nature of things, cannot be specified.

[53] Trade Union Act 1871, s. 14; Industrial Relations Act 1971, ss. 68, 72.

[54] s. 338.

[55] The obligation to publish the accounts was in many ways an advantage to the unions.

unions, so that it was estimated that almost nine out of ten union members belonged to registered unions.[56] Hence the provisions on union rules were very much part of the living law. Under the Industrial Relations Act, however, registration, though still "voluntary," acquired a completely new meaning. Non-registration carried with it the most serious disadvantages. Nevertheless, except for a very small minority, the unions left the Register, and faced these disadvantages and also the loss of the income tax exemption rather than submit to the enlarged powers of the Registrar over the rule book, and, more importantly, take any step by which they seemed to accept the Act to which they were bitterly opposed. Consequently, the provisions of the Act about union rules did not really matter in practice. What did matter were a number of principles for their internal organisation which applied to registered and unregistered unions alike, some of which—as we have already indicated—simply codified good practice, whilst others sought to saddle the unions with a burden they could hardly bear.[57]

The Registrar of Trade Unions and Employers' Associations who, under the 1971 Act,[58] had taken the place occupied by the Registrar of Friendly Societies under the Trade Union Act 1871,[59] has now in his turn been replaced by the Certification Officer appointed by the Employment Secretary after consultation with the ACAS[60] and the "register" has been replaced by the "list of trade unions" and the "list of employers' associations."[61] An organisation which is a trade union or an employers' association as defined by law[62] has a right to be entered in the appropriate list.[63] Hence the Certification Officer does not—except in connection with the "political fund"[64] and with trade union amalgamations[65]—have to "approve" the rules of an organisa-tion—in this respect the present situation resembles that under the Trade Union Act 1871, rather than that under the Industrial

---

[56] Cmnd. 3623, para. 789.
[57] See the "guiding principles" for organisations of workers and of employers in s. 65 and in s. 69, violation of which was an "unfair industrial practice" (ss. 66, 70). s. 65(7) was clearly unworkable.
[58] s. 63.
[59] s. 17.
[60] Employment Protection Act 1975, s. 7.
[61] Trade Union and Labour Relations Act 1974, s. 8, as amended by the 1975 Act and by the Amendment Act of 1976.
[62] *i.e.* by s. 28 of the 1974 Act.
[63] *Ibid.* s. 8(1) "entitled"; s. 8(2) and (3) "shall."
[64] Trade Union Act 1913, s. 4.
[65] Trade Union (Amalgamations, etc.) Act 1964, s. 1(4) and (5).

Relations Act 1971. The Certification Officer is not the guardian of internal union democracy, but he is the guardian of "publicity." To be "listed," an organisation must supply[66] a copy of its rules, a list of its officers, the address of its head office, and the name under which it is, or is to be, known, and one of the functions of the Certification Officer is to make sure that this is not identical with or deceptively similar to that of another organisation already listed.[67] His principal task, however, is to satisfy himself that the body asking to be listed is a trade union or an employers' organisation. To be a trade union, an organisation must consist wholly or mainly either of workers or of workers' organisations or their representatives, and one of its principal purposes must be to regulate the relations between workers and employers or their organisations, or, if it consists of workers' organisations, the relations between them.[68] To be an employers' association, an organisation must, *mutatis mutandis,* comply with the same requirements.[69] Clearly therefore, not only the Amalgamated Engineering Workers' Union or the Engineering Employers' Federation, but also the Trades Union Congress and the Confederation of British Industry fall within those definitions. So does the International Transport Workers' Federation.[70] The point here is that any organisation which satisfies these conditions has a right to be listed, and if the Certification Officer refuses to put it on the appropriate list, it can take the matter to the Employment Appeal Tribunal[71] which, in such a case, must decide not only whether the Certification Officer was right on the law, but also whether he had properly ascertained and interpreted the relevant facts.[72]

The present law, then, makes no attempt to guarantee union democracy, *i.e.* it does not prescribe to any organisation what degree of democratic control it wishes to infuse into its constitu-

---

[66] Trade Union and Labour Relations Act 1974, s. 8(4).

[67] *Ibid.* s. 8(5).

[68] *Ibid.* s. 28(1).

[69] *Ibid.* s. 28(2).

[70] *Camellia Tankers Ltd. S.A.* v. *I.T.W.F.* [1976] I.C.R. 274, at p. 290(C.A.).

[71] Trade Union and Labour Relations Act, s. 8(7); Employment Protection Act 1975, ss. 87, 88. The Employment Appeal Tribunal is a "superior court of record" (Sched. 6, para. 10) to which mandamus does not lie. Neither does it lie to the Certification Officer in view of the availability of the appeal to the Appeal Tribunal. Contrast the situation under the 1871 Act, under which the Registrar's obligation to register was enforced through mandamus: *R.* v. *Registrar of Friendly Societies* (1872) L.R. 7 Q.B. 741, a decision which is now obsolete.

[72] Employment Protection Act 1975, s. 88(3) (*a*). When the Certification Officer acts under the Trade Union Act 1913 or the Trade Union (Amalgamations, etc.) Act 1964, the appeal lies only on questions of law.

tion. It assumes that an organisation has some rules, at any rate if it is to be listed: in that event it must supply them to the Certification Officer[73] and thereby lay them open to public inspection.[74] And even an unlisted organisation is apparently expected to have rules, because the law says[75] that, whether listed or not, it must supply them to any person who asks for them. However, the law does not now (as the Trade Union Act 1871 did[76]) lay down a minimum of matters the rules must regulate (such as the objects on which money may be spent, the conditions under which benefits are paid or fines exacted, the appointment and removal of committees and officers, the manner of amending or rescinding rules, etc.). The Trade Union and Labour Relations Act 1974 contained a provision[77] (inserted by way of opposition amendment against the wishes of the Government) which did say what the rules had to deal with, but it did so in the most elaborate detail, in fact it repeated almost verbatim the relevant clause in the Industrial Relations Act 1971.[78] This provision was repealed by the Amendment Act of 1976,[79] but now the pendulum has swung in the opposite direction, and all vestiges of a prescribed content of the rule book have disappeared. The matter is however not very significant in practice, and this for four reasons. In the first place all unions that matter do in fact have elaborate rule books (if anything some of them are too long rather than too short), and all unions which were, before the coming into force of the 1971 Act, registered under the 1871 Act, or, whether registered or not, were affiliated to the TUC on September 16, 1974, were listed automatically.[80] Secondly, as regards its financial administration, each organisation, whether listed or not, is subject to very detailed statutory provisions,[81] which deal with accounts, accounting records and audit; and each of them must send to the Certification Officer, and thereby make publicly available, an Annual Return of

---

[73] 1974 Act, s. 8(4) (*a*).
[74] 1975 Act, s. 9.
[75] 1974 Act, s. 11(4).
[76] s. 14 and Sched. 1.
[77] s. 6.
[78] Sched. 4.
[79] s. 1(*b*); s. 8(6) of the 1974 Act had to be amended accordingly by a consequential amendment: 1976 Act, s. 1(*c*).
[80] 1974 Act s. 8(2)—except those which did not appear to the Certification Officer to be trade unions or employers' associations. Those registered under the 1971 Act were also automatically listed. The relevant part of the Act came into force on September 16, 1974: Trade Union and Labour Relations Act (Commencement) Order, S.I. 1974 No. 1385.
[81] 1974 Act, ss 10, 11, 12, and Sched. 2, Pt. 1.

its affairs[82]; special provisions apply to members' superannuation funds.[83] Thirdly, no trade union can claim exemption from income tax or other taxes for its provident income and funds, unless the benefit payments to which they are applied are expressly authorised by its rules.[84] And fourthly, as we shall see, the courts are increasingly inclined to use the principles of the common law to ensure that the constitution of an organisation is applied without discrimination, thus, to a limited extent at least, filling any gap which might be opened by the absence of statutory guarantees in this respect.

What, then, is the *raison d'être* of the Certification Officer and his lists? Or, which is the same question, why should any organisation bother to get on to the list at all? To this there are at least four answers. The first two are of importance to employers' associations as well as to trade unions, the third and the fourth (by far the most important ones), do not concern employers' associations in practice. In the first place, it used to be very important in a given case whether an organisation was a trade union or an employers' association or not, and this particularly because if it was, it could not—one exception apart— be made liable in tort,[85] as we shall have to explain in the next chapter. If it is listed, that is in itself evidence that it is a trade union or an employers' association and it can prove that it is listed simply by producing a certificate obtained from the Certification Officer.[86]

Secondly, the machinery for the vesting of union property in newly appointed trustees is very much simpler if the union or employers' organisation is listed than if it is not.[87] All trade unions[88] and many employers' associations are unincorporated associations[89] whose property must be vested in trustees. Hence, if the organisation is listed, the life of those concerned with the technicalities of its property administration is made much easier.

---

[82] *Ibid.* s. 11(2).
[83] *Ibid.* Sched. 2, Pt. 2.
[84] Income and Corporation Taxes Act 1970, s. 338(2), as amended by Finance Act 1974, s. 28(1) (*b*).
[85] 1974 Act, s. 14, now repealed by s.15(1) of the Employment Act 1982.
[86] *Ibid.* s. 8(10).
[87] *Ibid.* s. 4.
[88] Except so-called "special register bodies," *i.e.* (1974 Act, s. 30(1)) certain professional bodies which were companies under the Companies Act 1948 or chartered corporations, and included the regulation of labour relations among their purposes, and were registered in a "special register" under the Industrial Relations Act 1971, s. 84, *e.g.* the British Medical Association, the Royal College of Nursing, the Association of Headmasters.
[89] See below, p. 284.

Thirdly, however—and this is a matter of major importance—the income tax privilege to which we have already referred applies now to listed unions and to them only.[90] A listed union is, under certain conditions, exempt from income tax and corporation tax on income (except trading income) and from capital gains tax if the income or the gain is applicable and applied for purposes of provident benefits, *i.e.* sickness, accident, out of work, old age, or funeral benefit, also compensation for loss of tools. The payment must be expressly authorised by the rules.

Fourthly—and this too is a fundamental point—as we have already seen, it is of central significance whether a trade union is "independent," *i.e.* a real and genuine union or a creature of the employer or employers. In connection with *e.g.* (until recently), union recognition, with rights to union activity, with the operation of the closed shop, this is vital. The law, however, makes it impossible for a union to prove that it is independent, unless it is listed.[91] If it is (and only if it is) it can ask the Certification Officer for a certificate of independence. On such an application he must make the necessary inquiries and either issue the certificate, or, giving his reasons, refuse to do so[92] (in which case the applicant union can appeal to the Employment Appeal Tribunal,[93] whilst, in the event of the certificate being granted, no one, and especially no other union, can appeal[94]). This method of proving its independence is, however, for a union not just one method, but rather it is the only method available by law. If the question of the independence of a union arises in a court, or the Employment Appeal Tribunal or the Central Arbitration Committee, or in an industrial tribunal, or before the ACAS, and there is no certificate of independence, the court, tribunal or authority must stay its proceedings until the Certification Officer has issued a certificate or refused to do so. In such a case the matter may be submitted to him by the court or authority concerned directly.[95] Once a certificate has been issued the matter is conclusively decided, and

---

[90] Income and Corporation Taxes Act 1970, s. 338, in conjunction with Finance Act 1974, s. 28.
[91] Employment Protection Act 1975, s. 8(1) and (4).
[92] *Ibid.* s. 8(5) and (6). Note that (s. 8(3)) all applications for a certificate are, before being disposed of, laid open to public inspection for at least one month so that other unions can raise objections. Once the certificate is granted, however, there is no appeal (*General and Municipal Workers' Union* v. *Certification Officer* [1977] I.C.R. 183, E.A.T.).
[93] *Ibid.* s. 8(9), s. 88(3) (*b*). This appeal can be supported with arguments of law or of fact. See above, p. 213, where the recent case-law is considered.
[94] See n. 92. This is a regrettable gap in the law.
[95] *Ibid.* s. 8(12).

no one can question the union's independence. Conversely, if it is refused, withdrawn or cancelled, the union is precluded from asserting its independence.[96] It is a matter of major importance that this question of the genuineness of a union is withdrawn from the courts and other authorities and that its decision is concentrated in the hands of the Certification Officer under the expert control of the Employment Appeal Tribunal. It must be obvious that these provisions seek to guarantee (as far as this is possible) that labour relations in this country remain free from being distorted by "dependent" unions and thus respond to the challenge of the ILO Convention (No. 98) which condemns interference by either side of labour relations with the other side's organisations.

Compared with the problems of autonomy and of democracy, it is of minor importance whether trade unions and employers' associations are endowed with "corporate personality." Corporate personality is a technical device of the law to ensure that a body of individuals can, as an entity, enter into contracts, own property, be liable in contract and tort, sue and be sued in a court, be prosecuted for an offence, and be subject to the enforcement of judgments. Whether these practical results are achieved through the technique of corporate personality or through some other technique is a matter devoid of general interest. To some extent it is a matter of convenience in property administration and in litigation, but it has nothing to do with the principle of union autonomy. Nevertheless, and somewhat surprisingly, in continental countries legislators and lawyers attach an altogether exaggerated importance to this problem, so that it even appears in one of the relevant ILO Conventions.[97] The present law[98] says that a trade union—except a so-called "special register body"[99]—neither is nor shall be treated as[1] a corporate body—and if by mistake it gets on to the register of companies, or of industrial and provident societies or friendly societies, that registration is void.[2] An employers' association,[3] however, may choose whether or not it

---

[96] *Ibid.* s. 8(11). The certificate is "conclusive evidence" that the union is independent, its refusal, withdrawal or cancellation is conclusive evidence that it is not.

[97] No. 87, Art. 7. The question looms large, *e.g.* in the French books.

[98] Trade Union and Labour Relations Act 1974, s. 2(1).

[99] See above, n. 88, and see for further explanation, Hepple and O'Higgins, *Employment Law* (4th ed., 1981), para. 29.

[1] For the consequences of this formulation see *E.E.T.P.U.* v. *Times Newspapers Ltd.* [1980] 1 All E.R. 1097.

[2] 1974 Act, s. 2(3) and (4).

[3] *Ibid.* s. 3(1).

wants to be incorporated, *i.e.* be a company under the Companies Act or, like a trade union, be an unincorporated association. Trade unions and such employers' associations as are unincorporated have[4] nevertheless full capacity to enter into contracts, to sue and be sued in a civil court and are liable to be prosecuted and subject to the enforcement of civil judgments against them. Their property must vest in trustees holding it on trust for the association—all this by positive provisions of the law which apply to listed and unlisted bodies alike. And, as has been the law since 1871, the common law rules on restraint of trade cannot stand in the way either of the enforcement of a contract to which a trade union or employers' association is a party or of a trust.[5] In this simple way the law solves a problem which in the past gave rise to endless debates, academic and otherwise, to a whole literature and to examination questions without number.[6]

What follows from all this as far as our central problem of democracy and autonomy is concerned? Not only is there nothing in the present law to force democracy down the throat of any union, the law has even largely receded from its earlier insistence on the exercise of the constitution-making power of the unions so as to give an articulate regulation to certain fundamentals. When discussing freedom of organisation, we said that it is a freedom which may have to be protected against employers and also against the unions themselves, and we also said that freedom to organise is meaningless unless it comprises the freedom to be active in the interest of the organisation to which one belongs. We have seen how the law seeks to protect that freedom against interference by the employer, and we have also seen how (within their very limited possibilities) the courts protect the freedom to be a member of a union against the union itself. We must now link the problem of freedom to engage in union activity with that of union autonomy. How far—this is the critical question—does the law guarantee to a union member that freedom and how far does it thereby encroach upon the autonomy of the union? The present statute law is silent, with the notable exceptions of the legislation against race[7] and sex

---

[4] *Ibid.* s. 2(1), s. 3(2).
[5] *Ibid.* s. 2(5), s. 3(5).
[6] For a survey of the controversy see Grunfeld, *Modern Trade Union Law* (1966), Chap. 3. In *Bonsor* v. *Musicians' Union* [1956] A.C. 104 the House of Lords was divided on the question whether and in what sense a registered union had corporate personality, but nevertheless their Lordships arrived at a unanimous conclusion that the union was liable for damages.
[7] Race Relations Act 1976, s. 11(2) (c).

discrimination[8] which precludes an association from unequal treatment of candidates for an office or membership of a committee, or as participants of elections, by reason of race or sex. But otherwise it was left to the courts to prevent arbitrary discrimination in matters such as these, and altogether in all matters concerning the rights arising from membership.

When dealing with the right to membership—the right to remain a member—the courts have, as we have seen, only two avenues of approach towards a prevention of discrimination: one is the enforcement of the union rules themselves, the other is the rule of "natural justice." What applies to the right to membership equally applies to the rights arising from membership. The courts cannot intervene except on these grounds. To impose on a voluntary body any course of conduct is incompatible with its autonomy unless it has itself decided to adopt it or unless it is required by those two cardinal tenets *audi alteram partem* and *nemo judex in sua causa* to which we have referred before. The essential point is that discrimination can be prevented only by ensuring that a union applies the rules it has given to itself, and applies them in the light of the two cardinal rules of natural justice we have mentioned.

Rights arising from membership—as distinct from the right to be a member—can be of three types[9]: they can be rights to participate in the government of the union, rights to share in the services the union performs and the benefits it bestows, and the right not to be interfered with in matters in which the individual should be free to decide. This is no different from the rights of a citizen as a citizen. He too has rights of participation (voting, standing for election, serving on a jury), rights to services and benefits (protection by the police, social security benefits, share in health, education, housing, judicial services) and negative freedoms (from arrest and search, from censorship, etc.). In this country it is only the first of these three emanations of union membership which is liable to lead occasionally to conflicts in practice. Discrimination in benefits does not seem to occur and the question of a members' right to "equal representation"—so central in the United States—has not arisen.[10] A union rule or practice seeking to restrict a member's freedom to institute, prosecute or defend proceedings in court or to give evidence was declared illegal by a—now repealed—

---

[8] Sex Discrimination Act 1975, s. 12(3) (c), provided that in this case as in that of the previous note one interprets discrimination in participation as a "detriment," as one should.

[9] These are the three classical types of "public rights" distinguished by George Jellinek, *System der subjektiven öffentlichen Rechte*, (2nd ed., 1905), pp. 94–193.

[10] *Oddy* v. *TSSA* [1973] I.C.R. 524 (N.I.R.C.) is perhaps an exception.

provision of the Industrial Relations Act,[11] but it seems to be clear that any court would come down with a heavy hand on such an attempt to "oust" the jurisdiction of the courts or to interfere with their procedure. Any such rule would be void as being against public policy, and for the same reason no voluntary body can, however its rules are worded, exclude the ultimate jurisdiction of the courts on matters concerning members' rights.[12] As regards their freedom of political decision, the problem is settled by the Trade Union Act 1913.[13]

As regards participation, however, we must be careful not to go too far in insisting on the analogy with the freedom to engage in union activity enforced against the employer. Any interference by the employer with lawful union activity violates the principle of freedom of organisation, but the role of the union and of its constitution is to determine the activities the individual is called upon to exercise. The union is and must be free—this is a matter of autonomy—to lay down the rules which determine how individuals are selected (not necessarily elected) for this purpose, and to apply them. This process of application of the union's rules, however, may be subject to judicial control, and the individual's freedom to engage in union activity confers upon him, in relation to the union itself, the right to vote and to stand for union office or committee membership, and not to be deprived of either, except in accordance with the constitution of the union and with "natural justice." It is indispensable that the law should to this extent control access to the exercise of power inside the unions. They are an essential part of our Constitution because they are the only organs through which the workers as workers, that is the vast majority of the nation, can participate in the shaping of their own destiny. This cannot mean that each of them shares in the making of decisions, but it must mean that the selection of those who do must be governed by rules and not by procedures invented *ad hoc.* The union must be free—autonomous—in making these rules, but once made they must be applied without discrimination to every member. This is the irreducible minimum of democratic control in trade union law.

In view of the role the unions play in the Constitution, what happens inside each of them has the same public importance as

---

[11] s. 65(10).

[12] See, *e.g. Lee* v. *Showmen's Guild* [1952] 2 Q.B. 329 (C.A.), and, decisively, *Lawlor* v. *Union of Post Office Workers* [1965] Ch. 718; *Leigh* v. *N.U.R.* [1970] Ch. 326. The courts are now constantly acting on this principle which seems to be beyond dispute.

[13] See above, p. 247, n. 40 and the recent decisions there cited.

what happens inside an administrative authority. Hence the courts
are right in applying to internal union decisions the principles
governing the review of discretionary decisions in public
administration,[14] whether the matter in issue is the regularity and
revocability of an election to a union office,[15] the admission of a
member to nomination as a candidate for membership of an
executive council or for the office of union president,[16] the voting
procedure at a national committee,[17] the decision of a district
committee on personal grounds to refuse credentials to a member
elected to be a shop steward,[18] or the disciplinary dismissal of a full
time officer who is also a union member.[19] It is through insisting on
a strict observance of the union's own rules and of the elementary
rules of decency which bear the ancient name of "natural justice"
that the courts can and do make up for the lack of a statutory
guarantee of an equal opportunity to participate in the making of
union decisions. Might one on the other hand not enter a plea to
the courts, and perhaps also now to the industrial tribunals, that
when exercising these important powers of intervention, they
should keep in mind the limits of the individualist perspective on
the relationship between the union and the member, limits
ultimately based in the social claim of the union to function as the
means of expressing and achieving collective goals. If some would
see it as natural for trade unions to subordinate the interests of
individuals to their collective aims, might it not also be kept in
mind that it is all to easy for the courts to view the claims of the
individual member plaintiff as more attractive than those of the
association.[20] These are the extremes which all concerned have a
responsibility to avoid.

---

[14] See the fundamental (though dissenting) judgment of Lord Denning M.R. in
    Breen v. *A.E.U.* [1971] 2 Q.B. 175: the difference of opinion in the Court was
    not on the principles to be applied, but on the interpretation of the evidence.
[15] *Brown* v. *A.E.W.U.* [1976] I.C.R. 147.
[16] *Watson* v. *Smith* [1941] 2 All E.R. 75; *Leigh* v. *N.U.R.* [1970] Ch. 326. See
    Kidner, "The Right to be Candidate for Union Office," (1973) 2 I.L.J. 65.
[17] *Weakley* v. *A.U.E.W.* [1975] C.L.Y. 3453.
[18] *Breen* v. *A.E.U., supra*, n. 35; *Shotton* v. *Hammon et al.* (1976) 120 S.J. 780.
[19] *Taylor* v. *National Union of Seamen* [1967] 1 All E.R. 767; *Stevenson* v. *United
    Road Transport Union* [1977] 1 All E.R. 941 (C.A.).
[20] Consider, for instance, the judgment in *Esterman* v. *NALGO* [1974] I.C.R. 625.
    In *Porter* v. *National Union of Journalists* [1980] I.R.L.R. 404, the House of
    Lords applied the balance of convenience test for deciding whether to grant an
    interlocutory injunction in a manner which made scant concession to the union's
    interest in maintaining an effective disciplinary process. In this they were
    expressing the widespread judicial hostility towards the closed shop as a sanction
    operating in support of internal union discipline.

We have thus described and evaluated the legal regime that has hitherto applied to the internal government of trade unions. We have seen that it has for the most part been shaped by an abstentionist or minimalist approach which tends to maximise the autonomy of trade unions in fashioning their constitutions and conducting their internal affairs. It has been the counterpart of the notion of the collective laissez-faire which used to be thought to represent the approach of the state to collective bargaining. There are clear signs of the development of a far more interventionist and restrictive approach to trade union government, an approach which concerns itself with maximising the claims of the individual worker *vis-à-vis* the union. For some time now, as we have seen, this approach has given rise to policies of controlling and restricting the closed shop. The same approach is now also giving rise to a new interventionism directed towards guaranteeing more effective democracy within trade unions. As we saw in relation to the closed shop, it is an approach based on a model according to which trade unions are seen as tending to coerce the individual into patterns of behaviour to which he may object and to use the power derived from that coercion to achieve an advantage against employers which is seen as distortive of a true balance which would otherwise result from the operation of labour market forces. Hence this approach sees an advantage in individualism as a corrective both to the internal and the external exercise of trade union power; and so far as the internal exercise of power is concerned, individualism is increasingly identified with trade union democracy.

At the time of writing, the Department of Employment has, following the issue early in 1983 of a Green Paper[21] on Trade Unions, announced an intention[22] to propose legislation on democracy in trade unions, to be introduced in the Parliamentary session of 1983–1984, and to deal with the three issues of trade union election, strikes, and the political activities of trade unions. It is intended that the legislation will require elections to the governing bodies of trade unions to comply with the principles that: (i) voting must be secret and by ballot paper; (ii) there must be an equal and unrestricted opportunity to vote; and (iii) every union member should be able to cast his vote directly (rather than, for example, via delegates to a union conference). With regard to strikes, it is proposed that if a trade union orders or endorses industrial action by its members in breach of their contracts of

---

[21] *Democracy in Trade Unions* (Cmnd. 8778, 1983).
[22] House of Commons Statement by the Secretary of State for Employment, Mr. Tebbit, July 12, 1983 (Parly. Debates, H.C., Vol. 45, col. 773).

employment without first consulting those members in a secret ballot, the union should lose immunity from the normal civil law consequences of its action.[23] (It is also intended to "consult in due course" on proposals for loss of immunity for industrial action in breach of adequate procedure agreements in specified essential services). With regard to the political activities of trade unions, it is proposed to amend the 1913 Act to require that political objectives and funds should be submitted to ballot at least every ten years. It is also intended to invite the TUC to discuss arrangements which trade unions themselves might make to ensure that their members are fully aware of their statutory rights to contract out of the political levy and are able to exercise those rights freely and effectively; and a readiness is expressed, if the unions are not willing to make such arrangements, to legislate for this purpose.

The significance of these proposals for the matters discussed in this Chapter is very considerable. We have seen elsewhere in this book in relation to collective bargaining, and we shall see it again in relation to industrial disputes, that a change in the degree of interventionism of our labour laws does not merely result in an increase or decrease in the intensity of legal activity; it also alters the emphasis, the preoccupations, and indeed the whole balance and structure of the labour law system. It is surely a powerful instance of this phenomenon that trade union democracy, which under the abstentionist tradition has always taken a back seat, should come so much to the fore as the basis for the individualistic interventionism that now seems current. It is clear from the proposals just outlined that we are likely in the near future to see measures bearing heavily upon the industrial dispute and collective bargaining activities of the trade unions, and upon their contribution to the party political system and hence to the process of government itself, presented and evaluated in terms of the goal of internal trade union democracy. It is to be questioned whether the existing discourse on this topic is ready to carry the weight that thus may be placed upon it.

---

[23] See below pp. 363 *et seq.*

CHAPTER 8

TRADE DISPUTES AND THE LAW

WE have postponed the discussion of strikes to the end. It is of course a very important subject, but it is not central. To think of industrial relations in terms of strikes or of labour law in terms of strike law is absurd. It is as if one was thinking of commercial relations in terms of insolvency and of commercial law in terms of bankruptcy and compulsory liquidation. Or, if you like, of international relations in terms of war. Lawyers and journalists are prone to see society in terms of pathological situations: it is the pathological situation which produces the "news" as well as the "cases"—but a distorted image is the inevitable result.

There must of course be a strike law; there must also be a law of bankruptcy and a law of war. Industrial stoppages cause losses to the economy, and hardship to men and women. Everyone, except those on the lunatic fringe, wants to reduce their number and magnitude. But people do not go on strike without a grievance, real or imaginary. Sometimes they have ample justification for doing it, sometimes they do it wantonly. The important thing to do is to find out why strikes occur, and to remove their causes. It is more fruitful to promote collective bargaining and collective agreements and their observance than to sharpen the tools of repression. Such repression cannot be dispensed with, but it it is peripheral to the main purpose of labour law which is to redress any disequilibrium of power. This must in the first place be done by regulating its normal exercise, and only in the second place by suppressing its abuse.

More than 30 years ago Lord Wright said in a leading case[1]: "The right of workmen to strike is an essential element in the

---

[1] Lord Wright in *Crofter Harris Tweed* v. *Veitch* [1942] A.C. 435 at p. 463. For a systematic analysis of the problems discussed in this chapter, see K. W. Wedderburn, *The Worker and the Law,* (2nd ed., 1971), Chap. 8, to which we are much indebted; further: Aaron and Wedderburn (eds.), *Industrial Conflict and the Law: A Comparative Legal Survey* (1972); Kahn-Freund and Hepple, *Laws against Strikes,* Fabian Research Series, No. 305 (1972); and, for a survey of the English cases between 1871 and 1966, O'Higgins and Partington, "Industrial Conflict: Judicial Attitudes" (1969) 32 M.L.R. 53.

principle of collective bargaining." This is obvious. If the workers could not, in the last resort, collectively refuse to work, they could not bargain collectively. The power of management to shut down the plant (which is inherent in the right of property) would not be matched by a corresponding power on the side of labour. These are the ultimate sanctions without which the bargaining power of the two sides would lack "credibility." There can be no equilibrium in industrial relations without a freedom to strike. In protecting that freedom, the law protects the legitimate expectation of the workers that they can make use of their collective power: it corresponds to the protection of the legitimate expectation of management that it can use the right of property for the same purpose on its side. There is this important difference between the lockout and the strike: the strike is necessarily a concerted act; the lockout may, but need not be.[2] A single employer can lock out, just as he can be party to a collective agreement; a single worker cannot strike. As has been said before, every unit of management is by definition a "collective" unit.

But strike and lockout have in common that both are a waste of social resources. So is litigation in the courts. But just as the potentiality of litigation is indispensable to social relations in general, so the potentiality of the stoppage is indispensable to industrial relations in particular, and just as it is desirable to restrict to a minimum the actual incidence of litigation, so it is desirable to restrict to a minimum the number and the magnitude of stoppages.

There must be a freedom to strike. As we have said, this is obvious. It is equally obvious that it cannot be unlimited. It cannot be unlimited mainly for three reasons: first, there are cases in which the employer's interest in uninterrupted operation is exceptionally strong (one thinks of a ship on the high seas or in foreign waters; also of the cooling of blast furnaces); secondly, outside parties may need protection (this raises the issue of secondary action to which we shall return presently); thirdly, it may be necessary to ensure that the public obtains the essential supplies and services it needs—a matter of growing importance with the growth of service industries, and also with a rapid cultural change in the concept of what is "essential." The last point raises the problem of emergency legislation. This is not to say that these

---

[2] This is reflected in the definitions of "lockout" and "strike" in the Employment Protection (Consolidation) Act 1978, Sched. 13, para. 24(1)—definitions laid down, however, for the purpose of that schedule only (computation of period of employment).

are the only grounds on which strikes have been suppressed, nor that this has always and everywhere been done on these grounds. But they show why some restriction on the freedom to strike is unavoidable.

A strike may be unlawful by reason of its purpose or by reason of the means used towards its achievement. Thus, a distinction may be made between strikes for better wages and conditions, for union recognition, for the closed shop, for the redress of individual grievances, etc., and also between economic and political strikes. On the other hand, the attitude of the law may differ according as to whether it is an official or a wildcat strike, a strike in accordance with or in breach of existing collective agreements, and whether or not others have been induced to break their contracts, been intimidated, subjected to boycott, or to certain forms of picketing. The technique employed may in each case be criminal punishment, civil injunctions or orders for damages, or administrative measures (*e.g.* withholding of social security benefits). We shall say something about the freedom to strike itself, then about restrictions by reason of the objects of a strike, methods of action prohibited by law, and remedies available against those who use them. Much of what will be said applies to the lockout, but we do not assert that this is systematically the case.

1. THE FREEDOM TO STRIKE

A strike is a concerted stoppage of work. There are other forms of concerted industrial action—go slow, work to rule, overtime ban—but these are not strikes. There are countries, such as France,[3] which strongly insist on the right to strike, but exclude from it acts which, in addition to depriving the employer of the work or of part of the work, seek to saddle him with continued outlay for overheads and payment of wages without getting full value for it. We shall come back to this when discussing lawful and unlawful methods of industrial action. For the moment we are only concerned with the attitude of the law towards the freedom or right to stop work through concerted action.

In trying to define a strike we were careful not to make any reference to trade unions. We associate strikes and trade unions,

---

[3] The go slow (*grève perlée*) is not a lawful strike: see for the case law Sinay, *La Grève* (in Camerlynck's *Traité*, Vol. 6), pp. 201 *et seq.* and *Mise à jour 1979* pp. 56 *et seq.*; Camerlynck et Lyon-Caen, *Droit du Travail, loc. cit.,* (10th ed.) para. 798, p. 756; the strike presupposes a complete cessation of work. The position of the "work to rule" (*grève du zèle*) seems to be as obscure as it is in this country. See generally J.-C. Javillier, *Droit du Travail*, (2nd. ed., 1981), pp. 528–547.

but this is not a necessary association. The freedom to strike can be understood as a freedom of the individual or as a freedom of the organisation. For reasons to which we shall revert in a moment, the former is the prevailing attitude in France and in Italy. In those countries the distinction between "official" and "wildcat" strikes is therefore of minor significance.[4] In this country the Industrial Relations Act—in effect—restricted the freedom to strike to registered trade unions.[5] Contemporary West German law considers every wildcat strike as unlawful[6] (yet such strikes do occur in the Federal Republic). Our present law takes a completely different view: the legality of a strike does not depend on whether it is organised or even authorised by a union. The unofficial strike is not as such unlawful.[7] This is fundamental.

There can be unions which do not in fact authorise strikes. If they go further and renounce their freedom to do so, their credibility as collective bargaining partners may be open to serious doubt. On the other hand, and this is what matters here, there have always been and there will always be strikes organised by amorphous groups that are not trade unions, and spontaneous strikes not organised by anyone at all, or by groups formed ad hoc. There is a case for saying that in a sense trade unions resulted from strikes rather than the other way about.[8] To say the least of it, the question which came first, the union or the strike, is as meaningful as the same question about the chicken and the egg.

From all this it follows, and history shows it, that the law can permit strikes whilst trying to suppress trade unions, and that it can do the opposite. A complete denial or very severe restriction of the freedom to strike in any country may, however, indicate that the pretended freedom of organisation exists only on paper.[9] Nevertheless the freedom to strike and the freedom to organise

---

[4] See Folke Schmidt in Aaron and Wedderburn (eds.), *Industrial Conflict, loc. cit.*, pp. 47 and 55, Aaron, *ibid.*, p. 84.

[5] s. 96.

[6] For the theories of "social adequacy" and of "proportionality" see below.

[7] The subtle distinctions between "official union action," "unofficial union action" and "unauthorised non-union action" made in *Howitt Transport* v. *T.G.W.U.* [1973] I.C.R. 1, 5 became obsolete, but variations on this theme may now be played under the provisions of the 1982 Act. See below, p. 365.

[8] Sidney and Beatrice Webb, *History of Trade Unionism* (1926 ed.), pp. 23 *et. seq.*

[9] This is the view of the ILO Committee of Experts on the Application of Conventions and Recommendations, and of the ILO Governing Body Committee on Freedom of Association; Jenks, *The International Protection of Trade Union Freedom* (1957), pp. 369 *et seq.*; Valticos, *Droit International du Travail* (1970), para. 265.

are different things.[10] This is demonstrated by both French and British history, but, very oddly, in reverse. Freedom to strike in France stems from a law passed in 1864 under Napoleon III,[11] when the penal provisions against strikes were repealed, but, as we have said, the Loi Le Chapelier remained in force until well into the time of the Third Republic, and freedom to organise was not established until its repeal in 1884.[12] Between 1864 and 1884 nobody could be prosecuted for organising, let alone participating in, a strike, but he could (in theory at least) be prosecuted for forming a union. In this country the freedom to organise goes back to the repeal of the Combination Acts in 1824, but it is impossible to say that workers enjoyed an effective freedom to strike for the next half-century, that is, until the passing of the Conspiracy and Protection of Property Act in 1875. This statute can be called one of the foundations of the freedom to strike in this country.

The origin of the Conspiracy and Protection of Property Act 1875 sounds the *leitmotiv* of the history of much of the British law of labour relations: the clash between what the courts declared to be the principles of the common law, and what Parliament declared to be the principles of good social policy—in fact a clash of two policies, or, in the words of a leading Canadian authority "a see-saw vendetta between the courts and the legislature."[13] After the passing of the amended Combination Laws Repeal Act of 1825[14] strikers were frequently prosecuted, partly for offences under the Act itself (which was again amended in 1859)[15] and partly for the common law crime of "combining for the purpose of injuring another."[16] This doctrine of criminal conspiracy was developed by the courts after the repeal of the Combination Acts, though traces of it had existed before.[17] It was to the effect that the combination itself was an offence though the act contemplated by those who combined would not have been an offence if done by an

---

[10] *Collymore* v. *Att. Gen.* [1970] A.C. 538 (P.C.).

[11] Amendment of Arts. 414 and 415 of the Penal Code by the law of May 25, 1864. For details—also of the political background—see Sinay, *loc. cit.*, para. 41, pp. 94 *et seq.*; Durand and Vitu, *Droit du Travail*, Vol. III, pp. 779 *et seq.*

[12] See Chap. 7.

[13] A. W. R. Carrothers, *Collective Bargaining Law in Canada*, p. 57.

[14] See Chap. 7.

[15] Molestation of Workmen Act 1859.

[16] The *locus classicus* is the summing up by Erle J. in *R.* v. *Rowlands* (1851) 5 Cox C.C. 460. See also Sir W. Erle's Memorandum attached to the Eleventh and Final Report of the Royal Commission on Trade Unions (1869) of which he was Chairman.

[17] Holdsworth, *History of English Law*, Vol. VIII, pp. 378 *et seq.*, esp. p. 384.

individual. The result was, to quote the classical presentation by Sir James Fitzjames Stephen[18]:

> "to render illegal all the steps usually taken by workmen to make a strike effective. A bare agreement not to work except upon certain specific terms was, so long as this view of the law prevailed, all that the law permitted to workmen. If a single step was taken to dissuade systematically other persons from working, those who took it incurred the risk of being held to conspire to injure the employer or to conspire to obstruct him in the course of his business."

The element of concerted action—the essence of the strike—became the gist of the crime. A statute passed in 1871[19] (as a result of the Report of the first Royal Commission on Trade Unions[20]) tried to reform the law, but, the year after, Mr. Justice Brett (subsequently Lord Esher) held in *R. v. Bunn*[21] (one of the most momentous English court decisions of the nineteenth century) that the common law doctrine of conspiracy had survived the statute, and two men who had participated in a strike of stokers at a London gas works were convicted and sentenced for conspiracy. To understand the next act of this drama one must remember that in 1867 the urban male workers (who were householders) had obtained the franchise[22] and that the trade unions were beginning to be a political force. At the General Election of 1874 which led to the fall of the Gladstone Government and to its replacement by that of Disraeli, *R. v. Bunn* and the reform of the strike law played an important role,[23] and one of the consequences was the Act of 1875. This provided that two or more persons could not be indicted for conspiracy if the act they agreed or combined to do or to procure would not in itself have been a crime (such as an assault on a foreman or on a strike breaker, an act of sabotage, *i.e.* malicious damage to property, etc.), provided that it was to be done in contemplation or furtherance of a trade dispute.[24]

A century later the use of charges of criminal conspiracy again

---

[18] *History of the Criminal Law of England,* Vol III, p. 218.
[19] Criminal Law Amendment Act 1871.
[20] Eleventh and Final Report of the Royal Commission on Trade Unions 1869.
[21] (1872) 12 Cox 316.
[22] Representation of the People Act 1867.
[23] Clegg, Fox and Thomson, *History of British Trade Unions,* Vol. I, p. 45. On the political aspects of the Act, see Blake, *Disraeli,* p. 555; Webb, *History of Trade Unionism,* pp. 284 *et seq.,* and on the agitation during the General Election of 1874, pp. 286 *et seq.*
[24] Conspiracy and Protection of Property Act 1875, s. 3.

became a matter of public controversy. Within the area of trade disputes the objection was that more severe penalties were available for an agreement to commit an offence than for the offence itself.[25] Perhaps the main impetus for reform came, however, from outside the area of labour law where the principle applied by Mr. Justice Brett had not been restricted by the 1875 Act. After lengthy consideration,[26] the Government of the day in the Criminal Law Act 1977 generalised the principle of the 1875 Act so as to provide that in all cases of criminal conspiracy, guilt is incurred only if the course of conduct agreed upon will necessarily involve the commission of an offence[27]; and section 3 of the 1875 Act was repealed[28] as being redundant. The 1977 Act also limits the maximum punishment by way of imprisonment on conviction for conspiracy to the maximum term availble for the intended offence.

War legislation[29] and some exceptions (*e.g.* picketing[30]) apart, Disraeli's Act of 1875 removed the criminal law from the scene of industrial relations. This, one would have thought, was based on the view subsequently expressed by Stephen[31] that:

> "it is difficult to see how, in a case of a conflict of interests, it is possible to separate the objects of benefiting yourself and injuring your antagonist. Every strike is in the nature of an act of war. Gain on one side implies loss on the other, and to say that it is lawful to combine to protect your interests, but unlawful to combine to injure your antagonist, is taking away with one hand a right given with the other."

A few years later the same argument was taken up by Oliver Wendell Holmes in his celebrated dissenting opinion in the

---

[25] *R.* v. *Jones* [1974] I.C.R. 310 (C.A.).

[26] Law Commission, *Conspiracy and Criminal Law Reform* (Law Comm. No. 76, 1976).

[27] Criminal Law Act 1977, s. 1(1). However, a vestige of the special trade dispute protection remains in s. 1(3) which requires courts to ignore summary offences not punishable with imprisonment where the acts agreed upon are to be done in contemplation or furtherance of a trade dispute. This re-enacts the equivalent concession in s. 3 of the 1875 Act. Section 5 of the 1977 Act also retains some aspects of the common law of conspiracy, but these are not likely to be relevant to labour law.

[28] But only in England and Wales. The relevant sections of the Criminal Law Act 1977 do not apply in Scotland, where section 3 of the 1875 Act accordingly remains in force.

[29] *e.g.* S.R. & O. 1940 No. 1305—see above, Chap. 5.

[30] Conspiracy and Protection of Property Act 1875, s. 7; see below p. 346.

[31] *Loc. cit.,* p. 219.

Supreme Judicial Court of Massachusetts in *Vegelahn* v. *Guntner*.[32]

If the policy of the Act of 1875 was based on this view it was subsequently frustrated by the courts. Towards the end of the century and at the beginning of the twentieth century the same doctrine of conspiracy which the statute had scotched in the criminal law re-appeared in the law of torts.[33] This meant that those who acted on a combination or agreement to do something deemed by the court to be injurious to the public interest could be ordered to pay damages and, by an injunction, not to take the action or to stop it, or else suffer the penalties of contempt of court. In theory there is a big difference between the criminal law and the law of tort. In practice the difference is small: it is whether you go to prison by reason of conviction for a criminal offence or by reason of contempt of court. Committal for contempt may in fact be much more serious than conviction for an offence.

The law of torts, especially, but not only, the law of civil conspiracy, appears on the scene of labour relations in the 1890s,[34] that is, when after the turning point of the Dock Strike of 1889,[35] trade unions began to develop among the unskilled, and—particularly important—among the transport, including the railway, workers.[36] In a series of cases decided between 1893 and 1905[37] men involved in certain types of strike action were held liable for civil conspiracy, or for inducing others, especially fellow workers, to break their contracts. At one time there was an inclination to hold liable anyone who interfered with someone else's "freedom to dispose of his capital or labour," but the House of Lords put an end to this in 1897.[38] On the other hand in 1964[39]

---

[32] (1896) 167 Mass. 92; N.E. 1077.

[33] In *Quinn* v. *Leathem* [1901] A.C. 495 the House of Lords held that the 1875 Act had no effect on the tort of conspiracy. See *per* Lord Lindley at p. 542.

[34] *Temperton* v. *Russell* [1893] 1 Q.B. 715 (C.A.); see esp. the judgment of Lord Esher M.R.—the former Mr. Justice Brett—at p. 728. This appears to be the first case in which the doctrine of civil conspiracy was applied in labour relations. It initiated the development that led to the Trade Disputes Act 1906, just as the decision of the same judge in *R.* v. *Bunn* (1872), *supra*, n. 21, had initiated the development that led to the 1875 Act.

[35] Clegg, Fox and Thomson, *loc. cit.*, pp. 55 *et seq.*

[36] Webb, *History of Trade Unionism*, pp. 405 *et seq.*

[37] The most important cases were: *Temperton* v. *Russell* [1893] 1 Q.B. 715 (C.A.); *Taff Vale Railway* v. *Amalgamated Society of Railway Servants* [1901] A.C. 426; *Quinn* v. *Leathem* [1901] A.C. 495; *Giblan* v. *National Amalgamated Labourers' Union* [1903] 2 K.B. 600 (C.A.); *South Wales Miners' Federation* v. *Glamorgan Coal Co.* [1905] A.C. 239.

[38] *Allen* v. *Flood* [1898] A.C. 1, see below.

[39] *Rookes* v. *Barnard* [1964] A.C. 1129.

the House of Lords discovered the tort of intimidation by threatening to break a contract, and this was added to the list of types of action for which those preparing a strike could be made liable, but this was not yet known at the turn of the century. The situation was aggravated by the decision—this was the famous *Taff Vale* case of 1901[40]—that a registered union was liable to pay damages from its funds for torts committed by those acting on its behalf.

One of the most dramatic aspects of this story is how about a quarter of a century after the General Election of 1874 and the passing of the Act of 1875 a very similar scene was enacted, this time laid in the land of the law of torts, with the *dramatis personae* having changed their roles. This time the necessary reform resulted from a defeat—in 1906—of the Conservatives by the Liberals, coupled with the first appearance of the Labour Party in the Commons. The Trade Disputes Act of 1906[41] did for the law of civil conspiracy what the Act of 1875 had done for the law of criminal conspiracy. It also laid down that no one could be sued for a tort by reason of having induced someone else to break his contract of employment,[42] provided he had acted in contemplation or furtherance of a trade dispute, words which were for the first time defined in the Act.[43] Moreover, trade unions (registered or not) were exempted from tort liability altogether, or practically so.[44] The Act also dealt with the problem of picketing.[45]

This was the second pillar supporting the freedom to strike. The Act of 1875 protected it against criminal prosecution, the 1906 Act against civil action. That protection, as subsequent developments showed, was by no means complete, but when in 1964 the House of Lords held[46] that the 1906 Act did not cover the tort of intimidation by threatening a breach of contract, Parliament passed in the following year a statute[47] to stop the gap. This was

---

[40] See above, n. 37.

[41] s. 1, repealed by the Industrial Relations Act 1971, but re-enacted now, in a modified form, in the Trade Union and Labour Relations Act 1974, s. 13(4).

[42] s. 3. See now s. 13(1) (*a*) of the 1974 Act, as amended by s. 3(2) of the Amendment Act of 1976. The 1906 Act also dealt with the tort of "interference" which, in *Allen* v. *Flood,* the House of Lords had held not to exist (see *supra*, n. 38). See s. 13(2) of the 1974 Act, repealed in 1982.

[43] s. 5. Now s. 29 of the 1974 Act, as amended by s. 1(*d*) of the Act of 1976 and by the 1982 Act. See below.

[44] s. 4. Later s. 14 of the 1974 Act, repealed in 1982.

[45] s. 2. See now s. 15 of the 1974 Act, amended in 1980.

[46] *Rookes* v. *Barnard, supra.*

[47] Trade Disputes Act 1965, repealed, but in substance re-enacted in s. 13(1) (*b*) of the 1974 Act, as amended by s. 3(2) of the 1976 Act.

passed by a Labour majority: the statutes which in effect were the foundation of the freedom to strike were passed by Conservative, Liberal, and Labour majorities in 1875, 1906, and 1965 respectively.

However, more recently the simple picture of a "vendetta between the courts and the legislature" has become complicated by the appearance of Parliament, when under the control of Conservative majorities, in the role of restricting the immunity of workers and unions from civil liabilities in connection with industrial action. Thus, the Conservative Government of 1970 to 1974 passed the Industrial Relations Act 1971 and the Conservative Government, elected in 1979, the Employment Acts 1980 and 1982, whilst the intervening Labour Government attempted to restore the legislative framework established by the Acts of 1875, 1906 and 1965 in the Trade Union and Labour Relations Acts 1974 to 1976. The approaches to labour law reform in 1971 and 1980 were, however, rather different ones. The Industrial Relations Act represented a new and comprehensive statutory framework of labour law. As part of the new design, the common law liabilities were excluded where defendants had acted in contemplation or furtherance of an "industrial dispute," but in their place were established statutory "unfair industrial practices." Some of these "unfair industrial practices"—and indeed the ones that proved most controversial in the Act's brief life—were based on common law notions of inducing breach of contract,[48] but others were aimed at the purposes of the industrial action, such as action to upset a recognition order made by the National Industrial Relations Court[49] or to compel an employer to enter into a closed shop agreement declared void by the Act.[50] However, the difficulties encountered in enforcing these statutory liabilities, first against individual shop stewards and then against trade unions as vicariously liable for the acts of their members,[51] led to disillusion

---

[48] Industrial Relations Act 1971, ss. 96 and 98.

[49] *Ibid.* s. 55(3).

[50] *Ibid.* s. 33(3) (6).

[51] *Midland Cold Storage* v. *Turner* [1972] I.C.R. 230 (N.I.R.C.); *Midland Cold Storage* v. *Steer* [1972] I.C.R. 435; *Churchman* v. *Joint Shop Stewards' Committee* [1972] I.C.R. 222 (C.A.); *Heatons Transport (St. Helens) Ltd.* v. *T.G.W.U.* [1972] I.C.R. 285, 308 (H.L.); *General Aviation Services (U.K.) Ltd.* v. *T.G.W.U.* [1976] I.R.L.R. 225 (H.L.); *Con-Mech (Engineers) Ltd.* v. *A.U.E.W.* [1973] I.C.R. 620, [1974] I.C.R. 332, 464 (N.I.R.C.). The literature on this fateful period is extensive, but see especially Weekes, Mellish, Dickens and Lloyd, *Industrial Relations and the Limits of Law* (1975), Chaps. 4 and 7; Thomson and Engleman, *The Industrial Relations Act* (1975), Chap. 5; Davies,

even within the Conservative party with the new approach embodied in the Act, and it was repealed by the Labour Government elected in 1974.

Disillusion within Conservative Party ranks with the 1971 Act survived sufficiently long and sufficiently strongly to influence significantly the shape of the Employment Acts, which have two points of distinction from the earlier Act. First, they are not an attempt at comprehensive reform, but only at reform of the law relating to a limited number of what were perceived by the Government as abuses of trade union power. In relation to the law of industrial conflict this meant, however, rather extensive changes; in particular, reform of the law concerning picketing and secondary industrial action and the liability of trade unions as such. Second, the method of reform chosen was to accept the existing structure of the legal rules but then, by amendment, to shift the balance of advantage within that structure away from trade unions and workers. Thus, in the area of industrial conflict, no statutory "unfair industrial practices" are introduced; but in the case of picketing and secondary industrial action and elsewhere the extent of the statutory protections against the underlying common law liabilities arising out of the economic torts has been sharply reduced, as we shall see below.

Because the legislators in the 1980 and 1982 Acts sought to remain within the legislative framework of industrial conflict law established by the Trade Union and Labour Relations Acts 1974 to 1976, which themselves aimed to restore the principles of the Acts of 1875, 1906 and 1965, there is a continuity in the approach of our law to this topic over a period of more than a century, with the possible exception of the period 1971 to 1974. The statutory framework may have been more or less liberal, more or less restrictive, at different times over that century, but the continuity has existed in the form in which the freedom to strike appears in the statute book. In other countries, and also in international conventions such as the European Social Charter[52] (not in any of the ILO conventions), that freedom is expressed in positive terms,

---

(1973) 36 M.L.R. 78; Hepple, "Union Responsibility for Shop Stewards" (1972) 1 I.L.J. 197; Wedderburn, (1973) 36 M.L.R. 226 and (1974) 37 M.L.R. 187; Davies and Anderman, "Injunction Procedure in Labour Disputes—II" (1974) 3 I.L.J. 30; Lewis "Con-Mech: Showdown for the N.I.R.C." (1974) 3 I.L.J. 201.

[52] Art. 6, para. 4, ratified by the United Kingdom. Art. 8(1)(d) of the International Covenant on Economic, etc. Rights 1966, guarantees the right to strike provided it is exercised in conformity with the laws of the particular country.

as a freedom, sometimes, as in the French[53] and Italian[54] Constitutions, as a "right" to strike.[55] In this country it appears in the form of immunities and, until recently, of privileges. There is no rule proclaiming this freedom; there is merely a series of exceptions from rules of the common law, as it was held by the courts to exist. We shall see how very important this is from a practical point of view.[56]

No country suppresses the freedom to strike in peace time, except dictatorships, and countries practising active racial discrimination. Yet there are wide differences in detail. Let us single out three problems. How far have public servants the right to strike? How far is that freedom restricted to ensure that, in view of the nature of the work or of the services withheld, its exercise does not create excessive injury to the employer or to third parties? How far is it limited in case of emergencies?

On the question[57] whether (and what) public servants have the freedom to strike, otherwise closely related legal systems may differ most fundamentally. Thus, both German and French law consider as enjoying a special status those public servants who are called *Beamte*[58] or *fonctionnaires*,[59] words untranslatable into English for the reason that the concept itself is based on an historical development in which this country and the United States

---

[53] Preamble to the Constitution of 1946 which is incorporated in the present Constitution of 1958.

[54] Art. 40 of the Constitution of 1947.

[55] The Bonn Basic Law which (see above. Chap. 7) guarantees in Art. 9, para. 3, the freedom of organisation did not originally contain any reference to the right to strike (whereas two of the *Länder* Constitutions, Bremen and Hessen, do). However, in 1968 Art. 9, para. 3, was amended so as to add a provision by which certain emergency measures may not be directed against industrial action (*Arbeitskämpfe*) taken by organisations on either side for the protection and development of conditions of employment and economic activity (*zur Wahrung und Förderung der Arbeits-und Wirtschaftsbedingungen*). This formula is in some respects narrower and in others wider than the British formula "in contemplation or furtherance of a trade dispute."

[56] The implications of this form of expressing the legal rules are brilliantly analysed by Lord Wedderburn of Charlton, "Industrial Relations and the Courts" (1980) 9 I.L.J. 65. The consultative document, *Trade Union Immunities*, Cmnd. 8128, 1981 (Chap. 4), discusses "an alternative system of positive rights," but makes only modest claims for such an approach.

[57] For a comparative analysis see Wedderburn in Aaron and Wedderburn, *Industrial Conflict, loc cit.*, pp. 364 *et seq.*

[58] This is well explained in W. H. McPherson, *Public Employee Relations in West Germany*, Institute of Labor and Industrial Relations, University of Michigan (1971), pp. 32 *et seq.*

[59] Durand and Jaussaud, *Droit du Travail*, Vol. I (1947), para. 174 *bis*, para 176, pp. 222 *et seq.*, pp. 226–227.

did not participate. The term "established public servant" vaguely indicates what is meant, but gives no inkling of the aura of sacrosanctity which surrounds the status of a *Beamter* in Germany. The *Beamte* is a bearer of "governmental authority" and his status carries with it a special relation of submission and therefore of fidelity to the State. With this the idea of a strike is generally held to be incompatible.[60] But although the French *fonctionnaire* is very similar to the German *Beamter,* there is no doubt that he has the freedom to strike,[61] although subject to considerable restrictions imposed by administrative regulations and recent legislation.[62] In this country public servants, whether established civil servants or not, have never been subjected to any special disabilities in this respect,[63] except the members of the police[64] and of the armed forces, and possibly those of the postal services.[65] One must, however, remember that a servant of the Crown used, in theory, to be able to be dismissed at will, however unreal this principle might look in practice.

Restrictions on the freedom to strike by reason of a person's status must be carefully distinguished from those imposed by reason of the functions a person exercises at a given moment, the nature of the services he renders or the consequences to the community of a stoppage. Thus two major exceptions from the freedom to strike can be explained from the nature of the services rendered by the workers. Seamen aboard and seamen abroad have

---

[60] For a full conspectus of the case law and the very considerable literature and of the numerous variations of this theme, see the excellent monograph by Wolfgang Däubler, *Der Streik im öffentlichen Dienst* (1970), pp. 24–30, and especially Ramm, *Das Koalitions- und Streikrecht der Beamten* (1970), pp. 24–30. The prevailing view is succinctly formulated by Nipperdey (Hueck-Nipperdey, *Grundriss des Arbeitsrechts* (4th. ed., 1968) para. 69, III) who says that *Beamte* have no right to strike and that this follows from the relation of fidelity based on public law which links the *Beamte* with the State.

[61] It was recognised by the Conseil d'Etat in the leading case of *Dehaene,* July 7, 1950, D. 1950, 538.

[62] On the complex *jurisprudence* of the Conseil d'Etat, and on the law of July 31, 1963 and subsequent regulations, see Javillier, *op. cit.,* pp. 539–547.

[63] See the very interesting evidence of H.M. Treasury to the Royal Commission, Minutes No. 10, December 14, 1965, Questions 1615–1672. And see Hepple and O'Higgins, *Public Employee Trade Unionism in the United Kingdom* (Institute of Labor and Industrial Relations, University of Michigan, 1971), pp. 175 *et seq.*

[64] Police Act 1964, s. 53.

[65] The Post Office Act 1953, s. 58, forbids any officer of the Post Office, contrary to his duty, wilfully to detain or delay, or procure or suffer to be detained or delayed, any postal packet. Is this directed against strikes or only against the go-slow, work to rule, etc.? See Hepple and O'Higgins, *loc. cit.* p. 176, n. 58.

no freedom to strike. A seaman is by statute[66] entitled to terminate his employment in a ship by leaving it in contemplation or furtherance of a trade dispute after 48 hours' notice, but only if at the time of the notice "the ship is in the United Kingdom and securely moored in a safe berth." These provisions and some others[67] on discipline on board etc. restrict the seaman's freedom to strike. There are provisions of this kind in other countries too,[68] and on principle they can be explained from the nature of the sea service. The other exception to the freedom to strike has a much wider scope. Anyone, employer or worker, commits a criminal offence if he breaks a contract of employment (*e.g.* by a sudden strike or lockout) and knows or has reasonable cause to believe that, as a result, human life is likely to be in danger, serious bodily injury is likely to be caused or valuable property is likely to be exposed to destruction or serious injury.[69] This has been on the statute book for more than a century, but no one who gave evidence to the Donovan Commission had heard of a prosecution under this provision. This, incidentally, does not mean that such provisions are useless.

As a result of some recent disputes in the public services, *e.g.* in the civil service in 1981, in the health service in 1982 and in the water industry in 1983 renewed attention has been given to proposals in the Green Paper, *Trade Union Immunities* (1981),[70] to restrict the right to strike, either of certain groups of workers or where the industrial action has certain consequences. This would

---

[66] Merchant Shipping Act 1970, s. 42, (as amended by Trade Union and Labour Relations Act 1974, Scheds. 3, 5). The Act was the result of the Pearson Report, the Final Report of the Court of Inquiry into certain matters concerning the Shipping Industry, Cmnd. 3211, 1967. See its para. 328.

[67] s. 30, as amended by Merchant Shipping Act 1974, s. 19(4); s. 34, as amended by Merchant Shipping Act 1974, s. 19(5). s. 29 and s. 31 of the 1970 Act were repealed by s. 19(3) of the Merchant Shipping Act 1974.

[68] All such provisions raise the problem of compatibility with the ILO Convention concerning Forced or Compulsory Labour of 1930 (No. 29) and with the Convention concerning the Abolition of Forced Labour of 1957 (No. 105). See Valticos, *Droit International du Travail* (Camerlynck's *Traité*, Vol. 8), para. 288, p. 285. Similar problems arise under Art. I(2) of the European Social Charter.

[69] Conspiracy and Protection of Property Act 1875, s. 5, not applicable to seamen. The special provisions which were applicable by s. 4 of the 1875 Act to public utility (gas, water, electricity) workers were repealed by Sched. 9 of the Industrial Relations Act 1971.

[70] Cmnd. 8128, 1981, paras. 306–338. On July 12, 1983 the Secretary of State for Employment announced in the House of Commons that he intended to "consult on the need for industrial relations in specified essential services to be governed by adequate procedure agreements, breach of which would deprive industrial action of immunity." H.C. Deb., Vol. 45, Col. 773.

amount to a generalisation of principles which hitherto have played only a minor role in the law of industrial conflict, as is witnessed by the very small number of workers at present in Britain who do not benefit from the full protection of the trade dispute immunities and by the relative unimportance in practice of section 5 of the 1875 Act. Nevertheless, it is clear that the search for methods of settling pay disputes in the public sector that are neither inflationary nor productive of industrial conflict is becoming increasingly important for the success of governmental economic policies. There is thus a growing temptation for government to introduce into English law some type of general restriction upon the right to strike of public employees. As we have seen, such restrictions are well established in France, Germany and (in a different way) in America. However, in those countries the restrictions, which are of long standing, derive from old-fashioned notions of the sovereignty of the state and are in the course of being relaxed.[71] English law has always been able to distinguish between the state as legislator and the state as employer. The new proposals suggest that English law may soon find it difficult to distinguish between the state as employer and the state as the protector of the public interest.

But this leaves us with the problem of emergencies.[72] No government can stand by idly if the people are exposed to starvation owing to a stoppage in the supply of food. But this is not all. Modern life, especially urban life and its complexities, make it impossible to restrict emergency legislation to the crude case of a threat of actual starvation. It may have to intervene where the population is, to use the clear if clumsy phrase of the statute,[73] deprived of the "means of locomotion". "Locomotion" by railway or road vehicle, and also vertically, by lift, is an essential of life. So is, of course, the distribution of fuel, light and water. All this is included in the definition of an "emergency" in the Emergency Powers Act of 1920 which—except for the brief interlude of the Industrial Relations Act 1971[74]—has for more than half a century been our only source of law on this matter. This definition of an "emergency" is very difficult. What is an emergency in one country is not necessarily an emergency in another; one of the

---

[71] For the U.S.A. see Smith, Edwards and Clark, *Labor Relations Law in the Public Sector* (1974), especially Chap. 1. For France and Germany see nn. 60 and 62 above.
[72] For detailed comparative discussion see Wedderburn in Aaron and Wedderburn (eds.), *Industrial Conflict, loc. cit.,* pp. 342 *et seq.*
[73] Emergency Powers Act 1920, s. 1(1).
[74] ss. 138–145.

most dire threats to the life of the community in this country is a dock strike, but the United States can contemplate a strike of the "longshoremen" with slightly greater equanimity. A threat to public order can of course also cause an emergency but this does not raise any particular issue connected with labour disputes. Physical violence, riots and that sort of thing must be checked by the law, whoever adopts such behaviour and for whatever reason. We are concerned with economic emergencies.

Our Act of 1920 and the American Taft-Hartley Act of 1947 differ in the definition of an emergency, and, far more fundamentally, in the techniques used to protect the community from its consequences. The 1920 definition[75] is strictly in terms of actual or impending

> "events of such a nature as to be calculated, by interfering with the supply and distribution of food, water, fuel, or light, or with the means of locomotion, to deprive the community, or a substantial proportion of it, of the essentials of life."

The American definition of an emergency is a "threatened or actual strike or lockout" which "will, if permitted to occur or to continue, imperil the national health or safety."[76] Through the reference to safety this covers situations not within the British Act of 1920, such as (possibly) a steel strike[77] which may imperil safety, but not health. Neither definition covers purely economic disadvantages to the nation. Altogether, even on a wide interpretation, comparatively few strikes are likely to come within either definition, but those that do are apt to be of major importance, not necessarily because of the number of workers involved, but as regards the actual or potential consequences.[78]

The two enactments use different methods in coping with these emergencies. The Act of 1920 seeks to secure the essentials of life

---

[75] The definition was amended by the Emergency Powers Act 1964, which substituted the reference to "events" for that to human action so as to cover emergencies caused by natural disasters, such as a catastrophic flood.

[76] Labor-Management Relations Act, s. 206, restricted—so as to comply with the constitutional limitation of the legislative power of Congress—to strikes and lockouts in industries engaged in interstate and foreign commerce, but in view of the wide interpretation the Supreme Court has given to the Interstate Commerce Clause of the Constitution, this covers the major part of the economy. Similar (but not identical) provisions apply under the Railway Labor Act 1926, as amended; this also covers air transport.

[77] This was the great and enormously controversial problem of *United Steelworkers* v. *U.S.*, 361 U.S. 39 (1969).

[78] The repealed emergency provisions in the Industrial Relations Act 1971 used a very much more comprehensive definition.

to the community[79] and this is the object of the regulations the Government can make on the basis of a royal proclamation of emergency. For this purpose they can do all sorts of things: requisition goods or premises, regulate prices, send in the troops to perform essential services, etc., but they cannot[80] make it a criminal offence to participate in a strike or to persuade others to do so. Nor does the Act provide for an injunction against the strikers or their leaders. It is of course an intended by-product of a proclamation of emergency that the effectiveness of the strike as an economic weapon is reduced, and sometimes the threat of a proclamation or the mere proclamation (without its use for the making of regulations) is enough to put an end to a strike. But the professed object of a proclamation of emergency is not to get the strikers back to work, but to alleviate the injurious consequences of their action.

The Taft-Hartley Act, however, imposes a "cooling-off period" during which the strikers may not quit or must return so that an attempt can be made to settle the dispute. This is preceded by a fact-finding inquiry initiated by the President.[81] On receiving the report (which must not contain any recommendations for settlement)[82] an injunction can be obtained by the Attorney-General forbidding the strike or ordering the strikers back to work,[83] and the parties must then try to settle the matter.[84] If this does not happen within sixty days, the National Labor Relations Board organises within the next fifteen a ballot among the workers on whether or not to accept the employer's last offer. After a further five days the ban on the strike is lifted. During this cooling-off period of eighty days the public is constantly informed about the progress (or lack of progress) of the matter: this is a deliberate attempt to mobilise public opinion for a settlement. In one sense these provisions were reasonably successful[85]: the large

---

[79] s. 2(1). On the practice of the use of troops in industrial disputes, see C. J. Whelan, "Military Intervention in Industrial Disputes" (1979) 8 I.L.J. 222.

[80] *Ibid.* Second Proviso.

[81] Labor-Management Relations Act, s. 206.

[82] This is different under the Railway Labor Act.

[83] Labor-Management Relations Act, s. 208.

[84] *Ibid.* s. 209.

[85] L. H. Silberman, "National Emergency Disputes—The Considerations Behind the Legislative Proposal" (1970) 4 *Georgia Law Review* 673: in his article the author also investigates the success or failure of the corresponding provisions under the Railway Labor Act and seems to affirm the conclusion of a committee of the Section of Labor Relations Law of the American Bar Association which in 1966 reported that the "efficacy" of these provisions had "diminished almost to vanishing point." (Summers and Wellington, *Labor Law,* p. 836).

majority of the cases in which the procedure was used between 1947 and 1972 were settled during or after the cooling-off period. In another sense they were a failure: there was not a single case of a ballot in which the workers accepted the employer's last offer: across the Atlantic this ballot looks like a rather futile ceremony. Did those who drafted these (otherwise not at all unreasonable) provisions really expect that the workers would vote against the leaders of their unions? The two Canadian provinces of Alberta and British Columbia which have—or at one time had—similar strike ballot provisions, had the same experience. The only effect of such provisions is to make it more difficult for the union leaders to arrive at a settlement.[86]

The emergency provisions of the Industrial Relations Act 1971 which included the cooling-off period and the strike ballot were used by the government on one occasion,[87] but no settlement was achieved during the cooling-off period and the compulsory ballot resulted in an overwhelming vote to continue industrial action. After that, no more was heard of these emergency provisions.

2. LAWFUL AND UNLAWFUL PURPOSES

(a) Two approaches

One can see strikes and the freedom to strike in two different perspectives. On one view the power to use and to withhold one's labour is a fundamental human freedom of the individual. It is available for all purposes not contrary to law, just as one can use one's property as one likes, except where the law forbids it. Hence workers are entitled to withdraw their labour by concerted action for any lawful object, even one having nothing to do with labour relations, *e.g.* to exercise political pressure, to demonstrate against measures taken by the Government or by others, and also of course for any purpose connected with their relations with management. But the industrial purposes are, on this view, only incidental and not essential to this freedom. This attitude belongs to the political and to some extent the legal traditions of, *e.g.*

---

[86] See Anton, *The Role of the Government in the Settlement of Labour Disputes*, pp. 201 *et seq.*

[87] The railway dispute in the Spring of 1972, *Secretary of State for Employment* v. *A.S.L.E.F.* [1972] 2 Q.B. 443, 455; [1972] I.C.R. 7, 19 (N.I.R.C. and C.A.). See also Thomson and Engleman, *op. cit.,* pp. 114–118.

Italy,[88] and also of France,[89] although the courts there do not act on this principle, in so far as political strikes are concerned.[90]

It is not the attitude which has ever prevailed in this country, or, as far as one can see, in the United States, or in Germany. Here the strike is seen as the ultimate sanction available to the workers in labour relations, and linked with collective bargaining and with grievances at the place of work. This seems to be the general doctrine underlying all our relevant legislation, from the Conspiracy and Protection of Property Act of 1875 to the recent statutes, and clearly also such American legislation as the Norris-La Guardia Act of 1932.[91] It does not have to go to the length to which this doctrine has been driven in Western Germany. There a principle has been developed over the last 25 years, originally known as the principle of "social adequacy"[92] and now[93] in a modified form as that of "proportionality." A strike is *ipso facto* a civil delict (tort) giving rise to liability for damages, unless it is conducted in the absence of an existing collective agreement and after the failure of negotiations by a party capable of entering into a collective agreement against a party capable of doing so and with the aim of achieving an agreement. This narrows the range of

---

[88] Giugni, *Diritto Sindicale* (1969), p. 173: The strike is recognised to be a means towards the development of the human personality of the worker and towards the advancement of the effective participation of the workers in the organisation of the economic and social relations within which they work. Also p. 176: The right to strike belongs to the *"diritti pubblici di libertà."* This appears to be generally accepted in Italy. See also Riva Sanseverino, *Diritto Sindicale, loc. cit.*, para. 165, p. 425; Mazzoni, *Rapporti Collettivi di Lavoro,* pp. 292 *et seq.* and *Public Prosecutor* v. *Antenaci* (1974/5) 1 I.L.L.R. 51 (*Corte Constituzionale*).

[89] Sinay, *La Grève* (Camerlynck's *Traité*, Vol. 6), paras. 30–32, esp. pp. 56 *et seq.*

[90] *Ibid.* para. 82 *bis–*88, pp. 179 *et seq.*, esp para. 85, p. 187 and *Mise à jour 1979* pp. 54 *et seq.* The leading case is Cass. Soc., March 23, 1953, D. 1954, 89. See Javillier, *op. cit.*, p. 531.

[91] Norris-La Guardia (Anti-Injunction) Act 1932, which (s. 1) is restricted to cases "involving or growing out of a labor dispute." The definition of a "labor dispute" in s. 13 (*c*) is by no means identical with that of a "trade dispute" in the Trade Union and Labour Relations Acts 1974–1976, but the differences are of detail, not of principle. In the Labor-Management Relations Act, s. 13, the word "right" clearly denotes the "freedom" to strike.

[92] This is judge-made law, based mainly on the decision of the Great Senate of the Federal Labour Court of Jan. 28, 1955 (B.A.G.E. 1,291). For a succinct statement of the theory of "social adequacy," see Hueck-Nipperdey, *Grundriss,* para. 70, V (pp. 291–295). For a sharp criticism, Ramm, *Der Arbeitskampf und die Gesellschaftsordnung des Grundgesetzes* (1965), pp. 38 *et seq.*

[93] Leading decision of the Great Senate of the Federal Labour Court of April 21, 1971 (B.A.G.E. 23, 292). See also the decisions of the Federal Labour Court of June 10, 1980, applying the principle of proportionality to defensive lockouts (B.A.G.E. 33, 140; 33, 185; and 33, 195).

lawful strike purposes in a way which has never been accepted in this country or, as far as one can see, in the United States, in Canada or in Australia. It renders unlawful a strike conducted by workers on the shop floor, *e.g.* to induce the employer to comply with safety regulations.

The difference between the approaches to the strike as a sanction in labour relations and as a fundamental human right is not a mere matter of political theory, nor is its practical importance restricted to the political strike. If the worker has a "right" to strike, he has more than a mere "freedom" from criminal or civil liability or administrative intervention. He has a positive right which he cannot bargain away, especially not by the contract of employment. The exercise of the right has priority over any contractual obligations he may have incurred, and, as we shall see presently, this may have important practical consequences.

The United Kingdom has ratified the provision of the European Social Charter[94] by which the States Members of the Council of Europe "recognise the right of workers and employers[95] to collective action . . . including the right to strike." This applies only to conflicts of interest and not to conflicts of right such as a dispute about the interpretation of an existing agreement as distinct from the making of a new one. The right is guaranteed "with a view to ensuring the effective exercise of the right to bargain collectively" and it appears under the heading "The Right to Bargain Collectively." In the Charter therefore the "right" to strike is an institution complementary to collective bargaining, not a fundamental human right (as such it would in any event not have been germane to the Social Charter). The Charter does not, however, codify the German doctrines of "social adequacy" or of "proportionality": it does not restrict the right to strike to situations in which collective negotiations have been tried and have failed.

(b) The development of English law

We have seen that the initial response by the courts to the growth of trade unions and of the strike weapon was to fashion a liability in conspiracy—first criminal, later tortious—which was explicitly based upon the unlawfulness of the purpose of the combiners. An agreement to inflict economic harm upon an employer by way of industrial action would very likely have been regarded as a criminal conspiracy before the Act of 1875 and as a

---

[94] Art. 6(4).
[95] It is a violation of the Charter to make the lockout illegal.

tortious conspiracy before the Act of 1906. These Acts, however, brought about a situation in which liability would arise only if the agreement to inflict economic harm involved the commission of a crime or a tort. The *purpose* of inflicting economic harm was no longer unlawful unless it was effected by unlawful *means*; the latter was now the gist of the illegality.

Perhaps because it was seen to be too open an intervention by the courts into industrial relations for them to declare the intentional but nevertheless peaceful infliction of economic harm unlawful by reason of its purpose, the courts themselves in the 1920s and especially during and after the Second World War developed a broad defence of justification to the tort of conspiracy which, quite apart from statute, would operate in most cases so as to relieve the courts of the task of assessing the acceptability of the combiners' purposes. The courts revised their own definition of the purposes which make an agreement or combination an unlawful conspiracy. To be an unlawful conspiracy, the combination must have an "unlawful" purpose, and as far back as 1891 the House of Lords decided that a cartel of shipowners which through undercutting of prices sought to drive an outsider out of a profitable branch of business was not an actionable conspiracy: competition was not an unlawful purpose.[96] It was not until after the First World War that the principle of this famous case was extended from trade purposes to trade union purposes. This development culminated in the decision of the House of Lords in 1941 in *Crofter Harris Tweed* v. *Veitch*.[97] In that case the Transport and General Workers' Union had in fact placed an embargo on the import of mainland-spun yarn into the island of Lewes—the dockers at Stornoway who were members of the TGWU refused to unload it—with the object of obtaining for the island spinners a secure and stable market among the island weavers and thus of obtaining from the island spinners what was in fact a closed shop, apart from a wage increase.

This was not an unlawful purpose, and hence no conspiracy by the union officials against the weavers. The union officials had acted in the bona fide and legitimate interest of the union members. In the words of Viscount Simon L.C.[98]:

> "The predominant object of the (union officials) in getting the embargo imposed was to benefit their trade union members

---

[96] *Mogul S.S. Co.* v. *McGregor, Gow & Co.* [1892] A.C. 25.
[97] [1942] A.C. 435. It was Scottish case, but the laws of the two countries are the same in this matter.
[98] At p. 447.

by preventing undercutting and unregulated competition, and so helping to secure the economic stability of the island industry. The result they aimed at achieving was to create a better basis for collective bargaining, and thus directly to improve wage prospects. A combination with such an object is not unlawful, because the object is the legitimate promotion of the interests of the combiners, and because the damage necessarily inflicted on the (weavers) is not inflicted by criminal and tortious means and is not 'the real purpose' of the combination."

Inherent in this there is, of course, the conscious attempt to single out a "predominant" purpose—a highly problematical enterprise. More than that, the courts continue to think that, in a matter of economic conflict, "it is possible to separate the objects of benefiting yourself and injuring your antagonist," which, as Fitzjames Stephen[99] so convincingly pointed out 90 years ago, is in fact a fallacy. However, in the *Crofter Harris Tweed* case, the House of Lords gave a version to this doctrine which made it more suitable to be applied to hostile action in labour relations. Lord Simon distinguished between the object of benefiting the members and[1] "a combination . . . to demonstrate the power of those combining to dictate policy or to prove themselves masters of a given situation," a policy, if you like of "showing the flag," thumping the table, punishing dissidents for the sake of punishment. Two cases decided subsequently to the *Crofter* decision seem to show that this can be used as a line to separate what is an actionable conspiracy from what is not. The first[2] was not a case of a strike, but it is instructive. A number of local union members and their committee took gratuitously vindictive action against a member who had refused to participate in a one-day demonstration strike, and the court held them liable for conspiracy. In the other case[3] musicians and their union used a strike and boycott to force the owner of a dance hall to give up a colour bar against "non-white" customers, and this, the Court of Appeal held, was not actionable conspiracy at common law. To hound the plaintiff in the first case from pillar to post and to try to prevent him from getting a job was vindictive "prestige" policy; to put down the

---

[99] See above, n. 31, p. 297.
[1] At p. 445.
[2] *Huntley* v. *Thornton* [1957] 1 W.L.R. 321; [1956] 1 All E.R. 234.
[3] *Scala Ballroom (Wolverhampton) Ltd.* v. *Ratcliffe* [1958] 1 W.L.R. 1057; [1958] 3 All E.R. 220 (C.A.). This was, of course, many years before the enactment of any legislation against racial discrimination.

colour bar in the second case was the pursuit of a legitimate trade union interest. The line between what is and what is not a lawful purpose at common law appears to run somewhere between these two cases.

It would be an exaggeration to say that the redefinition of this line by the House of Lords in 1941 made the statutory immunity from liability for civil conspiracy superfluous. Cases may perhaps be possible in which people who act "in contemplation or furtherance of a trade dispute" would nevertheless not be covered by the rule which at common law protects those who act in furtherance of a legitimate trade union interest[4] but the two things are not very far apart. The *Crofter* case has narrowed the gulf between what is a lawful purpose at common law and what is a lawful purpose under the relevant statutes; it has not abolished that gulf. Apart from being expressive of a judicial attitude towards trade unions and industrial disputes which differs remarkably from that prevalent before the First World War, and again since the mid-'sixties, the *Crofter* case set the seal of the House of Lords on the rule, developed in earlier cases,[5] that the pursuit of the closed shop was not an unlawful purpose. This was recognised as one of the methods of creating "a better basis for collective bargaining."

Apart from the tort of conspiracy the other bases of liability in the common law of the economic torts are derived from the illegality of the means used: inducing breach of contract, intimidation, interference with business by unlawful means and so on. We shall examine these in detail below,[6] but we have already noted that the development of these heads of liability by the courts would have restricted severely the legal freedom of workers to engage in industrial action, had not Parliament provided some protection against them as well as against the liability for conspiracy.[7] These statutory protections presuppose that those

---

[4] This possibility was strengthened somewhat by the holding by the House of Lords in *N.W.L. Ltd.* v. *Woods* [1979] I.C.R. 867, 878, 889 that a genuine connection between the dispute and the matters listed as falling within the statutory definition of a trade dispute was all that was required to enable the defendants to claim the statutory protection and that it was not necessary for them to go further and show that the trade object was the sole or even predominant object of the defendants' action, but see now the amendment made by the 1982 Act, s. 18(2)(*c*) to the statutory definition of trade dispute. This is discussed below, p. 318.

[5] *White* v. *Riley* [1921] 1 Ch. 1 (C.A.); *Reynolds* v. *Shipping Federation* [1924] 1 Ch. 28.

[6] pp. 325 *et seq.*

[7] Above, p. 299.

involved have acted "in contemplation or furtherance of a trade dispute." This "golden formula"[8] was first introduced in the Conspiracy and Protection of Property Act 1875 and first defined in the Trade Disputes Act 1906.

The definition contained in the 1906 Act, although changed in detail by later statutes, laid down the structure of the golden formula, which subsequent legislators have not sought to disturb. That definition required that for a trade dispute to exist there must be a dispute between the relevant parties—in 1906 between "employers and workmen or between workmen and workmen"— and the dispute must be connected with the relevant subject matter—in 1906 "the employment or non-employment, or the terms of employment, or with the conditions of labour, of any person."[9] The definition in the Industrial Relations Act 1971[10] was more explicit and differed from the 1906 definition in one very significant respect: it omitted any reference to disputes between "workmen and workmen." The Trade Union and Labour Relations Act 1974 also contained an elaborate definition of trade dispute, but without the restrictive aspects of the 1971 definition.[11] However, that definition was rather narrowly construed by the Court of Appeal in the period 1976 to 1979,[12] and in 1982 Parliament itself moved to restrict the definition in the Employment Act 1982.[13] It is, thus, clear that over the past decade the question of the appropriate scope of the statutory immunities against the common law liabilities has given rise to a series of reformulations of the golden formula. However, no matter how broadly or narrowly that fomula has been conceived, it has functioned so as to provide, by reference to their purposes, a defence to those engaged in industrial action against common law liabilities, whether the latter have been posited upon unlawful purposes or unlawful means.

(c) What is a trade dispute?

As a consequence of the British tradition of viewing the right to strike as an adjunct to collective bargaining, the golden formula, no matter what the details of its provisions, has always had to

---

[8] Prof. Wedderburn's expression: *The Worker and the Law* (2nd ed.), p. 327.
[9] Trade Disputes Act 1906, s. 5(3).
[10] s. 167(1).
[11] s. 29(1). Disputes are covered if they relate to either individual or collective labour relations.
[12] See Davies and Freedland, "Labour Law" in McAuslan and Jowell (eds.), *Lord Denning, the Judge and the Law* (1984).
[13] s. 18, amending s. 29 of the 1974 Act.

perform one crucial function, *viz.* to mark off the area of industrial relations, within which industrial action would be to at least some extent protected from common law liabilities, from other areas of social relations, in which resort to industrial action was not perceived as having any special claim to protection. But just as the line between lawful and unlawful purposes in the common law of conspiracy has not proved an entirely easy one for the courts to draw,[14] so also the distinction between strikes for a purpose connected with industrial relations and strikes for other purposes has proved elusive. In this context it is often said that a "political" strike is not a strike "in contemplation or furtherance of a trade dispute." What this is intended to indicate is that the strike is not within the definition if its sole or predominant purpose is to bring pressure to bear upon the Government or some other public authority, unless the action the strikers seek to prevent or to promote is or would be that of the authority as employer. Similarly, a strike to protest against governmental action already taken or against the failure to take it would be classified as "political." What, however, do we mean by "political" in a marginal situation? A strike to demonstrate against some planned legislation would be "political" and not "in contemplation or furtherance of a trade dispute." This would probably still be true if the legislation directly affected the relations between the strikers and their employers, but this is debatable, and it has been debated in this country[15] and abroad.[16] A strike to protest against an arrest made by the police would not be "in contemplation or furtherance of a trade dispute," but here too there may be doubtful borderline cases, *e.g.* if those arrested were pickets who, in the course of a

---

[14] See above p. 312.

[15] *Associated Newspaper Group Ltd.* v. *Flynn* (1970) 10 K.I.R. 17. *Express Newspapers Ltd.* v. *Keys* [1980] I.R.L.R. 247; *Sherrard* v. *A.U.E.W.* [1973] I.C.R. 421.

[16] In the German Federal Republic in connection with the newspaper strike of May 1952 in which Nipperdey and Hueck developed the doctrine of "social adequacy" in a professional opinion presented to the Courts. Subsequently Professor Nipperdey became President of the Federal Labour Court and the Court adopted that doctrine. In Italy an exception to the prohibition of political strikes is made if the strike is linked with the workers' own interest in labour legislation (Decisions of the *Corte Costituzionale*, No. 123 of December 28, 1962, No. 31 of March 17, 1969, No. 1 of January 14, 1974, and No. 290 of December 27, 1974, discussed by Prof. Treu in *International Encyclopaedia for Labour Law and Industrial Relations*, Vol. 6, "Italy," pp. 168–170). In Sweden the Labour Court has upheld a demonstration or protest strike with political aims, in the absence of express prohibition in the collective agreement or serious harm to the employer's business (A.D. 1980 No. 15).

strike for higher wages, had been arrested for having wilfully obstructed a constable in the execution of his duty.[17]

The term "political" cannot be defined with precision. It is not a legal term of art whose definition is prescribed by law, nor has it—either among political scientists or in popular usage—a generally accepted meaning.[18] What is more important, however, is that even if a course of action, and especially of industrial action, is clearly "political," that does not necessarily mean that it is not covered by the immunity—though "political," it may still be "in contemplation or furtherance of a trade dispute." The issue of "political" strikes arose in *Duport Steels Ltd.* v. *Sirs*[19] in 1980. The steel union struck in pursuit of a wage claim against the British Steel Corporation, which was in a parlous financial condition. The strike made little headway, and the union decided to withdraw its members in the private sector of the industry, although it had no wage dispute with the private sector employers, in order to put pressure on the Government, which exercised fairly close control over the finances of the Corporation, to provide the money to the Corporation which would enable the Corporation to improve its pay offer. The House of Lords, assuming for the sake of argument that the extension of the dispute to the private sector was an expression of a conflict between union and Government rather than between union and private sector employers, nevertheless held that the extension was made in furtherance of the dispute between the union and the Corporation, which was undoubtedly a trade dispute. To their lordships this analysis was so clear (though it had not been grasped by the Court of Appeal) that the main arguments in the case were concentrated on other issues,[20] but the case serves to re-emphasize the fact that a "political" element in a dispute does not *ipso facto* deprive that dispute of its character as a trade dispute. In other words: the term "political strike" is not only indistinct, but also useless, because even where the strike is unquestionably "political," it may still be a trade dispute or it may not.

How could one expect anything else in a world in which the political and the economic spheres of life are indistinguishable?

---

[17] Police Act 1964, s. 51(3). See below, p. 348.

[18] See Roskill L.J. in *Sherrard* v. *A.U.E.W.* [1973] I.C.R 421 at p. 435, who pointed this out in a different context.

[19] [1980] I.C.R. 161 (H.L.).

[20] The finding in favour of the defendants would now very probably be upset because of the provisions of s. 17 of the Employment Act 1980. See below, p. 333.

Whatever the political colour of the Government, it is involved in industry, and the organisations of both sides of industry are involved in government. Is not every major industrial problem a problem of governmental economic policy? Is it not true that, not only in publicly owned industries, governmental decisions on wages policies[21]—whether statutory or not—on credits and on subsidies, on the distribution of industry and on housing and town planning, and on a thousand other things, affect the terms and conditions of employment at least as much as decisions of individual firms? Where is the line between a strike to induce an employer to raise, or not to reduce, wages, and a strike to press the government for measures which would enable the employer to do so? This was the great controversy about the legality of the General Strike of 1926,[22] the unsolved problem of whether the unions who struck in sympathy with the locked-out coal miners did so in order to induce the mine owners to withdraw a notice to reduce wages or struck to induce Mr. Stanley Baldwin and his Government to renew a subsidy which would enable the coal owners to comply with the miners' request.[23] It is all very well for a lawyer to speak about a "predominant purpose." In a somewhat less dramatic setting the question of 1926 arose afresh in 1951 in connection with a dock strike in the Mersey; partly for getting what was called the "Dockers' Charter" (which would have been a trade dispute) and partly to bring pressure to bear on the dockers' own union (which would not). The jury which was supposed to convict or to acquit clearly did not understand what "predominant purpose" meant in the law of criminal conspiracy.[24] This problem has not been solved by subsequent legislation. It is insoluble.

Nevertheless, so long as one views the justification for strike action as being its connection with industrial relations in general and collective bargaining in particular, the line between political and industrial purposes must continue to be drawn, no matter how

---

[21] See—in another context—*Sherrard* v. *A.U.E.W., supra.*

[22] Goodhart, *Essays in Jurisprudence and the Common Law,* Chap. X I, pp. 226 *et seq.*; Simon, *Three Speeches on the General Strike.*

[23] See Julian Symons, *The General Strike* (1957).

[24] *Annual Register 1951,* p. 34. The indictment had two counts: (1) for common law conspiracy under which the jury could only convict if the accused had not acted in contemplation or furtherance of a trade dispute (because of s. 3 of the 1875 Act); (2) for an offence under Art. 4 of S.R. & O. 1940 No. 1305, under which the jury could only convict if the accused had acted in contemplation or furtherance of a trade dispute. The Attorney-General invited them to decide what was the predominant purpose. They convicted on *both* counts. The Attorney-General entered a *nolle prosequi.* Order 1305 was revoked.

unsatisfactory the manner of doing it may be. And the line may be located so as to give greater or lesser scope to protected industrial purposes as against unprotected, non-industrial purposes. Under the definition in the Trade Union and Labour Relations Act 1974 the dispute had to be "connected with" the approved subject matter of a trade dispute. This was the phrase that had been used in the 1906 Act and it was given a wide interpretation by the House of Lords in *N.W.L.* v. *Woods*,[25] where their Lordships required only a genuine connection between the dispute and the relevant subject matter and not that the industrial purpose be the predominant one. In the Employment Act 1982[26] the Government decided to substitute the phrase "relates wholly or mainly to"—which had been used also in the 1971 Act—because it felt the need to "ensure that disputes which were mainly political or personal in character and had only a slight connection with the subject of a trade dispute fell outside the trade dispute definition."[27] It remains to be seen whether the courts will find the notion of a predominant purpose any easier to apply under the statutory definition than they have in the common law of conspiracy.[28]

With regard to industrial purposes matters are more clear-cut. The history of the legislation since 1906 allows us, again, to discern two approaches. The first is that of the 1906 and 1974 Acts. All industrial purposes should be brought within the definition of trade dispute and so benefit from whatever protection against the common law liabilities Parliament has thought fit to confer. The aim of the definition of trade dispute thus becomes to describe an area of legal protection which is coterminous with the social phenomena of industrial relations. The alternative approach is to use the definition of trade dispute so as to exclude from protection certain types of dispute, which, whilst clearly industrial, are regarded on other grounds as not deserving of protection. The Employment Act 1982[29] takes three such types of dispute outside the definition.

First, like the 1971 Act, but unlike the 1906 and 1974 Acts, disputes between workers and workers are not included within the definition. This may remove from protection disputes as to union

---

[25] [1979] I.C.R. 867.
[26] s. 18(2)(*c*).
[27] Department of Employment, *Working paper on proposed industrial relations legislation*, November 1981, para. 37.
[28] Above, p. 312.
[29] s. 16.

membership and demarcation disputes, where the employer may be regarded as uninvolved and so should be free to seek legal remedies against those organising industrial action. But in fact few such disputes do not develop in such a way as to involve the employer, *e.g.* by way of a demand that he sack the non-unionist or allocate the work to a particular group of employees. At that point the dispute is also a dispute between employer and workers and so protected. The experience of the Industrial Relations Act 1971 suggests that a firm division between worker and worker disputes, on the one hand, and worker and employer disputes, on the other, can be maintained only at the cost of some artificiality.[30]

Second, disputes between employers and workers fall as a result of the 1982 Act within the definition of trade dispute only if the workers are employed[31] by the employer in question. No such restriction can be found in the previous definitions. This is not a way of removing protection from secondary industrial action: so long as employees of the primary employer are in dispute with their employer, action taken by employees of a secondary employer, even if they are not in dispute with the secondary employer, would be in furtherance of the primary dispute.[32] The requirement does, however, prevent a union from pressing a claim against an employer on behalf of its membership as a whole where the employees of the employer in question are not in dispute with him.[33] The issue has arisen mainly in relation to the campaign against "flags of convenience" which has been waged for a number of years by unions affiliated to the International Transport Workers' Federation.[34] The I.T.F. represents the seafarers' unions of the advanced industrial nations; the "flags of convenience" ships are usually crewed by men from developing countries, who are prepared to accept much lower wages. In consequence, the demand made by the I.T.F. of the ship-owner that he should pay rates found in western Europe is often, not merely not supported by the existing crew, but actively opposed by them.

Third, it has become a commonplace that we are living in a world in which the scope and force of the law is circumscribed by national boundaries which bear no relation to the international

---

[30] See *Cory Lighterage* v. *T.G.W.U.* [1973] I.C.R. 339 and *cf. Langston* v. *A.U.E.W.* [1974] I.C.R. 180.

[31] Or are former employees whose employment was terminated in connection with, or whose termination gave rise to, the dispute; s. 18(6).

[32] *Cf. Duport Steels Ltd.* v. *Sirs* [1980] I.C.R. 161, above p. 316.

[33] Hence the necessity also to repeal s. 29(4) of the 1974 Act, making a dispute with a trade union necessarily a dispute to which workers are party.

[34] See *N.W.L.* v. *Woods* [1979] I.C.R. 867.

scope of economic activities. This is partly, but only partly, a problem of multinational corporations, yet this is the most important example. If the entire corpus of labour law is designed to promote an equilibrium of power of management and organised labour, then it completely misses its function in the international sphere. Here internationally controlled management is confronted by national organisations, and we can see no more than the beginnings of their effective international co-operation. The law can do little to promote it, but one of the steps it can take in the interest of international equilibrium is to remove such obstacles as prevent the use of the pressure power of labour in a country enjoying a high level of organisation in the interest of the workers of another, badly organised, country and especially in developing countries.[35]

In 1974 the Government wished to make it clear that such disputes were within the definition of trade dispute by enacting that there was to be a trade dispute "even though it relates to matters occurring outside Great Britain." By Opposition amendment, however, the qualification was added that those taking action in Britain must be likely to be affected themselves in relation to a trade dispute matter by the outcome of the dispute abroad.[36] Those additional words were deleted in 1976[37] but in 1982 the Employment Act[38] reintroduced them. The qualification amounts to a denial of international solidarity; protection is afforded only when those taking action in this country have an industrial interest of their own for so doing. Both the second and third restrictions derive from a view of industrial relations as essentially a fragmented activity, as a matter for particular employers and their employees, and not as raising issues of general concern to employees organised in trade unions.

(d) Other unprotected purposes

The golden formula lays down the basic criteria which those who wish to claim the statutory protections against the economic torts

---

[35] See on these problems: ILO, *Multinational Enterprises and Social Policy* (Geneva, 1973); H. Guenther (ed.), *Multinationals in Western Europe: the Industrial Relations Experience* (1976); Northrup and Rowan, *Multinational Collective Bargaining Attempts* (1979); Wedderburn, "Multi-National Enterprise and National Labour Law" (1972) 1 I.L.J. 12; Davies, "Labour Law and Multi-National Groups of Companies" in Klaus Hopt (ed.), *Groups of Companies in European Laws* (Berlin, 1982).
[36] Trade Union and Labour Relations Act 1974, s. 29(3).
[37] Trade Union and Labour Relations (Amendment) Act 1976, s. 1(*d*).
[38] s. 18(4).

must meet. The formula operates by reference to the purpose of the defendants in furthering an actual or contemplated trade dispute. It therefore affords an obvious way for legislators to proceed who wish to distinguish between protected and unprotected purposes. However, as a matter of technique it is not necessary that unprotected purposes be identified by way of amendment of the golden formula. The Industrial Relations Act 1971 imposed limitations on industrial sanctions even when used in contemplation or furtherance of trade, or, as the Act said, "industrial" disputes as defined by the Act itself.[39] Thus, the 1971 Act prohibited all strikes (and also other types of industrial action) aimed at achieving or maintaining the closed shop in any of its forms,[40] and it severely restricted any such action for the purpose of obtaining union recognition.[41]

By the Employment Act 1982[42] industrial action directed at the imposition of union membership or recognition requirements is also rendered unprotected, even though such action is taken in contemplation or furtherance of a trade dispute. The Act removes protection in three related situations. We have already seen[43] that clauses in contracts for the supply of goods or services requiring all or part of the work for the contract to be done by union or non-union members or requiring a supplier to negotiate or consult with a union or union official are rendered void. Section 14 renders unprotected industrial action aimed at securing the incorporation into the contract of any such void clause. Persons contracting for the supply of goods or services are also put under a statutory duty not to fail to include a person on a list of approved contractors, nor to fail to invite tenders from or to permit a person to tender, nor to fail to contract with a person, and not to terminate a contract, on the grounds that the work for the contract may be done by members or non-members of a union or on the grounds that a person does not negotiate or consult with a union or union official. Industrial action to induce a breach of this statutory duty is also declared to be unprotected. Finally, secondary industrial action is unprotected which has the effect of interfering with the supply of goods or services, which takes the form of inducing employees to break[44] their contracts of employment, and which is carried out because those doing work in connection with the supply are

---

[39] s. 167(1).
[40] s. 33(3).
[41] ss. 54 and 55.
[42] s. 14.
[43] Above p. 269. Employment Act 1982, ss. 12–13.
[44] And certain analogous acts: see s. 14(2).

members or non-members of a union or because the supplier does
not negotiate or consult with a trade union or official. Thus, to
take a simple example, a union official who calls upon his members
to black supplies coming to their employer from another employer
who runs a non-union shop is engaging in unprotected activity if
the reason for the blacking is the non-union status of the supplier's
employees.

(e) The definition of "trade dispute" and unlawful means

Just as it has proved possible to remove protection from
industrial purposes which were regarded as illegitimate in ways
other than by amendment of the golden formula, so conversely it
has proved possible to remove protection from means regarded as
illegitimate through the interpretation of the trade dispute
formula. The golden formula is not, however, well adapted to this
end and it is perhaps significant that its use in this way was the
work of the courts, especially the Court of Appeal, in the period
after 1976, and that when Parliament in the Employment Act 1980
came to adopt the policy of the Court of Appeal, it did not do so
via amendment to the definition of trade dispute. The history of
this piece of judicial activism is as follows.

We have already noted that by 1976 Parliament had laid down a
definition of trade dispute which not only reversed the exclusion of
"worker and worker" disputes from the 1971 Act's definition, but
which also explicitly attempted to counter some of the restrictions
upon the statutory definition contained in judicial decisions and
dicta.[45] As we shall see in the next section, by 1976 Parliament had
also provided immunity from a wide range of civil liabilities for
those acting within the golden formula. The width of the immunity
was in nominal terms, though probably not in functional terms,
greater than had existed before the passing of the Industrial
Relations Act 1971 or even than had existed in 1906 after the
passing of the Trade Disputes Act of that year. The immunity was
thought by Parliament to need to be wider in nominal terms
because of the developments in the underlying common law
liabilities which had occurred during this century and which are
considered in the next section. Only a wider nominal immunity
would provide workers with a freedom to strike functionally
equivalent to that which had been provided in 1906.

As we have already had cause to remark,[46] the development of a

---

[45] For a discussion of the 1974–1976 formula, see Simpson " 'Trade Dispute' and
'Industrial Dispute' in British Labour Law" (1977) 40 M.L.R. 16.
[46] Above, pp. 295–300.

legal freedom to strike in this country has been the result in large measure of a clash between the principles of the common law as declared by the courts and principles of good social policy declared by Parliament. The latest round of this battle, which occurred between 1977 and 1980, showed, however, some novel features. First, and most important for our present purposes, whereas in the past the clash of policies had expressed itself largely—though not exclusively—through judicial development of substantive common law liabilities which outflanked the then existing statutory protections, now in the late 1970s battle was joined on the interpretation of the scope of the statutory protections, in particular on the question of when a person could be said to have acted "in contemplation or furtherance" of a trade dispute. The Court of Appeal, with the Master of the Rolls in the van, found itself reacting to the extension of the nominal immunities of defendants in trade disputes and to the potentiality of industrial action to inconvenience those not directly involved in the dispute by adopting an avowedly restrictive approach to the new legislation. The immunities "are to be construed with due limitations so as to keep the immunity within reasonable bounds. Otherwise the freedom of ordinary individuals—to go about their business in peace would be intruded upon beyond all reason."[47] From this standpoint the Court of Appeal developed two main restrictive approaches, though each was presented in a number of slightly differing ways, which need not now concern us. The first was to say that, where the Court found the defendants' demands upon the employer unreasonable, the defendants could not be said to be acting in furtherance of a trade dispute, because, it was sometimes added, the unreasonableness of their demand showed that their real objective was not a trade objective but some other "extraneous" goal.[48] The second line of reasoning arose in response to action taken by defendants against employers other than the employer against whom the initial demand in the dispute was made (the "primary" employer).

Where the Court found that the "secondary" employer was too remote from the primary employer, it would hold that the action

---

[47] *Express Newspapers Ltd.* v. *McShane* [1979] I.C.R. 210, 218 (C.A.). See also the remarks of Ackner J. in *United Biscuits (U.K.) Ltd* v. *Fall* [1979] I.R.L.R. 110, 113 "that totally unlimited construction of these words 'in furtherance of a trade dispute' would mean that Parliament was writing a recipe for anarchy." For an analysis, see Ewing "The Golden Formula: Some Recent Developments" (1979) 8 I.L.J. 133.

[48] See *Star Sea Transport Corporation of Monrovia* v. *Slater* [1978] I.R.L.R. 507 (C.A.); *PBDS (National Carriers) Ltd.* v. *Filkins* [1979] I.R.L.R. 356 (C.A.).

taken against the secondary employer was not action taken in furtherance of the primary dispute because, in the Court's view, there was insufficient likelihood that the secondary action would significantly aid the defendants' cause against the primary employer.[49] The Court would be particularly likely to conclude against the defendants if their action was imposing large costs on the secondary employer or the public. The second approach involved the Court in substituting for a subjective test of furtherance (*i.e.* did the defendants act for the purpose of furthering the primary dispute?) some form of objective test in which the Court assessed the rationality of the means used by the defendants to further their purposes.

The second novel feature of this clash between Parliamentary intention and judicial policy was that Parliamentary intention was ultimately vindicated by the courts themselves, that is, by the House of Lords in a trilogy of cases in late 1979 and 1980. The policy of their lordships was most trenchantly expressed by Lord Scarman and was in sharp contrast to the restrictive approach of the Court of Appeal. "So far as the Act of 1974 is concerned, the legislative purpose is clear: to sweep away not only the structure of industrial relations created by the Industrial Relations Act 1971 . . . but also the restraints of judicial review which the courts have been fashioning one way or another since the enactment of the Trade Disputes Act 1906."[50] Thus, the first line of reasoning developed by the Court of Appeal was rejected by their Lordships. Immunity was not forfeited because compliance with the defendants' demands by the employer "is so difficult as to be commercially impracticable or will bankrupt the employer or drive him out of business."[51] Nor did it matter that the defendants might have an extraneous objective, even a predominant one, provided there was a genuine connection between the subject-matter of the dispute and the list of trade objects in the statutory definition.[52] Their Lordships also rejected, although not unanimously, the objective test of furtherance developed by the Court of Appeal. It was sufficient, for the defendants to claim the protection of the golden formula, that they acted with the purpose of furthering the

---

[49] *Beaverbrook Newspapers Ltd.* v. *Keys* [1978] I.C.R. 582 (C.A.); *Express Newspapers Ltd.* v. *McShane* [1979] I.C.R. 210 (C.A.); *United Biscuits (U.K.) Ltd.* v. *Fall* [1979] I.R.L.R. 110. *Duport Steels Ltd.* v. *Sirs* [1980] I.C.R. 161, 169 represented a variation on this theme. See above, p. 316.

[50] *N.W.L. Ltd.* v. *Woods* [1979] I.C.R. 867, 886, *per* Lord Scarman.

[51] *Ibid* at p. 878 *per* Lord Diplock.

[52] *Ibid.*

primary dispute in the honest belief that their actions would do so.[53]

Although a majority of their Lordships thus affirmed the subjective test, some of them clearly found the policy laid down by Parliament in 1976 "intrinsically repugnant to anyone who has spent his life in the practice of the law or the administration of justice,"[54] and the results of applying that policy in practice constituted an invitation to the differently composed Parliament of 1980 to reverse that policy. This invitation was accepted by the Government which added to its Employment Bill then before Parliament a clause restricting the range of civil immunities available in respect of "secondary action."[55] Thus, as we shall see in the next section, the third novel feature of this episode came about: Parliament acted to ratify—albeit not by narrowing the statutory golden formula as such—a restrictive judicial policy that the judges themselves had, ultimately, been unable to sustain.

3. LAWFUL AND UNLAWFUL METHODS[56]

(a) Economic torts and crimes

It goes without saying that there are acts which the law must forbid and, as best it can, suppress, quite irrespective of the purpose for which they are done. An assault remains an assault, malicious damage to property remains just that, and physically obstructing the highway or access to a factory or a power plant remains a public nuisance, no matter whether it is done in contemplation or furtherance of a trade dispute or for any other purpose. By the same token a sit-down strike or a "work-in" is a trespass,[57] whatever its objective. No one has ever tried to argue that the freedom to strike includes the freedom to commit or to threaten physical violence to persons or property, or, more generally, what one may call common as distinct from specifically economic crimes or torts.

---

[53] *Express Newspapers Ltd.* v. *McShane* [1980] I.C.R. 42 (H.L.).

[54] *Duport Steels Ltd.* v. *Sirs* [1980] I.C.R. 161, 177, *per* Lord Diplock. Contrast Lord Scarman, who thought it would be "a strange and embarrassing task for a judge to be called upon to review the tactics of a party to a trade dispute": *McShane, op. cit.* at p. 65.

[55] Employment Act 1980, s. 17.

[56] See Aaron, *Methods of Industrial Action,* Chap. 2 of Aaron and Wedderburn (eds.), *Industrial Conflict, supra*; Heydon, *Economic Torts,* (1978) Chaps. 2 and 3.

[57] Though not actionable in Scotland in the absence of damage: *Plessey Co. Ltd.* v. *Wilson* [1982] I.R.L.R. 198, noted by Miller (1982) 11 I.L.J. 115.

Our problem is different. It is concerned with the use of economic pressure in contemplation or furtherance of a trade dispute. As we have seen, English law has left it to the courts to trace the line between what is allowed and what is forbidden in the pursuit of economic advantage, and since (roughly) the middle of the nineteenth century they have discovered, formulated or invented a number of rules of conduct in the course of economic conflicts. Anyone who violates these rules commits a tort, *i.e.* he can be subjected to an injunction enforceable through the penalties of contempt of court, and to an order for the payment of damages. The principal types of "economic" tort relevant in our context are (i) conspiracy to do that which, if done by an individual, would be lawful but which the courts consider to be injurious to a public interest—originating in decisions of the Court of Appeal of 1893[58] and of the House of Lords of 1901,[59] (ii) inducing a breach of contract, first discovered to exist as a tort in 1853[60] and developed as a rule governing conduct in labour disputes since the beginning of this century,[61] (iii) interference with anther person's trade, business or employment or his right to dispose of his capital or labour, stigmatised as unlawful in 1867 by a judge in a memorandum addressed to a Royal Commission of which he was chairman,[62] but declared not to be a tort in the absence of unlawful means by the House of Lords 30 years later,[63] and (iv) intimidation by threatening a breach of contract, a tort formulated by the House of Lords in 1964.[64] None of these types of conduct was made unlawful by Parliament: this is judicial legislation, and it is judicial legislation not exclusively but principally concerning labour relations. The role of Parliament was different: it sought to protect the freedom to strike by creating exceptions to these rules where the acts stigmatised by the courts as unlawful were done in contemplation or furtherance of a trade dispute. These exceptions were narrowly interpreted by the courts and new exceptions had to be formulated by statute to redress the balance. The tendency of the courts to look at the statutory immunities through a powerful microscope engendered a technique of statutory draftsmanship which made a secret science of a

---

[58] *Temperton* v. *Russell* [1893] 1 Q.B. 715.
[59] *Quinn* v. *Leathem* [1901] A.C. 495.
[60] *Lumley* v. *Gye* (1853) 2 E. & B. 216.
[61] *Taff Vale Railway* v. *Amalgamated Society of Railway Servants* [1901] A.C. 426; *South Wales Miners' Federation* v. *Glamorgan Coal Co.* [1905] A.C. 239.
[62] See above, n. 16, p. 295.
[63] *Allen* v. *Flood* [1898] A.C. 1.
[64] *Rookes* v. *Barnard* [1964] A.C. 1129.

branch of the law more than many others in need of being understood by those bereft of the benefit of a legal training. We shall make no attempt to conceal here the extraordinary complexity of the law. It is advisable to get a glimpse of the intellectual tergiversations in which the law involved itself by omitting to proclaim a right to strike. A network of immunities can precariously serve as a substitute for a general principle, but the network is apt to become a labyrinth. Any attempt to present this matter as anything but technical in the extreme must be deprecated.

As we have said, the exceptions to common law liabilities laid down in statutes were either immunities or privileges. By an immunity we understand an exemption from liability of those—whoever they are—who commit certain acts, *e.g.* inducing others to break contracts. By a privilege we mean a provision exempting from liability certain persons or groups of persons, *e.g.* trade unions from tort liability. It is, however, not quite correct to speak of these immunities and privileges in terms of exemptions from liability. Most—not all[65]—of them are, or at least were originally, expressed in terms of procedure, not of substantive liability. Certain acts are "not actionable in tort"[66] (immunity). "No action in tort shall lie" against certain persons (privilege).[67] We shall point out presently that this distinction between an exemption from substantive liability and an exemption from proceedings in court is more than an academic quibble.

The freedom to strike thus remains hidden in the interstices of procedural immunities and privileges. This, as we have argued, creates extraordinary complexities, but its procedural formulation is not a feature peculiar to this particular fundamental freedom. As a result of British constitutional developments since the second half of the seventeenth century fundamental rights have generally been expressed in this way: to discover the freedom from arbitrary arrest you have to search the ramifications of the law of habeas corpus.[68] In recent years interest has been shown in some quarters in expressing fundamental constitutional propositions as positive rights—perhaps in a Bill of Rights—and the consultative docu-

---

[65] Not the one which refers to picketing. See Trade Disputes Act, s. 2; Trade Union and Labour Relations Act 1974, s. 15 (as amended). This immunity covers criminal prosecutions as well as civil actions.

[66] *Ibid.* s. 13(1), and (4).

[67] *Ibid.* s. 14. Now repealed by the Employment Act 1982 s. 15 (see below pp. 363 *et seq.*).

[68] This is, of course, one of the subjects developed at length in Dicey's *Law of the Constitution;* see esp. Chap. 5.

ment, *Trade Union Immunities,*[69] considers the application of this approach to the "right to strike" in particular. However, for the present at least the law remains unchanged. The complexities we have mentioned arise from the clash between the policies of Parliament and of the courts which has given its imprint to the law of labour disputes.

(i) Conspiracy

We have already seen that no one can be either prosecuted in a criminal,[70] or sued in a civil,[71] court for "conspiracy," *i.e.* for participating in an "agreement or combination" to do or procure the doing of an act, if the act itself, done by an individual, is not (in the case of a criminal prosecution) itself punishable as a crime or (in the case of a civil action) actionable as a tort, provided also in the case of the civil liability that the act is done in contemplation or furtherance of a trade dispute. Thus a group of people threatening others with physical violence "in contemplation or furtherance of a trade dispute" can still be prosecuted for criminal or sued for civil conspiracy, because if there had been only one person involved, he would have been criminally and civilly liable. But people cannot be prosecuted or sued for agreeing to refuse to work on a new machine because for an individual to do so is neither a criminal offence nor a civil tort. The fact is that (and the history of the matter bears it out) the crime as well as the tort of conspiracy in the absence of an agreement to commit a crime or a tort, arising simply because that which was agreed upon was what the judge saw as a violation of a public interest, was developed almost entirely in connection with labour disputes: it was the "collective" element of the strike which stigmatised it in the eyes of previous generations of judges.[72] This, then, is what we call an "economic" crime or tort. It is of cardinal importance that this vast extension of the judicial power (which happened mainly after the repeal of the Combination Acts) has been redressed by legislation, but this did not entirely solve the problem of conspiracy as an economic tort and its effect on labour disputes.

Conspiracy is an agreement to pursue an unlawful object (whether the means be lawful or not), or to pursue a lawful object by unlawful means. The statute creates an immunity for those

---

[69] Cmnd. 8128 (1981), Chap. 4.
[70] Criminal Law Act 1977, s. 1
[71] Trade Union and Labour Relations Act 1974. s. 13(4).
[72] Compare the more realistic analysis by Lord Diplock in *Lonrho Ltd.* v. *Shell Petroleum Co. Ltd.* [1981] 2 All E.R. 456 (H.L.).

whose agreement would have been stigmatised as unlawful by the courts solely on the ground that its purposes were considered to be contrary to the public interest as understood by the judges. If the means used are in themselves unlawful, the lawfulness or otherwise of the object is irrelevant. In other words: if the individual participant in the agreement would have been liable for what he agreed to do, had he done it by himself, then the agreement to do it is an actionable conspiracy, even if the act agreed upon is in contemplation or furtherance of a trade dispute. To induce someone else to break a contract (or to procure such a breach), to intimidate by a threat of a breach, etc., are, as we have already mentioned and shall further explain, acts which, if done by an individual in contemplation or furtherance of a trade dispute, are not usually actionable. But if, though not actionable, they are unlawful all the same, is not an agreement to do any of these things in contemplation or furtherance of a trade dispute an agreement to use unlawful means towards a lawful end and therefore an actionable conspiracy? Let no one say that to hold that it is would manifestly be contrary to the intentions of the legislature. In the light of previous case law this argument could not be expected to carry much weight, since the intention of the legislature cannot be gleaned from a literal construction of the the text.

To preclude actions for civil conspiracy arising from mere economic pressure exercised in the course of a trade dispute it was therefore necessary to make clear that an act is not unlawful which, if done by an individual, is not actionable by reason of one of the statutory immunities. This was done in the 1974 Act "for the avoidance of doubt."[73] Gratuitously, but presumably *ex abundante cautela,* the statute added that it was not an unlawful means for the purpose of establishing liability in tort, *i.e.* for conspiracy, possibly also for intimidation. It was further said that a breach of contract, *e.g.* of a contract of employment, in contemplation or furtherance of a trade dispute was not, for the purpose of establishing tort liability, "unlawful" either, so that those who struck in contemplation or furtherance of a trade dispute, but without the contractual or statutory notices, could not by reason of "unlawful means" be made liable for conspiracy. In *Rookes* v. *Barnard*[74] a breach of contract was held to be an unlawful act for the purposes of the law of intimidation; could not the same happen in relation to the law of conspiracy? Hence the need for this new provision. Yet the 1980

---

[73] *Ibid.* s. 13(3).
[74] *Supra.*

Act[75] repealed this provision of the Trade Union and Labour Relations Acts. This was done, apparently, for fear that the repealed provision might undermine the new liability for secondary action created by the Act. However, the repeal is a general one and not just for the purposes of the secondary action provisions, and so the uncertainties against which Parliament in the Acts of 1974 to 1976 attempted to guard were revived. Very soon after the passing of the 1980 Act the Court of Appeal used the argument as to unlawful means in order to establish liability in tort (albeit not in conspiracy). The subsequent rejection of this argument by the House of Lords has probably laid it to rest so far as acts declared "not actionable" by the 1974 Act (as amended) are concerned,[76] but the possibility of using a breach of contract in this way has yet to be tested.

(ii) Inducing breach of contract

A comparable inter-play between Parliamentary and judicial law-making occurred in relation to the tort of inducing another person to break a contract or of interfering (or inducing someone else to interfere) with its performance. Here however the story is a bit more complicated. The courts discovered in 1853[77] that it is a tort at common law to induce another person to break his contract with a third party, unless there is justification for this inducement. In deciding that this was a principle of the common law, the courts merely generalised a far more ancient principle according to which a "master" had an action against a third party who "procured that a servant should unlawfully leave his service"[78] ("master" and "servant" being the old expressions for employer and employee). The principle originated in labour law, in a body of labour law whose fundamental concepts were still strongly influenced by a notion of "service" being based on a status rather than a contract. It originated in labour law, and labour law was the field in which it was destined to play its principal role. A rule, designed to help land-owners and farmers, especially at times of a scarce labour

---

[75] Employment Act 1980, s. 17(8).

[76] *Hadmor Productions Ltd.* v. *Hamilton* [1981] I.C.R. 690 (C.A.); [1982] I.C.R. 114 (H.L.). See below p. 338. See also *Lonrho Ltd.* v. *Shell Petroleum Co. Ltd.* [1981] 2 All E.R. 456 (H.L.), where Lord Diplock suggested the surely too broad rule that the test of a predominant purpose to further the combiners' own interests (above, p. 312) would prevent liability arising in conspiracy even where the means used by the combiners were criminal.

[77] *Lumley* v. *Gye* (1853) 2 E. & B. 216.

[78] Erle J. in *Lumley* v. *Gye, supra.*

market, became one of the most serious limitations on the freedom to strike. In view of the prevalence of customs (incorporated in contracts of employment) by which both employer and employee broke their contract of employment if they terminated it without notice,it was, in many industries, an actionable breach of contract for workers to stop work without notice, and consequently an actionable tort to induce them to do so. Since it is often impossible to conduct a strike on any other basis, this was a matter of major importance. This was all the more so because there was a tendency to expand the range of this liability. From the beginning it was established that it was as unlawful to "procure" a breach by indirect means as it was to "induce" it by direct influence. Thus, quite apart from being liable for "inducing" the strikers to break their contracts of employment, those organising a strike could be liable for "procuring" breaches of contract by their employer who, owing to the strike, was unable to perform the contracts he had made with his customers. This principle remained alive despite certain limitations which the Court of Appeal put on it in 1952[79] but which subsequent decisions in the 1960s[80] tended to erode. The significance of this tort of "inducing" or "procuring" a breach of contract was not, however, restricted to the two situations of inducing breaches of contracts of employment by the strikers themselves and procuring breaches of commercial contracts by their employer. It operated, thirdly, in connection with what is known as "secondary action," *i.e.* a threat to stop work for one of the employer's customers, suppliers or sub-contractors unless he ceased to buy from, sell to, or work for, the employer against whom the strike was directed. If this involved the cessation of the supply or of the acceptance of goods or services under an existing contract, there was again an occasion for applying the principle that it was unlawful to induce or to procure a breach of contract. In 1969 the potentiality of this was very much extended when the Court of Appeal decided that, to establish the tort, a breach of contract was not required if it could be shown that performance had been interfered with, although (*e.g.* owing to a clause in the contract exempting both parties from liability in the event of a

---

[79] *D.C. Thomson & Co. Ltd.* v. *Deakin* [1952] 1 Ch. 646.
[80] See esp. *Stratford & Son* v. *Lindley* [1965] A.C. 269; *Emerald Construction Co.* v. *Lowthian* [1966] 1 All E.R. 1013 (C.A.); *Torquay Hotel* v. *Cousins* [1969] 2 Ch. 106 (C.A.); but see—more recently—*Camellia Tankers Ltd.* v. *I.T.F.* [1976] I.C.R. 274, and the comments thereon by Prof. Wedderburn (1976) 38 M.L.R. 717.

strike) there was no breach.[81] The matter may, however, go further: the mere threat to induce or to procure a breach or an interference with the performance of a contract may be covered by this liability.[82]

The present law can only be understood in the light of this historical development and in the light of this threefold impact which the tort of "inducing" or "procuring" a breach of contract or of interfering with its performance can have on the on the law governing labour relations. The Trade Disputes Act 1906 dealt only with a portion of this area of potential impact. It laid down[83] that an act done in contemplation or furtherance of a trade dispute was not to be actionable on the ground only that it induced some other person to break a contract of employment. Of the three possible fields of application of the common law principles to which we have referred, the 1906 Act covered only one, *viz.* the inducement (which might be regarded as covering procurement) of breaches of contract by the strikers or (in the case of a lockout or of the dismissal of substitute workers engaged during a strike) by the employer. In its original form the Trade Union and Labour Relations Act 1974 adopted the same wording,[84] but in this respect it was decisively amended by the Amendment Act of 1976.[85] This did two things: it deleted the words "of employment" and thus, acting on a recommendation of the Donovan Commission,[86] expanded the immunity to the inducement or procurement of breaches of commercial contracts,[87] *i.e.* to the second and third of the types of situation in which these principles can become relevant to labour relations: breaches of contract by the employer as against his customers, and breaches of contract by third persons as against the employer. In this sense, therefore, it was the 1976 Amendment Act which extended the statutory immunity to secondary action. Further, however, that Amendment Act added the words: "or interferes or induces another party to interfere with

---

[81] *Torquay Hotel* v. *Cousins, supra.* An alternative explanation of the decision is that there was a breach despite the exemptions clause. This is difficult to accept. The decision of the Court of Appeal was confirmed in *Merkur Island Shipping Corp.* v. *Laughton* [1983] I.C.R. 490 (H.L.).

[82] This is suggested by *Rookes* v. *Barnard* [1964] A.C. 1129.

[83] s. 3 first limb.

[84] s. 13(1) (*a*).

[85] s. 3(2).

[86] Cmnd. 3623, para. 893.

[87] And also to contracts between an employer and an "independent" contractor, *e.g.* a worker on the "lump," eliminating borderline difficulties like those in *Ready Mixed Concrete Ltd.* v. *Cox* (1971) 10 K.I.R. 273 and in *Emerald* v. *Lowthian, supra,* n. 80, p. 331.

its performance," thus ensuring that the immunity would cover cases in which industrial action would impede performance without thereby occasioning a breach of contract, owing, *e.g.* to an exemption clause excluding such breach.

It was to be expected that a Conservative Government, which had successfully secured in 1974 that the Trade Union and Labour Relations Act follow the wording of the 1906 Act by confining the immunity to contracts of employment, might seek to reverse the decision of 1976 to delete the words "of employment" when it came to power in 1979. After the re-assertion by the House of Lords of the subjective interpretation of the test of "furtherance" of a trade dispute in early 1980,[88] during a major strike in the steel industry, it became inevitable that the Government would act by adding an additional clause to its Employment Bill then before Parliament. That clause[89] did not seek, however, to effect a simple re-insertion of the words "of employment" into the 1974 Act. Rather the Act seeks, for the first time in English law,[90] to produce a definition of secondary action and to remove a large part of the immunities of the 1974 Act[91] from such secondary action if that action cannot be justified on one of the three tests laid down in the Act.[92] The continuity with the common law liabilities emerges, however, when one sees that the 1980 Act operates by removing the protections of the 1974 Act in respect of inducing breach or interference with performance of contracts (and threats to do so),[93] thus reviving the underlying common law liabilities. In short, the 1980 Act does not contain a concept of secondary action which is a new statutory concept divorced from common law notions as to when liability is incurred; rather, it defines a new set of circumstances in which familiar common law liabilities are again pressed into service to delimit the boundary between lawful and unlawful industrial methods.

In somewhat more detail, the 1980 Act removes the protection

---

[88] See above.

[89] Now Employment Act 1980, s. 17.

[90] The problem is, of course, one long known in U.S. labour law. See National Labor Relations Act, s. 8(b) and (e), and Lesnick, "The Gravamen of the Secondary Boycott" 62 Columbia L. Rev. 1363 (1962), and Levin, " 'Wholly Unconcerned': The Scope and Meaning of the Ally Doctrine under section 8(*b*)(4) of the NLRA" 119 U. Penn. L. Rev. 283 (1970).

[91] The immunities affected are those contained in s. 13(1) of the Trade Union and Labour Relations Act 1974. The union privilege in s. 14 was not touched by the 1980 Act, although it was subsequently repealed by the 1982 Act.

[92] Employment Act 1980, s. 17(3)–(5).

[93] The tort of intimidation and the statutory immunities existing in relation to it are discussed below.

of the 1974 Act in respect of inducing breaches of contract[94] other than of contracts of employment, where one of the factors relied upon to establish the liability is unjustifiable secondary action. Because of the requirement that liability must depend upon unjustifiable secondary action, the Act is in principle a lesser restriction upon the pre-existing law than a simple re-insertion of the words "of employment" would have been. The significance of this statement depends, however, upon the definitions of secondary action and justifiability adopted by the statute. As to the former, this is defined, somewhat confusingly, in terms of inducing breach[95] of a contract of employment with an employer who is not a party to the trade dispute. Thus, although a plaintiff in a secondary action case is ultimately attempting to show inducement by the defendants of breach of a commercial contract, he must show that liability in respect of the commercial contract depends upon inducement of breach of a contract of employment (which act cannot, of itself, be the subject of a complaint, since the protections of the 1974 Act still apply in respect of the contract of employment).

The element of "secondariness" is provided by the requirement that the employer party to the employment contract must not be a party to the trade dispute. A simple example of a case apparently caught by the 1980 Act would be where a union official calls upon his members employed by a supplier to the primary employer to black supplies to the primary employer, provided that the blacking by the employees was a breach of—or at least an interference with—their contracts of employment and that the blacking led to the supplier being unable to fulfil the terms of his supply contract with the primary employer.[96]

However, the Act contains three bases upon which secondary action can be justified and thus continue to be protected by the full force of the 1974 Act. One of these gateways is of general

---

[94] The non-application of s. 13(1)(*a*) of the 1974 Act means that protection is removed also in respect of interference and inducement to interfere with the performance of a contract, but it is convenient in the text to use "breach" to include interference falling short of breach.

[95] Or interference or inducement to interfere with performance of a contract of employment or threats to break or interfere with or to induce breach of or interference with performance of a contract of employment: s. 17(2). This exactly parallels the range of actions granted immunity by s. 13(1) of the Trade Union and Labour Relations Act 1974, except that, of course, the latter is not confined to contracts of employment.

[96] Whether or not the supplier was put in breach of this supply contract, *supra* n. 81.

significance; the other two are of more limited import.[97] Under the general justification immunity is maintained if the principal purpose of the secondary action is "directly" to disrupt the supply of goods or services between the primary employer and the employer party to the employment contracts in question. Supply between two persons is defined as supply in pursuance of a contract between them, and disrupting supplies "directly" between two persons is defined as disruption "other than by disrupting supplies by or to a third person."[98] The action must also be likely to achieve its purpose.[99] This general justification is designed to implement what the Government termed in the working paper on secondary industrial action[1] the "first supplier, first customer" principle; *i.e.* a relatively generous interpretation of secondariness that leaves as legitimate targets of industrial action the immediate contracting suppliers to and customers of the primary employer. This definition of justifiable action would thus appear to leave the actions of the union official in the example given above covered by the full 1974 immunities, and would appear to place him at risk only if he sought to spread the dispute beyond the first supplier to, say, that supplier's own suppliers.[2]

The rather weak definition of secondariness in the secondary action section of the 1980 Act is, as we shall see, in sharp contrast to the very strict definition adopted in the picketing provisions of the same Act, for there the touchstone of legality is that the picketing should be at the pickets' own place of work. The pickets lose the immunities provided by the 1974 Act if they picket elsewhere, even if the other place is some premises of their employer other than their own place of work, *e.g.* another plant of

---

[97] The general justification is in the Employment Act 1980, s. 17(3). Under s. 17(4) of the Act, the general justification discussed in the text is extended to embrace associated employers of the primary employer but only if the associated employer is receiving or supplying goods or services that, but for the dispute, would have been supplied to or by the primary employer. Under s. 17(5) of the Act there is a special provision for pickets, which is discussed below.

[98] Employment Act 1980, s. 17(6)

[99] *Ibid.*, s. 17(3)(*b*). See generally, Wedderburn (1981) 10 I.L.J. 113.

[1] Department of Employment, February 19, 1980, para. 18.

[2] As, for example, in *Express Newspapers* v. *McShane, supra,* where in a primary dispute with provincial newspaper employers the union sought to secure the cessation of the supply of copy from the Press Association (a first supplier) to the provincial newspapers by instructing its members employed by national newspapers to black P.A. copy. The action at the national newspapers would appear to have been unjustifiable secondary action, but query whether it led to any breach of a commercial contract between the national newspaper employers and the P.A.

a multi-plant company. The 1980 Act may thus be said to express the Government's view that picketing is an activity with very little claim to the protections of the 1974 Act, whereas other forms of industrial action are entitled to those immunities unless aimed at very remote employers. This may prove to be only a provisional view, however, since the Green Paper on trade union immunities discusses various further ways of restricting secondary action.[3] Moreover, the extent of the draftsman's success in effecting the "first supplier/first customer" exemption will only become clear when the complex formula in the legislation, especially the definition of "directly," is subject to judicial scrutiny in the context of particular cases.[4] Finally, there are two situations in which it is tolerably clear that the 1980 Act does not take a generous view, even in the absence of picketing. In the case of "worker and worker" disputes, the Act operates so as to put at risk even action taken by employees against their own primary employer, because their employer is not a party to the dispute if the dispute is purely between workers. The Act also operates harshly upon what might be described as "sympathetic" as opposed to "secondary" action, *i.e.* action taken against another employer not in order to disrupt business relations between the two employers (none may in fact exist) but in order to express support for the employees of the primary employer in their dispute with that employer. Such action is caught by the secondary action provisions of the 1980 Act.[5] Even where business relations do exist between the employers, the industrial action would seem not to be capable of benefiting from the general justification for secondary action because its principal purpose is not the disruption of supplies. Thus, sympathetic action even at first suppliers or first customers would be caught by the Act.[6] In both these instances the 1980 Act anticipated the narrowing of the definition of trade dispute by the 1982 Act.[7]

We have seen how the tort of inducing breach of contract has been expanded in scope by decisions that the tort includes forms of interference with the performance of contracts falling short of

---

[3] *Trade Union Immunities,* Cmnd. 8128, 1981, paras. 138–164.

[4] A strict approach was adopted in *Marina Shipping Ltd.* v. *Laughton* [1982] I.R.L.R. 20 (C.A.), noted by Prof. Wedderburn in (1982) 45 M.L.R. 317, and in *Merkur Island Shipping Corp.* v. *Laughton* [1983] I.C.R. 490 (H.L.).

[5] *Express Newspapers* v. *Mitchell* [1982] I.R.L.R. 465.

[6] Any argument that the organisers of the sympathetic action did not intend to procure breaches of commercial contracts between secondary and primary employers would seem unlikely to succeed after *Emerald Construction Co.* v. *Lowthian, supra.*

[7] See above pp. 318 *et seq.*

breach.[8] By an analogous process of extension the courts have come to see inducement of non-performance of duties other than those derived from contracts as capable of being tortious. Into this category have been placed fiduciary duties[9] and statutory duties.[10] This development is not yet well established, but if it became so, it would undermine the protections conferred by the Acts of 1974 to 1976, since those protections are framed in terms of inducing breaches of contract.[11] In one case[12] it was suggested that liability for inducing breach of statutory duty was not even a liability arising in tort.

(iii) *Interference*

It was the policy of the 1906 Act to create a "catalogue" of economic torts which would not give rise to liability if committed in contemplation or furtherance of a trade dispute—and for many years those interested in these matters were under the impression (proved by the House of Lords in 1964 to be mistaken[13]) that this catalogue was complete. One item in this catalogue of "economic torts" was the tort of "interference with the trade, business or employment of some other person or with the right of some other person to dispose of his capital or his labour as he wills." It was Sir William Erle, the Chairman of the first Royal Commission on Trade Unions[14] who, in a Memorandum submitted to the Commission and published with its Report, had expressed the view that such a tort existed at common law, but in 1897[15] the House of Lords decided that it did not exist.[16] However, it was not until the 1920s[17] that this meaning of the 1897 case was clarified by subsequent decisions, and in 1906 it was not at all clear—there were decisions or at least judicial utterances to the contrary.[18] This

---

[8] *Supra*, n. 81.

[9] *Prudential Assurance Co. Ltd.* v. *Lorenz* (1971) 11 K.I.R. 78.

[10] *Meade* v. *Harringay L.B.C.* [1979] 1 W.L.R. 637 (C.A.); *Associated Newspapers Group Ltd.* v. *Wade* [1979] I.C.R. 664 (C.A.).

[11] Trade Union and Labour Relations Act 1974, s. 13(1).

[12] *Associated Newspapers Group Ltd.* v. *Wade, supra.*

[13] *Rookes* v. *Barnard,supra.*

[14] See its Eleventh and Final Report, 1869.

[15] *Allen* v. *Flood* [1898] A.C.1.

[16] Contrast the situation in the German Federal Republic, where "interference with an organised and operating concern" is considered as a tort by virtue of the Civil Code, para 823(1), and this is the principal basis of delictual liability in connection with trade disputes.

[17] *Ware and de Freville* v. *Motor Trade Association* [1921] 3 K.B. 40 (C.A.); *Sorrell* v. *Smith* [1925] A.C. 700.

[18] *Gibland* v. *National Amalgamated Labourers' Union* [1903] 2 K.B. 600.

explains the appearance in the 1906 Act of the immunity from a tort which nine years before the highest court had declared to be non-existent. Since then, the House of Lords has made it clear that it can overrule its own decisions.[19] To repeat in a statute a ruling previously given by the House of Lords in its judicial capacity is not superfluous, and it was therefore of importance that the 1974 Act declared[20] "for the avoidance of doubt" that an act done by a person in contemplation or furtherance of a trade dispute was not actionable in tort on this ground only.

However, as a result of a possibly misunderstood implication in a Scottish case[21] that the 1974 Act gave protection against liability for interference with business even when unlawful means were used, the government in the 1982 Act decided to repeal the relevant subsection of the 1974 Act, thus throwing defendants in trade disputes back upon the common law decision of 1897 and exposing them to the risk of a judicial change of mind.[22] The decision of the House of Lords in 1897 clearly does not cover the situation where the interference with trade or business occurs through *unlawful* means. Such interference will, of course, be tortious if the unlawful means themselves consist of the commission of a tort, *e.g.* inducing breach of contract or intimidation. Indeed, as we have seen in our discussion of conspiracy, the repeal of section 13(3) of the Trade Union and Labour Relations Act 1974 by the 1980 Act created the risk that the commission of a tort in respect of which immunity is granted by the 1974 Act might nevertheless count as unlawful means for the purpose of tortious liabilities such as interference with business by unlawful means. In *Hadmor Productions Ltd.* v. *Hamilton*[23] the majority of the Court of Appeal exploited this possibility to hold that a union official, who had threatened to instruct members employed by Thames T.V. to black the transmission of programmes produced by the plaintiffs, had committed this tort as against the plaintiffs, the

---

[19] Practice Statement [1966] 1 W.L.R. 1234.
[20] s. 13(2).
[21] *Plessey Co. Ltd.* v. *Wilson* [1982] I.R.L.R. 198, noted by Miller (1982) 11 I.L.J. 115, pointing out the differences between England and Scotland in the matter of trespass. The Scottish court based itself upon a dictum by Lord Diplock in *Hadmor Productions* v. *Hamilton, infra,* n. 24a, and apparently repeated by him in *Merkur Island Shipping Corp.* v. *Laughton, supra,* n. 4, but the dictum seems inconsistent with the decision in *Rookes* v. *Barnard, infra,* n. 28.
[22] Not a small risk since *Allen* v. *Flood* has not met with universal approval even in recent times. See *Rookes* v.*Barnard* [1964] A.C. 1129, 1216, *per* Lord Devlin, but contrast *Lonrho Ltd.* v. *Shell Petroleum Co. Ltd.* [1981] 2 All E.R. 456.
[23] [1981] I.R.L.R. 210.

unlawful means being the threat to induce the members to break their contracts of employment. Thus, even before the secondary action provisions of the 1980 Act had been tested in the courts, the Court of Appeal outflanked the carefully drawn defences of justifiability in that Act by resort to the common law.[24] For this reason the House of Lords[24a] rejected the argument accepted by the Court of Appeal. The latter had in effect made the consequential repeal of section 13(3) by section 17(8) of the 1980 Act the main thrust of that section. The opportunity was taken by their Lordships to settle the underlying argument by holding that acts declared "not actionable" by section 13 could not constitute unlawful means for the purposes of establishing liability in tort. However, this is merely to exclude one form of unlawful means—albeit an important one. It seems that the unlawful means need not necessarily themselves be tortious, though it is unclear exactly what kinds of unlawfulness will count. Breach of the restrictive trade practices legislation[25] and aiding and abetting a person to disobey the terms of an injunction[26] have been held to constitute unlawful means. The main question is how far unlawful means extend beyond wrongs which are not independently actionable.[27]

(iv) *Intimidation*

We have said that in 1964 it became clear that the catalogue of economic torts in the 1906 Act was incomplete. That year saw the decision of the House of Lords in *Rookes* v. *Barnard*,[28] in which it was held that a person was liable in tort if he intimidated another person by threatening him with a breach of contract (not necessarily a breach by himself). This was of great importance in practice. It showed that a person could be liable for intimidation, without having threatened to commit either a crime or a tort, by

---

[24] Although the industrial action was aimed at Hadmor in part, the dispute was with Thames and it was the employees of Thames who took the action. This was not secondary action as defined by s. 17(2) of the 1980 Act. See above, p. 334.

[24a] [1982] I.C.R. 114.

[25] *Daily Mirror Newspapers Ltd.* v. *Gardner* [1968] 2 Q.B. 762 (C.A.); *Brekkes Ltd.* v. *Cattel* [1972] Ch. 105.

[26] *Acrow (Automation) Ltd.* v. *Rex Chainbelt Inc.* [1971] 1 W.L.R. 1676 (C.A.)

[27] The decision of the House of Lords in *Lonrho Ltd.* v. *Shell Petroleum Co. Ltd.* [1981] 2 All E.R. 456 suggests that independently actionable unlawful means are a necessary ingredient for liability. This approach is criticised in P. Elias and K. Ewing, "Economic Torts and Industrial Action: Old Principles and New Liabilities" [1982] C.L.J. 321.

[28] [1964] A.C. 1129.

reason of having threatened to break a contract. The plaintiff had lost his job because he had left the union which had a closed shop agreement with the employer. The other employees, under the leadership of the three defendants (two union officials employed in the same office and a full time union officer) had informed the employer that they would, from a certain moment, refuse to work alongside the plaintiff. The threat to strike was held to be a threat to break the contracts of employment, and this on the particular ground that a no-strike understanding between the union and the employer was admitted to be incorporated in those contracts—it will be observed that this would be impossible now because of the provision[29] (discussed in Chap. 6 above) that a no-strike clause in a collective agreement must comply with stringent formal require-ments if it is to be regarded as incorporated in the individual contracts of employment. This, however, does not dispose of the significance of *Rookes* v. *Barnard* because in the event of a strike without the contractual or statutory notices the breach of contract could be found in the absence of the notice, and third parties (suppliers or customers, or, as in *Rookes* v. *Barnard*, a displaced employee) could recover damages on that ground. It is true that in a subsequent case[30] the Court of Appeal held that this situation was, for a variety of reasons, not within the principle of *Rookes* v. *Barnard*, but later doubt was expressed as to the correctness of this decision.[31] In any event, the gap torn open in the safety wall erected by the Trade Disputes Act 1906 had to be closed. This, as we have seen, was done by the Trade Disputes Act 1965, which together with the Trade Disputes Act 1906 was repealed by the Industrial Relations Act 1971. It is now re-enacted in the Trade Union and Labour Relations Act 1974.[32] This says that no one is liable in tort on the ground only of having threatened that a contract will be broken, whether he is a party to it or not—one remembers that of the three defendants in *Rookes* v. *Barnard* one was a full time union official who did not, of course, threaten to break a contract, but threatened that others would do so. Moreover since the threat of a breach of contract had in *Rookes* v. *Barnard* been held to be an actionable intimidation, it was to be anticipated that the courts would hold the same about a threat to induce a breach. Thus, a union officer or a shop steward could be

---

[29] Trade Union and Labour Relations Act 1974, s. 18(4) and (5). See above, Chap. 6, p. 176.
[30] *Morgan* v. *Fry* [1968] 2 Q.B. 710.
[31] *Simmons* v. *Hoover Ltd.* [1976] I.R.L.R. 266 at p. 269 (E.A.T.).
[32] s. 13(1) (*b*), as amended by s. 3(2) of the Amendment Act 1976.

made liable by a plaintiff in the situation of Mr. Rookes if he had announced to the employer that he would ask the other employees to stop work without notice unless the plaintiff was dismissed. This is the reason why the 1974 Act (like the repealed 1965 Act) also refers to a threat by a person "that he will induce another person to break a contract." The immunity from liability for "inducing" a breach[33] might not have comprised that from liability for the "intimidation" involved in threatening to induce it. This was, of course, the unlawfulness suggested in *Hadmor Productions* v. *Hamilton*.[34]

In *Rookes* v. *Barnard* the defendants were held to be liable on the ground that they had procured the plaintiff's dismissal by threatening the employer with breaches of contracts of employment. Would it not be conceivable that in a similar situation representatives of the union might intimate to one of the employer's customers that his men would be called out on strike unless he placed before the employer the alternative of either dismissing the non-unionist or not obtaining performance of the customer's contract? In other words, to have a "copper bottomed" scheme of immunity from the economic torts it was necessary to do for the tort of intimidation what, as we have seen, was done for the tort of inducing a breach of contract, *i.e.* to extend it from contracts of employment to all contracts, including commercial contracts. It was also necessary to cover not only a threat that a contract would be broken, but also a threat that its performance would be interfered with without breach and a threat to induce another person so to interfere. These things were done by the Amendment Act of 1976.[35] However, like the protection in respect of the tort of inducing breach of contract, that created in the Acts of 1974 to 1976 against the tort of intimidation is now qualified in various ways, notably by the secondary action provisions of the 1980 Act. No protection now exists in relation to threats to break or interfere with or to induce another to break or interfere with a commercial contract, where liability for the intimidation depends upon unjustifiable secondary action. Secondary action itself is defined, as we have seen,[36] so as to include threats to break or interfere with or to induce others to break or interfere with contracts of employment. Thus, in the example given above, the union official would prima facie appear to lose

---

[33] s. 13(1) (*a*) of the 1974 Act.
[34] See above p. 338.
[35] s. 3(2).
[36] Above, p. 334.

the protection of the 1974 to 1976 Acts, but might be able to bring himself within the general justification of secondary action contained in the 1980 Act.[37]

(v) *Duress*

Recently a profound new development has taken place in the law of restitution, which is outside the law of torts and also, therefore, strictly outside the immunities provided by the Acts of 1974 to 1976, even as amended by the Employment Acts.[38] The facts arose out of another dispute in the I.T.F. campaign against flags of convenience. The defendants had managed to secure the blacking by tugmen of the plaintiffs' ship when it was berthed in a British port and in order to secure her release the plaintiffs signed a collective agreement with the defendants' union and made certain payments to the union. Having secured the ship's release the plaintiffs then claimed the agreement to be void and the payments to be recoverable on grounds of duress to their property. Thus, essentially the same situation of a threat to break or induce breach of contracts of employment unless the person threatened acted to his own or a third party's disadvantage has been argued over the last two decades to give rise to liability in three separate ways. In *Rookes* v. *Barnard*[39] the House of Lords accepted that this situation constituted the tort of intimidation and Parliament had to provide immunity; in *Hadmor Productions* v. *Hamilton*[40] the threat was argued to constitute unlawful means for the purpose of the tort of interference, but the House of Lords eventually rejected the argument; and in *Universe Tankships Inc. of Monrovia* v. *I.T.F.* the House accepted the threat as constituting duress. However, their Lordships then went on to apply the trade dispute defences by analogy and thus to protect the majority of the payments made to the union,[41] though with the narrowing of the trade dispute definition in the 1982 Act, in particular by requiring

---

[37] Employment Act 1980, s. 17(3).
[38] *Universe Tankships of Monrovia* v. *I.T.F.* [1982] I.C.R. 262 (H.L.).
[39] Above, p. 339.
[40] Above, p. 338.
[41] Strictly much of the decision was *obiter* since the parties to the litigation had agreed that the blacking of the ship amounted to duress and that the trade dispute definition indicated the boundary line between legitimate and illegitimate economic pressure for the purposes of the law of restitution. The parties also agreed that the back pay paid to the union for distribution to the crew and the entrance and membership fees paid to the union for itself were covered by the definition; the point for decision was whether a payment to the union's welfare fund was covered and the majority held that it was not.

a dispute to exist between the employer and his employees, future defendants may not escape liability in this situation.

(b) Picketing

The question what are lawful and what are unlawful methods of industrial action has been very much discussed in connection with picketing. The reason is clear: it is here more than anywhere else that permissible economic pressure and impermissible physical force are liable to get mixed up. We have in the course of the past few years been able to observe a curious semantic change. The word "picketing" seemed to acquire a new meaning. During the national coal strike—the first general stoppage of the coal mines since 1926—which began on January 9 and ended on February 25, 1972[42] the miners extended their system of picketing to coal sites, ports and power stations. The "picket" lasted around the clock, and it was designed to prevent any coal from getting to or leaving these places. This in itself was in accordance with the traditional and accepted meaning of "picketing," *i.e.* in the words of the 1974 Act[43] (which were similar to those in the 1906 Act),[44] the attendance by one or more persons in contemplation or further-ance of a trade dispute at or near a place where another person works or carries on business or happens to be (except his residence)[45] for the exclusive purpose of peacefully obtaining or communicating information, or of peacefully persuading a person to work or not to work. As long as the miners did not go beyond exchange of information and "persuasion," and as long as the information was exchanged with, and the persuasion directed to, say, men loading or unloading coal or coke on to or from lorries, they were engaged in picketing as this word has been understood for at least a century. If however the persuasion became physical compulsion or prevention, if the picket line became a road block, this was something else than picketing—it is common knowledge that it did, at least at certain times and places. Moreover—and this can be regarded as even more serious—if, whether by persuasion

---

[42] See (1972) 10 Brit. J. of Ind. Rel. 309. See also the instructive article by Wallington, "The case of the Longannet Miners and the Criminal Liability of Pickets" (1972) 1 I.L.J. 219. This deals with Scots law, which, however, is not different from English law on the relevant points.

[43] s. 15.

[44] s. 2.

[45] The 1974 Act, s. 15, like the repealed s. 134 of the Industrial Relations Act 1971, removed from the immunity picketing at a person's home (which had been included in the immunity under the 1906 Act). This section of the 1974 Act was drastically revised by the Employment Act 1980, s. 16. See below p. 349.

or by physical means, the pickets tried to prevent fuel oil from reaching an electrical power station, they were engaging in an activity which had no longer anything to do with industrial relations at all. Why should the supply of oil be prevented? In order to cut off the supply of electricity from industry and from households. By interrupting the flow of coal, the miners brought pressure to bear on the Coal Board but by preventing the electricity industry from using oil as a substitute for coal, they brought pressure to bear on the consumer. It was as if, in the course of a railway strike, pickets had surrounded the bus depots to prevent people from using road vehicles as substitutes for their normal railway trains in order to get to their work. The prominence which picketing has gained in public discussion in the course of the past ten years or so derives partly from this dual change in the meaning of the word. Or, more precisely: that which is today widely discussed as "picketing" is not "picketing" as this word was understood until fairly recently.

[In the above passage Kahn-Freund expresses two, analytically distinct, misgivings about picketing during the past decade. The first concerns the use of "physical compulsion or prevention." The law has never gone beyond permitting peaceful persuasion. That pickets, on the other hand, do on occasion form the intention of preventing persons from crossing picket lines who have not listened or will not listen to persuasion, is beyond doubt. Since the police generally take the view that it is their duty to ensure that those who wish to cross picket lines are free to do so, the result may be violent confrontation between pickets and police. Such confrontations are not, however, necessarily or even typically linked with secondary picketing. The most notorious recent example of such picketing occurred at Grunwick Processing Laboratories Ltd. in 1976 and 1977. This involved picketing by ex-employees at their former place of work, and, although the strikers received massive support from trade unionists employed elsewhere, the location of the picketing was nevertheless the premises of the primary employer.[46] Whether such violent confrontations are a more common feature of picketing in the 1970s than of, say, picketing in the last decade of the nineteenth and the first decade of the twentieth centuries (*i.e.* the last

---

[46] By virtue of s. 16 of the Employment Act 1980, the pickets who were not former employees of the company would no longer enjoy the trade dispute immunities in respect of their picketing (see below) and to this extent could be regarded as "secondary pickets," but this does not seem to be the sort of secondary picketing Kahn-Freund had in mind, to judge by his example of the miners.

occasion when picketing was extensively used as an industrial weapon by trade unionists) is difficult to say.[47] It may simply be that one is reacting to a contrast between a period when picketing was not a much used sanction (the 1950s and 1960s) and a period of greater use of picketing in the 1970s.

Kahn-Freund's second misgiving is expressed in respect of picketing by miners of oil-fired power stations, which he characterises as "no longer anything to do with industrial relations at all" and, moreover, as "not picketing as the word was understood until fairly recently." The second objection is largely a terminological one, but the first might be thought to give insufficient recognition to the role of Government in controlling the finances of nationalised industries, and more generally in controlling the level of wage settlements even in the private sector if it is operating an incomes policy. The action of picketing power stations generally was indeed taken by the miners in order to put pressure on the community and thus on the Government, but was taken because the Government was perceived as controlling the level of wage settlement the National Coal Board could offer. The miners' action was still related to "industrial relations" but to a model of industrial relations in which the employer could no longer decide freely upon its own wage levels and, moreover, in which the employer, backed by the resources of the Government, was, at least in the short-term, impervious to any economic pressures that could be brought against it. The counterpart to the determination of wages by Government through the political process was the union's need to bring political pressure upon Government. The recognition of these matters does not necessarily lead one to the conclusion that industrial action which has a widespread impact on the community should be unrestricted by law, but it does lead one to an understanding that there is here a genuine problem of industrial relations that needs to be faced.[48]]

Picketing occupied a comparatively unimportant place[49] in the

---

[47] For a discussion of picketing at the turn of the century see Clegg, Fox and Thompson, *op. cit.*, pp. 307 *et seq.*

[48] In a later book, *Labour Relations: Heritage and Adjustment* (1979), Kahn-Freund was himself to call for a new type of collective bargaining, derived from the Labour Government's "Social Contract," which would have allowed for a more explicit working out of the political elements in wage bargaining.

[49] Around the turn of the century the problem was central, but apparently the only cases decided in Great Britain (the situation in Ireland was very different) between 1945 and 1971 which were reported are *Piddington* v. *Bates* [1961] 1 W.L.R. 162 and *Tynan* v. *Balmer* [1967] 1 Q.B. 91. One refers to a freakish situation in the printing industry, the other refers to a white collar union.

practice of labour relations and labour law in this country during the period between, say, the First World War and the late 1960s, far less important than the role it played in the nineteenth and early twentieth centuries, and has always played in the United States,[50] in Canada,[51] and in Ireland.[52] In a sense picketing is a phenomenon which characterises an early stage of union development. As unions establish themselves and achieve recognition, perhaps also as their internal lines of communication improve, the importance of picketing diminishes, especially if employers abandon the habit of looking for alternative labour in the event of a strike. For some time in this country picketing was practised mainly by white collar unions still struggling for recognition. As long as short spontaneous strikes played a more significant role than protracted stoppages (as was the case in the 1960s and early 1970s), picketing was naturally not very significant. It has become more significant lately with the change in the prevailing strike pattern in the course of the past few years.[53]

Before the Trade Disputes Act 1906[54] there was a big controversy (including two conflicting decisions of the Court of Appeal[55]) on what was "peaceful" picketing and what was not. This was principally of importance in connection with one of the sections of the Conspiracy and Protection of Property Act 1875 which is still in force.[56] This makes it a criminal offence, *inter alia*, to "watch or beset" the place where a person resides, works, carries on business or happens to be, or the approach to it, with a view to compel that person to do or not to do something which he is entitled not to do or to do, provided this is done wrongfully and without legal authority. The wording of the Act was not clear and

---

50 See, *e.g.* National Labor Relations Act 1935, s. 8 (*b*) (7), amended by the Landrum-Griffin Act of 1959. The volume and complexity of the American case law on picketing is terrifying. See the Index References in Summers and Wellington, *loc. cit.,* p. 1220.

51 Carrothers, *Collective Bargaining Law in Canada,* Chap. 5; Christie, *The Liability of Strikers in the Law of Tort (Comparative Study in the Law of England and Canada),* pp. 35–61.

52 See Citrine-Hickling, *loc. cit.,* pp. 532–540, 557–579 where the Irish cases are analysed.

53 *Kavanagh* v. *Hiscock* [1974] I.C.R. 282; [1974] 2 Q.B. 600 provides the perfect illustration: protracted strike of electricians at a big building site, use of alternative labour by the employer, attempts by pickets to dissuade alternative workers from continuing to work there. The classical pattern.

54 s. 2.

55 *Lyons* v. *Wilkins* [1896] 1 Ch. 811; [1899] 1 Ch. 255; *Ward, Lock & Co.* v. *Operative Printers' Assistants Society* (1906) 22 T.L.R. 327.

56 s. 7.

this ambiguity affected not merely criminal liability, but also civil liability, *i.e.* the threat of injunctions and committal for contempt of court. The main problem was whether picketing ceased to be "peaceful" once the conveying of information became an attempt to persuade.

This problem was solved by the 1906 Act —and this is now repeated in the 1974 Act,[57] which declares to be "lawful" (*i.e.* exempts from criminal as well as civil liability) the conduct of those who attend at or near a place "for the purpose only of peacefully obtaining or communicating information, or of peacefully persuading any person to work or not to work." However, the status in the common law of the somewhat ludicrous distinction between: "There is a strike on here" and "Don't go in there" was never clarified and has recently again become of importance with the restriction of the statutory protection to those picketing at their place of work.[58] It is an unrealistic distinction, quite different from that between verbal persuasion and physical compulsion which must be clear to every sane human being.

A real problem, however, arises from the revolutionary change in transport which has occurred in the course of a few decades. What does picketing mean in a place at which the workers arrive by car or at which goods arrive and from which other goods leave in lorries or vans? A picket can talk to a pedestrian, but not to a man at the steering wheel. In order to do so, he would have to induce the driver to stop. It was suggested to the Donovan Commission[59] that the law should be changed so as to permit this, but the Commission refused to recommend this[60] and the law has not been changed. Clearly, therefore, this stopping of vehicles is unlawful,[61]—it is the offence of "obstructing free passage along the highway." It is a little difficult to understand why a decision of the House of Lords[62] was required to confirm so obvious a proposition. The proposition is obvious because the law does not establish a "right" to picket any more than a "right" to strike, but

---

[57] s. 15. The wording of the corresponding s. 134 of the Industrial Relations Act 1971 was different. See Drake, "The Right to Picket Peacefully" (1972) 1 I.L.J. 212.

[58] See below. The issue was raised but not settled in *The Mersey Dock & Harbour Co.* v. *Verrinder* [1982] I.R.L.R. 152 and in *Hubbard* v. *Pitt* [1975] I.C.R. 308 (C.A.).

[59] By the Society of Labour Lawyers, Minutes of Evidence No. 63, p. 2816; in a modified form by the TUC: see its evidence paras. 536–537.

[60] Cmnd. 3623, para. 874

[61] Highways Act 1980, s. 137. The purpose does not matter.

[62] *Broome* v. *D.P.P.* [1974] A.C. 587; [1974] I.C.R. 84.

merely an immunity from criminal or civil liability for peaceful picketing itself,[63] and not from liability for another offence which may be committed in the course of picketing.

"Obstructing free passage along the highway" is one such offence—what is perhaps even more serious is that "obstructing a police constable in the execution of his duty" is another.[64] This offence is committed by a picket whenever he disobeys a policeman's instructions, provided in giving them the policeman acts in what the court eventually decides to have been a reasonable manner in order to prevent a breach of the peace.[65] Experience has shown that this may enable a policeman to control the number of pickets. Cases decided in the course of the last 15 years seem to show that this is potentially perhaps the most serious limitation on the freedom to picket under the present law.

In fact, there is a wide range of ordinary criminal offences available to the police to enable them to preserve order on picket lines. These cover the whole spectrum of threats to public order, from obstruction through abusive or insulting behaviour to assault and criminal damage. In consequence, the specific criminal provisions in the 1875 Act designed to control the behaviour of pickets seem to be rarely used by the police, who prefer to invoke the ordinary criminal law. It also follows that the problem for the police in maintaining order on those, rather few, picket lines that are not peaceful is one of law enforcement rather than one of law reform.[66] However, the widespread and sometimes disorderly use of picketing that has accompanied a small number of national disputes over the last decade generated strong pressure for law reform and for more vigorous enforcement of the existing laws. As far as the criminal law and the police are concerned, those pressures expressed themselves principally in the issuance by the Secretary of State under powers conferred upon him by the Employment Act 1980[67] of a Code of Practice on Picketing. That Code does not in itself change the criminal law, though it must be taken into account by any court when it appears relevant to any question before the court.[68] The Code is partly a description of the

---

[63] This point was emphasised by Lord Salmond in *Broome* v. *D.P.P., supra*, and by Lord Widgery C.J. in *Kavanagh* v. *Hiscock* [1974] I.C.R. 282.

[64] Police Act 1964, s. 51(2), replacing Prevention of Crimes Amendment Act 1885, s. 2.

[65] *Piddington* v. *Bates* [1961] 1 W.L.R. 162; *Tynan* v. *Balmer* [1967] 1 Q.B. 91.

[66] See House of Commons, Employment Committee, Session 1979–80, Minutes of Evidence, February 27, 1980, H.C. 462–ii.

[67] Employment Act 1980, s. 3.

[68] *Ibid.*, s. 3(8).

current law (both criminal and civil) and partly a statement of "best practice" addressed to picket organizers and pickets, though very much "best practice" as seen from the point of view of a need to preserve public order rather than from the point of view of how most effectively to achieve the pickets' goals within the law. The most controversial point in the Code is its celebrated suggestion, somewhat watered-down in the final version, that picket organisers "should ensure that in general the number of pickets does not exceed six at any entrance to a workplace; frequently a smaller number will be appropriate."[69] Since the Code makes it clear that this advice is not designed to entrench upon the police's discretion to require a smaller or permit a larger number of pickets in the pursuit of their duty to preserve the peace, it is not certain how helpful this advice will be to the picket organiser or, in general, what impact the Code will have on police behaviour. Indeed, it is not clear what impact the Code may have upon pickets and picket organisers, since much of its advice, *e.g.* to maintain close liaison with the police or to identify authorised pickets, is not directly related to any criminal offences the pickets may be at risk of committing.

The pressures for law reform, on the other hand, expressed themselves in the 1980 Act mainly through alterations to the civil law, and here radical restrictions have been introduced on the scope of the immunities afforded to pickets. We have seen how the 1974 Act declared it to be lawful to attend at or near a place "for the purpose only of peacefully obtaining or communicating information, or of peacefully persuading any person to work or not to work" where this was done in contemplation or furtherance of a trade dispute.[70] In addition, however, pickets benefited from the general immunity for those acting in contemplation or furtherance of a trade dispute against the torts of inducing breach of contract, intimidation, etc., discussed above.[71] These two provisions were independent of one another, so that, for example, a picket who exceeded the bounds of the specific picketing section and obstructed access of lorries to a factory would no doubt render himself liable to be arrested for obstruction of the highway, but would not render himself liable to a suit for inducing breach of contract at the instance of the lorry driver's employer, because he

---

[69] Code of Practice on Picketing, para. 31. The Draft Code had provided that it would be "rare" for the appropriate number to exceed six.
[70] Trade Union and Labour Relations Act 1974, s. 15.
[71] *Ibid.*, s. 13.

would not have lost the protection of the general immunity.[72] Consequently, as far as the civil law was concerned, the main effect of the specific picketing protection was to exclude a number of rather nebulous civil liabilities which were not contained in the list of torts against which general immunity was granted, such as nuisance or trespass.

The 1980 Act has operated upon this arrangement in two ways. First, the specific picketing immunity is now largely confined to those picketing at their own place of work and to trade union officials accompanying pickets whom the officials represent.[73] We have seen that the previous law provided no real protection in respect of criminal liabilities stemming from obstruction etc., so that this change will probably not increase the risk of criminal charges to which pickets are subject, although in formal terms a narrowing of the criminal immunity has taken place. As far as the civil law is concerned, the narrowing of the protection in respect of the property-based torts is over-shadowed by the confining of the immunity in respect of the economic torts, which has been achieved by the second change made by the 1980 Act. This change consists in making an express link for the first time between the specific picketing immunity and the general immunity, to the effect that those pickets who exceed the terms of the specific immunity lose also the general immunity with regard to the economic torts.[74] Consequently, workers who picket other than at their own place of work or who, though picketing at the right place, exceed the permitted purposes of communicating information or persuasion, render themselves liable, for example, to actions for inducing breach of contract, perhaps at the suit of the employer whose premises are being picketed, perhaps at the suit of that employer's customers or suppliers.[75] The changes contained in the 1980 Act

---

[72] There would have been a potential liability for interference with business by unlawful means, (*viz.* the obstruction) against which s. 13 of the 1974 Act would have conferred no protection even before 1980, but in fact no decision seems to have been put on this basis.

[73] Employment Act 1980, s. 16(1), substituting a new s. 15 in the 1974 Act. Those who work other than at any one place or whose place of work is such that picketing there is impracticable may picket at any premises of the employer from which they work or from which their work is administered.

[74] *Ibid.*, s. 16(2).

[75] Those who are picketing within the confines of the new s. 15 in pursuit of a dispute with their own employer are, however, protected from the impact of the new secondary action provisions: *ibid.* s. 17(5). If their dispute is not with their own employer, then the pickets will have to satisfy the secondary action requirements as well.

thus represent a policy of seeing the civil law as playing an important role in the regulation of picketing, alongside the criminal law which has traditionally performed that function. Or, in other words, it is a policy of seeing employers[76] as having an important role in regulating picketing as well as the police. Whether employers in general will prove willing to take out injunctions to enforce their rights remains to be seen.

In the United States the emphasis in distinguishing between lawful and unlawful picketing[77] is very much on its purposes; in this country it is on its methods and since 1980 upon its location. Once it is clear that pickets are acting "in contemplation or furtherance of a trade dispute," there can—one exception apart[78]—be not much further difficulty about the legality of the purpose, not since the repeal of the Industrial Relations Act 1971. If they do *not* act "in contemplation or furtherance of a trade dispute." if, *e.g.* they act in connection with a "political" strike, they are very likely to be criminally liable by reason of "watching and besetting,"[79] while a decision of the Court of Appeal (in a matter not connected with labour law)[80] suggests that they may be subjected to injunctions by reason of nuisance.[81]

In one respect, however, the purpose of the picketing is crucial in this country, even if the picketing is "in contemplation or furtherance of a trade dispute." The 1974 Act,[82] repeating the formula of the 1906 Act, restricts the statutory immunity to the purposes of "peacefully obtaining or communicating information" and of "peacefully persuading any person to work or abstain from working." It does not cover persuasion to buy or not to buy. It is confined to producer picketing and does not extend to consumer picketing. This limitation of the immunity now codified in the 1974 Act may perhaps be one of those restrictions on the freedom of industrial action which are intended to protect third parties, though it is difficult to see that the members of the public really suffer through consumer picketing. The real reason is that

---

[76] As in *United Biscuits (U.K.) Ltd.* v. *Fall* [1979] I.R.L.R. 110.
[77] See n. 50 *supra*, and Aaron, in Aaron and Wedderburn (eds.),*Industrial Conflict, loc. cit.*, at pp. 108 *et seq.*
[78] See below.
[79] s. 7 of the Conspiracy and Protection of Property Act 1875.
[80] *Hubbard* v. *Pitt* [1975] I.C.R. 308.
[81] The proposition is very dubious. It raises difficult problems of the law of nuisance, public and private. See Wallington, "Injunctions and the Right to Demonstrate" [1976] C.L.J. at pp. 95 *et seq.*
[82] s. 15.

consumer picketing was not within the range of vision of those who drafted the 1906 Act. It is still not nearly as important in this country as in the United States, but its importance may be growing with the increasing unionisation of the retail, catering and hotel trades. The Donovan Commission recommended[83] that the protection of "peaceful persuasion" should be extended to consumer picketing, but this has not been carried into effect.

(c) Breach of contract and wrongful dismissal

If workers or their unions use methods of industrial action which the law forbids, the sanctions are—normally—the liability to pay damages for tort, the compulsion to comply with an injunction, also for tort, or—more rarely—criminal liability. Industrial action on the part of workers may also, however, involve a breach of contract, especially (but not only) if they go on strike without giving the requisite contractual or statutory notices. This we shall discuss presently. What is, however, equally important is that certain forms of industrial action, other than a strike, are in themselves breaches of contract, notice or no notice. A go slow is always a breach of contract. It is an implied undertaking of the worker that, in so far as he is capable of doing so, he should work at a reasonable speed. If he deliberately slows down his work, he breaks his contract.[84] The overtime ban raises more difficult problems which can only be solved by looking carefully at the relevant collective agreements to see whether the employer is entitled to demand overtime, and, if he is not, by looking at the practice of the plant to see whether the employer has successfully imposed on the workers a rule that they must work overtime to a given extent. The particulars which the employer has to furnish to the worker in writing[85] should be of some help, but a number of cases have shown how difficult such questions are in practice.[86] This, however, is a difficulty in ascertaining the facts; there is no doubt about the law. But when we come to the work to rule, we

---

[83] Cmnd. 3623, para. 875.

[84] See Aikin, (1963) 1 Brit. J. of Ind. Rel., 260; Napier, "Working to Rule: A Breach of the Contract of Employment" (1972) 1 I.L.J. 125, but neither Mrs. Aikin nor Dr. Napier has been able to find any direct judicial authority.

[85] Employment Protection (Consolidation) Act 1978, s. 1.

[86] *Camden Exhibition and Display Ltd.* v. *Lynott* [1966] 1 Q.B. 555 (C.A.) and the cases which have arisen under the redundancy payments legislation. See Grunfeld *The Law of Redundancy* (2nd. ed., 1980) pp.366–376. For the factual situation see Whybrow, *Overtime Working in Britain,* Royal Commission Research Paper No. 9, esp. Chap. 4.

are confronted with a legal problem of considerable magnitude.[87]
We are, of course, concerned with rules made by the employer,
not rules made by the union. These rules the worker is expected to
obey. Why? By what authority can the employer request the
worker to adopt a certain course of conduct?

One possible answer might be that he imposes the rules in his
capacity as owner or occupier of the premises, but it does not seem
that this is a possible explanation of a rule which concerns the
handling of anything not physically connected with the premises
themselves. How can one say that the Railways Board makes a
rule on the checking of engines or of compartment doors of
departing trains in its capacity as owner of the station? The rules,
as Lord Denning said,[88] are "instructions to a man as to how to do
his work." This is the essence of the matter, but if it is, it is very
difficult to agree with Lord Denning that "these rules are in no
way terms of the contract of employment." It is only as an
employer, *i.e.*—from the legal point of view—by imposing a
contractual obligation on the worker, that the employer can insist
on their observance. He has no other authority to do so. Hence it
follows that, on principle, it is a breach of contract not to observe
any of them. But from this premise one must not jump to the
conclusion that a work to rule is not, or, at least, cannot be a
breach of contract. In the case arising from the cooling-off and
strike ballot emergency orders occasioned by the railway dispute
in the Spring of 1972, to which we have already referred,[89] the
courts had, for reasons which are no longer of interest, to decide
whether a work to rule on the railways was a breach of the
contracts of employment. The decision of the Court of Appeal that
there had been a breach was right. But the reason was that in
observing certain rules, *e.g.* about safety, the workers were
deliberately breaking another which was to the effect that they had
to "make every effort to facilitate the working of trains and
prevent any avoidable dealy." It was not only, as Lord Denning
pointed out, that they put an unreasonable construction on certain
rules—they certainly did that too—but that they construed the
rules in their entirety in such a way as to necessitate their violation.

---

[87] On this too see Mrs. Aikin's Note and Dr. Napier's Article, above n. 84. Dr.
Napier gives a very interesting analysis of the effect of the decision of the Court
of Appeal in *Secretary of State for Employment* v. *A.S.L.E.F.* (No. 2) [1972] 2
Q.B. 455 See also Kahn-Freund, "The Industrial Relations Act 1971—Some
Retrospective Reflections" (1974) 3 I.L.J. 186.

[88] [1972] 2 Q.B. at p. 491; [1972] I.C.R. at p. 54.

[89] *Secretary of State for Employment* v. *A.S.L.E.F.* (No. 2) [1972] 2 Q.B. 455;
[1972] I.C.R. 19.

It is not necessary or desirable in order to arrive at a sensible solution of this problem to postulate a duty on the part of the worker to promote "those commercial interests in which he is employed,"[90] *i.e.* the duty of a partner without a partner's rights. The solution of the problem is in the power of the employer himself. It depends entirely on the way he formulates the rules. If he does not take the precaution (which the Railways Board had taken) of making it explicit that the observance of one rule must not frustrate the operation of a general rule such as one we have quoted, it may well be that in a concrete case—differing from that before the Court of Appeal—a work to rule may not be a breach of contract. One should also point out that if the observance to the letter of a rule would have been a breach of contract, then its non-observance cannot be a breach of duty, contractual or otherwise. If at every stop the station master or someone acting for him checked each door of each compartment of each train to see that it is securely shut, the entire railway system would grind to a halt very quickly. To observe a rule to do this may be a breach of the duty to prevent any avoidable delay. But if it is, how can the station master then be responsible—criminally, or civilly, in contract or in tort—if a door was not properly shut and an accident happened as a result? And if he is not, what—one may very well ask—is the good of such a rule? Despite the decision of the Court of Appeal, this remains a problem of immense difficulty—it is a meagre comfort that it has apparently proved to be as intractable across the Channel as in this country.[91]

Let us now assume that no such question of industrial action short of a strike arises. What is the effect of the strike on the contracts of employment?[92] This question has for a long time been in the centre of the discussion in France and to some extent in other continental countries,[93] whilst in this country it did not receive much attention until fairly recently. Does a strike or a lockout put an end to the contracts? Does it suspend them? Do

---

[90] Buckley L.J. at [1972] Q.B. 499; [1972] I.C.R. 62.

[91] See Latournerie, *Le Droit Français de la Grève* (1972), pp. 305–306, who marshals the arguments on both sides. They are almost verbatim the same as those advanced in this country. There is no decision.

[92] See Blanc-Jouvan, "The effect of industrial action on the status of the individual employee" in Aaron and Wedderburn (eds.), *loc. cit.*, Chap. 4; Foster, "Strikes and Employment Contracts" (1971) 34 M.L.R. 275; England, "Loss of Jobs in Strikes: The Position in England and Canada Compared" (1976) 25 I.C.L.Q. 583.

[93] See O'Higgins, "The Right to Strike—Some International Reflections," Carby-Hall (ed.), *Studies in Labour Law* (1976), p. 110.

those taking part in a strike break their contracts so that the employer may dismiss them without notice? Or does he, by doing so, in his turn break the contract? And whether he does or not, can he be liable for unfair dismissal if he has dismissed a worker who has gone on strike or been locked out?

At this point the difference between a "right" and a mere "freedom" to strike becomes decisive. If—as in France[94] and in Italy[95]—the workers have a "right" to strike then they cannot, by exercising it, break their contracts. Moreover, if the contract was terminated by a strike or if the mere fact that there was a strike allowed the employer to terminate it, the right to strike would be frustrated, because the workers could exercise it only at the risk of sacrificing their jobs. Hence—and this conclusion was drawn in Italy[96] as well as in France[97]—the contract of employment is only suspended by the strike, and after its end the employee is entitled to re-instatement with full seniority. In France this was the conclusion accepted on general principles by the (then) highest Court of Arbitration as early as 1939,[98] subsequently by inferior courts,[99] then by the *Cour de Cassation*[1] on the basis of the constitutional guarantee of the right to strike, and finally codified by a statute of 1950.[2] *La grève ne rompt pas le contrat de travail, sauf faute lourde imputable au salarié.* This gives *carte blanche* to the courts to define "grave misconduct" (*faute lourde*) and they have made much use of it. In particular they have held that the "grave misconduct" may be found not only in the personal behaviour of the individual worker on strike, but also in the unlawfulness of the purposes pursued or the methods adopted by the strikers in general[3]: many of the problems we have discussed in

---

[94] Preamble to the Constitution of 1948, incorporated in that of 1958.

[95] Art. 40 of the Constitution of 1947.

[96] Riva Sanseverino, *Diritto Sindicale* (1964), para. 173, p. 452.

[97] Sinay, *La Grève* (Camerlynck's *Traité de Droit du Travail*), Vol. 6, para. 109, pp. 246 *et seq.*: Durand and Vitu, *Traité de Droit du Travail*, Vol. 3 (1956), paras. 288 *et seq.*, pp. 820 *et seq.*, esp. paras. 291 *et seq.*, pp. 832 *et seq.*; *cf.* Javillier, *op. cit.*, pp. 525–527.

[98] *Cour Supérieure d'Arbitrage*, May 19, 1939; *Droit Social*, 1939, 199. (Conclusions P. Laroque).

[99] Cases: see Sinay, *loc. cit.*, p. 247, n. 2; Durand and Vitu, *loc. cit.*, p. 836, n. 2.

[1] The two decisions of the Cour de Cassation of June 18, 1951, *Droit Social*, 1951, 530 *et seq.* (1st and 6th cases), analysed by Durand and Vitu, *loc. cit.*, pp. 839 *et. seq.* were based on the law before the statute of Feb. 11, 1950.

[2] Law of Feb. 11, 1950, Art. 4, now *Code du Travail*, 1974, Art. L. 521–1.

[3] But the notion that mere participation in an unlawful or abusive strike can on the individual level constitute *faute lourde* is criticised by many writers, *e.g.* Javillier, *op. cit.*, p. 553.

connection with English law of tort appear in a very similar form in France in the law of contract.

From our point of view one of the most interesting aspects of the French development is that—much more recently—it has had a counterpart in this country. Here too the question has been ventilated whether the strike terminates or suspends the contracts and whether the strikers break them by striking or the employer breaks them by dismissing them without notice. No one had in this country referred to a "right" to strike in the sense in which the word is used, *e.g.* in France[4] until this very same problem about the contract of employment arose which made it a practical issue there. In the 1960s a number of judges expressed doubts[5] whether a worker intended to, and therefore did, terminate his contract of employment by giving the usual strike notice, or whether he merely announced his intention of breaking the contract by refusing to work. In *Morgan* v. *Fry*[6] two members of the Court of Appeal held that a strike notice merely suspended, *i.e.* neither terminated nor broke, the contract and in this context Lord Denning M.R. expressly referred to the "right to strike."[7] This dictum, however, was an isolated event, and later the Employment Appeal Tribunal expressed the view that *Morgan* v. *Fry* did not yield a general principle.[8] The Industrial Relations Act had attempted to codify the view taken by the majority of the Court of Appeal in 1968[9] but this provision has not been re-enacted in the legislation of 1974 and 1975.[10] Consequently the problem of the effect of the strike on the contract of employment remains obscure, and it is likely that the "right to strike" remains—despite Lord Denning's dictum—a political rather than a legal concept, just like the "right to work." In other words, we may still adhere to the somewhat old-fashioned view that the worker who gives the proper notice terminates the contract and that the worker who does not, breaks it.

If this is the proper view, then most strikers break their

---

[4] In his dictum in the *Crofter* case (above, n. 1 at p. 291) Lord Wright used the term "right to strike" in a much looser sense.

[5] Donovan L.J. in *Rookes* v. *Barnard* [1963] 1 Q.B. 623 at pp. 682–683; Lord Devlin in *Rookes* v. *Barnard* [1964] A.C. 1129 at p. 1204; Lord Denning M.R. in the Court of Appeal in *Stratford* v. *Lindley* [1965] A.C. 269 at p. 285.

[6] [1968] 2 Q.B. 710.

[7] At p. 725.

[8] *Simmons* v. *Hoover* [1976] I.R.L.R. 266 at p. 269 (E.A.T.).

[9] s. 147.

[10] In effect it has been replaced by the rules on unfair dismissal and unfair non-re-engagement. See below.

contracts and can be dismissed. The dismissal itself is no breach. But, under the provisions of the Employment Protection (Consolidation) Act 1978[11] a dismissal can be "unfair" although not "wrongful." If it is, the employer may be liable to reinstate, to re-engage, or to compensate the worker.[12] Hence it is important that the statute gives a very clear answer to the question: can dismissal during a strike or lockout, though lawful, be "unfair"? On principle the answer is "no." The Act treats strike and lockout situations on the same principle. The principle is that the employer is not liable for unfair dismissal during a strike or lockout.[13]

This principle is, however, subject to two most important exceptions. The two exceptions express connected policies. The first arises from the need for protecting active unionists and strike leaders from discriminatory treatment. If the employer dismisses all strikers without exception or if he locks out all the workers involved, this question does not—at this stage—arise. But if his dismissals are selective,[14] if even one of the strikers or those directly interested in the dispute which engendered the lockout has not been dismissed, then the possibility of discrimination has to be considered. In that case the dismissals may be "unfair," with the consequences to which we have referred in a previous chapter. The rule is: dismissals during a strike or lockout cannot be "unfair." The first exception is: if they are selective, they can be. All this applies whatever the motivation of the strikers, and even if their action was purely defensive.[15] Of course, if at the time of the dismissal the workers had already told the employer that they wanted to return, the dismissal may be unfair whether it was "selective" or not.[16]

The difficulty in applying this general rule and its exception arises from the need to define the boundaries of the group all of whose members must be dismissed if the industrial tribunal is to be deprived of its jurisdiction to consider claims for unfair dismissal. This is particularly true in relation to a lockout when all those "directly interested" in the dispute must be dismissed (whether or not a particular interested employee has been locked out or not).[17] But it may in some circumstances be difficult to know whether a

---

[11] Pt. V. [12] ss. 67 *et seq.*
[13] s. 62. [14] s. 62(2).
[15] See the decisions of the E.A.T. in *Thompson* v. *Eaton Ltd.* [1976] I.C.R. 336 and *Marsden* v. *Fairey Stainless* [1979] I.R.L.R. 103.
[16] *Heath* v. *J. F. Longman (Meat Salesmen) Ltd.* [1973] I.C.R. 407, a decision of the N.I.R.C. under s. 26 of the 1971 Act which retains its importance under the present legislation.
[17] s. 62(4)(*b*)(i). See *Fisher* v. *York Trailer Co. Ltd.* [1979] I.C.R. 834 (E.A.T.).

particular employee was on strike or engaging in other industrial action and so is within the group.[18] In relation to strikes, however, the main controversy has concerned the time by reference to which the group of strikers must be identified. Under the provisions in operation before 1982 the employer had to dismiss all the employees who had at any time taken part in the strike.[19] This would include those employees whom the employer had persuaded to return to work, perhaps indeed under the threat of dismissal, if the employer subsequently decided to dismiss those employees who would not return. By an amendment contained in the 1982 Act the employer, in order to protect himself, need dismiss only those on strike at the date of the complainant's dismissal and, moreover, only those strikers employed at the same establishment as the complainant.[20] The latter reform strengthens the tendency we have already noted in relation to the definition of trade dispute for the legality of actions taken in the course of industrial disputes to be judged on a fragmented basis under the 1982 Act.[21] Moreover, the whole reform of the 1982 Act in relation to the dismissal of strikers places at risk the active unionist and strike leader, whom it was the original policy to protect, because it is precisely these persons who are most likely to continue the struggle even though some of their fellow workers have decided to give in.

The second exception is linked with what we have said about the effect of a strike or lockout on the contracts of employment. If the employer dismisses a worker during the strike or lockout, the contract is legally terminated. Legally, but not socially. Socially it is in fact suspended, *i.e.* the workers expect to be re-engaged when the strike is over.[22] The law to some degree protects this expectation of re-engagement (not re-instatement) by treating a refusal to re-engage as if it were a dismissal.[23] Not to be re-engaged means to be finally dismissed. And if the refusal to re-engage is "selective"—as it almost invariably will be—then those who do not get

---

[18] *McCormick* v. *Horsepower Ltd.* [1981] I.C.R. 535 (C.A.); *Coates* v. *Modern Methods and Materials Ltd.* [1982] I.R.L.R. 318 (C.A.); *Williams* v. *Western Mail and Echo Ltd.* [1980] I.C.R. 366 (E.A.T.).

[19] s. 62(4)(*b*)(ii). See *Stock* v. *Frank Jones (Tipton) Ltd.* [1978] I.C.R. 347 (H.L.).

[20] Employment Act 1982, s. 9(3), amending s. 62(4)(*b*)(ii) of the 1978 Act.

[21] Above, p. 320.

[22] Hence, whether the worker's old contract of employment is continued after a strike or lockout (re-instatement) or the parties enter into a new contract (re-engagement), the continuity of the period of employment is not broken by a strike or lockout for the purpose of the employment protection legislation: 1978 Act, Sched. 13, para. 15.

[23] s. 62(3); *Edwards* v. *Cardiff C.C.* [1979] I.R.L.R. 303.

their jobs back can claim that they have been unfairly dismissed, and—which is what matters in effect—that their employer's refusal to take them back is discriminatory. The industrial tribunal will, in the event of selective refusal to re-engage, have to be satisfied that the employer acted reasonably in refusing to re-engage the particular worker, in the light of his conduct and other circumstances.

In short: the provisions of the legislation on unfair dismissal by selective re-engagement come in their practical effect very close to that of a rule by which a strike or lockout merely suspends the contracts of employment, except for those who cannot by reason of some misconduct claim to return to their jobs. In details there are differences: in practical effect our law has, through these provisions, come very close to the continental systems to which we have referred. It is a reminder that, in similar social circumstances similar results can be achieved through different legal techniques, a reminder also that if one does not see the common law (*e.g.* the law of contract) and the law enacted in statutes as one, one can only get a distorted image of the law.

However, the British law does leave strikers exposed to one risk; the dismissal of the whole workforce and its replacement by a new one are not unknown employer responses to industrial action, and against such employer acts the law of unfair dismissal leaves the strikers in principle unprotected. Yet in France a striker would be protected in such circumstances.[24] The British law is perhaps more akin to that of the United States, where, unless the employer has contributed to causing or prolonging the strike by committing an unfair labor practice, he is free to hire replacements, even permanent replacements if need be, for his striking employees, despite the guarantee in the National Labor Relations Act that "employees shall have the right . . . to engage in other concerted activities for the purposes of collective bargaining or other mutual aid or protection . . . ", which thus has been limited to the prohibition of discriminatory discharges or refusals to rehire.[25]

---

[24] H. Sinay, *La Grève, Mise à jour 1979* pp. 98–99; unless perhaps the strike is "*illicite ou abusive*," where the *Cour de Cassation* has developed the much criticised doctrine of "*la faute lourde collective.*" See J.-C. Javillier, *Droit du Travail* (2nd. ed., 1981), p. 552–553.

[25] National Labour Relations Act, s. 7; *N.L.R.B.* v. *Mackay Radio & Telegraph Co.* 304 U.S. 333 (1938): *N.L.R.B.* v. *Erie Resistor Corp.* 373 U.S. 221 (1963). U.S. law permits even partial replacement of the strikers provided those strikers not re-hired are not selected for discriminatory reasons. In the U.K., the tribunals would have jurisdiction to consider the fairness of the employer's actions in such a case, but might nevertheless conclude in his favour. The issue has not yet arisen for decision.

4. REMEDIES

(a) The labour injunction

Shorn of its irritating technicalities, the law of tort, as applied to collective labour relations, can be seen as potentially serving two purposes: the first is the use of the courts in order (if necessary by physical constraint) to prevent workers or their representatives from organising or conducting a strike or other industrial action. The technical instrument for this is the injunction, and, more particularly, the very speedy remedy of the interlocutory injunction. The second purpose is the enforcement of claims for damages against the accumulated funds of the trade unions. Claims for damages against individual workers can be ignored, not because they are legally impossible but because their practical significance is nil. Since the injunction and the liability of the unions for damages are the only aspects of tort liability in our context that matter in practice, we need not be surprised to find that in countries such as France or Italy, where the unions do not normally dispose of any attachable funds and where the injunction and the law of contempt of court are unknown (in the sense in which the common law knows them), the problems we are now concerned with are hardly discussed at all.

We shall first say something about the labour injunction and then say something about the liability of the unions. In this country no court will grant an injunction unless the party which applies for it can satisfy the court that a breach of contract or trust or a definable tortious act or the violation of a concrete right is threatened, and even if it is, the grant of the injunction is in the discretion of the court,[26] *i.e.* the court has no overall discretion to grant injunctions: given the violation of a right (or its threat) the court will exercise its discretion; in the absence of such violation, it has no discretion. This is why the technicalities we have discussed are so very important in practice.

In the United States, however, during the crucial period between, say 1880 and 1932, a very remarkable transformation occurred: the rule that the court could, in its discretion, refuse an injunction was turned upside down so as to become a rule that the court could, in its discretion, grant an injunction.[27] "The injunction became the predominant device of judicial intervention

---

[26] *Doherty* v. *Allman* (1878) 3 App. Cas. 709.
[27] Summers and Wellington, *Labor Law* (1968), p. 168. Some dicta in *Duport Steels Ltd.* v. *Sirs* [1980] I.C.R. 161 (H.L.) (see below n. 40) can be interpreted in this way.

in labour disputes.''[28] Its enormous power and significance derived from the habit of granting temporary (*i.e.* interlocutory) injunctions against union action and of doing so *ex parte, i.e.* on the application of an employer without hearing the labour side. Until the passing of the Norris-La Guardia Act in 1932 (which put an end to this) the entire practice of labour relations and labour law in the United States was—this is no exaggeration—dominated by the labour injunction. It cannot have often happened in human history that judges wielded such power over fundamental social issues.

Nothing comparable ever happened in this country. Nevertheless, experience has shown that an injunction (or under the 1971 Act a restraining order, much the same thing) and its enforcement through the sanctions for contempt of court can be a formidable weapon.[29] It is an indispensable weapon, both in its permanent and in its especially important interlocutory form. It may be the only method of preventing irreparable damage by unlawful action and this may be threatened (or already have been taken) in contemplation or furtherance of a trade dispute, *e.g.* by physically blocking the highway or access to a factory, shop, building site, power plant through "mass picketing." The law does not, in such situations, deprive the court of its power to grant (in its discretion) an interlocutory injunction to stop or to prevent such conduct. It does not, however, permit the court to grant it *ex parte*[30]; not even the National Industrial Relations Court was under the 1971 Act allowed to do so. If the party against whom the injunction is sought claims (or would, in the opinion of the court, be likely to claim) to have acted in contemplation or furtherance of a trade dispute, he must be given notice of the proceedings and an opportunity of being heard—at least all reasonable steps must be taken to ensure that he is given it.

There is, however, a further problem. As we have said, the interlocutory injunction is a formidable device, especially in all matters concerning labour disputes: a temporary prohibition is likely to have permanent effect. Here, if anywhere, the alternative may be "now or never"—the preservation of the status quo (which is the significance of an interlocutory injunction), *i.e.* the

---

[28] *Loc. cit.,* p. 166.

[29] See the *Con-Mech,* case, above n. 51, p. 300.

[30] Trade Union and Labour Relations Act 1974, s. 17(1). However, often no more than 24 hours' notice is given to the defendants. For a detailed analysis of the developments before and under the 1971 Act see Anderman and Davies, "Injunction Procedure in Labour Disputes" (1973) 2 I.L.J. 213, and (1974) 3 I.L.J. 30.

postponement of action, may mean its abandonment. Unless those proposing to act can claim their immunity at this "interlocutory" stage, *i.e.* unless they are allowed to argue that they are acting or propose to act "in contemplation or furtherance of a trade dispute," these immunities may in practice be useless. Whether they were able to do so was, however, by no means certain as the law stood under the 1974 Act. Early in 1975, in a piece of judicial legislation of quite exceptional importance[31] (which had nothing to do with labour law) the House of Lords re-defined the conditions under which a court can grant an interlocutory injunction. It held that, to obtain an interlocutory injunction, a party does not have to convince the court that it has a prima facie case in its favour. "The court no doubt must be satisfied that the claim is not frivolous or vexatious; in other words that here is a serious question to be tried." But, so the House of Lords held, it is not the function of he court, at this preliminary stage and on necessarily incomplete evidence, to gauge the chances of either party of ultimately being successful. What the court has to gauge is the balance of convenience and inconvenience. The plaintiff's need for protection against injury for which he could not be adequately compensated by damages has to be weighed against the defendant's risk of not being able to be compensated by damages for the injury resulting from an interlocutory injunction.

One would have thought that on this reasoning an interlocutory injunction could hardly ever be granted in a labour dispute because there, as we have said, the question is likely to be "now or never." However, in May 1975, the Court of Appeal (by a majority of two to one) rejected this reasoning in a case[32] concerning picketing which had nothing to do with labour relations. This made it likely that, if confronted with a motion for an interlocutory injunction in a case arising from a labour dispute, the court would refuse to consider whether eventually the defendant was likely to succeed by relying on the statutory immunities protecting action "in contemplation or furtherance of a trade dispute" and would decide solely on the "balance of convenience." This might have frustrated the practical effect of these immunities. Hence it is of importance that an amendment was added to the Trade Union and Labour Relations Act later in

---

[31] *American Cyanamid Co.* v. *Ethicon* [1975] A.C. 396.
[32] *Hubbard* v. *Pitt* [1975] I.C.R. 308. See Wallington, "Injunctions and the Right to Demonstrate" [1976] C.L.J. 86, where the "now or never" point is developed most persuasively.

1975 by the Employment Protection Act[33] to remedy this defect. By this amendment it is declared "for the avoidance of doubt" that when asked to grant an interlocutory injunction the court must, in exercising its discretion, "have regard" to the question how likely it is that the party against whom it is claimed will succeed with the defence that he acted in contemplation or furtherance of a trade dispute, provided he has raised that defence.

Even the statutory provision did not settle the matter. Having had regard to the likelihood of the trade dispute defence succeeding, the court still had to decide what weight should attach to its finding, for the amendment was not expressed so as simply to re-instate the test of a prima facie case. The Court of Appeal felt itself free in appropriate cases to grant an injunction if the balance of convenience favoured the plaintiff, even though it might have found that the defendant was more likely than not to succeed on the trade dispute defence.[34] The House of Lords, however, in the same trilogy of cases in which it re-asserted the broader interpretation of "in contemplation or furtherance of a trade dispute," also recognised the significance of the "now or never" point in relation to industrial disputes.[35] It was held that "in the normal way" an injunction should not be granted if a likelihood of success on the trade dispute defence had been demonstrated, but sufficient flexibility has been left for the recognition of "abnormal" cases that one can be fairly confident that this tale has not reached its conclusion.[36]

(b) The trade union privilege

Whilst the injunction problem is much more important than it looks, that of the unions' own legal liability looks much more important than it is. The Trade Union Act 1871,[37] had merely clarified the existing law by laying down that a union as such was not a criminal conspiracy in restraint of trade—this is renacted in the Trade Union and Labour Relations Act 1974[38] Because of the decision of the House of Lords in the *Taff Vale* case in 1901,[39] the

---

[33] Trade Union and Labour Relations Act 1974, s. 17(2), inserted by Employment Protection Act 1975, Sched. 16, Pt. III, para. 6. For its dramatic parliamentary history see Wallington, *loc. cit.,* p. 90.

[34] *Star Sea Transport Corporation of Monrovia* v. *Slater* [1978] I.R.L.R. 507 (C.A.).

[35] See especially *N.W.L. Ltd.* v. *Woods* [1979] I.C.R. 867, 879 *per* Lord Diplock.

[36] *Duport Steels Ltd.* v. *Sirs* [1980] I.C.R. 161 (H.L.).

[37] s. 2. See *R.* v. *Stainer* (1870) L.R.I.C.L.R. 230, and Citrine-Hickling *Trade Union Law* (3rd ed.), pp. 99–100.

[38] s. 2(5); s. 3(5) (a).   [39] [1901] A.C. 426.

Trade Disputes Act 1906[40] exempted trade unions (which then included most employer's associations) from practically all tort liability, no matter whether the act had been done in contemplation or furtherance of a trade dispute or not. This provision thus established a privilege, not a mere immunity. It gave rise to a storm—it was a storm in a teacup. With the advantage of hindsight one can say that it would have made little difference[41] if that provision had been left out of the 1906 Act. What mattered were the immunities from certain kinds of conduct in contemplation or furtherance of a trade dispute. If those acting for a union were covered by one of those immunities, the union could not—even without the union privilege—have been vicariously liable for their acts. If they were not and were held liable, the union usually paid in fact without being liable to do so, as, *e.g.* in *Rookes* v. *Barnard.*[42] and also if someone acting on its behalf committed a tort unconnected with labour relations, *e.g.* injured someone through negligently driving a car or van of the union. The Donovan Commission[43] recommended the abolition of the union privilege, and the Industrial Relations Act 1971 did abolish it. It was, however, re-introduced by the Trade Union and Labour Relations Act 1974,[44] and this in a form which made it clear that the union[45] or employers' association[46] was exempted not only from liability for damages, but also from injunctions,[47] which for some time had been in doubt[48] under the 1906 Act. In two respects, however, the privilege of exemption from tort liability was reduced to an immunity from liability for action in contemplation or furtherance of a trade dispute: the first was negligence, nuisance or breach of (especially but not necessarily) statutory duty resulting in personal injury; the second was breach of a duty imposed in connection with the ownership, occupation, posses-

---

[40] s. 4.

[41] It did make some difference: see *Vacher* v. *London Society of Compositors* [1913] A.C. 107.

[42] [1964] A.C. 1129.

[43] Cmnd. 3623, paras. 902–909.

[44] s. 14.

[45] If the union was a special register body it applied only to acts done or threatened or intended in connection with the regulation of relations between employers or their associations and workers or trade unions.

[46] If it was incorporated the same applied as to unions which were special register bodies.

[47] s. 14(1) (c).

[48] The matter was however clarified by *Torquay Hotel Co.* v. *Cousins* [1969] 2 Ch. 196 (C.A.)

sion, control or use of property, *e.g.* a claim by a neighbour of a trade union branch that its activities give rise to excessive noise.

As we said above, the attempt to recover damages in the event of strikes, etc., out of union funds is a matter of great importance. It is, however, comparatively unimportant whether the union pays because the court has ordered it to do so or because it wants to protect those who have acted for it. Nevertheless, the Government decided in the 1982 Act again to repeal the union privilege,[49] thus putting unions in a position where they have to rely upon the general immunities for those acting in contemplation and further-ance of a trade dispute. Since, however, unions did not in practice seek to rely upon the privilege outside the area of trade disputes as previously defined, the substitution of immunity for privilege was not as such the significant thing. It is the coupling of the removal of the privilege with the narrowing of the general immunities that can be seen as putting union funds at risk, especially in relation to picketing, secondary action, and those disputes now excluded from the area of trade disputes.[50] That risk is by no means eliminated by the provisions placing a limit on the amount of damages recoverable from a trade union in a single set of legal proceedings[51] or those protecting certain types of union funds from attachment for the payment of damages and costs[52] or those specifying which committees and officials of the union the union is vicariously responsible for.[53] Further, in proposals announced in July 1983, the Government stated its aim of legislating so as to make the trade union's immunity from liability in tort depend upon its having balloted the members concerned in cases where the union has authorised or endorsed the industrial action.[54]

However, the question still remains of whether the change in the legal position of the union will encourage more employers to sue for damages.[55] It was no doubt the case under the previous legal

---

[49] Employment Act 1982, s. 15(1).

[50] See above, p. 349 *et seq.*, 333 *et seq.*, and 318 *et seq.*

[51] s. 16. More than one set of proceedings may, of course, arise out of a single dispute.

[52] s. 17, notably the union's political and provident benefit funds. Neither s. 16 nor s. 17 would operate if the union were being fined for being in contempt of court.

[53] s. 15(2)–(7). The statutory rules apparently aim to impose a lesser liability upon the union in respect of the actions of its lay officials, notably shop stewards, than did the common law rules developed in *Heatons Transport (St. Helens) Ltd.* v. *T.G.W.U.* [1972] I.C.R. 308 (H.L.). See above p. 300.

[54] Department of Employment, *Proposals for Legislation on Democracy in Trade Unions*, 1983, pp. 3–4. See above, Chap. 7, p. 289.

[55] Employers will no doubt often wish to join the union in claims for injunctions if there is doubt about which are the relevant officials of the union who are responsible for organising the unlawful action.

regime that if an employer sued a full-time union official (or even perhaps an important lay official) for damages, then the union would in practice stand behind the official and pay the award out of its own funds. Nevertheless, it was also the case that damages claims against individuals were very rarely pursued. The litigation was concerned almost wholly with the interlocutory stages, the granting or refusal to grant interim injunctions and appeals from the interlocutory decisions. The issue was very rarely pressed to a full trial of the action, at which point alone damages could be awarded. Will the removal of the union privilege alter plaintiffs' perceptions of the utility of seeking damages? The arguments are evenly divided. No doubt, employers are often interested only in getting the unlawful industrial action stopped by injunction and would not wish to rake over cold embers months or even years later at a full trial. Certainly, during the period 1972 to 1974, when the Industrial Relations Act operated to remove the union privilege, only one out of 33 applications by employers for relief from industrial action was taken to a full hearing for damages. On the other hand, a case decided after the Act had been repealed but arising whilst the Act was still on the statute book, illustrated neatly the sort of employer who has nothing to lose and a lot to gain by seeking damages. There a Canadian company, prevented from operating effectively at Heathrow Airport, withdrew from the United Kingdom entirely and sued the T.G.W.U. for the loss inflicted, which was put at £2 million.[56] Such an employer has no continuing industrial relationships in the United Kingdom to protect, and a union in the position of the T.G.W.U. which could still claim the benefit of the union privilege might be tempted not to stand behind its officials.

A REMINDER OF RECENT EVENTS

1964 *Rookes* v. *Barnard* [1964] A.C. 1129.
1964 General Election. Small Labour Majority.
1965 Trade Disputes Act 1965.
1965 Donovan Commission appointed.
1966 General Election. Larger Labour Majority.
1968 April: "Fair Deal at Work."
1968 June: Donovan Report published: Cmnd. 3623.
1969 January: "In Place of Strife": Cmnd. 3888.

---

[56] *General Aviation Services (U.K.) Ltd.* v. *T.G.W.U.* [1976] I.R.L.R. 225 (H.L.). The union was held not to be vicariously liable for the unofficial acts of the joint shop stewards' committee at the airport.

1969/1970 Government—Trade Union Negotiations.

1970 April: Labour Government's Industrial Relations Bill.

1970 June: General Election. Conservative Majority.

1971 Industrial Relations Act 1971.

1974 February: General Election. No clear majority. Labour Minority Government.

1974 Summer: Trade Union and Labour Relations Act 1974. Repeal of Industrial Relations Act, but Government defeated on a number of Amendments.

1974 October: General Election. Conservative Statement that 1971 Act will not be restored in the event of Conservative victory. Election results in small Labour majority.

1975 Employment Protection Act 1975.

1976 Trade Union and Labour Relations (Amendment) Act 1976.

1977 Bullock Report published: Cmnd. 6706.

1978/1979 Industrial action in a number of industries, notably road haulage and public services.

1979 April: General Election. Conservative Government elected with large majority.

December: Employment Bill introduced into Parliament after various Working Papers issued by Department of Employment. House of Lords decision in *Express Newspapers Ltd.* v. *McShane.*

1980 January–March. Strike in steel industry. House of Lords decision in *Duport Steels Ltd.* v. *Sirs.* Secondary action clause added to Employment Bill.

August: Unemployed total exceeds two million.

October: Act in Force.

November: Codes of Practice on picketing and closed shop in force.

1981 January: Green Paper, Trade Union Immunities, Cmnd. 8128, published.

Civil Service Strike.

1982 Health Workers Industrial Action.

September: Unemployed total exceeds three million.

December: Majority of provisions of Employment Act 1982 in force.

1983 January: Green Paper, Democracy in Trade Unions, Cmnd. 8778, published.

February-March: Water Workers' Strike.

June: General Election. Conservative Government returned with increased majority.

July: Government publishes proposals for legislation on trade union democracy.

INDEX